ON THE TRAIL OF THE
JFK ASSASSINS

ON THE TRAIL OF THE JFK ASSASSINS

A GROUNDBREAKING LOOK AT AMERICA'S

MOST INFAMOUS CONSPIRACY

DICK RUSSELL

A Herman Graf Book
SKYHORSE PUBLISHING

Skyhorse Publishing books may be purchased in bulk at special discounts for
sales promotion, corporate gifts, fund-raising, or educational purposes. Special
editions can also be created to specifications. For details, contact the Special Sales
Department, Skyhorse Publishing, 307 W. 36th Street, 11th Floor, New York,
NY 10018 or info@skyhorsepublishing.com.

www.skyhorsepublishing.com

10 9 8 7 6 5 4

Paperback ISBN: 978-1-61608-086-0

Library of Congress Cataloging-in-Publication Data

Russell, Dick.
On the trail of the JFK assassins: a groundbreaking look at America's most
infamous conspiracy/Dick Russell.
p. cm.

Includes bibliographical references.

ISBN 978-1-60239-322-6
1. Kennedy, John F. (John Fitzgerald), 1917–1963—Assassination.
2. Conspiracies—United States—History—20th century. I. Title.
E842.9.R8723 2008
364.152'4—dc22
2008025299

Printed in the United States of America

To all those who still grieve him

Contents

Acknowledgments   XI

Introduction: *Case Open*   1

1. *The Village Voice, September 1, 1975*
   "Professor Popkin & the Robot Assassin:
   'Dear President Ford: I Know Who Killed JFK. . .'"   5

2. The Programming of Luis Castillo   17

3. *The Village Voice, December 8, 1975*
   "JFK Assassination Probe: CBS Leaves a Skeptic Skeptical"   29

4. The Media, the CIA, and the Cover-Up   34

5. *The Village Voice, December 15, 1975*
   "Senator Schweiker Reopens Assassination Probe:
   The Finger Points to Fidel, But Should It?"   41

6. The Takedown of the House Investigation   49

7. *Argosy Magazine, April 1976*
   "An Ex-CIA Man's Stunning Revelations on 'The Company'
   [and] JFK's Murder" [*Argosy* interview: Gerry Hemming]   59

8. Off the Beaten Path: Spooks Galore   69

9. *The Village Voice, April 26, 1976*
   "New Assassination Questions: 'What Was in the CIA's
   Declassified JFK File?'"   76

10. A Visit to CIA Headquarters   87

11. *The Village Voice, June 21, 1976*
    "Cubans Connected to JFK Murder—But Which Cubans?"   89

12. A Cuban Exile and a CIA Break-In   95

13. *Harper's Weekly, September 6, 1976*
    "The Vindication of Jim Garrison"   97

14. Memories of an FBI Informant 109

15. *Harper's Weekly, July 21, 1976*
"Assassination Assignation:
Captain Sam on the Death of a President" 113

16. Who Was 'Captain Sam'? 118

17. *The Village Voice, August 23, 1976*
"Is the 'Second Oswald' Alive in Dallas?" 119

18. The Lingering "Double Oswald" Mystery 125

19. *New Times Magazine, June 24, 1977*
"Three Witnesses" 133

20. *The Village Voice, October 3, 1977*
"Loran Hall and the Politics of Assassination" 139

21. Discovering Antonio Veciana 145

22. *The Village Voice, August 14, 1978*
"This Man Is a Missing Link" 147

23. The Man Who Knew Too Much 151

24. *Gallery Magazine, March 1981*
"The Man Who Had a Contract to Kill Lee Harvey Oswald
Before the Assassination of President John F. Kennedy" 152

25. The Paisley Puzzle 166

26. *Gallery Magazine, May 1981*
"The Spy at the Bottom of the Bay" 167

27. A Visit to the KGB's Inner Sanctum 182

28. *Los Angeles Times Book Review, February 7, 1993*
"Confessions of a Conspiracy Theorist" 191

29. *Boston Magazine, November 1993*
"From Dallas to Eternity" 194

30. *High Times Magazine, January 1994*
"'Case Closed': A Fraud on the American People" 202

31. The Reflections of Marina Oswald Porter   205

32. *High Times Magazine, March 1996*
   "Oswald and the CIA"   211

33. *High Times Magazine, August 1996*
   "JFK & the Cuban Connection: Havana's Spies Spill the Beans"   218

34. A Man Named "Bob": New Clues in the Nagell Saga   225

35. Oswald—A "Manchurian Candidate"?   236

36. Encountering the CIA's "Black Sorcerer"   238

37. Oswald: The Mysterious Formative Years   249

38. Russia and Beyond   258

39. Programmed to Kill?   267

40. An MKULTRA Field Operative Talks   273

41. Two Caskets, Two Autopsies,
   Two Brain Exams: The Disappearing Evidence   278

   Index   299

Acknowledgments

My thanks, first, must go to my tolerant wife Alice, for once again putting up with my foraging of old files and my re-immersion in the dark side of American history. It was my Australian actor/screenwriter friend, Lachy Hulme, who suggested that I assemble an anthology of my published writings on the Kennedy assassination through the years, along with new material that I'd not used in my first book, *The Man Who Knew Too Much*. Also, my thanks to Herman Graf at Skyhorse Publishing, who served as an editor on several of my earlier books, and had faith enough to commission this latest one. And to my literary agent and longtime friend, Steven Schwartz, along with his lovely wife (and agent) Sarah Jane Freymann.

A number of indefatigable JFK researchers have helped out along the trail. They include my long-ago colleague Jeff Cohen, who read several of the chapters, and Anthony Summers, who read and offered his expertise on the "mind control" material. Also, my thanks to Larry Hancock, Rex Bradford, Kate Willard, John Judge, Joan Mellen, and Ed Sherry.

Many years ago now, it was *Village Voice* editor Judy Daniels who believed in my efforts to get at the truth, and later Steve Hager at *High Times*. I thank Jennifer McCartney at Skyhorse for her astute editorial judgment. And my old fraternity brother Greg Rieke for his encouragement, along with Mark Lentine.

Finally, I must extend my gratitude to the late Mary Ferrell and Bernard Fensterwald, Jr., whose counsel on this American tragedy can never be equaled.

ON THE TRAIL OF THE
JFK ASSASSINS

Introduction: *Case Open*

Forty-five years since the assassination of President John F. Kennedy on November 22, 1963, the mystery of what really happened in Dallas continues to haunt the imaginations of millions of Americans. Consider the events of the past two years alone:

- A new study by Italian weapons experts, test-firing the identical Mannlicher-Carcano rifle said to have been used by Lee Harvey Oswald, concluded that it would have been impossible even for an accomplished marksman to fire three shots quickly enough to have killed the president. Thus, Oswald could not have acted alone.[1]
- Another study, by researchers at Texas A&M University, conducted a chemical and forensic analysis on the type of ammunition Oswald used. It found that the bullet fragments involved in the assassination are not nearly as rare as experts had reported. Thus, evidence said to rule out a second gunman proves fundamentally flawed.[2]
- E. Howard Hunt, Jr., the Watergate burglar who had long denied any knowledge of the assassination, revealed in his autobiography—and, shortly before his death, in more detail to his son—that he was aware of a conspiracy involving Vice President Johnson, the CIA, Cuban exiles, and a "French gunman" on the grassy knoll.[3]
- The CIA continued to stonewall a court order to explain its refusal to release records on George Joannides, in 1963 the chief of psychological warfare operations at the agency's Miami station and the case officer for a Cuban exile group (the DRE) with long-established ties to Oswald.[4]
- The Dallas County district attorney's office discovered a trove of records about the assassination inside an old safe in a courthouse. The transcript of an alleged conversation between Oswald and his slayer, Jack Ruby, discussing a plot to kill the president, was apparently not a "smoking gun"

---

[1] Italian rifle study: *London Sunday Telegraph*, February 2, 2007, "Oswald 'Had No Time to Fire All Kennedy Bullets'" by Tim Shipman.

[2] Texas A&M bullet study: *ScienceDaily*, May 17, 2007.

[3] Hunt: *Rolling Stone*, posted March 21, 2007, "The Last Confessions of E. Howard Hunt" by Erik Hedegaard.

[4] Joannides: *The Huffington Post*, October 22, 2007, "'Denied in Full': Federal Judges Grill CIA Lawyers on JFK Secrets" by Jefferson Morley.

but a "recreation" for a possible movie. However, the announcement made headlines around the world.[5]

At the same time, several new books have appeared. *Reclaiming History*, the 1,600-page tome by prosecutor Vince Bugliosi, purports to be the last word and has "established beyond all doubt that Oswald killed Kennedy." Given the other revelations in 2007, Bugliosi seems to have ended up with considerable egg on his face.

Brothers, by David Talbot, gives a well-researched view of Robert Kennedy's unresolved quest to learn the truth about who killed his brother, including new evidence about the probable involvement of anti-Castro Cuban exiles.

Former Secret Service agent Abraham Bolden, in *The Echo from Dealey Plaza*, describes his knowledge of a plot against Kennedy in Chicago several weeks before Dallas. When he learns of evidence being withheld from the Warren Commission, Bolden ends up being charged with conspiracy to sell secret government files and spending six years in prison.

In *Our Man in Mexico: Winston Scott and the Hidden History of the CIA*, journalist Jefferson Morley and Scott's son, Michael, delve into Scott's surveillance programs that monitored Oswald's movements in Mexico City and how the CIA then kept the Station Chief out of the loop in the months leading up to the assassination.

My own book, *The Man Who Knew Too Much*, first published in 1992 and reissued in a revised, updated edition in 2003, was the first to examine the role of Winston Scott in the Oswald saga. I had been the first investigative journalist to devote myself full-time to the unresolved questions about the assassination. For almost two years, in 1975 and 1976, I traveled to a number of locations across America, following leads, seeking out and interviewing many individuals with professed knowledge about what happened in Dallas.

This book is, in part, a compilation of what I uncovered. It brings together, for the first time, all of my published articles on the assassination, as they appeared at the time in *The Village Voice*, *New Times Magazine*, *Harper's Weekly*, and other periodicals. It is also a memoir of what life was like for a journalist following this bizarre, circuitous trail. And it includes new material developed in the course of my investigation, information that I hope will prove useful to other researchers—and leave the reader with the inescapable conclusion that the truth has yet to surface about that infamous day in American history.

How did my interest first come about? I was walking down the crowded hall between classes at my high school, junior year, in suburban Kansas City when Ralph Underwood—a casual acquaintance whom I otherwise would probably not remember by name or face—suddenly turned and said to me: "Did you hear?

---

[5] Assassination file: *Dallas Morning News*, February 17, 2008, "Dallas County DA's Office Finds Cache of JFK Memorabilia" by Jennifer Emily.

Kennedy's been shot." In those days, I was not all that interested in politics, but the news still cut through me like a knife. At first I didn't believe him. My next class was American History. What was unfolding in Dallas played through a loudspeaker into ours and all the other classes, by way of the radio.

I remember a number of my fellow students that day, the intellectuals, discussing the future of the country. I was not in their league, and stood off to the side and listened. I remember a guy on the school bus saying caustically, "Well, I guess that puts Vaughn Meador out of a job." (Meador was a comedian who specialized in imitating Kennedy on LP records). I got home and turned on the TV, which I watched for much of the weekend. I saw Ruby shoot Oswald live, sitting with my parents in our TV room den. We couldn't believe it. It rained like hell that entire weekend in Kansas City. I still see the rain falling as vividly as if it was yesterday. More vividly, actually.

The years went by. I went off to the University of Kansas, and became a sportswriter. In the spring of 1970, after only six months at my dream job with *Sports Illustrated* in New York, I resigned and took off with a portable typewriter and a backpack to see the world. I was on a boat, bound for Jordan from Egypt, late in 1971 when I struck up conversation with an elderly man named James Arthur Duff. He turned out to have been an old friend of CIA Director Allen Dulles, and had himself made some forays for the Agency. Over the course of several days together, during which we visited the ancient city of Petra and other sites of antiquity, Duff told me his theory on the Kennedy assassination: that Madame Nhu had orchestrated it, in revenge for the administration's having killed her husband, Diem, the leader of Vietnam.

Something seemed to be pulling on me, especially after I ended my wanderings deep in the Sinai Peninsula. One afternoon, a stranger approached me and asked that I follow him. He said he wanted to show me something. We walked to the edge of the Red Sea, where Moses is said to have parted the waters. The stranger pointed to a large rock. It clearly showed Kennedy's profile.

"Who carved that?" I asked.

"No one," the stranger said, "it has always been there." And walked away.

A few years later, in 1975, I was freelancing in New York City for a number of publications. *The Village Voice* gave me the go-ahead to write about the Assassination Information Bureau (AIB), formed by a small group of young people to spread the word about revelations starting to surface about the CIA's involvement in plots to kill Fidel Castro and other foreign leaders.

One of the AIB's founders, Dave Williams, rang me up that June. He said that a remarkable story was breaking out west, through a well-known assassination researcher named Richard Popkin. The editor of the *Voice*, Judy Daniels, gave me a hundred dollars out of her own pocket and a hundred more from the accounting department—travel was still cheap in those days—to get me to San Diego.

Before heading for the airport, I remember engaging in a verbal jousting with Clay Felker, then-publisher of the *Voice*. Felker believed that all conspiratorialists were crackpots, but he was willing to let Daniels send me anyway. Bidding Felker goodbye, I said: "If I get a signed confession, I'll call you."

The story that follows, published that autumn of 1975 on the cover of *The Village Voice*, marked my initiation into this strangest of all possible quests.

1

The Village Voice, September 1, 1975

"Professor Popkin & the Robot Assassin: 'Dear President Ford: I Know Who Killed JFK. . .'"

SAN DIEGO—There is no longer any doubt in my mind that the world has gone mad, and I with it. The story you are about to read is not fantasy, it is lunacy. And it is absolutely true. How to begin? Perhaps with the telegram.

This telegram was dispatched at approximately 1 AM, Thursday, June 19, to Gerald Ford, White House:

> "I have documents indicating that U.S. intelligence agencies had a laboratory producing robot murderers (Manchurian Candidates) and that at least one of them took part in the assassination of John F. Kennedy. The programmer of this robot murderer is presently at large. I will provide the information to you at your convenience."

The sender was Richard H. Popkin, author of *The Second Oswald* and professor of philosophy. A reputable, scholarly gentleman who lectures at Oxford and the Sorbonne, edits the *Journal of the History of Philosophy*, co-directs the International Archives of the History of Ideas, and once translated Pierre Bayle's seventeenth-century dictionary.

Unfortunately, this will not be the full tale of how the absentminded professor found unopened a five-year-old letter from an Oriental hypnotist, flew off to meet with him, and ultimately barricaded himself in a hotel room with a thousand pages of the hypnotist's explosive research. Popkin is currently at work building his case and will then attempt to negotiate a deal with a variety of interested media—from television networks to major publishing houses—for the greatest sum possible. Therefore, I was permitted to see the documents only on the condition that I would sign a pledge not to reveal their contents.

At this point, I can tell you that I've spent the better part of the past six weeks investigating the veracity of Popkin's evidence. I did this for Popkin himself. He needed someone to verify certain leads in the Midwest, and he paid the expenses of a young Los Angeles investigator and myself to check the leads out. I personally have met the mysterious hypnotist and have done enough legwork to be convinced—with certain reservations—of the story the documents tell. The attorney general's office is not convinced, the Church Committee might yet be.

But all that must wait. This chronicle is necessarily but a footnote to the history of "The Popkin Papers." If sometimes the tone seems disrespectful or even totally disconnected from such incredible subject matter, it can't be helped.

The account that follows is a journal of five days spent in the Richard Popkin household overlooking San Diego bay. Five days of bizarre telegrams, bugged telephones, and strange conversations with Jim Garrison, Dick Gregory, and Bernard Fensterwald. Five remarkable days in which the author of *The History of Skepticism* first concluded he had found the solution to one of the darkest puzzles of recent times.

● ● ●

SATURDAY. Stepping out of the San Diego airport, I am confronted by a fervent, bearded young man thrusting a leaflet in my face: "WHO SHOT KENNEDY? by Moses David." It is copyrighted by the Children of God, and a tiny circle in the upper right-hand corner says: "donation suggested." I give the fellow a nickel and hail a cab.

Yesterday morning, the tip-off that "something huge is happening in California" had come from an acquaintance at the Assassination Information Bureau in Cambridge. He didn't know exactly what Professor Popkin had unearthed, but along the grapevine that monitors the assassination business, the rumors had never been so electric.

After about an hour of busy signals, I had managed to reach the professor by phone. "I'm in a slight state of hysteria," he began, and proceeded to tell of *two* JFK assassination plots in 1963—the first foiled by a double agent, the second including a killer programmed somewhere in the Midwest. He said he'd give the story only to those "who've been on our side," that the *National Tattler* had already mentioned six figures and could *Village Voice* come close to such an offer? If not, I was still welcome to come observe history-in-the-making. They even had a spare bed.

So I had headed West. After all, what was beyond possibility anymore? The CIA had hired mob hit-men to try to bump off Fidel Castro. The army had been "turning on, tuning in, and dropping out" ten years before Timothy Leary. The navy supposedly had run an assassin training school. If Nelson Rockefeller and the Nightly News were willing to reveal this much, what other horrors might be twisting slowly, slowly in the conspiratorial wind of Watergate?

For some time, a growing segment of the country had been turning back the clock to November 22, 1963. Finding out who really killed JFK, RFK, and MLK had become far more than the pastime of a few "lone nuts" asserting the innocence of a few other "lone nuts." Indeed, a considerable chorus had begun wondering if America was *run* by lone nuts.

Was it merely a bunch of people getting off on their own paranoia? A lot of hucksters and false prophets gleefully boarding another media bandwagon? Partly, maybe. Still, a gut feeling persisted that somewhere in the muck of the last 12 years, a truth did wait to be discovered. And if Richard Popkin had found it. . . .

Thus do I find myself riding past the Pacific Ocean on a cool summer evening, reading a nickel message from the Children of God: "Save yourselves from this untoward generation of vipers who would destroy the Earth!"

The Popkins' ranch-style home sits on a hillside in the plush suburban environs of La Jolla. The Del Charro, where J. Edgar Hoover used to huddle with cronies, is now a vacant lot a few hundred yards down from their picture-window. Dr. Popkin (henceforth to be called "the professor") is sitting with a few guests at a dining room table cluttered with manila folders, disheveled typescript, and a collection of mailgrams.

The first impression he exudes is one of hair. Wildly curling black hair with specks of gray, bushy eyebrows, and gray sideburns. A prominent nose on a long thin face overlaps a bristly mustache. He has a tendency to mumble into his thin beard, causing some to refer fondly to him as "Snuffy Smith." He wears glasses, suspenders, and baggy pants. Fifty-one years of manic energy.

His wife Julie, dark-haired, bespectacled, and pleasant, offers me the last of some steak and informs I'm the fifth visiting journalist of the week. *Newsday's* Marty Schramm, who in 1973 broke the exclusive about Bebe Rebozo's wheeling-dealings, led the way for lamb chops on Monday evening. Next came Howard Kohn of *Rolling Stone*, renowned for exposing Detroit police corruption. Then a CBS team of Lee Townsend and Brooke Janis, working on a two-hour assassination special for the fall. *New Times'* Robert Sam Anson was due in a few days. The *National Tattler* had been visited personally by the professor in Chicago.

Seymour Hersh, he is saying as I sit down, will soon be sorry he hadn't shown more tact on previous associations. In the meantime, tonight's Western Union message is almost ready.

"Do you want to call it in?" the professor asks me. "To have the fun of listening to what happens?"

A fellow who is book review editor of the *Journal of the History of Philosophy* suggests it might be dangerous.

"Anybody can get away with it," the professor replies. "They're in the business of selling telegrams. They'll make $20 out of this one."

I consent to go as far as listening in on another extension. The professor dials, intimating that he's sure the phone is tapped.

"I'd like to send a telegram to President Ford."

"Go ahead, sir."

"I have documents indicating that Fidel Castro tried to foil the plot to assassinate John F. Kennedy, but that the FBI prevented him from stopping the assassination. I will present these documents to you at your earliest convenience."

He asks this also be mailgrammed to Henry Kissinger, Frank Church, Howard Baker, George McGovern, John McClellan, Nelson Rockefeller, Mike Mansfield, Edward Levi, Clarence Kelley, Bernard Fensterwald, Fidel Castro, Dick Gregory, Richard Dudman of the *St. Louis Post-Dispatch* and David Rosenthal, a former student who keeps a collection.

"Night letter or cable, sir?" asks Western Union.

This done, the professor ushers me quickly into his office, also my temporary bedroom. I'm asked to examine the other journalists' statements of silence and write one of my own. Then, and only then, will I be able to examine the documents. Signing my pledge of allegiance, I am spirited back to the living room for a "crash course."

The utmost caution is required, the professor says recklessly. At this moment somewhere in the Midwest, there is a stakeout on the house of a man who helped program one of the JFK assassination team. And in Los Angeles, at a secret residence, is the ex-CIA man who knows all about the earlier plot in 1963.

Two hours later, nearly staggering into bookcase in which is prominently displayed a volume titled *The Historian as Detective*, I take a set of the documents to my room. Begin to read about a spy who came in from the cold. A young Latin ready to kill at the utterance of key words. There is a tape transcript from a deep-trance deprogramming session carried out by a hypnotist employed by the intelligence service of U.S. ally. The wildest imaginings of John le Carré, Len Deighton, and Richard Condon—can it be?

Confused, but feeling the thread of a certain diabolic logic, finally I fall asleep. My last conscious thought takes in my sleeping quarters. A wall-to-wall sprawl of papers whose catacombs might conceivably alter the face of recent history. In the living room, the professor is playing pinochle.

● ● ●

SUNDAY. The clacking of typing keys had come pulsing through my bedroom door at approximately 4:15 AM. At breakfast, sitting with his wife Julie and thirteen-year-old daughter Sue, I am told the professor had felt a sudden need to finish a letter about Napoleon's emancipation of the French Jews in 1806. Julie had curtailed the brainstorm, and he was now sleeping in.

The new theory about Napoleon's Messianic complex was another of his current interests. Julie says it's always been his passion "to uncover material never before seen." It started in Bibliothèque nationale de France in 1952 with some forgotten documents that led him to a whole unsuspected strain of philosophical skepticism beginning with Descartes, the fuel for a book that "didn't make him a popular figure, but a respected one."

The Second Oswald was similarly skeptical and scholarly. It appeared in 1966 as one of the early alternatives to the Warren Commission inspired by reading Bertrand Russell on a midnight train and dedicated "To my mother who has always encouraged my interest in the unknown and unexplained."

(Mother Zelda, I later learned, is a renowned writer of Jewish mystery novels. The professor's father was, incidentally, one of America's pioneer public relations men, having arranged Einstein's tour of the U.S. and managed Alf Landon's New York campaign and promoted Harry Houdini. Today the professor's brother performs similar services for the Red Cross disaster service and writes books about earthquakes.)

The Second Oswald also certified the professor as a big-league assassination buff, and over the years he had become a kind of data bank of the dark side, annually hibernating at universities until about the Ides of March.

Springtime was when something always seemed to build. Two years ago, the professor had learned of a Secret Army Organization of San Diego right-wingers with mislaid plans to terrorize the 1972 Republican Convention (published in *Ramparts*). Last year, it was a possible government plot on Nixon's life.

This particular spring had seen a succession of disappointments. First he'd put together a story for Universal Press Syndicate identifying Robert Bennett, a former E. Howard Hunt associate, as Woodward and Bernstein's "Deep Throat," but few papers seemed interested. Next he zoomed off to Toronto to check out a man claiming new film evidence about the JFK assassination, but then everybody involved clammed up. So it was back to Washington University in St. Louis and the humidly humdrum life of a Professor of Philosophy and Jewish Studies, until. . .

"If I hadn't been nagging him about cleaning his study," Julie is saying—it is almost noon, audible stirrings in the bedroom—"none of this would have happened. Dick never sorts his papers. His mind is very orderly, but the flesh is different. Well, finally he agreed to try and suddenly he was in the kitchen shouting 'Look at this letter! It will boggle your mind!'"

The elusive letter, from a long-ago admirer of his Oswald book who'd been secreting his own sensational documents in sealed plastic under a washer-dryer in Canada for the last five years, was a scenario from the professor's fondest nightmares. Shakily, he had dialed the old phone number. The chain reaction that followed, he was currently living through. We all were.

Before flying off to make history, the professor had packed up in St. Louis and prepared to move the family back to summer in San Diego, where he chaired the university philosophy department through the 1960s. Then they all headed up to New York for a quick visit to his mother before she left for Israel. There, the night they put Zelda on her plane, a young colleague was called in for the first of numerous special missions.

"In addition to philosophy, this young man is a great bugger," Julie recalls. "My husband has coteries of faithful helpers everywhere. So, on our wedding anniversary, we spent the evening tapping in on Dick's conversation with Dick Gregory. That was also the night of the first telegram." For a time, Popkin had taken to bugging his own phone, taping his conversations for history.

"He's been pretty caught up in telling people he's making history," Sue adds. "The first couple times he sent telegrams, he told the operator *she* was making history."

About this time, the professor is emerging, wandering into the kitchen in pajamas to the tune of a jangling phone. It's Jim Garrison.

"Your reputation will be vindicated in a few days," the professor is saying. "Unfortunately you can't produce Ferrie or Shaw except in the graveyard. . . . I'll be called as a witness, that's for sure. . . . I sent another telegram last night. I didn't put you on the list because it costs a dollar for every one, but I'll read it to you. . ."

Jim Garrison feels like he's being vindicated at last, he says, hanging up. He ponders momentarily about getting a set of all the telegrams to Frank Church immediately, then remembers: "Washington doesn't work on weekends. That's why Pearl Harbor worked so well."

Within a half hour, we are driving to his office at U.C. San Diego to Xerox documents and dictate letters. Also he has a long-postponed paper to work on about the philosophical basis of racism. Everyone here is working on papers. Julie is doing one on Drugs and Keats. The professor has begun calling me his Boswell.

Evening floats in on the vapors of a spent copying machine. All the visiting media have been given copies of the documents, even though they're forbidden to use them. Tonight, some people called the Dykstras are having a dinner party and Herbert is coming. Herbert Marcuse, philosopher-hero of the New Left and instructor of Angela Davis in the late 1960s, brought from Brandeis to San Diego by none other than the professor.

Waiting for a chili relleno soufflé in a living room on La Jolla's outskirts, as seventy-seven-year-old Herbert Marcuse walks in with his mid-thirties girlfriend Ricki. An aristocratic white-haired gentleman with a paunch and a cane, full of vinegar. He and the professor face each other across the chip-and-dip. Marcuse slams a palm down and cries, "What is most important is to get it out!"

The professor talks at dinner about the Secret Service. He became familiar with their ilk during his investigation of the Secret Army Organization. Suddenly he gets up and beckons his hostess and the wife of his book review editor into a bedroom. Picking up the phone, he gets the number of the local Secret Service and dials.

"Hello, I have knowledge of a plot to assassinate President Ford." Brief silence. "Well, is Mr. Perez in? I'll talk to him about it. He's not? Well, I'll call back then."

A wide grin crosses the professor's face as he hangs up. It seems to say: See? I told you so. They could care less. "If Perez heard my name, he'd have to leave the country," he adds. "He knows I connected him with the Secret Army."

Dinner is over and Herbert Marcuse is lying on a heat pad on the couch. His back is bothering him, Ricki is making him comfortable. The professor starts preparing his nightly telegram, one pointing up newfound Warren Commission fallacies. He asks Marcuse if he'd like to receive a copy. However, Marcuse, who is hard of hearing, thinks it's a telegram about assassinating Ford and is concerned about getting involved. Things are getting confusing.

"Why does he do it?" Marcuse demands. "Those people get telegrams like this every day!"

The professor explains that the *Sacramento Bee* is publishing the full texts of his telegrams. The professor also wants a dollar from Marcuse to add his name to the list of recipients.

"Did anyone watch CBS News to see if there was anything?" the professor asks everyone.

Our hostess is selected to read the telegram to the operator. Julie is trying to get her husband to stop talking. He says he wishes she'd quit arguing with him. Marcuse is making a joke about Oswald's wife sleeping with Earl Warren.

Soon it is time to depart. The professor meets Marcuse at mid-room, beside the couch.

"Got the dollar?" he asks.

"Keep up the good fight, old man," Marcuse says, and obliges.

• • •

MONDAY. Another long day of Xeroxing at the office. On the way home, the professor takes me downtown to see his bank, where a set of documents is kept in his safe-deposit box. The Southern California First National Bank, La Jolla branch. The bank is apparently a prime local attraction. The bench outside faces the bank, not the street. Inside are artificial olive trees, gold and lavender swivel chairs, ostrich plumes in the corners, a Mexican tapestry on the wall behind the tellers, little picnic-type waiting tables with multicolored director's chairs, and a free coffee dispenser. The professor is seeing an official about setting up the Richard H. Popkin Foundation with the money he'll soon be getting.

"Give me something my wife can sign right away," he instructs. "In case I get bumped off, like Sam Giancana." He winks at me.

Back in the car, he realizes his address book is missing. "I remember getting some cigarettes out of my pocket. Well, if it's not at home, we'll just commit suicide. I've got more spies in there than a CIA man." (The address book was later discovered in his bedroom.)

He remembers he should try to reach Peter Dale Scott in Berkeley. Scott is one of the more meticulous buffs, his latest manuscript running somewhere in the neighborhood of 3,000 pages.

"A very good researcher, but he can't tone it down," says the professor. "He's a medievalist by trade—*Beowulf*—a timeless view. We'll call him tonight and see what he thinks of the telegrams. He knows I'm not crazy, that I wouldn't say anything unless I had the evidence, though I am a trifle less cautious than he."

It's 6 PM when we arrive home, and Dick Gregory has just phoned. Gregory, who lectures all over the country, had kindly footed a portion of the professor's traveling bill in the interest of truth. Gregory also has a demonstration planned for the White House lawn, and the plan is for the professor to present his documents in Washington concurrently.

The professor reaches Gregory at home in Rhode Island. He's just received letters from John C. Keeney (acting assistant attorney general, Criminal Division) and Philip Buchen (counsel to the president). Why they are addressed to Gregory, I'm not sure. Anyhow, they acknowledge the first telegrams and inform tactfully that the White House has passed the buck to the attorney general's office, which Mr. Keeney writes would be pleased to review the material.

The professor seems to take the replies a bit further. "I'm going to ask a bodyguard to accompany me to Washington," he says.

"That's beautiful," says Gregory.

I am being allowed to monitor the conversation.

The professor:	"I'm afraid to go myself. I want a bodyguard and I'm at their disposal if they send one, and with you present."
Gregory:	"Let's be careful with that. They might say they'll send someone to pick it all up."
The professor:	"I'll say I'll show it only to the President and attorney general."
Gregory:	"Let's play with it. Don't concentrate on it. They made their move, now ours is the next move. Okay, if we decide to go the bodyguard route, that's my suggestion, not yours, you follow me?"

The professor: "Let me tell you something completely different. I'm sending you off a paper, 'The Philosophical Basis of Racism,' I think you'll enjoy it."

Gregory: "We're in good shape, doctor. You know what's gonna wipe you out, don't you? When you see White House stationery with words like Martin Luther King, John F. Kennedy, assassinations. CIA. It's amazing what a telegram can do, isn't it?"

The professor: "Would you have believed back at Christmas we'd be at this stage?

Gregory: "Okay. I gotta get outta here, hit the highway. Peace and love."

The professor: "I'm not gonna send off more telegrams after this."

Gregory: "Keep 'em hoppin'."

The professor: "I'm going to demand to see only the President or Levi."

Gregory: "But that's not protocol. The minute you force the President's hand . . . We can do it, but it'll have to be worked a different way. Cleverly worded. Only 'Someone that would speak for the President.'

The professor: "And also someone who's not implicated. We don't want to give this to co-conspirators, don't want to go the way Sam Giancana went."

Gregory: "Have you heard the latest news on that? The cops have admitted they heard the shots outside, but they thought it was beer cans popping."

The professor: "Beautiful. Lone nut beer cans now." (A pause) "They can send Air Force One out here for me if they want.

Gregory: "Probably the only safe way you can travel."

End of conversation. In the kitchen professor looks at his Boswell—me—apologetically. "I'm sorry," he says, "somehow we lost the bug that goes on the phone. Then you wouldn't have to take notes. I'll get over here tonight to replace it."

He picks up again to call his literary agent in New York. "Hello, Cyrilly? The White House has invited Dick Gregory and myself to come present our evidence."

Cyrilly Abels, who among others handles Katharine Anne Porter, Eldridge Cleaver, and the professor's mother, reports that *Rolling Stone*'s owner hasn't shown much interest. The *Newsday* man sent a memo to his boss, who wasn't in today.

"I warned you not to count on more than you should," says Julie. "What about the *Tattler*?"

"Cyrilly called, but they closed at five o'clock."

Another call, this time to Howard Kohn of *Rolling Stone*, who refers to nego-tiations there as "an Armenian rug deal." The professor takes a tranquilizer. We sit down for dinner.

A former student drops by. She has brought along her mother Ethel, who begins talking about her husband, who was in military intelligence in Mexico City but killed in a plane crash in Panama in 1953. Aroused, the professor goes into his office and comes back with copies of E. Howard Hunt's *Undercover* and a Hunt biography *Compulsive Spy*. He begins looking up where Hunt might've been at the time, but this project keeps getting curtailed by the ringing phone.

Searching vainly in a closet for more papers, he mumbles: "I wish you'd stop cleaning house every day. It's not helping."

At last, the professor and I settle down to our second taping session, a com-plete chronology of his life since spring.

"Starting tomorrow, every expense is coming out of the institute," he says at midnight. "Friday we'll draw up corporation papers. Saturday my accountant will be down. The addition to *The History of Skepticism* may have to wait until fall. I intend to offer the library here my archives in exchange for a wing. It's a monstrosity, totally underused. We may go back and forth between St. Louis and San Diego. Well, I'll take my ginger ale and sleeping pills now."

• • •

TUESDAY. First thing in the morning, CBS News calls about a possible inter-view with Daniel Schorr. The professor is inspired to the phone once more. Bill Turner, onetime FBI man turned assassination scholar in San Francisco, appar-ently agrees to serve as bodyguard for the Washington excursion. The bad news is that the stakeout in the Midwest has been lifted for lack of action. There's also some advice from Bernard Fensterwald, the Washington lawyer with such diverse clients as James McCord and James Earl Ray.

"Fensterwald says I'm crazy to go into the President's office with Gregory," the professor is telling me in the car. "He thinks Gregory might tell the Presi-dent about flying saucers or something. But I'm too committed to Greg. Fen-sterwald is my lawyer, I want his advice, but there are times I must make up my own mind."

More bad news. The *National Tattler* has apparently gotten a call from a Russian-sounding name with a bad conscience and sent its reporter "off to God-knows-where to meet him. There's every reason in the world now for the real assassins to send these guys on a wild goose chase."

We are driving to the office of his local lawyer. Roger Ruffin, the man who put financier C. Arnholt Smith behind bars. A quick trip to talk about the founda-tion. One of Ruffin's secretaries has found a key to the professor's safe deposit box in the parking lot, where he had lost it earlier. The professor is grateful.

Back at the house, a call to Donald Freed in L.A. to compare notes about hypnotized assassins. Freed, co-author of *Executive Action* with Mark Lane, has a new book coming out about the programming of Sirhan Sirhan.

"I stayed up until 4:30 last night marking passages in the documents for you," the professor tells him. "Just don't get your movie out before I get my story out!" (Freed is seeing Orson Welles these days about movie rights.)

Outside, the ocean breezes sponge the air. A few students are dropping by once again, veterans of Watergate. That means they spent hours in the professor's garage helping clip and file the newspapers. It's getting dark when the doorbell rings again and, casually, Julie goes to answer it. The professor turns to me confidentially, whispering: "Don't you think she should be a little more careful?"

All perspective is fading. I remember a conversation about ex-neighbors, how Barry Goldwater used to haunt La Jolla and Earl Warren even lived next door. I remember the professor wondering aloud: "Is Care CIA?" I remember the Midwest stakeout starting up again with some students from the *New German Critique*, a radical journal.

The last thing I recall is sitting on my bed transcribing a taped interview with a CIA man about murder attempts on Castro. The professor is on the floor below, sifting through reams of files. A car is screeching up outside. Anxiously, I peer out the windows. I walk around in a zombie-like state checking that all the doors are locked.

• • •

WEDNESDAY. A girl named Jan arrives to assist with the files. I try to pack around her. Jason Epstein of Random House calls to talk about a book. Sue is helping comb her father's hair and fix his suspenders while he talks, so he can go to the hospital and visit a friend with an amputated leg. More calls. John Molder of the *Tattler*. *New Times* can't afford any grandiose fee, but Anson is coming down tomorrow anyway.

On the way to the airport, the professor is wondering about the ethics of letting the National Endowment for the Humanities fund his project on "Milleniarism and Messianism." He's read a *Penthouse* article that the NEH is really a CIA front.

Before I know it, I am standing before airport security. "Is that a typewriter?" A tingle of paranoia swivels up my spine.

But the guards allow me to board.

• • •

EPILOG. And this is only the beginning. First of all, the professor passed up his joint venture with Dick Gregory, a lucky thing since Gregory went and got himself arrested. The professor did keep eventual appointments in D.C. with aides of the attorney general and the Church Committee. He also suffered a slight breakdown of nerves, but has recovered splendidly. The attorney general's office pretty much gave him the brush. The Church Committee showed interest and took copies of some of the documents to look into on their own.

In the meantime, nobody has yet broken the true story contained in "The Popkin Papers." Popkin is currently holding back letting his agent handle negotiations with the media, while he and his team of investigators continue to make their case ready for public acceptance.

In fairness to the professor—a loveable gentleman whom I don't mean to slander or malign—the days since have brought greater calm and reality to both his life and mine. If after reading this chronicle, you hold doubts about his credibility, try putting yourself in the place of an eighteenth-century scholar born under the sign of Capricorn who falls upon the last piece of a jigsaw puzzle five years late to solve a twelve-year-old murder with implications of mind-warp. Then put yourself in the place of his Boswell. Then go read William Burroughs.

2

The Programming of Luis Castillo

My close encounter with Professor Popkin in the summer of 1975 marked the beginning of my quest to solve the Kennedy assassination. Eventually, my focus would be on the second of Popkin's theses: "And in Los Angeles, at a secret residence, is the ex-CIA man who knows all about the earlier plot in 1963." His name was Richard Case Nagell, and he would become the main subject of my book *The Man Who Knew Too Much*.

At the time, though, I was most intrigued by the "Manchurian Candidate" idea. The longer I gazed down that rabbit hole, the more plausible it became. It would have seemed too fantastic, except for this: In 1974, after revelations first surfaced in the press about the CIA's having conducted operations against American citizens in violation of its original charter, President Ford had formed a commission to investigate further. Its report, issued in June 1975, contained a bombshell. It described how, starting in the late 1940s, the CIA "began to study the properties of certain behavior-influencing drugs (such as LSD) and how such drugs might be put to intelligence use. . . . The drug program was part of a much larger CIA program to study possible means for controlling human behavior." The report went on that "all of the records concerning the program were ordered destroyed in 1973, including a total of 152 separate files."[6]

In this instance, Professor Popkin not only had over 500 pages of transcripts detailing "deprogramming" sessions conducted in the Philippines, but the hypnotist himself had flown into San Diego from Canada to reminisce about what transpired there in 1967. Victor Arcega had been enlisted by Philippine intelligence to look into the case of a man being held in custody for spying. During three months that included more than 90 hours of taped sessions under hypnosis, Arcega had unlocked what he called a "zombie" state inside the mind of Luis Angel Castillo—a form of conditioning that caused Castillo to perform acts and deliver messages at the utterance of certain key words and phrases. A Puerto Rican-American born in 1945, Castillo was an apparent victim in the 1960s of individuals connected with U.S. intelligence, forging in him through drugs and hypnosis a multiple-personality who could serve as a courier and potential assassin. Arcega had also discovered a possible link to the Kennedy assassination.

---

[6] *The Nelson Rockefeller Report to the President by the Commission on CIA Activities*, June 1975, Government Printing Office.

Over the course of that summer of 1975, along with another young researcher named Jeff Cohen (later to become a well-known media critic and cable news commentator), I reviewed the documents at Popkin's home and conducted a series of taped interviews with Arcega there and in L.A. There seemed no question that the transcripts of Arcega's ninety-some hours with Castillo were authentic. Finally, Cohen and I traveled through the Midwest seeking to verify names and places described in trance by Castillo; they were real. We also spent several days with Castillo's family in Chicago, and later tracked down his ex-wife, all of whom added further corroboration for the existing material.

Here was what we learned initially: In February 1967, using a passport bearing the name of Antonio Eloriaga, Castillo was deported to the Philippines from New Mexico, allegedly for overstaying an American visit and stealing a car. One month later, having made suspicious contact with members of the left-wing Huk guerrilla movement, he was brought to Manila for interrogation by the Philippine National Bureau of Investigation. Administering truth serum, the authorities discovered Castillo's real name and began to observe a peculiarity in certain of his behavioral reactions. So Arcega, a businessman whose brother was a high official in Philippine intelligence, was called in to exert his skills with hypnosis.[7]

On April 6, Arcega was using a calming method of induction that describes a scene of windows and trees when, inadvertently, he triggered something about "a tunnel" and "a man shot in the head." Castillo remembered nothing of the time, place, or victim's name—but this was the tale he related while in deep trance:

He had met four or five men at an airport and been driven to a building in a black car. Covered by a "Spanish" guy on his left and an American behind, he had walked to a room on the second story. There the American produced a rifle from a black suitcase, assembled it and set the scope at 500 yards, and handed it to Castillo. His instructions were to shoot at a man seated beside a lady in the back seat of an open car, in the middle of a "caravan."

Someone would flash a small mirror from a building across the street to let him know when the car was approaching. Two flashes would signal that he should start firing. He was then left alone in the room until, after a time,

---

[7] Luis Castillo background: The transcripts of Arcega's interviews begin on March 2, 1967, and conclude September 1, 1967, and are in the author's possession. Further background was drawn from *Harper's Weekly*, Volume LXIV, No. 3150, December 8 and 15, 1975, "Hypnotist's Notes: Was Luis Castillo a Back-Up Rifleman in the JFK Assassination?" by Jim Hougan. Articles on the Castillo case appeared on the wire services at the time: AP, *Chicago American*, April 22, 1967, "Ordered to Shoot JFK in 1963, Says Cuban Agent" and UPI, *New York Daily News*, April 22, 1967, "Dallas Cops Shrug at 'Plot' Tale." Articles also appeared in the Filipino press, beginning with: *Manila Times*, April 22, 1967, "'JFK Plotter' in Manila!" by Alberto Rous, followed by *Manila Times*, April 23, 1967, "Marcos Bares Hunt for Spies"; *Manila Times*, April 26, 1967, "Eloriaga Found!"

the American returned and said: "They got him already. Let's get out of here." Castillo remembered getting into a car with two other men, sitting in the back, and someone giving him a shot. When he woke up, he was in a hotel room with a woman he knew well. Later that evening, he was taken to a "college or resort area," where three doctors made him "feel good." Then he was in a car again, riding past a wooded area along a highway.

Beyond this point in the trance, Castillo would begin suffering a terrible pain in his stomach, his head would spin, and he would begin muttering the word, "blue."

At this same time in 1967, Jim Garrison's conspiracy probe was getting underway in New Orleans. Arcega, who knew little about the Kennedy assassination but enough to realize the implication of Castillo's words, obtained a list of Garrison's suspects from a newspaper and fed some of them to Castillo under hypnosis. As Arcega recorded in his summary of these sessions:

"David Ferrie. Upon mention of this name, the subject suffered the usual stomach pain, the spinning of the head, and weight on the legs. While such a reaction is significant, the point was temporarily abandoned for later exploration, to avoid breaking the trance depth. . . .

"Lee Harvey Oswald. The subject knew his name well. But when confronted with the newspaper clipping, he said the man did not look like Oswald at all. (Awake, after trance, the subject recognized Oswald from the same picture.)"

There were other, less familiar names, many recalled by Castillo without any prompting, including that of the woman in the hotel room who "controlled the subject's work and life like a nightmare." There was also mention of meetings in Chicago, and a "strip of airfield not far away from the Bay of Pigs."

Philippine authorities alerted the U.S. FBI in Manila. Late in April, a leak to the *Manila Times* brought headlines: JFK PLOTTER IN MANILA! It had a picture of Castillo and the story was picked up by American wire services, but quickly disappeared from view. Meanwhile, Arcega requested tight security and total secrecy around his continuing sessions with Castillo. These would last through June 25, almost on a daily basis, accompanied by tapes, transcriptions, and Arcega's elaborate summaries for Filipino intelligence.

Although Arcega himself expressed early reservations about the truth of Castillo's revelations about the Kennedy assassination—writing about the possibility of disinformation or faking by the subject—as time passed it became obvious that Castillo was indeed in the Philippines on some kind of espionage mission. He recalled in trance countless contacts and places, both in the Philippines and other countries like Cuba and South Vietnam.

This young man of average intelligence, and a long history (according to FBI files) of trouble with the law back home, could not possibly have memorized such a wealth of data—some of it highly classified—from books. The problem was the sifting of truth from false information. For Arcega managed to unlock as many as three separate identities at work inside Castillo's mind, identities whose knowledge sometimes overlapped but often obscured what the other parts "knew." Yet Castillo seemed to remember nothing before the age of 18.

During the deprogramming, Arcega made sure that Castillo always had access to notebooks and pens, as he was constantly doodling, or writing the same words or phrases over and over, including his own name. In his summaries, Arcega referred to this as "automatic writing."

The most frightening aspect was Arcega's gradual unraveling of a pattern of key words—seemingly innocuous words like "sand" and "flowers"—that would set Castillo walking through a "zombie" state that always ended with his firing an imaginary gun, first at someone else and then into his own head. Beneath the elaborate cover of identities, Castillo had come to the Philippines apparently to assassinate President Ferdinand Marcos at the nation's Independence Day celebration on June 12. Hearing about this, Marcos himself once came to get a look at his potential assailant, through the barred windows of the Veterans Memorial Hospital where Arcega had Castillo transferred for tighter security.[8]

As Independence Day approached, Arcega wrote: "Special attention was given to the subject's mental states and behavior in relation to June 12 at 12 o'clock noon. As this date and hour neared, he was discovered to have been marking his detention cell wall with such things as '44 hours to go,' '43,' '42,' canceling one for the other. Counting down to '0,' the zero hour was found to be 12 o'clock of Independence Day. . . ."

Arcega went on to relate how, at precisely noon, Castillo went into a spontaneous "zombie" state lasting for two hours and culminating in a suicide attempt. At the parade grounds, there was the tightest security in Philippine history. That evening, "during the interrogation from 4 to 11 PM, the subject disclosed operational data as CIA."

After weeks during which Castillo had referred in trance to his American programmers as Communist agents, he now began describing them as CIA operatives. Why would the CIA have wanted to eliminate Ferdinand Marcos? Arcega's analysis was that an assassination allegedly committed by one of the Huks (with whom Castillo was openly associated) would lead to a complete crackdown on Communist insurgency by a new Philippine president, a man more inclined to be a CIA puppet than the independent-thinking Marcos.

Besides a few anonymous "doctors" whom Castillo recalled being with him, the central figures behind his mission were a man and a woman from separate areas of Wisconsin: the man gave the orders, the woman conducted the preparatory "sessions." In FBI interviews that summer of 1967, both James M. and Jean B. admitted that Luis Castillo had worked for them as a kind of chauffeur but denied any involvement with him beyond that. The FBI had also visited

---

[8] Marcos visit: Interview with Victor Arcega, June 1975.

Castillo's mother and stepfather on two occasions, yet never told the family that their son was in the Philippines and in fact once said he was "in another part of the country, maybe in jail."

Equally curious was the FBI's arrest record on Castillo, which had recently been obtained by Professor Popkin. There it was noted: "On February 2, 1967, he was deported to the Philippines from New Mexico."[9] Yet Castillo, at that time, was traveling under a passport bearing the name of Eloriaga. And, having never been a Philippine resident, he could not have been "deported." It turned out that Antonio Reyes Eloriaga was also a real person, born in Manila on August 29, 1944. According to the *Manila Times*, Castillo had had specific orders to contact Eloriaga in Chicago and assume his identity, then have himself arrested and deported.

Arcega maintained that the FBI in Manila had tried through several sources to disrupt or block his interrogation, once trying to have Castillo given LSD in lieu of any more hypnosis. By then, the two had established a rapport. For the initial weeks, Castillo had refused to believe he'd been hypnotized to undertake various missions—until, finally, Arcega played a tape of him walking through the "zombie" state. Horrified, Castillo had broken down and asked that the sessions continue until the whole truth could be unlocked.

Arcega's efforts with Castillo were ultimately curtailed. He was told that Castillo had been beaten by another prisoner and now refused to submit to any more sessions. After late June 1967, Arcega heard no more about Castillo's fate.

At the end of that year, the hypnotist left the Philippines with his family for Los Angeles, where he gained employment as a proofreader for the *Herald Examiner* newspaper and contemplated writing a book about the Castillo case. He brought along most of the transcripts, although the tapes themselves stayed behind with Filipino intelligence. Early in 1968, Arcega's brother sent him a clipping from the *Manila Times*. It contained only one paragraph: Luis Castillo had been deported back to the United States.

On the night of June 5, 1968, Arcega was working the late shift at the paper when Robert Kennedy was assassinated. Early the next morning, Arcega received a caller at his home claiming to be a local newsman. The caller wondered whether Arcega might know if the accused killer, Sirhan Sirhan, was a Filipino.

For a time, Arcega considered offering his services for placing Sirhan under hypnosis. He was chillingly aware of the similarities between Sirhan and Castillo: the dilated eyes, the trembling, the disorientation when Sirhan was taken into custody. When later placed under hypnosis by a team of psychiatrists, he had again exhibited the same symptoms. The psychiatrists termed Sirhan highly suggestible, even having some experience "experimenting with hypnotic states of mind."

---

[9] FBI arrest record: In author's possession.

Sirhan remembered nothing about the assassination. The last thing he recalled was having coffee with a woman wearing a polka dot dress, whom other witnesses allegedly saw whispering into his ear shortly before he opened fire in the pantry of the Ambassador Hotel. Sirhan's doctors would spend considerable time analyzing what they called his "automatic writing." Like Castillo, Sirhan constantly wrote words and phrases over and over, including his own name.

It all weighed heavily on Arcega. In 1969 he packed up his family again and moved to Canada. And there he remained in obscurity, until Professor Popkin rediscovered his letter in the spring of 1975. Jeff Cohen and I, in our many hours with Arcega, found him to be sincere and scientific in his approach, with no reason we could surmise to be concocting a fictional story.

In my research, I came upon a book titled *Hypnotism* by an expert in the subject named G. H. Estabrooks. In a chapter on "Hypnotism in Warfare," he speculated about a man who, in normal waking state (Personality A), has been programmed to be a rabid communist. Personality B has been hypnotized to be a violent anti-communist, yet possesses all the information known to Personality A. "The proper training of a person for this role would be long and tedious," Estabrooks wrote, "but once he was trained, you would have a super spy compared to which any creation in a mystery story is just plain weak."

He went on to describe how such a subject could be placed in a country like Cuba. "Convinced of their own innocence, they would play the Fifth Column role with the utmost sincerity," and no physiological test could detect someone prepared in this way. "We might have to test, train and work with him for six months," Estabrooks continued, describing a subject's potential as an intelligence courier.

For us, the question became: What happened to Luis Castillo? Was he still alive? And how much of what he had said to Arcega could be verified? Setting out with some financial aid from Professor Popkin, using "code names" among ourselves (Jeff was "Slim," I was "Ryan"), on the Fourth of July, we flew to the Midwest.

Over the course of two weeks, we checked out every piece of Castillo's trance recollections that dealt with people and places—and it all turned out to have basis in fact. The likely site of some of his "programming" was an isolated cottage near a lake outside Milwaukee, which was still owned by Mrs. Jean B. Castillo had indeed worked nearby at a "flower factory" called Halton & Hunkel, and had chauffeured Mrs. B home from work each day. Although her father had supposedly been a laborer there, and Mrs. B a "rose grader," we discovered that the two of them owned fifteen pieces of property around the Wisconsin lake.

Castillo had been among a number of migrant workers employed by Halton & Hunkel, whose Army-like barracks that once housed about 50 Latinos and Filipinos had been destroyed in 1970. The former personnel director we tracked down seemed also to recall a worker by the name of Eloriaga. It did not seem inconceivable that Castillo, Eloriaga, and others were itinerant laborers used as part of an intelligence network.

In Madison, Wisconsin, the man in Castillo's scenario—James M.—had been placed under surveillance earlier in the summer by an investigator for Washington attorney Bernard Fensterwald, Jr. In his report, Ken Smith said he'd confronted the man, who displayed "nervousness and irritability and repeated denials of any knowledge of psychology or anything related. He repeated several times that he was an editorial writer who wrote for the food trade publications."[10]

Smith went on: "I called Wilbur Emery, a former police chief in Madison during the 1960s and now retired. He vaguely recalled that in the early- to mid-1960s he had reports that some local citizens were engaged in behavioral studies of dissidents and it was thought that they were moderate right-wingers. He had his deputy, Inspector Herman Thomas, look into the matter and they determined that they were not an organization but termed themselves 'concerned citizens.' He referred me to Mr. Thomas who is now retired and his recollections were much the same."

It would still be more than two years before the University of Wisconsin–Madison issued a press release (October 5, 1977) that "announced the recent receipt of documents pertaining to two research projects funded by the Central Intelligence Agency (CIA) and conducted at the University from 1959 to 1962. The projects were part of activities funded through various 'cover' agencies by the CIA as part of Project MKULTRA. . . . Names of individuals, organizations and institutions have been obliterated by heavy black markings on the documents. . . .

"Of the two Wisconsin projects, one—as explained by the principal investigator—had as its general aim 'an intensive study of the process of change in personality and behavior as it occurs in schizophrenic and normal individuals during the period of psychotherapy.'"[11] Could they, perhaps, also have been studying how to *make* someone's personality schizophrenic?

In Chicago, Cohen and I found Castillo's parents, who were still living at the address listed in a 1967 FBI report that Arcega had obtained. They were able to clarify their son's fascination with cloak-and-dagger activities. More than once, Castillo had told his mother he was a "secret agent." On another occasion, he'd shown his younger stepbrother a container, saying: "This I got to deliver. It's microfilm." (In the Philippines, Castillo's courier mission had concerned the delivery of microfilm, according to the transcripts.)

Although they knew little about their son's recent life, the family was sincere and had nothing to hide. For years, Castillo had been the black sheep of the family, in and out of juvenile detention centers. The last they had seen him was October 1974, less than a year earlier, when he'd dropped by asking for money.

---

[10] Smith report: In author's possession.
[11] Press release: "CIA Releases Research Documents to UW-Madison," October 5, 1977.

The chronology they offered of his life over the past dozen years went like this:

As a teenager, sometime in 1963 Castillo had been arrested for stealing a car. But the owner, a doctor Luis seemed to know in Chicago, chose not to press charges.

Sometime in 1966, during one of his periodic visits, he began talking about making a trip to Cuba.

They knew nothing of his travels to the Philippines, despite two visits paid them by the FBI in 1967, until Luis showed up unannounced at their door. "He said he was beaten in the Philippines and they tried to kill him over there," his mother remembered. "He said the CIA helped him get back from the Philippines," recalled his stepfather, who went on: "When he came back, he was using strange words, goofy. He'd smoke half a cigarette and then toss it away and then ask me for a cigarette. I don't smoke."

In June 1971, Luis was convicted in Missouri of two robbery attempts and sentenced to concurrent six-year terms.[12] His only visitor during 37 months in jail was a woman whom he'd married in 1970 and then separated from a month later. On August 1, 1974, termed a model prisoner, Castillo's sentence had been commuted by Missouri governor Christopher "Kit" Bond.

By the last time he returned home, he'd become a religious fanatic. He'd given his mother a book, *The Desire of Ages*, and said he was planning to write one about his own religious experiences. He had temporarily reconciled with his wife. Claiming that his drinking bouts drove him to violence, she was then granted a divorce on December 5, 1974.

We decided to wait on confronting either of Castillo's alleged "controllers"— Jean B. and James M.—or to pursue trying to find Castillo himself. At least not until we'd pinned down a book contract. Random House agreed to fly Arcega in from Canada to a meeting in New York. In mid-September 1975, I met him at the airport and we drove to an apartment where editor Jason Epstein awaited, along with Bob Silver (editor of the *New York Review of Books*) and an expert in hypnosis from Columbia University, Dr. Herbert Spiegel.

Spiegel, who hoped eventually to be asked to "deprogram" Sirhan, immediately launched into a monologue about the need for corroborative evidence. He said it was possible, even probable, that Castillo was possessed of a vivid imagination and thus had fantasized all of this. Arcega and I countered him, trying to show that the bigger picture indicated just the opposite. Spiegel admitted he was playing devil's advocate, that he had heard about the use of hypnosis by intelligence agencies, but insisted that "self-programming" was equally likely. That swayed Epstein to remain cautious about making any publishing commitment. He wanted Castillo located, but would not front any money to help find him.

---

[12] Castillo conviction: Divorce file, *Castillo v. Castillo*, 74D20558.

The next day, I took Arcega to a lunch with Richard E. Sprague, the leading gatherer of photographic evidence about the Kennedy assassination. Castillo's in-trance description of the back stairway fit the Daltex Building in Dallas to a T—and it was possible to fire from the second floor, if Castillo had meant to say the distance was 500 feet instead of 500 yards.

Having been unable to convince the publishing world of the veracity of Castillo's story, Arcega returned to Canada feeling like a failure. For our part, we briefly continued the quest. Cohen, in fact, was able to find Castillo's ex-wife in Chicago, with whom he had two lengthy conversations.[13] "We got along very well," he wrote me in May 1976. "She is friendly and talkative, but is now a little scared."

When they first met, around February 1968, she recalled Castillo "living with somebody called Poppa, a man who sounded very old, and talked about religion a lot." (Arcega's notes from a June 12, 1967 session with Castillo contained the following passage: "The subject repeatedly asserted no one would ever know who his Papa was, and his real name.")

Castillo's ex-wife told Cohen: "Lots of things didn't add up about Luis. I didn't know what to think. He always seemed to have money. He said, 'I'm an alley cat. I don't want you to meet my friends.' He said that he knew cops, mob types, government people. He told me never to ask questions about his work.

"One day, I was in a hypnosis seminar. I told Luis that night that I didn't get hypnotized. He said, 'How do you know?' He said people could hypnotize you so you'd be hypnotized forever and you could do things without knowing that you were doing them.

"He was left handed, but he showed me how he could write with both hands. His favorite color was blue, he said. He talked about coded writing when I first met him, and at the end, in late '74. He said he'd teach me how to write in scramble, in code. He'd write backwards, he'd write in number codes. He said he could write a letter in code, and I wouldn't know what it meant.

"Two guys from the FBI came to talk to me, probably in 1969. They asked questions like, 'How long have you known him? Does he come to your home? Where is he? We have to talk to Luis. We have to know where he is.'

"Luis told me that he'd been in jail and then later [that] someone was in jail with his name. . . . I asked him what he did while the 'imposter' served his three years for him. He said he had to do work. 'What work?' I asked. 'Remember, I told you never to ask questions,' he said.

"He threw a tantrum in August or September '74, when he found out that I had another guy. He said he'd get me. He yelled through the door. 'If you don't let me in, I'll get the CIA, I'll get the CIA.' He was a little drunk. He was talking like he'd been brainwashed. This was the first time he mentioned the CIA.

---

[13] Interview with wife: May 10, 1976.

Later he said the reason he allowed no questions was because he worked for the CIA. That I could never lose him, because . . . they could find me.

"Luis was always well-dressed and walked around with a black leather briefcase. He had an almost photographic memory. He'd read a few pages of a book, hand the book to me, and recite it.

"He had little scratches on his stomach. He said he'd been shot at the tip of his tailbone."

What was learned in the aftermath of our investigation of Castillo only lent more credibility to the story we were piecing together. After the Rockefeller Commission's report appeared about the agency's having set out "to study possible means for controlling human behavior," a former State Department officer turned freelance writer named John Marks decided to file a Freedom-of-Information-Act request for any potentially surviving documents. At first Marks was told that everything had been shredded when Richard Helms resigned as CIA Director in 1973. Then, in the spring of 1977, the CIA informed Marks that several boxes of documents filed with the agency's financial records had been located. Some 16,000 pages on the CIA's behavior control effort were released; their contents made front-page headlines and became the basis of Marks' book, *The Search for the 'Manchurian Candidate.'* [14]

It had begun in 1949 with Project BLUEBIRD, which soon became Project ARTICHOKE and evolved into MKULTRA in 1953. The Cold War with the Soviet Union was going full-steam, and CIA memos of the period indicate fears that certain "uncommon drugs" as well as hypnosis were being utilized by the communists. During the Korean War in the early 1950s, the term "brainwashing" was coined by an American journalist—and CIA agent—named Edward Hunter. "The Reds have specialists available on their brainwashing panels, drugs and hypnotism," Hunter warned. The fact that the Americans were delving into the same realm was a closely guarded secret.

The Navy already had a program initiated in 1947 called Project CHATTER, which was looking into various truth drugs for interrogation methods. The Army was interested, too, and in 1952, drew up a "Memorandum of Understanding" with the CIA. Under Project MKNAOMI, the Army Chemical Corps based at Fort Dietrich, Maryland, entered into covert research to aid CIA efforts. Between 1955 and 1958, the Army later admitted administering the powerful hallucinogenic LSD to nearly 1,500 soldiers and civilians, often without their knowledge. At least into the early 1960s, the CIA's own LSD testing was conducted at 86 U.S. and Canadian hospitals, prisons, universities, and military installations, as well as on unwitting victims at domestic "safe houses" in Washington, New York, and San Francisco.

---

[14] CIA MKULTRA files: *New York Times*, July 21, 1977, "CIA Data Show Fourteen-Year Project on Controlling Human Behavior" by Nicholas M. Horrock.

The CIA was also keenly interested in the uses of hypnosis. A 1951 memo described several employees receiving "special private instruction" from experts in "H [hypnosis] techniques." The file, in question-and-answer format, was chilling:

Q—What percent of subjects can be subjected successfully to H techniques?
A—By the forceful or stage methods—85%. By the subtle or "relaxing" method—95%.
Q—Can a person under H commit an act against his religious or moral scruples or against his training and upbringing?
A—Yes—[deleted] stated that anything could be done by a person under H including murder.
Q—Can a person under H be forced to commit suicide?
A—Yes. [deleted] only stated this could be accomplished indirectly but implied it could be done directly.
Q—How long can post H suggestions be kept effective?
A—A long time—unknown periods—particularly if reinforced from time to time.
Q—Will an individual under H give up information he would not otherwise do?
A—Yes—apparently there is no limit to the amount of information that can be obtained given sufficient time.
Q—Can a really total amnesia be obtained in H—in post-H activity?
A—Yes—this apparently can be achieved regularly.

Many years later, I obtained two documents from a researcher into the CIA's behavior experiments. They pertained to MKULTRA Subproject 47, which was listed as having existed between 1955 and May 31, 1964. One study used "quantitative electroencephalographic analysis of naturally occurring (schizophrenic) and drug-induced psychotic states in human males." The drug was LSD.

A report published in the journal, *Clinical Pharmacology and Therapeutics*, stated: "Three groups of subjects were utilized in these studies. The first consisted of 21 volunteers from the New Jersey Reformatory at Bordentown. Most were first offenders. . . . Their age range was 21 to 30."[15]

In the transcripts of Victor Arcega's conversations with Luis Castillo, twice the hypnotist asks whether Castillo remembers being at Bordentown. Castillo says he does not.

A St. Louis police report, completed when Castillo was arrested there in the 1970s for theft, contains the information that he had been sent to a "reformatory" in New Jersey in 1964.

---

[15] Report: *Clinical Pharmacology and Therapeutics* 4 (1), 1963, pp. 10–21. Also, *New York Times*, August 2, 1977, "Private Institutions Used in CIA Effort to Control Behavior." "Dr. Carl Pfeiffer, a pharmacologist now associated with a private treatment center in New Jersey, conducted LSD experiments for the CIA on prisoners at the Federal penitentiary in Atlanta and the Bordentown Reformatory in New Jersey between 1955 and 1964."

This constituted the strongest evidence I had come across to indicate that Castillo had indeed been part of the MKULTRA program. Had he also been a back-up rifleman in the Kennedy assassination? He would, after all, only have been eighteen at the time. But if he was not an actual participant, he seemed to have been at least programmed with such information (or disinformation) as part of some type of experiment—perhaps to determine his retentive capacities, or to obscure the mission that he was really on in the Philippines.

Victor Arcega, however, believed that Castillo really had been part of a "hit team" in Dallas that day. And this would not be the last time in my research that the CIA's mind control efforts would raise their ugly head.

For the time being, though, *The Village Voice* wanted me to critique the latest media "revelations" on the assassination, and I sat in front of my TV taking copious notes on a CBS special.

3

The Village Voice, December 8, 1975

"JFK Assassination Probe: CBS Leaves a Skeptic Skeptical"

It was a classic case of guilt by omission. Or, at best, an exercise in "benign neglect." Last week's CBS Reports Inquiry into the assassination of John F. Kennedy, the result of a supposedly exhaustive six-month study, promised a scalpel's probe and delivered two hours of mascara.

CBS finally let itself off the hook by joining the chorus of calls for a new investigation by Congress. But its first program was a kind of "Ode to Expertise," a parade of scientists behind charts and microscopes, an attempt to pronounce the last word on Oswald-as-lone-gunman. Consider, however, what CBS failed to mention about its team of specialists:

- Itek, a photo-analysis corporation hired to examine the frames of the original Zapruder film, is a Rockefeller company that gets 60 per cent of its contracts from the government. According to Maurice Schonfeld, former managing editor of UPI Films writing in the *Columbia Journalism Review*, Itek's knowledge about things like development of bomb sights is sought mainly by the military and the CIA. Itek's Chairman of the Board, Franklin A. Lindsay, was once named by Soviet spy Kim Philby as a CIA plotter. (Lindsay said yesterday he has never confirmed or denied this.) Lindsay's assistant, Howard Sprague, writes Schonfeld, has also been a CIA employee. And this CBS study was Itek's third purporting to show no photographic evidence of conspiracy in the JFK assassination. The others were for UPI and *Life Magazine*.
- Dr. James Weston, the president-elect of the American Academy of Forensic Sciences asked by CBS to analyze Kennedy's wounds, is the *only* recent Academy president still satisfied with the original Warren Commission conclusions about two shots striking from the rear. Outgoing Academy president Robert Joling, as well as four other past presidents, have called for a review of all medical and scientific evidence by a new independent panel of forensic experts.

- Dr. Alfred G. Ólivier, called on by CBS to uphold the controversial belief that a single bullet could emerge so unscathed after hitting both Kennedy and John Connally, is a *veterinarian* at Edgewood Arsenal. His lone approving voice has been called gospel by the Warren Commission, Rockefeller Commission on CIA activities, and now CBS.

As for the critics whose evidence might indicate more than one assassin, CBS gave them short shrift. Despite a total of six hours of interviews with photo researcher Josiah Thompson and former Academy president Dr. Cyril Wecht, the strongest conclusions of both men wound up on the cutting room floor.

Here is what a truly open CBS inquiry might have said about the main bones of contention:

Oswald's marksmanship: If a man could fire three shots from a clumsy, single-shot Mannlicher-Carcano rifle like Oswald's in 5.2 seconds—the time CBS calculated between the first and fatal shots on the Zapruder film—then Oswald could indeed have been the only gunman. So CBS set up a simulated situation with a moving target, and four marksmen did achieve what many critics had long contended was impossible. But CBS said nothing about the results of its other seven marksmen, and gave no indication of cumulative scores or number of practice rounds.

Another question about the law of probability focuses on just when the first shot may have struck Kennedy. The Zapruder film doesn't tell, because 15 frames (slightly less than a second) are obscured by the limousine's passage behind the Stemmons Freeway sign. If Kennedy was hit just before emerging again into Zapruder's lens, the likelihood of Oswald's hitting his target is even more suspect, since CBS starts its 5.2-second computation much earlier. CBS didn't bother raising that issue.

The single-bullet theory: The Warren Commission's contention of three shots, one of which struck the curb, depends totally on the first shot passing through both Kennedy and John Connally. If Kennedy and Connally were hit by separate bullets, that means there were *four* shots altogether—one too many for a single marksman to get off in 5.2 seconds. But is it possible for a single bullet to hop, skip, and jump into seven different angle wounds in the two men?

CBS refuted the doubters on this issue by claiming it was impossible to tell precisely how Kennedy and Connally were sitting when struck. This time, the network chose to *use* the temporary obstruction of the freeway sign in the Zapruder film to make its point. If the men changed position in that time frame, CBS said, the strange trajectory could well have occurred. Had CBS consulted available films taken from other angles, it would have been obvious that neither man moved enough in that less-than-a-second interval to allow the otherwise impossible flight of the so-called "magic bullet."

The program's experts also maintained that a slight visible movement on Connally's part right after Kennedy is hit indicates that the same bullet is striking *him*. Josiah Thompson and Dr. Wecht painstakingly showed CBS how, more than a second later in the Zapruder frames, Connally *clearly* reacts—his right shoulder collapsing, cheeks puffing, hair dislodged. Connally's own doctor believes *that* is the momentum of a bullet hitting him, while the earlier movement is a startled reaction to *hearing* a shot hit Kennedy. Connally agrees. In fact, he told that to CBS in an earlier interview where he also stated his feeling that all the shots did come from the rear. CBS chose to use the latter segment but eliminated Connally's remarks about different bullets.

CBS also eliminated Dr. Wecht's discussion of the implausibility of the single bullet's remarkably pristine condition, if indeed it could do what the Warren Commission claimed. That bullet, as CBS showed, is scarcely damaged by all its travels. Not one scientist has ever come up with a bullet in such good condition in simulated experiments with cadavers. Yet CBS took the word of veterinarian Oliver that it *could* happen, and ignored Wecht's telling words.

The fatal shot: The strongest argument for conspiracy in the Zapruder film is also the hardest to watch. It clearly shows the top of the president's head being blown off, and the force catapulting him backward and to the left. That final impact obviously came from somewhere in *front* and to the *right* of the president—somewhere along the area known as the grassy knoll.

Yet Itek's image enhancement technique claims to show a perceptible forward movement of Kennedy's head *before* the backward "reaction" sets in. If so, it was invisible in CBS's rendering. CBS backed this with the hypothesis that Jacqueline Kennedy may have inadvertently pushed her husband backward. This is preposterous, since the film shows no real reaction on Mrs. Kennedy's part until 10 frames *after* the fatal shot.

For further evidence, Dan Rather asserted that the greater portion of the president's brain matter flew forward, indicating once again a shot from the rear. This statement is contradicted by almost every witness in the motorcade. Both policemen riding *behind* the limousine were splattered, one so hard he thought he'd been shot, and two skull fragments also went flying backwards. In front of the president there was only slight falling debris.

On CBS, the Zapruder film was never shown all the way through at speed, nor was much of the other vast photographic evidence examined in detail. There was no mention of something Itek acknowledged in its earlier work for *Life Magazine*—a strange figure visible in other films, standing at the base of the retaining wall perpendicular to the fateful Elm Street.

Nor was there mention of new technological tools like the Psychological Stress Evaluator (PSE), which concluded from voice tapes of Oswald after the shooting that he was telling the truth about not shooting anybody in Dallas.

And no mention of the possibility that Oswald was framed, although considerable speculation exists whether the window boxes and spent cartridges were arranged *later* on the sixth floor of the Texas School Book Depository.

The second program, which dealt with Oswald's relationships with the FBI and CIA and the chance of conspiracy, was better—as far as it went. But Jack Ruby, Oswald's slayer, was left out entirely. No discussions of Ruby's previous connections with the mob, FBI, Dallas police, Castro's Cuba, possibly even Oswald himself—despite two months of CBS research last spring for a *60 Minutes* segment titled "The Oswald-Ruby Connection." That program was canceled when the fall specials were announced, its research supposedly turned over to the new production unit.

There are countless smaller points. Why, in interviewing ex-CIA official Victor Marchetti, didn't CBS ask abut the meeting he attended in 1968 with then-director Richard Helms? At the height of Jim Garrison's conspiracy investigation in New Orleans, Marchetti has Helms conceding that Garrison's two principal figures—accused conspirators Clay Shaw and David Ferrie—were indeed once CIA contact employees. The Garrison probe wasn't mentioned once by CBS.

How does this happen? Why should CBS blatantly ignore so much crucial evidence and uphold the government-appointed Warren Commission? Can this be another example of the kind of Byzantine media-government relationship *Variety* suggests in its latest issue in which it alleged an offer of favored treatment from former CBS president Frank Stanton to the Nixon White House in exchange for help in a lawsuit against the CBS documentary "Selling of the Pentagon?" (Stanton has denied initiating the 1971 meeting.)

Perhaps not. But, curiously, these current CBS programs are almost identical—in score and cast—to the network's first series of specials eight years ago. It's basically the same production staff and commentator coming to the same conclusions. Back in 1967, up until the last minute most of the producers anticipated a script raising grave doubts about whether Oswald acted alone. Then, abruptly, something changed. CBS backed the Warren Commission right down the line, and one producer, Bob Richter, was so astounded that he resigned.

Richter, who now has his own documentary production company, says of the latest CBS effort: "It seemed a form of unusual advocacy journalism, especially the first program. I'd say they almost seemed to be defensive. They should have said, here's the evidence and here's what the experts say—experts who disagree. A third conclusion ought to have been considered for the evidence: Not proven."

Both Dr. Wecht and Thompson privately wonder if the script didn't again undergo last-minute editing from CBS higher-ups. After calling him twice to go over word for word what Rather would say about Wecht's statements, Wecht says CBS then "cut the heart of my presentation."

The November 24 issue of *Time Magazine* also devoted five pages to "Who Killed JFK? Just One Assassin." The article, of course, didn't touch on Time-Life's long suppression of the original Zapruder film vaults. Nor did it mention former editor Richard Billings who, like Richter at CBS, resigned in outrage in 1968 when *Life* thwarted the investigation they'd assigned him.

According to photo research expert Richard Sprague, who was gathering material for Billings, the *Life* team was suddenly ordered to stop all work on the JFK assassination. "All of the research files, including the Zapruder film and slides and thousands of other film frames and photographs, were locked up tight," Sprague has written. "No one at the magazine was permitted access to these materials and no one outside was ever allowed to see them again."

As *Life* eventually did with the Zapruder film, CBS made a big deal about showing the interview in which LBJ expressed his own doubts about the Kennedy case. Although segments were originally kept off the air at LBJ's request, their content had long since been widely reported. So in the main had CBS's look at intelligence ties. But the one startling revelation—an interview with Robert McKeown about Oswald's approaching him to buy *four* high-powered rifles—wasn't pursued very far. Nor were other men besides McKeown with equally important tales, whom CBS made no effort to track down.

The strongest insight came from the films of Lee Harvey Oswald himself. In the midst of chaos at police headquarters, he possessed an almost uncanny calm, as if certain that this rather bizarre circumstance would soon be cleared up and the truth made known. And from the old footage of Oswald's days in New Orleans, the distinct feeling remains that his espousing the Marxist cause has a motive behind it, that he wasn't speaking for himself but for someone else.

The question that must yet be answered is—who?

4

The Media, the CIA, and the Cover-Up

In the many years that have passed since my critique of CBS's news special, not much has changed in terms of the major media's emphasis on the official Oswald-did-it-alone scenario, and its unwillingness to acknowledge (much less to investigate) possibilities of a conspiracy. When Gerald Posner's book, *Case Closed*, was published in 1993, it was widely praised by reviewers as the last word on the assassination (a later article in this book provides my own critique). In 2007, Vincent Bugliosi's *Reclaiming History*, a 1,612-page tome essentially regurgitating the Warren Commission, received similar accolades. Even PBS joined the chorus this year, with "Oswald's Ghost" on *American Experience* leaning heavily against the "conspiracy buffs." The reasons behind this are worth exploring, even forty-five years later, for they tell us quite a bit about the corporate media's abandoning its role as watchdog of democracy and becoming more like the government's lap-dog.

On November 22, 1963, the initial dispatch by the *Associated Press* had reported: "The shots apparently came from a grassy knoll in the area."[16] While this news dominated most of the early reports from Dallas, it was quickly supplanted by the Texas School Book Depository where Oswald supposedly fired all the shots from the sixth-floor window.

Dan Rather, at the time a local news reporter in Dallas, had been the first journalist to see the twenty-second-long "home movie" taken by dressmaker Abraham Zapruder. Rather proceeded to tell a national TV audience that the fatal shot drove the president's head "violently forward." In fact, the footage showed precisely the opposite.[17] In his book, *The Camera Never Blinks*, Rather later defended his "mistake," saying it had happened because his viewing of the film was so hurried.

Yet no one was able to question this in 1963, because Time-Life immediately bought the Zapruder film for $150,000—a small fortune at the time—and then fought to keep it out of the public domain. The *Life Magazine* publisher, C. D. Jackson, was "so upset by the head-wound sequence," according to

---

[16] Associated Press story: *New Times Magazine*, Fall 1976, "The Media and the Murder of John Kennedy" by Jerry Policoff.
[17] Dan Rather: *Extra!*, March 1992, "The Plot to Kill JFK."

Richard Stolley, then the magazine's L.A. bureau chief, "that he proposed the company obtain all rights to the film and withhold it from public viewing at least until emotions calmed."[18]

It may have been more than a matter of Jackson's being "upset." As reporter Carl Bernstein wrote in a 1977 article for *Rolling Stone* ("The CIA and the Media"): "For many years, [Time-Life founder Henry] Luce's personal emissary to the CIA was C. D. Jackson, a Time Inc., vice president who was publisher of *Life Magazine* from 1960 until his death in 1964. While a *Time* executive, Jackson co-authored a CIA-sponsored study recommending the reorganization of the American intelligence services in the early 1950s." He also "approved specific arrangements for providing CIA employees with Time-Life cover. Some of these arrangements were made with the knowledge of Luce's wife, Clare Boothe."[19] (Herself a member of the Committee to Free Cuba, immediately after the assassination Mrs. Luce disseminated information implicating Oswald that she'd received from a group of CIA-backed Cuban exiles whom she supported.)[20]

Life then published a story headlined END OF NAGGING RUMORS: THE CRITICAL SIX SECONDS (December 6, 1963), purporting to show precisely how Oswald had succeeded in hitting his target. Supposedly based on the Zapruder film, the magazine claimed that the president had been turning to wave to someone in the crowd when one of Oswald's bullets struck him in the throat. However, this was patently false: that sequence did not appear in the film.[21]

From the moment of his arrest in the Texas Theater, Oswald was damned as guilty by the media. CAREER OF SUSPECT HAS BEEN BIZARRE, the *New York Times* headlined. LEFT-WING LUNACY, NOT RIGHT IS SUSPECT, said the *New York Herald-Tribune*. EVIDENCE AGAINST OSWALD DESCRIBED AS CONCLUSIVE, bannered *Time Magazine*.

Wrote media critic Jerry Policoff years later: "Thus, the press' curiosity was not aroused when a 7.65-caliber German Mauser mutated into a 6.5-caliber Italian Mannlicher-Carcano; or when the grassy knoll receded into oblivion; or when an entrance wound in the President's throat became an exit wound (first for a fragment from the head wound and then for a bullet from the back wound); or when a wound six inches below the President's shoulder became a wound at the back of the neck. The press was thereby weaving a web that would inevitably commit it to the official findings."

---

[18] C. D. Jackson: Policoff, op. cit.
[19] Jackson and CIA: *Rolling Stone*, October 20, 1977, "The CIA and the Media" by Carl Bernstein.
[20] Mrs. Luce and Cuban exiles: *Not in Your Lifetime* by Anthony Summers (N.Y.: Marlowe & Company, 1998), pp. 322–24.
[21] *Life* article: Policoff, op. cit.

Three months before *The Warren Report* came out, the *New York Times* ran a Page One exclusive: PANEL TO REJECT THEORIES OF PLOT IN KENNEDY DEATH. The "paper of record" then printed the whole report as a forty-eight-page supplement in late September 1964, collaborating with Bantam Books and the Book-of-the-Month Club to publish both hardcover and paperback editions.[22] "The commission analyzed every issue in exhaustive, almost archaeological detail," reporter Anthony Lewis wrote.

The *Times* also put together another book, *The Witnesses*, which contained "highlights" from testimony before the Warren Commission. All these were designed to buttress the lone-gunman conclusion. In one instance, a witness who reported having seen a man with a rifle on the sixth floor had other portions of his testimony eliminated—namely, that he'd actually seen *two* men but been told to "forget it" by an FBI agent. Witnesses like Zapruder, who believed some of the shots came from in front, were not included.

Life Magazine devoted most of its October 2, 1964, issue to *The Warren Report*, assigning commission member (and future president) Gerald Ford the job of evaluating it. In 1997, the Assassination Records Review Board would release handwritten notes by Ford, revealing that he had misrepresented the placement of the president's back wound—raising it several inches to suggest he'd instead been struck in the neck—in order to make it fit the theory that a single bullet had hit both Kennedy and Texas Governor John Connally. Otherwise, the entire lone-assassin notion would have collapsed. Ford, it was also later revealed, served to keep FBI Director J. Edgar Hoover fully apprised of the commission's deliberations.

That same issue of *Life* underwent two major revisions *after* it reached the newsstands. One of its articles was illustrated with eight frames from the Zapruder film. But Frame 323 turned out to contradict *The Warren Report*'s conclusion about the shots all coming from the rear. So the issue was recalled, the plates broken and re-set (this was all pre-computer), and Frame 313 showing the president's head exploding became the replacement. A second "error" forced still another such change. When a Warren Commission critic, Vincent Salandria, asked *Life* editor Ed Kearns about this two years later, he replied: "I am at a loss to explain the discrepancies between the three versions of LIFE which you cite. I've heard of breaking a plate to correct an error. I've never heard of doing it twice for a single issue, much less a single story. Nobody here seems to remember who worked on the early Kennedy story. . . ."[23]

And so it went. Skeptics of *The Warren Report* were often labeled "leftists" or "Communists." By late 1966, however, books like Mark Lane's *Rush to Judgment* and Josiah Thompson's *Six Seconds in Dallas* had become best-sellers and led a

---

[22] *Times* coverage: Ibid.
[23] *Life* "errors": Ibid, sidebar "A Matter of *Life* and Death."

growing number of Americans to question *The Warren Report*. The *New York Times* launched a new investigation. "We will go over all the areas of doubt and hope to eliminate them," announced editor Harrison Salisbury. Houston bureau chief Martin Waldron, a member of the investigative unit, later said they'd found "a lot of unanswered questions" that the paper then wouldn't pursue. "I'd be off on a good lead and then somebody'd call me off and send me out to California on another story or something. We never really detached anyone for this. We weren't really serious."[24]

Life Magazine also took a fresh look at the case. DID OSWALD ACT ALONE? A MATTER OF REASONABLE DOUBT, an article in the November 26, 1966 issue was headlined. A re-examination of the Zapruder film, the magazine said, had reached the conclusion that the single-bullet theory didn't hold up; a new investigation was needed. This was to be the first of a series of articles but, in January 1967, editor Richard Billings says he was informed that "It is not *Life's* function to investigate the Kennedy assassination." Never again would either *Time* or *Life* challenge the official version of events. Billings resigned from the magazine and took a job with a newspaper in St. Petersburg, Florida.[25]

In 1967, CBS News did a four-part study that again upheld *The Warren Report*, led by Dan Rather. Warren Commission member John McCloy served as the network's behind-the-scenes advisor. The final program of the series closed with commentator Eric Sevareid comparing critics of the Warren Commission to advocates of the anti-Semitic "Protocols of the Elders of Zion."

It would be another decade before the *Rolling Stone* article by Carl Bernstein, of Watergate fame, would reveal just how extensive were those same media organization's ties to the CIA. Among the executives lending their cooperation to the spy agency were, besides Henry Luce, CBS's William Paley and Arthur Hays Sulzberger of the *New York Times* (the last having even signed a secrecy agreement with the CIA). "By far the most valuable of these associations, according to CIA officials, have been with the *New York Times*, CBS and Time Inc.," Bernstein wrote.

"Over the years, the [CBS] network provided cover for CIA employees, including at least one well-known foreign correspondent and several stringers; it supplied outtakes of newsfilm to the CIA. . . . A high-level CIA official with a prodigious memory says that the *New York Times* provided cover for about ten CIA operatives between 1950 and 1966."

Bernstein's article began by recounting how a leading syndicated columnist, Joseph Alsop, had gone to the Philippines in 1953 to cover an election, at the CIA's behest. It would be Alsop, transcripts of President Johnson's taped telephone conversations later revealed, who first urged LBJ to form the

---

[24] Waldron quote: Policoff article.
[25] Billings: Ibid.

Warren Commission to answer any unresolved doubts about the assassination. "Alsop is one of more than 400 American journalists who in the past twenty-five years have secretly carried out assignments for the Central Intelligence Agency, according to documents on file at CIA headquarters," Bernstein wrote. "Journalists provided a full range of clandestine services—from simple intelligence-gathering to serving as go-betweens with spies in Communist countries."

Bernstein listed a number of CIA officials who worked closely with journalists, including Allen Dulles, Richard Helms, Desmond FitzGerald, and Tracy Barnes—all of whom had roles in covering up the truth about the Kennedy assassination and anti-Castro plots. "James Angleton, who was recently removed as the Agency's head of counterintelligence operations, ran a completely independent group of journalist-operatives who performed sensitive and frequently dangerous missions; little is known about this group for the simple reason that Angleton deliberately kept only the vaguest of files."

Among the CIA's most valuable relationships in the 1960s, Bernstein went on, was a *Miami News* reporter who covered Latin America named Hal Hendrix. He regularly provided information about individuals within Miami's Cuban exile community. He was the conduit through which the CIA passed word to then-Senator Kenneth Keating that the Soviets were putting missiles in Cuba in 1962, and was awarded the Pulitzer Prize for his coverage of the Missile Crisis. Although Bernstein did not delve into this, on the afternoon of the assassination Hendrix had provided to a colleague in Dallas considerable, yet-unrevealed, information about Oswald's history—including his supposed defection to Russia and his activities with the Fair Play for Cuba Committee.[26]

In the wake of Bernstein's investigation, the *New York Times* published an article (September 13, 1977) headlined: NEWS ORGANIZATIONS SAY THEY FIND NO EVIDENCE THEIR EMPLOYEES MAINTAINED CIA RELATIONSHIPS. However, two weeks later, the CIA announced that "it had adopted a new regulation barring any use of American reporters or employees of American newsgathering organizations as adjuncts of agency intelligence operations."[27]

And, on Christmas Day 1977, no doubt with considerable egg on the faces of its editors, the *Times* kicked off a three-part series: "The CIA's Three-Decade Effort to Mold the World's Views: Agency Network Using News Organs, Books and Other Methods is Detailed." The newspaper conceded that "the CIA's propagandizing appears to have contributed to at least some distortion of the news at home as well as abroad." Revelations included the fact that the CIA "has at various times owned or subsidized more than 50 newspapers, news services, radio stations, periodicals, and other communications entities, sometimes in

---

[26] Hendrix: Summers, p. 83.
[27] CIA barring reporters: *New York Times*, December 3, 1977, "CIA Adopts Regulation Barring Use of U.S. Reporters to Aid in Spying" by David Binder.

this country but mostly overseas." Also, "nearly a dozen American publishing houses, including some of the most prominent names in the industry, have printed at least a score of the more than 250 English-language books financed or produced by the CIA since the early 1950s." And perhaps as many as one hundred American journalists "have worked as salaried intelligence operatives while performing their reportorial duties." That was one-fourth the number that Bernstein's article described, but still a major admission of complicity.

One freelance journalist named Daniel James had been provided "material and background" on Che Guevara's diaries by the CIA. James, then living in Mexico, said he was acquainted with Agency Station Chief Winston Scott (a key man in the Oswald cover-up), and has asked Scott for "anything that they could get for me or help me with." The *Times* articles failed to mention that, along with Clare Booth Luce, James was a member of the Committee for Free Cuba and had been among the first purveyors of incriminating knowledge about Oswald.[28]

Also ignored by the media was the January 1978 congressional testimony of Morton Halperin, then-director of the Center for National Security Studies, that among the CIA's manipulation of American opinion through the press were its attempts to discredit critics of the Warren Commission. Meanwhile, Richard Salant, the CBS News President already identified as a CIA collaborator, told *Variety Magazine* that October that he had no intention of making publicly available the network's seventy-plus hours of outtakes relating to the assassination—because no evidence existed to contradict the fact that Oswald acted alone.[29]

Of course, while there may have been some "bad actors" linked to intelligence agencies working inside mainstream media, perhaps an even bigger explanation of their near unanimous rallying in support of a flawed Warren Commission and its findings was the instinct of top news executives toward defending powerful institutions. And working journalists couldn't help but notice that colleagues who questioned the official findings ran into roadblocks, while those who were largely accepting saw their careers flourish.

As the years passed, the big media's efforts to disparage the naysayers continued unabated. After the House Assassinations Committee concluded late in 1978 that the president "was probably assassinated as a result of a conspiracy," the *New York Times* initially buried the story—"Experts Say That Second Gunman Almost Certainly Shot at Kennedy"—on page 37, alongside the classified ads. Later, a *Times* editorial said that the committee seemed "more interested in

---

[28] Daniel James and Oswald: *The Man Who Knew Too Much* by Dick Russell (N.Y.: Carroll & Graf Publishers, 1992), p. 403.
[29] CBS and outtakes: *Variety*, October 25, 1978, "JFK Outtakes Stay Private, Salant Says."

inflaming than informing."[30] Where there were intimations of conspiracy in the media, the finger pointed elsewhere—a CBS documentary, "The CIA's Secret Army," strongly hinted that Fidel Castro had ordered Kennedy's murder in retaliation for the attempts on his own life.

And, when Oliver Stone's movie *JFK* appeared to much fanfare in the early 1990s—the public outcry leading to President Clinton's creation of an Assassination Records Review Board to gather and release still-classified government files—the strongest attacks came from news outlets and journalists "with the longest records of error and obstruction in defense of the flawed Warren Commission inquiry," as the non-profit group Fairness and Accuracy In Reporting observed.[31]

So we are left with the troubling assertion of David Atlee Phillips, who has since surfaced as the CIA official most likely to have been involved directly with Oswald. There was, Phillips said, "a natural affinity between American journalists and American intelligence officers abroad. They perform tasks which are similar."

---

[30] *Times* on investigation: *Inquiry*, March 5, 1979, "Press Contortions."
[31] Media coverage: *Extra!*, op. cit.

5

The Village Voice, December 15, 1975

"Senator Schweiker Reopens Assassination Probe: The Finger Points to Fidel, But Should It?"

The death of a president is once again at hand. With CIA comic book plots on world leaders and Oswald notes in FBI wastebaskets, time stops at the edge of where it all began to go wrong.

In recent days, it's *seemed* like even the most diehard Warren Commission supporters have been endorsing the Senate's move to reopen the JFK assassination inquiry. First David Belin, the world's staunchest defender of the original conclusions as counsel for the Warren and later Rockefeller commissions, announced for reopening although anticipating the same results. Then the most famous ex-commission member—President Ford himself—told a press conference that "some responsible group or organization" should investigate "new developments."

But if those developments go beyond an FBI-CIA–White House cover-up and accusations of murder actually start flying, look for the main target to be Cuba. Not necessarily because Fidel Castro is guilty, but because he is convenient—and, in the wake of at least eight admitted CIA plots on his life from 1960 to 1965, even excusable.

For sure, Lee Harvey Oswald had some kind of relationship with several mysterious Cubans. That's never been any secret. Who they were working for, or who Oswald *thought* they were working for, is another question.

The recent CBS inquiry featured an interview with LBJ filmed in 1970, implying that Castro might well have conspired against Kennedy in retaliation. That same series had a startling clip of Robert McKeown, onetime gunrunner to Castro and his guerrillas in the Sierra Maestra Mountains, claiming Oswald approached him with a Latin-looking man shortly before the assassination and offered $4,000 for four high-powered rifles. Another recent story, originating with Clare Booth Luce, has a Cuban friend approaching her after the assassination and describing tapes of a pro-Castro conspiracy.

Now, suddenly, Belin's call for reopening (motivated, he says, "toward a rebirth of confidence and trust in government") centers on the failure to tell the Warren Commission about CIA plots against Castro.

U.S. Senator Richard Schweiker, the Pennsylvania Republican whose subcommittee investigation is the impetus behind the Ford-Belin turnaround, is another who seems to lean toward Castro as the culprit. But Schweiker rules out *no* possibilities—except the one that Oswald acted alone. The story of his own turnaround—and the mirror image he uses to describe it—is the most hopeful sign that the truth, at long last, will be known.

"The Kennedy assassination is a mirror image proposition," Schweiker says. "What makes it so hard to know what happened is that you're struggling to find the real focus in the mirror. And you really need two reversible ones."

How to read the mirrors? That's the puzzle that faces Schweiker's growing team of investigators as the likelihood mounts for a full congressional examination of JFK's murder. Mirror number one is cloaked by the reversible dagger of the intelligence business. Who was Oswald? Agent or double agent? FBI, CIA, KGB? None of those? All of those? Did he even know? Or were there two of him? Mirror number two spins to memories of an undeclared war on an island off the Florida coast. Who were the Cubans that Oswald was associating with? Pro-Castro or anti-Castro? Or did he even know?

Someone knew. Or so Richard Schweiker believes.

"The more witnesses we talk to, the more they raise the fact that the Warren Commission really is a house of cards. Now it's just prodding, pushing, shaking the tree enough to have it fall."

And could that mean—as the Bicentennial dawns—a TV spectacular to make Watergate pale? A daytime parade of soldiers-of-fortune, Cuban exiles, right-wing fanatics, mobsters, and spies?

"Only if the worst fears of the critics are realized," Schweiker hedges. "But they could be."

It was only October, after six months of swampy allegations of CIA-Mafia deals and FBI black bag jobs, when Frank Church's Senate Select Committee on Intelligence granted Schweiker his mandate—a two-man subcommittee, with Colorado Senator Gary Hart, to explore the probability of an intelligence agency cover-up during the Warren Commission investigation. That made theirs the first government body since the commission with power to review classified documents, subpoena witnesses, and grant immunity. Once the regular Senate intelligence hearings end on December 18, it may also become the first body ever to hold open hearings on who killed JFK.

Beyond CIA-FBI sins of omission about Oswald, it's not clear how far Schweiker's knowledge extends. Just who might be saying what is a closely guarded secret within the labyrinthine cubicles of the Senate auditorium, where outsiders are forbidden and four task forces are winding up 60 different projects on the warp-and-woof of the intelligence trade.

This much is certain: the JFK task force is gaining both momentum and manpower. Schweiker and Hart's full-time subcommittee staff is up from two to five members and, as other phases of the Church committee come to a close, more are likely to switch over.

"There are indications from Church," says Schweiker's personal aide Dave Marston, "that he will make available as much staff as the inquiry needs."

On the other side of Capitol Hill, where the JFK issue began gathering support many months earlier, things are more or less at a standstill. Congressman Tom Downing's House resolution to reopen the case does have over 80 sponsors, and a Henry Gonzalez proposal to examine all *four* shootings (the two Kennedys, King, and Wallace) has 53. But so far, Rules Committee chairman Ray Madden hasn't been too receptive, and even by combining the two resolutions, twice that many co-sponsors would be necessary to pass a vote on the House floor.

So the burden is really on the Senate, particularly Schweiker, whose staff has never seen him devote so much energy to any single issue. Marston, normally his legislative counsel, is now spending about 90 per cent of his time "running a brushfire operation" out of the senator's office. That means maintaining liaison with the subcommittee staff, tracking down new leads, and filtering potential witnesses through Schweiker's schedule. Another personal assistant devotes full time to receiving *all* kooks, spooks, and their possible truths in an outer office. A new assistant press secretary has been hired to devote half his day to the JFK inquiry, and a WATS line has been installed to handle cross-country calls.

In many ways, Schweiker seems an unlikely crusader. Not a dodger of issues—a liberal Republican who opposed Vietnam, Haynsworth, Carswell, and ultimately Richard Nixon—but a reserved and not-too-charismatic forty-nine-year-old who barnstormed Pennsylvania in an old school bus last year, and whose wife is the original Miss Claire of TV's *Romper Room*.

Now he's barnstorming the talk shows, telling of "the bankruptcy of American policy" in stooping to alliances with the Mafia. And with eight of the 11 Church committee senators consulting him "on a fairly regular basis," it's only a matter of time until he becomes the Sam Ervin of an old and painful psychic wound.

"I was one of the millions who believed *The Warren Report*," he said in his Senate office, "until a CIA agent came before our committee and testified he'd made arrangements with the Mafia to make a hit on Castro. We know a lot more since then, but that was so repugnant and shocking to me that I did a backflip on any number of things.

"I've learned more about the inner workings of government in the past nine months than in my 15 previous years in Congress. Now I don't know who killed cock robin, but we *don't* know what happened and we *do* know Oswald had intelligence connections. Everywhere you look with him, there are the finger-prints of intelligence."

But as Schweiker found during the month's recess he spent studying the JFK literature last August, in this case the fingerprints are as likely to obscure the truth as reveal it. What J. Edgar Hoover and Allen Dulles pretended not to know has probably long since been given to the shredder. Recently declassified minutes of Warren Commission sessions do point directly to a cover-up, but Schweiker realizes "a lot of stuff is not *in* certain files—the 'Do Not File' pro-cedure we've learned about. So when Hoover says his files *show* only three FBI contacts with Oswald, he could be narrowly telling the truth where in fact he's lying through his teeth."

Still, the most intriguing aspect of the Senate probe, initially anyway, is the chance for a peek at the 152 secret and top-secret documents still salted away in the National Archives. Included are the commission minutes and the reports submitted by various government agencies, many of which were assembled after *The Warren Report* and never even seen by the commission.

Citing reasons of national security, in 1964 Lyndon Johnson issued an order to keep these particular documents hidden for 75 years, until 2038. Since then, about 50 of the original two-hundred-plus have been released or recently pried loose by Freedom of Information suits. Two of those are the commission ses-sions where Dulles admits that Hoover might lie about the bureau's links with Oswald and where members agree the FBI refused to investigate conspiracy evi-dence because of a preconceived conclusion about Oswald—both instrumental in Schweiker's original call to reopen the case.

Of the 152 still-sealed documents, 107 are FBI and 23 are CIA reports. That includes 15 relating to Oswald's sojourn in the Soviet Union, 23 more about his trips to Mexico. Some of the titles are unbelievably tantalizing. There is a CIA document called "Oswald's Access to Information About the U2 (the high-flying spy plane)." Another is titled "Reports of Travel Activities, Lee Harvey Oswald as Marine." Plus two memos from then-CIA Director Richard Helms, an "Allegation That Lee Harvey Oswald Was Interviewed by the CIA in the USSR," and a "Reproduction of CIA Official Dossier on Lee Harvey Oswald."

The secret FBI reports contain information about Oswald from Louisville, St. Louis, Albany, Tampa, Norfolk, Cincinnati, Oklahoma, Cleveland, Chicago, and Washington. Not to mention 15 of the 23 Mexican files.

Then there is Jack Ruby. "Why did the FBI withhold for 12 years that he'd informed for them on nine occasions?" Schweiker asks. "This wasn't national security information, so why were they so sensitive? Also I'm certain there were extenuating circumstances in his activities running guns to Cuba. We were really running a secret war against Cuba, and we know the CIA was heavily involved. Ruby had to have been at least working for someone who was working for CIA."

Tucked away in those classified archives is material on Ruby's tax returns, social security records, long-distance phone calls—and a mysterious CIA report titled "Information on Jack Ruby and Associates."

All this, supposedly, is being made available to the Senate subcommittee—with a few ground rules.

"The agencies involved have not released the documents, they've given us access," Schweiker says. "You can't take documents away or photocopy them. The FBI originally had a rule we couldn't even copy them by hand. If you have a good photographic mind, you're all right. But until we have a case to make on it, why fuss about it?"

The CIA, say Senate staffers, has been more cooperative than the FBI, though Schweiker says both agencies have given "most of what we've asked for. Until we digest it and question witnesses, we won't know if there are any gaps. We've had to get specific and narrow with our requests, and we may be missing the target unknowingly."

How good are the chances of finding a bombshell to blow the case wide open? Schweiker offers a dubious "who-knows" shrug.

"Whether any single document would reverse it is a very questionable assumption," he says. "But until you remove the documents from the premises and go over them with a fine tooth comb . . . well, my personal opinion is that there have got to be leads and relationships there. It should all be put in a computer and integrated. A lot of the material is overclassified in my judgment. In 1964, they'd classify your tie if it walked through a secret security net. And with the Warren Commission proceedings, a lot of the documents were simply not put together in any meaningful way."

The most glaring problem was mislabeling of documents. Consciously pre-planned mislabeling, Schweiker believes, in the case of a 1960 Hoover FBI memorandum *already* raising the possibility of an Oswald imposter in the USSR. That vital document was listed under "A Message to State Department on Data Oswald."

"They completely buried it," Schweiker says angrily. "A statement of an Oswald imposter by Hoover ought to have waved red flags around every circuit, but nowhere is it listed like this in the index. So it doesn't surprise me when the Warren Commission says they never saw some material."

Another strangely classified series is seven FBI files on Mark Lane, the first and most vocal of the Warren Commission critics. Though Schweiker won't cite specifics, he does admit his discovery of "an ongoing effort by the White House to discredit the critics."

The first piece of evidence is a White House memorandum from LBJ aide Marvin Watson to the FBI, ordering the bureau to compile secret dossiers on seven prominent commission detractors.

"The FBI did turn those dossiers over, and in one instance there was derogatory sexual activity with photographs," Schweiker says. "The part we've uncovered happened in 1966 and 1967. What we don't know yet is how ongoing it was. There is some indication that this is the tip of the iceberg."

If the federal government would go to such lengths to vilify its opponents, what could it possibly have been hiding? Merely the fact that Oswald and Ruby had intelligence connections that would prove embarrassing? Or something far more terrifying?

The idea that Castro engineered the whole thing is indeed the *least* of all possible evils. And Schweiker, with apparent good intentions, is inclined to buy it.

"As soon as he heard about the attempts to assassinate Castro, he said we ought to look into the Warren Commission," Marston recalls. "I said 'why?' He said, 'If we're shooting at Castro, why isn't he shooting back?'"

Schweiker considers what Dulles didn't tell his fellow commission members about this "a cover-up of sensational proportions." And while insisting he doesn't subscribe to any *particular* theory, he does point to an *Associated Press* story of September 9, 1963 that has Castro threatening "to answer in kind" if the U.S. tried to "eliminate Cuban leaders."

"Nobody paid any attention then because nobody knew we *were* trying to kill Castro," Schweiker says. "But that statement had to have meaning, particularly to Allen Dulles. Nobody has ever investigated that."

That's all well and good, as far as it goes. But strangely, some kind words about Castro of late come from E. Howard Hunt, who admitted to the *Providence Journal* that while working for the Nixon White House, he interviewed a Miami woman who was in Castro's house when news of Kennedy's death came. Hunt's report, a copy of which went to the CIA, called Castro "morose" because the two leaders had reached "an understanding" about eventually renewing diplomatic ties.

Despite all the fingers to Fidel, Hunt's statement seems far more believable. At least according to revelations in the Church committee's 347-page interim report, "Alleged Assassination Plots Involving Foreign Leaders."

According to this, in the fall of 1963, America's number two man at the U.N.—William Atwood—"held a series of talks with the Cuban ambassador to the United Nations to discuss opening negotiations on an accommodation between Castro and the United States." The progress was reported regularly to the White House, where McGeorge Bundy says JFK was in favor of "pushing towards an opening with Cuba . . . perhaps wiping out the Bay of Pigs and maybe getting back to normal."

In November, a French journalist named Jean Daniel went off to see Castro as a quasi-official spokesman for JFK. The administration's dirty tricks—the death plots and sabotage plans—had apparently, as far as Kennedy was concerned, come to a close. The journalist was with Castro on November 22, 1963. That same day, according to the CIA's 1967 inspector general's report, "it is likely that at the very moment President Kennedy was shot, a CIA officer was meeting with a Cuban agent and giving him an assassination device for use against Castro."

The device was a poison pen, a ballpoint rigged with a hypodermic needle so fine that the victim wouldn't notice its insertion. The would-be assassin was a "highly placed Cuban official" codenamed "AM/LASH" who originally had wanted from the CIA "a high powered rifle with telescopic sights that could be used to kill Castro from a distance." Desmond FitzGerald, head of CIA covert Cuban operations, has assured AM/LASH his mission had the sanction of the highest officials in the land. Because Richard Helms, according to the CIA's own report, decided "it was not necessary to seek approval from Robert Kennedy for FitzGerald to speak in his name."

The CIA's own files claim "the situation changed when the case officer and FitzGerald left the meeting to discover that President Kennedy had been assassinated . . . it was decided that we could have no part in the assassination of a government leader (including Castro) and would not aid AM/LASH in this attempt."

However, the Senate report says assassination efforts involving AM/LASH did in fact continue into 1965. And with Johnson's assuming the presidency, William Atwood's diplomatic talks with the Cubans became less frequent and eventually ceased early in 1964.

Why should U.S. Intelligence, which desperately wanted Castro gone anyway, be so scrupulous about covering up a Castro retaliation against Kennedy? Was Castro—or his tie with Russia—so strong that this government then *feared* him? Nonsense. The Castro's-revenge motive is too easy. The devil plays subtler games.

Who then? In Schweiker's files, there is also a large sheaf on a right-wing extremist group called the National States Rights party. It contains government documents, some pages still withheld from the public, on a wealthy southerner named J. A. Milteer. On November 9, 1963, in Miami, a police informant "who has furnished reliable information in the past" has Milteer—an organizer for the party—telling him that a plan to kill Kennedy was in the works. Two weeks prior to the assassination, the informant passed that information to the Secret Service. Information about an assassination plan "from a window with a high-powered rifle."

Milteer, according to researchers in Texas, died several years ago. But dozens of others, some never called or even mentioned by the Warren Commission, are very much alive—and perhaps willing to talk.

"Some I was told would never talk at all, and I can't get them off the phone," says Dave Marston. "But you can do only the most preliminary things by phone. I've seen a large number of people here, and we hope to put more people in the field."

So far, the Senate staff hasn't talked to Oswald's wife Marina. Marston has spoken to his mother Marguerite by phone from Fort Worth: "She gave me the suggestion she's under surveillance continually, and that her son had some intelligence community connection she can prove—but that solution is always somewhere around the corner."

Progress is slow, but steady. As Marston says, "The Warren Commission was so compartmentalized, protected from the outside world. It's like the old story of how somebody wanted to confess but they had nobody handling confessions. The committee is more systematized, long-range."

And, to believe Schweiker, more open. Even the discredited case of New Orleans ex-District Attorney Jim Garrison isn't taken lightly. "We have some leads that obviously go to New Orleans and we're pursuing them," Schweiker says. "Whether it's Garrison's story or a contradictory one, I think we'll know in a couple months."

A couple months. That is Schweiker's timetable to find that single, sensational piece of news that will convince the most skeptical of his colleagues to rush ahead. Then will come the technical analysis ("If we had 100 staffers to turn loose, this would be a very important segment"), the feeding of all relevant material into a computer ("Ultimately it has to be done"), the appointment of a special prosecutor, and subpoenaing of witnesses.

The final irony, in an election year, will be the fateful effect on the lives of two public figures—Gerald Ford and Edward Kennedy.

Does Schweiker believe Ford's chances for reelection might hinge on the findings of his subcommittee? "It strictly depends on what we find out. I believe there was a cover-up, so where was it and by whom? I don't really know. The LBJ White House? CIA-FBI? Or into the Warren Commission? If he was involved in some cover-up, it will certainly hurt him.

"But I don't think this will become party politics. I hope it won't, because it could set us back another two years. It can cut both ways. If a cover-up went to the Warren Commission, it also went to the Johnson White House."

As for Ted Kennedy, Schweiker glances down at his desk, then up, and says evenly: "Senator Kennedy and I are good friends. He is chairman of the Health Committee and I'm the ranking Republican. Before I held my initial press conference, I wrote a personal note to him explaining why I was doing it and that I hoped he would read my statement. I knew in my own mind he would not want to see the case reopened, from his family's point of view. I didn't expect an answer. I phrased it in a way it didn't need one, unless he wanted to. He has not told me to cease and desist."

6

The Takedown of
the House Investigation

With all the interest generated by the Schweiker probe, the following March 1976 more than 100 congressional lawmakers sought the creation of a House Select Committee on Assassinations (HSCA) to look anew at the deaths of President Kennedy and Martin Luther King, Jr. Although the House Rules Committee initially squelched the attempt, on September 17 the full House passed the resolution.

Richard A. Sprague was named acting counsel and director of the HSCA. He was the former assistant District Attorney of Philadelphia, having led the investigation of Tony Boyle (former head of the United Mine Workers) that resulted in a murder conviction. Regarded as tough and uncompromising, before he would accept the new job Sprague had demanded and been assured complete freedom to conduct the investigation as he saw fit. By November, he'd hired a staff of 170, drawing many of them from homicide bureaus and DA's offices across the country. He'd also asked for a starting budget of $13 million, and begun issuing subpoenas.[32]

One of the first individuals called to testify was David Phillips, who in 1963 had been in charge of the CIA's Cuban operations in Mexico City. Phillips claimed that a CIA wiretap had recorded Oswald speaking with the Soviet Embassy three times, but the tapes had been "routinely destroyed" within a week after Oswald's late September trip to Mexico. However, Sprague then came across an FBI memo from the day after the assassination, referring to Dallas agents having listened to the tape and being "of the opinion" it was not Oswald's voice.

CIA photos of "Oswald" in Mexico City did not match either. So Sprague demanded all information about CIA operations there and full access to any employees involved with tape recordings, photographs, or transcripts. First the Agency balked, and then told Sprague he would first need to sign a CIA Secrecy Agreement. He refused, saying he would issue subpoenas.

And that is where things soon began to go sour for Sprague and the House Select Committee. At the close of 1976, the HSCA announced that preliminary

---

[32] Sprague background: *New Times*, December 1976, "The Man Congress Picked to Investigate the Assassinations" by Jerry Policoff. Also, *New York Times*, December 10, 1976, "Assassination Study Requests $13 Million" by David Burnham.

investigations had uncovered enough unresolved questions to keep moving forward. Then, on January 2, 1977, *New York Times* reporter David Burnham wrote a lengthy article claiming that Sprague's "judgment and actions have been subject to formal criticism on a number of occasions" by Pennsylvania authorities. A few days after that, Representative Don Edwards of California—an ex-FBI man who chaired the House Judiciary Subcommittee on Civil and Constitutional Rights—warned that some of the HSCA's investigative techniques were "wrong, immoral and very likely illegal." He was referring to alleged plans to secretly record potential witnesses remarks with hidden body transmitters and then do Psychological Stress Evaluation tests.[33]

Burnham continued his negative reporting on Sprague and the committee. After the Pennsylvania Supreme Court suddenly ordered a new trial in the murder case in which Sprague had successfully convicted Tony Boyle, Burnham inferred that it had been the result of a fix. The House Rules Committee, in early February, approved re-establishing the HSCA but only for two months and with a restricted investigative mandate. Not long after this, Texas Congressman Henry Gonzalez—chairman of the committee—suddenly demanded Sprague's immediate resignation, saying he had "engaged in a course of conduct that is wholly intolerable for any employee of the House." Burnham would later detail Gonzalez' charges that Sprague had violated House rules by continuing to work as a private attorney and refusing to file a statement of his outside income, while also failing to provide the FBI information about himself in a background check.[34]

For the next six weeks, Gonzalez continued to press his surprising crusade against Sprague. He shut off the HSCA staff's long-distance phones and rescinded their clearance to pursue classified information.

On March 18, 1977, Sprague wrote a memorandum "To File" recounting that an attorney, William Illig, had contacted him "after a luncheon meeting with his client, Dr. Burkley." Retired Navy Vice Admiral Dr. George Burkley had been the personal physician for President Kennedy. He rode in the Dallas motorcade, was present at Parkland Hospital, traveled with JFK's body aboard Air Force One, and attended the autopsy at Bethesda Naval Hospital. The Warren Commission never called him as a witness.

The physician had advised attorney Illig, wrote Sprague, "that although he, Burkley, had signed the death certificate of President Kennedy in Dallas, he had

---

[33] Edwards quote: *New York Times*, January 6, 1977, "Assassination Panel Is Warned on Its Techniques" by David Burnham.

[34] Sprague and Gonzalez: *Washington Post*, February 11, 1977, "Representative Gonzalez Trying to Fire Sprague" by George Lardner Jr.; *New York Times*, February 12, 1977, "Assassination Panel's Fate in Doubt As Sprague Faces New Allegations" by David Burnham; *Congressional Record*, Remarks of Henry Gonzalez, February 16, 1977, "The Reasons for the Firing of the Chief Counsel and Staff Director."

never been interviewed and that he has information . . . indicating that others besides Oswald must have participated. Illig advised me that his client is a very quiet, unassuming person, not wanting any publicity whatsoever, but he, Illig, was calling me with his client's consent and that his client would talk to me in Washington."

Sprague never had the opportunity. After he agreed to resign two weeks later, on March 30, the House voted to keep the HSCA in existence for another year.[35] Soon named as new chief counsel was G. Robert Blakey, a Cornell University law professor. Blakey's first step was to require all remaining staff to sign confidentiality agreements. Several were either fired or talked into quitting because the FBI wouldn't clear them. Others weren't allowed access to classified materials, pending CIA clearance. Those staffers who were permitted to read CIA documents had to submit any notes they took to the CIA for review.[36] The HSCA's new medical panel never took Dr. Burkley's testimony.

And, while the Blakey-led HSCA did conclude that a probable conspiracy pointed to the involvement of several Mob figures, the CIA would basically get a free pass in terms of complicity.

On May 25, 1978, I walked into Sprague's office in Philadelphia with a tape recorder. I wanted to know how he looked back on his short, unhappy tenure as chief counsel for the committee. Published here for the first time is a transcript taken from our interview:

In hindsight, how do you view what happened to you and the Committee?
I view it from a number of different angles. I am absolutely convinced that the Congress of the United States, as a totality, has not the slightest interest in a thorough, in-depth investigation into the assassination of President Kennedy or Martin Luther King, Jr. Putting the two together as a package deal was really to make the Black Caucus feel that they had input into the Democratic Party, and to make the people pushing the Kennedy probe feel that at last they've got their way. There was a presidential election coming up [won by Jimmy Carter in 1976] and it was good politics. I think that's the reason it went through in the waning hours of that particular Congress. And the appointment of [Tom] Downing as the first chairman, knowing that he was retiring, is indicative of the fact that there was no real intent. Furthermore, when the new Congress reconvened, [House Speaker] Tip O'Neill and others kept saying, "Well show us why it should continue"—yet we hadn't even really commenced the investigation. I am convinced that there are a number of Congressmen who are also subject to

[35] Sprague resignation: *Rolling Stone*, April 7, 1977, "Why Is the Assassinations Committee Killing Itself?"
[36] Blakey: *New Times*, September 4, 1978, "A Great Show, A Lousy Investigation" by Jerry Policoff and William Scott Malone.

pressures and so are effective blocks to an investigation. Some of these pressures come from investigative agencies of the federal government, others by various groups around this country. As a result, the Congress as an instrument is not really the place to have such a probe.

A second thing I feel is that for some reason—and to me it's the most fascinating part of my whole Washington experience—there is some manipulation of the press that's successful enough that it's not interested in a real investigation either. There was total dishonesty in the reporting of newspapers that I would otherwise have confidence in, such as the *New York Times* and the *Washington Post*, but in this area that degree of integrity and impartial reporting was not to be. Now whether it's because of subtle pressures upon them, or independent motivation by them, I do not have the answer. But, as a result, this attitude by the press was most successful in taking advantage of the attitude of Congress in general, and by individual Congressmen who were manipulated such that the press could achieve a tone to help kill the investigation.

The other area that I see with hindsight is that there is a greater ability to manipulate public opinion by certain agencies of government than I would have believed possible.

David Burnham particularly took you apart in the New York Times. *Did you ever come across any reason he would have had? He intentionally seemed to have distorted a number of things.*

I go beyond Burnham. It would be an interesting analysis by someone going to college, to get into the whys and wherefores of the reporting by the press. In Burnham's case, it's not just that he distorted or said things that weren't so. It's so obvious it was conscious. It was to such an extent that it had to be apparent to those on his paper who were in a superior position.

Let me illustrate here what I mean, because to me it's the most concrete example. One, as a prosecutor, I have never wiretapped and never secretly recorded any conversation with anybody. I wanted us to obtain recording equipment, for the purpose of our people in the field interviewing and getting the person's permission to tape record for the purpose of accuracy. If the person said no, we would not record it. The record will show that's exactly the way we used them. Three or four weeks after we made that request to Congress, stories were carried in the *Los Angeles Times*, the *Post*, and particularly by Burnham that I'd bought this recording equipment to surreptitiously record what witnesses are going to say. To this day, nobody has ever in fact produced anybody who said we did that. We must be the first group crucified not for what we did, but for what a reporter says we are going to do!

I immediately saw the potential of what could be created out of that. I had a meeting with the committee and stated exactly what I've said to you, and we called a press conference. Burnham was there, along with the *Los Angeles Times* and *Post* reporters, and the guy from the *Washington Star* [Jeremiah O'Leary, who would soon be named by Carl Bernstein as a CIA asset]. They didn't even carry our response. However, because of what had appeared before, Congressman Edwards out in California puts out this letter in which he crucifies us on the basis of their original stories for our improper constitutional manner of proceeding with the investigation. Burnham and the others carry big stories on Edwards' attack. We called another press conference, said again exactly what I've just said, and again our response isn't carried. Now it seems to me that someone in a supervisory position at the *New York Times*, for example, would say to Burnham: "All right, Edwards is saying this, but what does the committee say?" Yet it seemed to be of no interest to the superiors. It's also interesting that those attacks, without our response, then engendered other attacks carried in the press, again without our response, which then led to editorials. Not one editorial writer in the United States contacted our committee to ask for our side of it.

It is striking to note that, right after I resigned, Burnham was taken off the whole thing and someone else was put in his place. Was he put on the story to do a hatchet job? There is certainly an appearance of that. On a story getting this kind of national attention, I don't think anyone could get away with that distorted reporting without the connivance of superiors.

Of course, the Times *and many other media have a long history of not wanting anything more to come out about the assassination.*

That's right. I've become more interested in the media than the assassination. I'm a great believer, or have been, that it's up to you to get good people into public office. But if the public can't get impartial, thorough news, how can I damn the public? And where do you get this responsibility by the media?

What do you think happened to Congressman Henry Gonzalez? He seemed to flip.

I see that as an anomaly kind of situation. Despite all the attacks from Gonzalez, to me he is just a pathetic character in the broader drama here. I ascribe to Gonzalez a number of things, but predicated on an inferiority complex. Here's a Mexican-American guy who's been pushing and pushing for the Kennedy investigation, and finally the Congress goes through the charade, though not really intending to [do it]. Who do they make chairman of the committee but, as far as he's concerned, a blueblood—[Tom] Downing. This is an affront to Gonzalez. Well, Downing is a lame duck who's retiring and just about everybody on the committee would say to me, "There must be someone other than Gonzalez as chairman when Downing leaves." A number of them went to Tip O'Neill to express that, because they said Gonzalez just does not work with people. To what extent this got back to Gonzalez and raised further problems in him, I do not know.

Now what happens when Gonzalez *is* appointed chairman? Right off the bat, he wants to show that power emanates from him. I was starting to look into matters involving the FBI and the CIA. When this recording thing came up, Gonzalez, instead of responding "what a bunch of nonsense," said: Don't blame me, I wasn't chairman then, it was Downing. Gonzalez had been one of our biggest supporters of the budget, when we initially submitted it. But when people started attacking the budget, again he said, Oh, that was a stupid thing that happened under Downing. This became, I think subconsciously for Gonzalez, a way of getting back at his colleagues for appointing Downing. You know, had they appointed him in the first place, none of these problems would have occurred.

Then, of course, with the [budget] pinch that occurred, Gonzalez—again flexing his muscle—wants to get rid of some people who are working for us. Who does he pick on first? The Downing people that have been hired. Let me say this, he had some legitimate complaints about certain people. However, at this time most on the staff were working without any pay, on the promise that yes they will get reimbursed. I felt that if people are working for you on faith, that is no time to say to someone, "I'm firing you." I made it clear that there's a moral obligation to at least keep people on until they've been reimbursed for their time. I said that to the committee. Now here is Gonzalez, thwarted in the beginning by Downing, and with his first pronouncement as chairman, his chief counsel and the committee go against him. I think that, with his particular sensitivities, that set Gonzalez off. I don't think it's anything more than having been rubbed the wrong way. I don't see him as part of any conspiracy toward killing anything off.

In the course of your limited investigation, did you ever have the feeling that what you were dealing with in investigating Kennedy's death went beyond the assassination and into very sensitive areas of intelligence?

Yes.

In what way?

You know, it's interesting. This gets back to the press. When I was appointed, the *New York Times* wrote a very favorable editorial. The *Times* had always been very favorable to me in the Boyle prosecution in the Mine Workers case. This whole business à la Burnham, and the distortions, and then an editorial attacking my appointment for not have been thoroughly investigated, has to be taken in terms of time sequence. At that later stage of the game when the attacks started, I was raising questions concerning the connections, if any, between Oswald and the CIA, pre-Kennedy assassination. I was raising questions about the reliability of information that Oswald was in Mexico City, as opposed to being in Dallas that September. I was raising questions as to whether the information that the CIA had presented of the wiretaps [in Mexico] and so forth was, in fact, reliable. I was starting to raise questions concerning why it was that Oswald, as a defecting American returning to the United States from the Soviet Union, is not debriefed by the CIA. And who made the decisions not to touch him?

And I was making it clear, at this same time, that I would not sign any of the agreements with the CIA and FBI that other committees had signed (and that they want in general, and which the present committee has signed)—a non-disclosure agreement. They give you access to certain things provided they have control over your staff and can then control what thereafter gets released. I took the view that, for this to be a thorough, hard-hitting, impartial investigation, they could not control the staff or what gets disclosed. The purpose of the investigation is ultimate disclosure. I was also making it clear that I wanted to subpoena information from these agencies, as well as the people involved in the decision-making process, and I would not bargain in this area.

Because of where I was at, and the timing of these attacks, that convinces me that the motivation came to kill me off. They don't care about an investigation if it does not really tread on toes. Sprague, they felt, was going to tread on toes. Blakey, who is there now, is not going to tread on toes. Whatever they do today, you couldn't get a ripple out of the press across this nation. If I sneezed, it made headlines. And I think that they are very concerned about the way it might appear in terms of intelligence operations and an Oswald, in connection with the assassination, not saying it had any connection.

You interviewed David Phillips. Did you believe him?

I had questions about Phillips. As an investigator, I don't accept what anyone says. I want to draw them out and hear them, but I want to then proceed and see where there is corroboration—and where there is evidence that disproves as well—and then I'll decide after that.

What about George de Mohrenschildt? He certainly had connections with Oswald in Dallas, and perhaps with the intelligence agencies as well.

You have to understand, de Mohrenschildt had been in touch with us for a period of time, from Europe. He then came over here, and I observed his attempt to use things first as a publicity vehicle. However, that did not mean I did not want us talking to him. We were trying to locate him, when his death occurred. The night of his death, that's the night I ended up resigning. One of the last things I was setting in motion, when I got word about this, was that we immediately contacted the District Attorney down in Palm Beach, Florida, someone I had known, and I was arranging to send some people down there. To me, that was an area to be working on immediately. But I never got any further.

There are a lot of strange characters in this whole thing, and that's the shame of it—that there could not be a thorough, hard-hitting, full examination. It is most surprising that there can't be. Why shouldn't there be? I am convinced that the present committee is just going through a charade right now. They're going to have public hearings, but they're already writing the report.

Do you know that for a fact?

Yes.

What do you come away feeling about the assassination? Do you believe it must have been a conspiracy?

I did not get far enough to come away with any such opinion. I came away with the feeling that agencies of the United States government have an interest in preventing a full investigation, because at least in offshoots they are connected with some of the characters involved in the assassination. Beyond that, I don't know. I'm convinced that there is more of a connection between those agencies and Oswald than has ever surfaced.

You have to understand, I was just there six months. Here we're talking about the murder of a president and a civil rights leader. You don't even have a secretary yet, so what are you going to do? Obviously first you've got to find and recruit staff, spend time interviewing them. You're getting flooded with mail by applicants from around the country. So when the Congress asks at the end of three months, "What have you done?" it's idiotic. The only thing you've done basically is to formulate what kind of staff you're going to have. Now the one thing that I did do, I started hiring some people and, rather than have them sit around while I'm continuing with this administrative matter, I did put them into some very brief hit-and-miss areas of work. But I never got beyond that.

Did you ever go to Mexico City?

I sent people there.

One key group is Alpha 66, do you know if they were ever investigated?

Cuban exiles were part of the area that was being investigated when I was there, including that group. We did not get into any area enough to generate something that was really a lead.

Can you say any more about the direction the committee is taking now?

Well, Blakey has had the staff sign these agreements, subject to $5,000 penalties if they disclose anything. People are not on the staff if they're not approved by the CIA now. And Blakey is not spending money for in-depth field investigation, but has turned some funds back to Congress. They're using a guy like Dr. Spitz from Detroit as one of their experts on the autopsy. Spitz was found by the DA's office in Detroit to have misused his medical examiner's office. He was also used by the Rockefeller Commission [on CIA Activities], so you don't have people who are disinterested.

The tragedy is, the American people will probably take whatever they say as the last word now.

Oh sure. I think that the public interest is down drastically, and the fiasco—as I call it—in Washington has helped kill it.

Have you thought of writing a book about the fiasco?

I've kicked it around in my mind, it could be an interesting book. I sent one of the deputies to talk to the California delegation, about the connection between Ruby, Oswald and the underworld. A couple of members of the delegation raised their hands and asked, "Who's Jack Ruby?" I mean, that's some of the problem down there. Have you heard my story on Jim Wright, the House Majority leader? I had Bob Tanenbaum report to Wright on where we were going with the Kennedy investigation. After about ten minutes, Wright grabs Tanenbaum and says, "Wait a minute, you haven't gotten to the point. You haven't told me about Sirhan Sirhan!" Tanenbaum looks at Wright and says, "Sirhan Sirhan?!" And Wright says, "Yes, he's the shooter, he did the killing." Tanenbaum said, "Mr. Wright, that's the assassination of Robert Kennedy." Wright says, "Of course, of course." Tanenbaum says, "But we're investigating the assassination of President Kennedy, not Robert Kennedy." And Wright says, "Oh, yes, yes, I forgot that."

What about [House Speaker] Tip O'Neill, was he helpful?

Tip O'Neill, in my opinion, was not the least bit helpful. He talks out of all sides of his mouth equally well at the same time. I don't think he has any desire for an investigation, though he will articulate otherwise. He is close to the Kennedys, and I have been told that the Kennedy family did not want an investigation, on the basis that nothing can bring the president back to life. Anything that comes out, in terms of other matters, can only tarnish the image and therefore why do it? I have been told that when the Congress authorized this investigation, Helms [Richard, former director of the CIA], who was then our ambassador over in Iran, saw one of the Kennedys—I think it may have been the one who was married to [Peter] Lawford—and told her to convey back that the Kennedy family should have no interest in wanting this investigation to proceed. Whatever that meant. Obviously Helms himself was one of the people that I ultimately wanted very much to interview. But not until I would be thoroughly prepared.

Did you ever interview the CIA's former chief of Counterintelligence, James Angleton?

No, that's another one we were supposed to get to. Just like with the Yablonski case, people said right after the murder why don't you interview Tony Boyle? That would have been ridiculous at that time, because I did not have the wealth of information which I would need.

And Santo Trafficante, Jr., the Florida Mob boss?

That's another interesting example of a media distortion. We took him before the committee publicly, and he took the Fifth Amendment. We were blasted by the press as a side-show, and for doing it publicly. What they made no attempt to ascertain was, Trafficante's lawyer is the one that insisted on the public hearing. The reason was, he thought if we did it privately, we would leak word that Trafficante was talking. And he wanted it clear to all that he's *not* talking.

Look, I was not an assassination buff and I am not one. The advantage I thought that I could bring to this was a professionalism. I had no preconceptions. It did not matter to me whether there was a conspiracy or not, or whether there was involvement by government agencies or not. What did matter to me was the fact that there was enough lack of confidence in what the public felt occurred, and by the public about governmental integrity à la Watergate and everything else. I felt, this is a good opportunity to show the public that we can have decent public officials do a thorough, honest, impartial job. But the evaluation process was not to be done sitting off in a room, it was to happen via a public hearing so that others could evaluate it—are we missing points, are we covering them? If we did it well, it would get credibility.

I don't think the committee now has the courage to take a position on something like immunity.

Were you going to be able to?

I was going to fight for it. Done deal.

7

Argosy Magazine, April 1976

"An Ex-CIA Man's Stunning Revelations on 'The Company' [and] JFK's Murder" [*Argosy* interview: Gerry Hemming]

*G*erry Patrick Hemming has come in from the cold. Last year, this former mercenary and CIA contract agent (now a Miami private investigator) came to Senate investigators with perhaps the most remarkable revelations ever offered about the CIA's hits, plots, and plans. Now, in an exclusive Argosy interview, he has agreed to elaborate.

Hemming, a six-foot-six ex–Marine and Green Beret, knew personally Lee Harvey Oswald, Fidel Castro, Frank Sturgis, and Che Guevara.

The odyssey of Gerry Hemming began in the mountains of Cuba where, like many other adventurers in the days before Castro turned to the Communists, he came to aid Fidel's rebels in their efforts to overthrow the corrupt Fulgencio Batista. Eventually, he was assigned by Castro to work as an officer–instructor of a parachute regiment, later as an adjutant at a Cuban air base. By this time, he was really working against Castro for American intelligence. In the fall of 1960, discovered by Fidel and facing possible execution, he escaped.

After contacting the CIA to tell them all he knew about Castro's operations, Hemming settled in Florida. There he started Interpen, a specialized group that trained embittered Cuban exiles in special Florida camps for long-range penetration and guerrilla warfare against Castro's regime. He maintained a cadre of twenty-five instructors. And he began a long friendly-adversary relationship with the CIA, the Mob, the Hughes interests, Congress, and many wealthy and influential Americans.

For the last ten years, since Interpen disbanded in 1964, Hemming has worked for a NASA project in Africa; as a paid investigator on Jim Garrison's staff looking into the Kennedy assassination; and as part of a paramedic team that rescued survivors in the 1970 Peruvian earthquake.

Gerry Hemming was around for the tumult and the shouting, the hits and the misses. He was an insider who knew most of the secrets and the locations of the skeletons in the closet. Concerned that America may be drifting perilously close to a Gestapo-type state of mind, he has decided to talk.

ARGOSY: You've told Senate investigators that 1963 marked a startling change in your liaisons with certain groups and certain wealthy American citizens. And this change finally led to the dissolution of your group, the International Penetration Force. Could you elaborate on what happened then?

HEMMING: There were a helluva lot of weird things going on. We'd begun to encounter more and more organizations of people in different cities with one thing on their mind—initially, taking care of Castro and then doing something about the other "problem," that "guy" in the White House. You couldn't walk down the street without running into some kind of conspiracy. I don't doubt that there are a dozen people out there that are sure they are the ones who financed the Dallas job on Kennedy.

ARGOSY: Were offers to assassinate Kennedy actually made to you and your group?

HEMMING: Rather frequently.

ARGOSY: How many?

HEMMING: More than two dozen, by organized elements that had financial backing within the United States.

ARGOSY: What kind of elements? The right-wing? Minutemen types?

HEMMING: There might be a retired armed forces type, a guy from the Klan. These would only be casual conversations. When it came time to open up the attaché case with the money in it, it was usually a mixed group.

ARGOSY: You actually saw money on the line?

HEMMING: Oh yeah, more than once. Some of the cheapos talked about $100,000; one said they'd pay a million.

ARGOSY: So what did you do?

HEMMING: About that point, we would gracefully back out of it. Then we would later find out that they were trying to recruit our Cuban contacts for the same purpose.

ARGOSY: Do you think it's possible that the Kennedy killing involved some of the Cuban exile community?

HEMMING: Yes, very possible. It wasn't that hard a job. I've seen and been on the scene for harder jobs than what happened in Dealey Plaza. You had a hard core of characters in the Dallas Police and County Sheriff's Department that would blow somebody's head off at a whisper. When you've got people running around who have friendships with organized crime, Federal agencies, and have been in bed with so many people—well, when the assassination goes down, everybody's covering their tracks.

ARGOSY: Can you be specific about the offers you received to kill Kennedy?

HEMMING: Look, there are people who didn't have a goddamn thing to do with it, but they *think* they did because they were conned by other people. If they think somebody's gonna point the finger at them, they're gonna get 'em. And I'd like to stay alive.

ARGOSY: You told the Senate investigators that you believed in 1963 that Loran [Lorenzo] Hall was somehow involved. [Hall, an ex-CIA contract employee, right-wing politico and trainer of Cuban exiles for a Cuban invasion, was named by the Warren Commission as one of three men who may have been in Dallas with Lee Harvey Oswald in September 1963.]

HEMMING: Yes, the day of the assassination, I made a call to Texas from Miami. And I pointedly asked, is Lorenzo Hall in Dallas? I made the call about 1:30 or 2:00 in the afternoon. He was there. My contact had seen him in Dallas the day before.

ARGOSY: Why were you suspicious of Lorenzo Hall?

HEMMING: Because he left Miami with the stated intent to get Kennedy. And he had my weapon, a Johnson 30.06 breakdown rifle with a scope on it that had been prepared for the Bay of Pigs. I'd left it with a private investigator who had previously worked under Agency [CIA] auspices on the West Coast. Hall got the weapon when we ran short of funds on a return trip from L.A. to Florida, and we ended up using Hall's car.

ARGOSY: You were working closely with Hall?

HEMMING: He came out to work with our group in 1963. Then he ran afoul with some people, and immediately went to work with a group that I thought was infiltrated by Castro's agents. Hall ignored this. He siphoned off a couple of people who had worked with me in the past, and started organizing his own operation with [Frank] Sturgis and some other guys.

ARGOSY: Hall left Miami again shortly before the assassination? Could you be more specific about his plans?

HEMMING: He was gonna stop and look up a number of people. Some he'd met through me, others when he was in Cuba in

1959. One was Santo Trafficante's brother in St. Pete, and some others who operated under Meyer Lansky's auspices. [Lansky is the boss of the National Crime Syndicate.] And there were still other connections in Louisiana and Texas that had expressed an interest.

ARGOSY: In eliminating Kennedy?

HEMMING: Yes.

ARGOSY: And you believe Hall was directly involved. . .?

HEMMING: He knew how to do the job. We'd discussed various techniques as part of our schooling—techniques required for Havana, Port-au-Prince and other Latin American jobs. But I think somebody was trying to put him there [Dallas] so he'd be one of the patsies.

ARGOSY: You've said you believe Oswald was a patsy. Did you ever have contact with Oswald?

HEMMING: I ran into Oswald in Los Angeles in 1959, when he showed up at the Cuban Consulate. The coordinator of the 26th of July Movement [a Cuban organization] called me aside and said a Marine officer had showed up, intimating that he was prepared to desert and go to Cuba to become a revolutionary. I met with the Marine and he told me he was a noncommissioned officer. He talked about being a radar operator and helping the Cubans out with everything he knew. He turned out to be Oswald.

ARGOSY: What was your impression of him? Was he sincere?

HEMMING: I thought he was a penetrator [of pro-Castro forces]. I told the 26th of July leadership to get rid of him. I thought he was on the Naval Intelligence payroll at the time.

ARGOSY: What about Jack Ruby? Did you know of him? Supposedly he'd been involved in Cuban gunrunning and smuggling operations. . . .

HEMMING: From what I understand, Ruby was around way back in 1947 when Claude Adderley—the Hiroshima pilot—got involved in a plan to bomb Havana. He also had a connection to an intelligence-Mob type in Mexico who was running the operation. They all got hauled into Federal court, arms and equipment were confiscated, and someone told me that Ruby had some kind of involvement. And you can figure Ruby was acquainted with some of the people involved in the Kennedy operation in Shreveport, New Orleans, and Texas. He worked with the Chicago mob and some

Pittsburgh boys, and was in good with the Lansky people down in Havana.

ARGOSY: So you see a definite role for organized crime in the picture?

HEMMING: Look, going back to things concerning the overthrow of Batista in 1958, the Mob was trying to get their boys into Cuba—Sturgis, Johnny Devereux, Jack Canon, Herman Marx. They wanted people on both sides [with Batista *and* with Castro]. Later they operated the same way, trying to do the hits against Fidel through 1959 and 1960.

ARGOSY: The Mob was actually pulling those kinds of things in Cuba before the CIA's attempts on Castro's life?

HEMMING: Well, let's say they all know one another. They get along. Quite a few of the people who had worked for the Agency and had gotten into a little trouble, went to work for people that knew Mob people or [Howard] Hughes people. Everybody gets to know everybody else. And Castro was getting tired of the attempts on his life. And finally I think some of Fidel's boys had people in Mexico monitoring the JFK thing in 1963. Their presence was indicated.

ARGOSY: You mean that Castro might *also* have been involved in the Kennedy assassination?

HEMMING: Consider that Castro was faced with all these CIA-Mob hits; a lot of people were coming down on him. At a lower echelon, people in his own circle, wanting to do the "big guy" a favor, might've taken things into their own hands. I don't see Castro himself directing the thing. It could've been like Jeb Magruder and Gordon Liddy in Watergate—you know, "we've got to get rid of this Jack Anderson," so away Liddy goes with a grenade in his hand. The thing is, you had so many people planning the Kennedy thing, it was bound to come.

ARGOSY: Could one motivation have been to try to pin the blame on Castro in order to justify an immediate invasion of Cuba?

HEMMING: There are people crazy enough to think that that would be the outcome. If there had been enough fingers pointed in Castro's direction, Lyndon Johnson might've struck out at Havana in the belief that it was a KGB [Russian intelligence]-Castro operation. I was aware of a couple of the attempts on Fidel. We [Interpen] felt Castro was so clumsy that leaving him in power suited our purpose more than allowing Raul [Castro] or Che [Guevara] or some of the more hardcore

Communists to take control. Even the KGB attempted a coup against Fidel in '63 because they wanted the Party and not some wild-eyed guerrilla operation in control.

ARGOSY: Who was paying your way back then?

HEMMING: There were dribs and drabs from people connected with organized crime, some from the right-wing, and even some from quite liberal sources. An ex-dictator from Colombia sent us a monthly stipend because he envisioned someday using our [Interpen's] talents for his benefit. The same thing happened with an ex-dictator from Venezuela. Our job was mostly to introduce some Cuban exiles to people who had money, and also to show these exiles how to stay away from the suicide operations that other groups wanted 'em to do.

ARGOSY: You mentioned earlier that Howard Hughes' organization had its own operation in Florida that concentrated on Cuba. Can you go into more detail on that operation?

HEMMING: Getting research on the Hughes operation is well nigh impossible, but it was a sizeable organization. One Cuban exile organization was on a Hughes retainer handled by C. Osmant Moody, who's now, I think, southeastern director for one of Hughes' larger insurance outfits located in Miami. The guy's a millionaire himself.

ARGOSY: Do you know of any attempts to assassinate Castro that emanated from this Hughes network?

HEMMING: More than one. The group Moody had on retainer inserted numerous teams into Cuba, trying to do hits, and a helluva lot of people got killed. In 1961, eighty-eight of their people were executed by Fidel. Then I know of a job they were gonna do on Fidel in Miramar, Cuba, in 1964. There was a bad scene in Key West when one of the boats blew up and a guy got killed. For another hit, Sturgis' buddy Pedro Diaz Lanz was brought in to do the job, and he left for Cuba from Cay Sal. Cay Sal is technically part of the Bahamas, but the Hughes Tool Company has a ninety-nine-year lease on it. From Key West, Osmant Moody oversees it and a Bahamian named Robinson is stationed there. If strangers came on, he'd radio to Moody. You didn't go near Cay Sal unless it was cleared, either through Moody or the Agency. It was really a launching area place to run to when people have a rough time getting out. Of course, others who wanted to get out just went to an intelligence ship—a *Pueblo*-type vessel called USS *Oxford*—that moved up and down the coast.

ARGOSY: Did you know Robert Maheu, the Hughes man who served
             as the liaison between the CIA and the Mob on some of
             the other attempts on Castro? Or John Roselli, the Mob guy
             who was one of Maheu's contacts?

HEMMING: Names like Maheu didn't come up. John Roselli I knew—but
             I didn't know who he was. He was using the name Phil. These
             are guys who don't use their last names.

ARGOSY: Was the Hughes-CIA-Mob link around Cuba a wedding or
             a rivalry?

HEMMING: Convenience. You're not talking about Hughes himself on
             a lot of these things. But the interest of some lower- or
             middle-echelon Hughes people was to provoke situations
             and lobby where they could. There were things they could
             all make a buck on. It's hard to say what kind of operations,
             though.

ARGOSY: Anything else you can tell us about anti-Castro operations
             back then?

HEMMING: Well, if you want to get into the Senate's foreign assassina-
             tions report, the "B-1" that they mention as a CIA contact to
             assassinate Fidel is Manuel Artime. [Artime, a close friend
             of Howard Hunt, was among the exile leaders in the plan-
             ning of the Bay of Pigs invasion]. And "AM/LASH," the guy
             the CIA gave the poisons to for administering to Fidel, is
             Rolando Cubela. He's under house arrest in Cuba now. Hunt
             was in on that, too. Desmond FitzGerald [CIA Western
             Hemisphere chief] and some of his boys were running the
             "Z-R Rifle" Castro assassination operation the Senate talks
             about in its report.

ARGOSY: When you talked to the Senate, you also mentioned a remark-
             able situation around a former Florida governor named
             Ferris Bryant.

HEMMING: Yes, he was governor before Claude Kirk. Well, by early 1962
             we'd [Interpen] established a very good relationship with some
             very influential people in the United States. It had taken a lot
             of hard work, a helluva lot of talking and convincing. And
             some of this led us to Governor Bryant's staff. He, along with
             Senator [Kenneth] Keating and some others, were recipients
             of raw intelligence about Cuba, prior to the missile crisis. And
             he was concerned about the possibility of Florida suffering
             the first damage in any encounter. During the Southeastern
             Governor's Conference in September 1962, he'd planned to

bring some of the governors into our exile training camps, go public and say he was organizing a state militia to train American and Cuban exile volunteers, in case of any threat from Cuba. This was based on an old law instituted when Florida came into the union, which said that the state could have foreign dealings and its own small state department to conduct preventive warfare against the Indians. About this time, James Meredith unexpectedly walked into the University of Mississippi [creating a civil rights crisis] and this broke up the governor's conference. The Kennedy people moved in fast to get a hold of Bryant and brief him [tell him to keep quiet] about the imminent missile crisis. Afterwards, the Kennedy people got him to Washington, D.C. as Director of the Office of Emergency Planning. This gave him a seat on the National Security Council, a place where you can brief somebody to death. They put him "on the team."

ARGOSY: Then there was considerable advance warning on the missile crisis?

HEMMING: My group had started getting information from Cuba indicating tighter security activity, more than just antiaircraft missile defense operations, and enlargement of Russian facilities. These later were identified to be the SAM sites and mobile medium-range ballistic missiles. But as far as we were concerned, the missiles were never delivered to the island. Preparations were made, but our information indicated there never *was* a missile in Cuba. Kennedy was scammed. He was so suspicious of the CIA's photo-interpreters that he insisted that the Defense people take over. [CIA Director John] McCone was away on his honeymoon, and then his son-in-law got into a strange accident [keeping him away longer]. All kinds of things were going on while *somebody* was trying to provoke a confrontation between Cuba and the U.S. We were more than willing to go along with that—the night Kennedy went on TV, we'd launched a boat on an operation from Marathon Key to Havana province—but the crisis wasn't real. You look at who benefited from such things and you could see how they'd be engineered. I think Kennedy found out towards the end, and that's why things developed as they did.

ARGOSY: It seems we're getting back to the Kennedy assassination. One final thing that's surfaced in recent weeks—the Exner woman who had relationships with both Kennedy *and* Mobsters Sam Giancana and John Roselli.

HEMMING: Yes, this was the Mob penetrating the White House. When you talk about the Mob, you're not talking about a homogeneous unit. The only homogeneous part is Lansky's, but the Mob is mostly feudal warlords in major cities. Quite a few have developed their own CIAs. This is right in line with their penetration of law-enforcement agencies, which gives them access to things like judges and FBI documents. They've learned how to wire tap the FBI just like the FBI wire taps them. Their program has always been, naturally, to penetrate at the highest level. And they did. They did it very well. There were Cubans up in the White House, too—select Cubans kept on government retainers, who knew everything going on and at some point made Mob connections. Some stayed at Bobby Kennedy's house, and one dated Jackie's social secretary. They have since gravitated to good political positions in the U.S. and elsewhere. They became part of the political family up there. We [Interpen] monitored them, and used them like the Mob used them.

ARGOSY: Do you mind our asking how you came to possess all this information?

HEMMING: It's a very small world in this business. We're all the same people. You don't go outside a circle, you know? If you're involved in arms supply or whatever, it's always the same contacts. We had guys constantly working with us until they were picked up by the CIA. Then when the CIA dropped them, they'd come back to us. These Cubans' prime belief was that we were the *good* CIA guys. To stay in good with us, they'd even check with us *prior* to operations. So here I was, sitting in the street with people pouring in and out with all kinds of confidential information.

ARGOSY: Why have you decided to talk about it now?

HEMMING: These last ten years have been a tremendous education. South of the border you learn a lot of things you're not taught in school, and you can get past the propaganda if you know how to read it. I learned from one of my early contacts in intelligence—a gentleman who later killed himself—that if I wanted to stay alive, I had better never pass on anything that could be attributed to me. I should be an anonymous phone caller. If I didn't cover my tracks, he told me, I would soak up some lead. Since that time, I have basically just stuck my nose into things to find out if other people knew about them. I'd later find [using this method] that some who were supposed to know *didn't*, and others did, but did nothing about it. In my younger years, I felt they knew better than me, so I'd just keep my mouth shut. Now that the years have gone by, I find out *why* things happened in a certain way.

8

Off the Beaten Path: Spooks Galore

Gerry Patrick Hemming was one of many "spooks" I encountered once I stepped off the beaten path and into the netherworld that surrounded the Kennedy assassination. Did I find them all credible? Certainly not. Most, including Hemming himself, I came to believe spun together a mix of fact and fantasy. Sorting it all out could be well nigh impossible. However, my journalistic motto was basically, "I'll listen to you, and I'll believe you, until what I learn from others erodes your credibility."

It was a matter of slowly piecing the puzzle together, and the only way to do that was to track down as many leads as one could. In this chapter, I hope to get across a sense of what it was like following that trail. It certainly did not lack for "characters."

Was I sometimes scared? You're damned right.

September 1975. I'm standing in the phone booth of a Texaco station in El Monte, a suburb of L.A. "You wait for me there," says the voice at the other end. "What kind of car are you driving?"

"A '55 Chevy," I reply.

"Okay, have your car facing the street and ready to move. I'll be driving a green station wagon. I'll honk once, you follow me. Start watching for me in ten minutes."

Sitting in the front seat of the faithful old Chev, contemplating my future. By the time he arrives, it will be too dark to catch a glimpse of him. But from the photograph I saw in the rogue's gallery of the "other" CIA (the Committee to Investigate Assassinations), he's enormous.

A green station wagon slows to a crawl along the empty thoroughfare. One honk—off we go. Everybody else seems to have gone into hibernation. Seven PM and scarcely a soul around. Right turns, left turns, an endless maze to . . . where?

The man I'm trailing is Lawrence Howard, onetime soldier-of-fortune who, as the old cliché goes, would presumably just as soon kill you as look at you. A dozen years ago, the FBI had fingered him as one of three men who showed up one September day in 1963 at the Dallas home of Cuban refugee Sylvia Odio. His companions were said to have been a couple more anti-Castro activists named Loran Hall and William Seymour, the last of whom looked remarkably like Lee Harvey Oswald. After the president was shot, Mrs. Odio took one look at her TV screen, became certain that the assassin had been her September visitor, and promptly collapsed in shock.

The so-called "Odio incident" had long been a thorn in the Oswald-as-lone-nut conclusion. The fellow at the lady's door had been introduced as "Leon," and even been quoted by one of his companions as having told her how easy it would be to kill JFK. If it wasn't Oswald, many researchers had wondered if it were an imposter, somebody seeking to frame him ahead of time as a would-be assassin. If so, that made Lawrence Howard part of a conspiracy. Assuming, of course, that the FBI was right about the real identities of the trio who called themselves "Angel," "Leopoldo," and "Leon." Sylvia Odio disagreed. She thought the FBI's three suspects all bore some resemblance to her visitors, but weren't the real McCoys.[37]

Now we are approaching a cul-de-sac. I can see it coming about an eighth of a mile ahead. Either this is where Lawrence Howard lives, or he's got some message that he wants to deliver very privately. Happily, there are several houses at the end of the road. There—he's pulling into a gravel driveway at the apex of the turn-around. I pull in behind him.

Howard is now standing beside his car, a mountain of a man, very dark and very bearded. As I walk up to him, reluctantly he acknowledges my handshake, his eyes boring into mine. Without a word, he motions me forward and into the living room of a wood-frame, single-story house.

"Would you raise your pant leg, please?" A low monotone, almost a growl, coming from behind me. It's the most commanding "please" I ever heard. Quickly if queasily, I bend over and comply. "All right, now the other one." I can glimpse him hovering behind me, motioning with one menacing finger. "Okay. Now, would you lift the back of your jacket?"

Satisfied that I am unarmed, Howard motions me to sit down. As he lowers his 240-pound frame into a big easy chair, I spy a meaty hand slipping a pistol out from under his belt. It slides like a snake behind the side of the cushion. The hand follows, ready, willing and able. I look around the living room. It is filled with fast-draw trophies. The man's wife and daughter pass silently through the room, like shadows. "Would you like a beer?" he asks me.

"I keep my nose clean," Howard is saying as the wife extends a bottle of Bud to each of us. "I just take precautions, you understand?"

I nod.

"Now, what can I help you with?"

"The, ah, Odio-di incid-d-d-ent," I stammer. Really losing your cool, I silently reproach myself. Almost yodeled it, for Chrissake.

---

[37] The Odio "incident" has been reported in many books on the assassination, including my own, *The Man Who Knew Too Much* (N.Y.: Carroll & Graf Publishers/Richard Gallen, 1992), pp. 479–82.

"That all began with Loran Hall's big mouth," my suspect replies calmly. "He made statements to the FBI that we'd been to see Mrs. Odio—me, Seymour, and him. This is not true, because Seymour and myself were never in Dallas together. So later, he changed it to me and a Cuban friend of mine. Loran Hall has changed so many stories, I don't know what's going on. But there's no doubt in my mind that I never went to the home of any Cuban woman who I didn't know."

Why, Loran Hall hadn't really even been a part of their group, he scoffs. And Lawrence Howard begins to reminisce about the good old days, back when he had command of the "troops" on the Florida island called No Name Key. They had been a tight bunch, the soldiers-of-fortune who trained in the Keys. They were ex-Marines and ex-paratroopers who devoutly believed that a certain big island 90 miles from their shores was a threat to democracy. So they did survival training, and coached the Cuban exiles, and went on night raids along the Cuban coast.

"I suppose I was motivated by a desire to fight Communism, or adventure, perhaps mercenary, any number of things. We had different personnel qualified in different fields. Mine was infiltration, hand-to-hand combat, and—I almost hate to tell you this one—sight-and-kill."

Sight-and-kill. He chuckles. I smile weakly.

"At first, we were making our raids with the blessing of the CIA. We'd take boats into Cuba, drop off personnel and medical supplies, make a few strafings. After the government put the lid on and clamped down on us, we kept on anyway. There was a certain amount of bitterness, sure, but mostly directed against the various law enforcement agencies that stopped us. But no real animosity. It was just part of the game, you take your chances and sometimes you get caught. To my knowledge, there was no real anger toward President Kennedy. Aside from a little name-calling. No cries for retaliation, nothing like that."

Howard pauses, takes a long draw on his beer. The right hand still hasn't budged from its casual resting place at the side of the cushion. I'm beginning to wonder if memory makes the trigger finger grow fonder.

"But I suppose we look pretty good, don't we?" he continues.

As suspects, I presume he means. I check myself from shaking my head and shouting a very vocal "Of course not!"

Howard went on: "I mean, it's all a big question mark in my mind. I don't know if I was being used, set up, or what. I feel personally that Loran Hall got me into this mess. He'd come in from L.A., looked me up, convinced me that he could get financing for the types of operations we were involved in. The lid was down at the time, and everything had come to a grinding halt. So I decided to go back to the West Coast with him. We went through the Dallas area, holed up for a few days. Later, Hall did the same thing with Bill Seymour, my second-in-command. But we were never all together, you see.

"Then somebody signed my name in the register of the Dallas YMCA on November 22, the day Kennedy was shot. I'd like to see the handwriting on that signature. Now people are bugging me pretty heavy again. I'm getting calls from here and there. Well, I've already admitted my involvement in anti-Castro activities, as far as it went. But not this. Never anything like this. What it all boils down to is, I got a family, a couple grown daughters, and I don't want to go through it all again."

The fast-draw trophies on the bookcases, I've been noticing, are not all in the name of Lawrence Howard. Some are credited to his daughters. And his wife.

"Your whole family," I say, pointing to a big silver one, "they seem to be pretty good shots."

"Excellent shots," he replies. "But I don't want my family brought into whatever you're writing."

Have I said the wrong thing? His eyes betray no change in expression. He is imperturbable really. Even soft-spoken. Of course, given what he's sitting on—literally—maybe he can afford to be.

"Look, we're the perfect set-up to throw anybody off somebody else's trail. The public wants questions answered. I feel there will be a future investigation and they will try to toss us to the wolves. It'll all boil down to No Name Key, Howard and Hall. I really hope one day it will all be cleared up, and I'll be given a clean bill of health."

There's a quick movement of his right hand. I flinch slightly, but he seems not to notice. His hand moves off from the deadly object it's been cradling for almost an hour. He stands up. "Would you like another beer?" he asks.

"No," I say, "I suppose I should be going soon."

He walks into the kitchen to get one for himself. Obviously, he's decided he trusts me. Either that, or he realizes I'd scarcely know where to begin to aim. But I find that I trust him, too. To coin a bad phrase for this situation, he seems a straight shooter.

"Say, would you do me a favor?" I ask as he returns. "Could you, uh, show me what it is you've been sitting on that you could blow me away with?"

Lawrence Howard smiles. Reaching beside the cushion, in a flash he produces his prize.

".45 automatic," he says. "Very effective."

We start to laugh, the two of us. There's nothing like sharing a good laugh looking down the barrel of a .45 automatic with a guy whose forte is sight-and-kill.

I first heard of Gordon Novel through Mary Ferrell. She lived in Dallas with her husband Buck, and was the pre-eminent gatherer of all material related to the assassination. That included a card file with more than 30,000 names, and some 12,000 books.

When I first met Mary in the fall of 1975, she played me some tape recordings of her phone calls with Novel. She called him "the most dangerous boy—and one of the nicest I know." She dialed him up, and put us on the phone together. With Mrs. Ferrell's blessing, Novel agreed to meet with me in New Orleans.

I already knew this much about him: He'd been involved, back in 1961, in the burglary of a munitions dump outside New Orleans along with Sergio Arcacha-Smith and David Ferrie, whose names later surfaced as suspects in Jim Garrison's investigation. The stolen weapons had been destined for use in the Bay of Pigs invasion. In mid-March 1967, Garrison had subpoenaed Novel to appear before a grand jury. Novel flew the coop and took refuge in Columbus, Ohio, where he called Garrison's probe a "fraud" and the D.A. tried without success to extradite him. According to the *New Orleans States-Item* at the time, "The strongest CIA ties lead to Gordon Novel." He ended up being arrested in Columbus and posting $10,000 bond, after making trips to McLean, Virginia (where CIA headquarters was located) and Montreal. Ohio Governor James Rhodes said he'd agree to extradite Novel, only if he was granted immunity from being questioned about the Kennedy assassination.[38]

While en route to see Novel, I stopped to try to interview Oswald's mother, Marguerite, by simply knocking on her door in Fort Worth. To put it mildly, she was less than cooperative. Speaking through a closed curtain, she berated my ill manners, informed me she was on welfare and tired of people getting rich off her, then slammed the door saying: "Why don't you go ring Jackie Kennedy's doorbell?"

Novel, then in his late thirties, was a good-looking guy with close-cropped hair and a stubble of a beard and what I thought were very shifty eyes. He met me at the airport and, when he asked if I had a place to stay and I told him I didn't, said he'd drop me off at the Town and Country Motel. It happened to be owned by Carlos Marcello, boss of the New Orleans Mob. "I've known Carlos since I was a little bitty boy," Novel said. "Would you like to meet him?" "Oh sure," I said with bravado. Maybe lucky for us both, Carlos wasn't in. But I noticed some fellows eavesdropping on our conversation as Novel and I talked in the motel driveway.

We talked for hours that evening, in somebody's office whose name I've long since forgotten. We talked about UFOs (Novel was the first person I knew to mention a secret National Reconnaissance Office that keeps track of all the reported sightings), and about Watergate (Novel had plotted with Charles Colson, Nixon's "hatchet man," on how to wipe out the White House tapes with a magnetic laser beam).

Interestingly, especially in retrospect, was what he said about George H. W. Bush, who'd recently been named director of the CIA. When I opined that

---

[38] For the most up-to-date background on Novel, including his having been an informant for both the FBI and the Walter Sheridan investigation for Robert Kennedy, see Joan Mellen's *A Farewell to Justice* (Washington, D.C.: Potomac Books, Inc., 2005), pp. 190–91.

Bush was an outsider who probably didn't know what was really going on, Novel said: "Bush can keep the Texas politicians from lighting the fires that are stoked and ready to go." Which fires were those? I asked. "The Kennedy fires," he said, and added, "Congressman [Henry] Gonzalez from Texas is the one who submitted the first bill for a new investigation into the assassination. George Bush would be able to reach all around Texas, both in the Democratic and Republican camps, to keep the disgrace from latching into Texas."

Novel went on to recall how he'd first gotten involved with Garrison's investigation as someone able to "furnish electronic equipment to protect or secure Garrison's investigation from the prying eyes of other government agencies." He said he'd told Garrison about meeting David Ferrie briefly in 1960. And then Novel and Garrison had a falling-out: "I was accusing him of fraudulent actions in the preparation of his cases, and he was accusing me of anything he could." When the D.A. tried to extradite him from Ohio, he was able to avoid it because "I sued everybody."

Looking back over the transcript of our initial conversation today, not much seems too significant in terms of the Kennedy assassination. It appears highly unlikely that he knew much about it, beyond "educated speculation." Novel, though, was one of the best talkers I ever encountered—and he certainly knew people who knew people. We liked each other and, the next time I visited New Orleans, I stayed at the mansion on Lake Pontchartrain where he lived with his beautiful wife (an ex-*Playboy* model) and two young children named Spirit and Lucky.

Then, in February 1976, while Novel was in preparation to build a $200 million World's Fair "Expo '80" in New Orleans, he was arrested and accused of plotting to firebomb five downtown buildings on Mardi Gras Day. This was banner headline news for days in the Crescent City. Novel went on a hunger strike in jail, and got the initial charges dropped.

I saw him next in New York City. We met in a Hilton Hotel lobby and went for coffee. He said the Alcohol, Tobacco and Firearms agency was out to frame him. The cops had arrested his partner, a guy I'd met, accusing him of sticking a pistol out the window of his car and firing a shot at one of his own buildings.

Novel then handed me a cassette tape, and said I should play it in my recorder. It proved to be quite a telephone conversation, with an airline pilot named Gene who had called up offering Gordon the assistance of an "old-time assassin" if he needed one. "You talk to him, he'll come up with his credentials," Gene said.

"You mean his notches," Novel said.

It was Novel who brought up the name of a guy named Slew Montgomery.

"They got an earful if they got surveillance on this fucking phone," Gene replied.

"Man, I didn't come in yesterday's mail," Gordon said. He added that he'd been told by someone that "Slew Montgomery knocked off JFK."

Gene said his own assassin friend "knew Montgomery, but not well. . . . I seen the guy before, done business you know. I didn't mean that, let me rephrase that."

Later, Gene said, "Within four months of the time Slew died, four around here all had the same problem."

Later, Gordon added: "Look, I know what I was paid to interfere on Garrison and by who." Of the charges pending against him, "The federal government put a phony case together. You cannot pull rabbits out of hats if you ain't got no hats." Hence, no thank you Gene,, he didn't need a professional hitman.

As we walked past the Ziegfeld building on Sixth Avenue, Novel told me he was planning to enlist Garrison to defend him against the federal government.

Next I heard about Gordon, he was doing time somewhere in North Carolina. If you do an Internet search about him, you'll learn that he went on to become heavily involved in the UFO research community—and worked as an investigator for former Attorney General Ramsey Clark in a civil trial following the siege of David Koresh's Branch Davidian compound.

Gordon Novel always had a flare for the unusual.

9

The Village Voice, April 26, 1976

"New Assassination Questions: 'What Was in the CIA's Declassified JFK File?'"

WASHINGTON, D.C.—The CIA has finally bared half its cupboard on the Kennedy assassination. But if the agency hoped to end the dark rumors once and for all, they did not succeed. The question of an official cover-up is now larger than ever, and these documents could be the straw that finally breaks the Warren Commission's back.

Several weeks ago, when the CIA released 1,466 pages of files to Freedom of Information suits by lawyers David Belin and Bernard Fensterwald, Jr., first reports of the contents centered around Lee Harvey Oswald's apparent liaison with agents of the Russian KGB and Cuban intelligence during a September 1963 trip to Mexico City.

But the most revealing material really concerns the domestic side of the situation. The CIA's files raise serious new doubts about Oswald's murder weapon and whether he might once have been an American intelligence operative. They provide further insight into Jack Ruby's ties with Mob and Teamster leaders. They admit that Clay Shaw, the accused conspirator in Jim Garrison's New Orleans probe of the late 1960s, did indeed have "past CIA contact." And they bring Cuban machinations into closer focus.

This mountain of paper is, in other respects, largely what you might expect—an often-fascinating compendium of foreign reaction and foreign intrigue, with source's names and agency code-words dutifully excised. There are valuable historical footnotes—including a source's private conversation with Khrushchev, in 1964, who did not believe Oswald was a madman acting alone. For the real buff, there are numerous new theories and suspects—some utterly bizarre, some thought-provoking.

By and large, the CIA seemed diligent in pursuing all leads to a possible foreign conspiracy. This was, after all, its job. And taken at face value, the bulk of the documents leads one to believe that the CIA hierarchy knew only a little more about Oswald and the assassination than anyone else.

The trouble lies in the contradictions. Let's examine them, piece by piece:

The Oswald Rifle: From the beginning, there was great confusion about precisely what weapon had been found near Oswald's alleged sniper's nest. The first police reports described it as a German 7.65 Mauser bolt-action rifle. That was how it was generally labeled for the first 24 hours after the assassination, although another report called it a British Enfield. The CIA, these files show, as late as November 25, was still calling it a Mauser.

The Warren Commission, however, concluded that the only rifle Oswald owned was an Italian-made Mannlicher-Carcano. *The Warren Report* explains: "Police laboratory technicians subsequently arrived and correctly identified the weapon as a 6.5 Italian rifle." It's always seemed odd that the identification took so long since, as testimony also showed, the gun Oswald had obtained some months earlier from a Chicago mail-order house was clearly marked: "Made Italy, Cal. 6.5." If this was indeed the weapon found in the School Book Depository building, why the confusion?

A CIA analysis of November 28, 1963, adds a third dimension to the rifle puzzle. "The weapon which appears to have been employed in this criminal attack," wrote the CIA, "is a Model 91 rifle, 7.35-caliber, 1938 modification." Although by this time the weapon was being described as a 6.5-caliber, the analyst concluded, "the photographs from American sources appearing in the Italian press show another type of weapon—a 7.35-caliber."

The Warren Commission never mentioned this caliber of Italian rifle, but such a weapon does exist and, according to one intelligence source, is still used for sniper practice by NATO forces abroad. It is apparently superior to Oswald's smaller 6.5-caliber, and a much more likely and effective assassin's weapon—except Oswald didn't own one.

What conclusion can we draw from such confusion? Were the CIA and the Warren Commission evaluating the same rifle? And what about the earliest police reports about a Mauser? Unless we are ready to accept not one, but *two*, official errors in seemingly expert judgment, it is logical that either an additional rifle was discovered—or else Oswald's own 6.5 rifle was never in the depository building at all.

As if these implications weren't enough, the CIA's November 28 report makes mincemeat of the Oswald rifle's accuracy—even if it *was* actually fired at the presidential motorcade. In 1958, said the CIA, "the Italian military authorities decided to eliminate all the Model 91s (6.5- and 7.35-calibers) of various types which were no longer being issued and which were declared obsolete." An American company undertook to modify and purchase some 100,000 of these—at a wholesale price tag of $2.20 for serviceable 6.5 rifles and $4.50 for the 7.35-caliber.

However, the report continued, "The first lot of 7,000 'Model 91s' which Adam [Company] put on the American market had disastrous results. Many of them burst, with frequently fatal consequences, and many didn't fire. This forced Adam to withdraw all the rifles from sale and check them before putting them back on the market. After taking delivery of 100,000 rifles the Adam Company, with various excuses, did not accept any more."

The CIA analyst concludes: "It is suggested that you may desire to pass copies of this report to FBI. A copy has been made available to the FBI representative here for his information and with advice that it has been forwarded to Washington."

But if the FBI got the message, the Warren Commission apparently didn't. *The Warren Report* contends: ". . . the assassination rifle was an accurate weapon . . . in fact, as accurate as current military rifles. . . ." According to the CIA, that statement seems ridiculous. If Lee Harvey Oswald really assassinated the president with a 6.5 Mannlicher-Carcano, he couldn't have made a poorer choice of weaponry—and he must have been, despite many reports to the contrary, a quite remarkable shot.

Oswald and the CIA: Speculation about a possible Oswald-CIA link was raised, according to a CIA "Memorandum for the Record" of a meeting between its two top Clandestine Services officers and the Warren Commission, on March 12, 1964. Commission lawyer Howard P. Willens began by noting "that Mrs. Oswald had introduced a statement to the effect that she suspected her son to be a CIA agent. . . . [Staff officer] replied that he had not been. Mr. Willens then asked if there were any way of proving this. [Staff officer] first remarked that in him and [staff officer] the commission had the two Clandestine Services officers who certainly would know whether or not Oswald had been an agent for CIA in the Soviet Union. He then said that the commission would have to take his word for the fact that Oswald had not been an agent. Mr. Rankin interjected the view that the commission had not adopted this procedure with other agencies and wondered whether there was not some way to clarify this point more effectively for the commission. . . ."

Although neither CIA staff officer is identified, an intelligence source has named the agency spokesman as Richard Helms. This same CIA memorandum reveals for the first time that the commission was concerned about a book found in Oswald's possession which had certain letters cut out—"giving the impression that this might have formed the base or key for a cipher system. They asked whether it would be useful in our opinion to send this book to NSA [National Security Agency] for review. We assured them that NSA was the appropriate agency for this. . . ."

There is no further mention in these files of any NSA evaluation. But the question of Oswald's possible intelligence connections did not die, judging from a strange CIA memo to J. Edgar Hoover of March 2, 1965. This, remember, is six months after the release of *The Warren Report*. "It may be of interest to your office," the memo begins, "to note the following coincidences in the backgrounds of [deleted] and Lee Harvey and Marina Oswald." For public consumption, the "subject's name has been deleted throughout," but the CIA makes reference to his FBI file number and apparently had corresponded about him with the bureau on previous occasions.

Like Oswald, this "subject" had served as an enlisted man and technician in the United States Marines. He had then showed up in Minsk, USSR, in both 1958 and 1959, where as the only American he became acquainted with the son of a Soviet army general and "claimed to have attracted to himself a group of young Soviets who displayed an unusual curiosity about the standard of living in the United States and Western Europe and whose interests centered around girls, cars, having a good time, and listening to jazz music on the Voice of America." This "subject" then divulged this information in Copenhagen on May 3 and 4, 1961, to a CIA employee known to him as "a representative of American intelligence."

The CIA memo continues: "It is interesting that Oswald also reportedly considered himself to be an oddity as the only American residing in Minsk and attracted more or less the same type young Soviets as did [deleted]. It should be noted that Oswald listed among his close friends in Minsk a young Soviet named Pavel Golovachev, whose father ostensibly was a Soviet army general."

Oswald, who arrived in Minsk a few months after the other "subject" departed, would remain for over two years. The other fellow, by the CIA's own admission, served at the very least as an informant on Soviet activities after he left Russia. This memo appears to imply that Oswald was simply picking up where someone else left off. But why would the CIA send a memo to the FBI alluding to Oswald's similar role, but not getting specific? Had Oswald and the other Marine "subject" been sent to the USSR not by the CIA, but by some other U.S. agency like Naval intelligence?

Oswald and the Russians: The CIA apparently decided very early that Oswald was an unlikely Russian agent. In a memo of December 11, 1963, "Additional Notes and Comments on the Oswald Case," its analyst writes: "Longstanding KGB practice generally forbids agents serving outside the USSR to have any contact with domestic Communist parties or with Soviet embassies or consulates.... Yet Oswald blazed a trail to the Soviets which was a mile wide. He corresponded with the national headquarters of the Communist party USA—apparently with some regularity—and visited the Soviet Consulate in Mexico City....

"Certain facets of Oswald's activities in the USSR also argue strongly that the KGB would never have recruited him for a mission of any kind. . . . It is extremely unlikely that Oswald—with his Russian wife—was even seriously considered for subsequent repatriation to the United States as a KGB asset. As a re-defector from the USSR he would immediately be suspect and thus under surveillance by the FBI. . . ."

The Soviets, themselves, right up to the highest level of government, apparently believed Kennedy was the victim of a right-wing American conspiracy—

with Oswald in the role of a "patsy" whose background would point a false finger at the Communists. One of the most fascinating CIA documents is a May 27, 1964, memo to the Warren Commission describing a forty-five-minute "Discussion Between Chairman Khrushchev and [American CIA source] re: Lee Harvey Oswald."

The memo records Khrushchev as asking, "What really happened?" Then: "[Source] said in effect that the whole affair had taken place just as had been reported in the newspapers and presumably by the Soviet ambassador in Washington. Chairman Khrushchev was utterly incredulous.... When [source] said that ... in fact Oswald was mad, had acted on his own, ditto Ruby, Chairman Khrushchev said flatly that he did not believe this. He said he did not believe that the American security services were this inept.

". . . Chairman Khrushchev was completely convinced that the true story of the Kennedy assassination has not come out. [Source] said somewhat ruefully, 'I couldn't make a nickel with Khrushchev on this one.... [Source] got the impression that Chairman Khrushchev had some dark thoughts about the American right-wing being behind this conspiracy although Chairman Khrushchev did not articulate this in any clear fashion. . . .'"

It's not inconceivable that *both* American and Russian intelligence had something to hide. At different times, Oswald could have served as a kind of "freelance" agent or informant. For sure, his being allowed to leave the USSR with a Russian wife and very little hassle was an unusually generous Soviet procedure. And if Oswald *had* served two masters—neither of which would want it known, particularly after November 22, 1963—he thus became a perfect tool for anyone else who wanted to ensure an official cover-up.

There is another report which sounds similar to the CIA's "Operation 40," revealed last year by E. Howard Hunt. The February 1964, study of "Soviet Use of Assassination..." begins: "It has long been known that the Soviet state security service (currently KGB) resorts to abduction and murder to combat what are considered to be actual or potential threats to the Soviet regime. These techniques, frequently designated 'executive action' and known within the KGB as 'liquid affairs,' can be and are employed abroad as well as within the borders of the USSR. ... Foreign political leaders are also potential targets of Soviet executive action operations. ... There is, however, no evidence proving that any Western leader has been the victim of Soviet executive action."

In a lengthy chronology of Oswald's association with Soviet citizens, the CIA does identify a Soviet Consul with whom Oswald supposedly met September 28, 1963, in Mexico City as "a staff officer of KGB ... connected with the thirteenth, or 'liquid affairs' department, whose responsibilities include assassination and sabotage." But while the CIA spent countless hours tracing the activities of Valery V. Kostikov, the files show they could find nothing to indicate his pre-awareness of the Kennedy assassination.

Oswald and the Cubans: Given the aura of detente after the 1963 nuclear test ban treaty, it's always seemed doubtful that the Soviets wanted Kennedy eliminated. Cuba is another matter, particularly as revelations of CIA-Mob attempts to kill Fidel Castro have given rise to a "Castro's revenge" theory. But Fidel, as seen in CIA memos of November 25 and 29, reacted fast and furiously—and considered Kennedy's death "serious and bad news."

Castro's first speech after the assassination raised immediate questions about Oswald's motive. "Is he really guilty?" Castro asked on November 23. "Is he a scapegoat? Is he a psychopath? Or is he perhaps a tool of the most reactionary U.S. circles? Who is this man? Why did he go into action precisely when circumstances were least favorable for a left-wing fanatic to assassinate the U.S. President?"

Studying a second Castro speech four days later, the CIA wrote: "Textual analysis . . . neither proves nor disproves that the Cuban leader had advance knowledge of the assassination. . . . It does indicate that Castro—alert to the consequences which even the imputation of complicity would have for U.S.-Cuban relations—is fully read on the details of the shooting as they have been reported by the press."

Indeed, Castro sounds sometimes like the first of the assassination buffs. The CIA says: "Alluding to statements made early this week by doctors at the Parkland Hospital, Castro claims that no one in a position to do so has said whether there were one or two bullets used to kill the President. Castro declared that 'they cannot establish which are the entry and exit wounds,' implying that more than one assassin was involved, and that the President was struck both from in front and behind. . . ."

Castro's speeches notwithstanding, the CIA's most intensive early efforts concentrated on possible Cuban involvement. Curiously, some of the most persistent field reports spoke of complicity with the Chinese. A foreign diplomat, a source in Chicago, a letter to the U.S. embassy in Sweden, and even a letter postmarked December 2 from Havana, all conjured such a scenario. According to the CIA, the FBI was "very much interested in this allegation," particularly as it concerned contact with a Mexican and a Cuban who lived in Dallas at the time. A memo to the CIA director dated December 6, 1963, describes the foreign diplomat's claim that. "These men financed through bank located 14 Wall Street, New York City." Another memo, dated December 9, reports that the FBI "is endeavoring to run down the lead relating to the bank in New York. . . ."

There is no indication of what the FBI might have learned. Quite probably, most of such "source" reports were frauds. The CIA spent weeks tracking down a lead about Oswald's receiving $6,500 in Mexico's Cuban embassy, only to have the source confess he'd made it all up. Only two days after the assassination, an internal memo to Director John McCone said: "Rumors are now circulating among exile Cubans re: possible DGI [Cuban intelligence] involvement in

President Kennedy's death. Authors these rumors not identified but it clear this being done primarily in attempt provoke strong U.S. action against Cuba. . . ." The memo concluded there was only an "off chance" that the rumors might have substance.

That's the way Castro saw it, too, according to the CIA's study of his speech: "Castro rehearses the details of Oswald's 27 September application for a Cuban visa at the Cuban consulate in Mexico City and reports publicly for the first time the arrest of two employees of the consulate by Mexican police on 23 November. This was done, he charges, in order to fabricate a case against Cuba, and to provide a pretext for punitive action against the revolution. . . ."

The CIA's files do show that Oswald, in his efforts to get a Cuban visa in Mexico City, may have had contact with three Cuban intelligence officials at the embassy there. And after the assassination, Castro did put his intelligence service in Mexico on alert. A CIA memo to the Warren Commission of May 15, 1964, reports: ". . . orders were issued for all DGI components in the country to sort and package all documents according to whether they were *muy secreto* [very secret], *secreto* [secret] or *importante* [important]. The material, once consolidated, was to be held pending further instructions. All travel by DGI officers was suspended temporarily. In addition, DGI headquarters' personnel were instructed to remain in their offices or to keep the DGI aware of their whereabouts so that they could be reached immediately. The source does not know the reasons for these measures but believes it is logical that they were issued because of the possibility that the United States might have taken some type of action against Cuba and the DGI itself . . . the DGI files were restored to regular use about 3 December 1963."

Obviously, Castro was not resting easily. But his actions really seem more natural than suspicious. If Oswald's role in going to the Soviet and Cuban embassies was part of a plan to bait a trap in that direction, Castro had good reason to be paranoid. Immediately after the assassination, his own intelligence in Mexico would surely have informed him of Oswald's contact with them. Castro was no fool. He also had little reason, except for the simplistic "revenge" notion, to plot the death of a president who was rapidly working to ease U.S.-Cuban tensions.

The Mexico Mysteries: There has been speculation down through the years that the real Oswald never went to Mexico at all in September 1963. The question arose because the "Lee Oswald" who supposedly visited the Soviet embassy on October 1 was, according to a CIA station cable nine days later, "apparent age 35, athletic build, circa six feet, receding hairline, balding top. Wore khakis and sport shirt." Of course, slim twenty-three-year-old Lee did not match that description. So who was the man the CIA photographed and identified as Oswald? Perhaps someone carrying false Oswald papers and blazing a phony trail?

On the day of the assassination, when the CIA arranged to have one of these photographs delivered to the FBI, the agency has said it realized its mistake. The earliest message about the Mexico City photos has not been released. It's in the form of a personal letter signed "Best wishes" and appears to be an exchange with the FBI. It is dated November 22: "Reference is made to our conversation of 22 November in which I requested permission to give the legal attaché copies of photographs of a certain person who is known to you. At 6 PM Mexico time on 22 November, the ambassador decided that this was important enough to have a member of the legal attaché's office take copies of these pictures to Dallas, Texas. The naval attaché is making a special flight from Mexico City for this purpose. The legal attaché's officer who is going to Dallas has promised to mail this material to you for me. Copies of these photographs are also being sent by pouch which will leave Mexico City on the night of 22 November 1963."

What is the meaning of "a certain person who is known to you"? Did the CIA mean Oswald, and was being purposely cryptic in those tense early hours? Or, if the CIA knew by then that the photos were *not* of Oswald, did they fear this "certain person" was part of a conspiracy? Was the "certain person," if not Oswald, known to both the CIA and FBI?

A CIA memo to the Warren Commission of July 28, 1964, indicates that the CIA at least found out who the mystery man was—and wanted to bury the subject forever. "The Central Intelligence Agency recommends that this photograph not be reproduced in the commission's report," the memo says. "It could be embarrassing to the individual involved who as far as this agency is aware, had no connection with Lee Harvey Oswald or the assassination of President Kennedy." (The commission did reproduce the picture, without explanation. The man has never been identified.)

The mystery man is not the only unexplained mystery about Mexico and the assassination. Another memo has an FBI informant alleging that Oswald met there with a CIA man whose alias was Bill Medina; the CIA denies the rumor. Then there was an "alleged official of the American government" said to have been in contact with Oswald in Cozumel. And a student who reported Oswald saying, on a visit to a university campus, that it was "urgent he visit Cuba immediately and that Cuban embassy denied him visa."

The Mysterious Mr. Ruby: Although the CIA had "no indication that Ruby and Lee Harvey Oswald ever knew each other, were associated, or might have been connected in any manner," the agency had plenty of indication that Mr. Ruby wasn't as simple a fellow as the Warren Commission wanted us to believe.

Ruby himself acknowledged making a trip to Havana in September 1959, a few months before the borders closed. Besides visiting a nightclub one night, it's never been known just what he did there. But as early as November 27, 1963, according to a CIA memo to the director, a British journalist named John Wilson aka Wilson-Hudson had told a strange tale at the American embassy in London. While working in Cuba and being jailed by Castro in 1959, the journalist recalled, he had met an American "gangster-gambler named Santo who could not return to the USA because there were several indictments outstanding against him. Santo opted therefore to remain in prison for a period of time paying Castro in dollars for his rather luxurious and definitely non-prisonlike accommodations. . . ." While Santo was in prison, Wilson says, "Santo was visited frequently by an American gangster type named Ruby."

The CIA didn't put much stock in the journalist's story. The fact remains that an infamous "gangster-gambler" and narcotics trafficker named Santo Trafficante *was* in a Castro jail in 1959. Under Batista's regime, he had handled the Havana casinos for crime boss Meyer Lansky. And Ruby, as even the FBI finally conceded, had long had peripheral ties to the mob.

This is not the only mention in the CIA's files of Ruby and Cuba. Reports from two sources claimed that Ruby had flown into Havana from Mexico City sometime in late 1962, "frequenting a tourist store owned by man named Solomon Pratkins." The CIA rather hazily denied these rumors, saying: "Information available to this office fails to confirm that subject left Mexico City for Habana, or arrived in Mexico City from Habana by air anytime during 1962."

Another source, a Polish citizen, gives the improbable story of having met Jack Ruby in Tel Aviv, where Ruby was "described as high NKVD [Russian] official who recruiting for NKVD from among members Polish army." Such a role seems incredible, but this wasn't the only report linking Ruby to a journey to Israel. Here is how an undated CIA memorandum puts it:

"A reliable source who is well versed in labor affairs informed me today that Jack Ruby (formerly Rubenstein) was sent to Israel last year with a delegation of American trade unionists, having been placed on this delegation by [deleted] of the Teamsters' Union. While in New York he was also in contact with [deleted] reported to be an official of the Histadrut (Israel Federation of Labor).

"2. It was also stated that the AFL-CIO has a record that subject applied last year in New Orleans to the AFL-CIO office there for a job as a union organizer."

Jack Ruby, good-time nightclub operator? According to ex-CIA agent Philip Agee's book, *Inside the Company*, the Israeli Histadrut is regularly used in CIA "labor operations" for "specialized training within the social-democratic movement."

Where Ruby is concerned, as with Oswald, a lot of people may have had a lot of secrets to protect. He had been, the FBI admitted in 1975, a bureau informant. He was no stranger to labor, the mob, and Cuban affairs. He was a most convenient fellow, for anyone who wanted a quick "case closed."

The Garrison Investigation: Very few believed Jim Garrison when he claimed Clay Shaw had worked for the CIA, and ranted that the agency was going out of its way to curtail his investigation. When his conspiracy case collapsed in 1969, Garrison faded into obscurity. Shaw traveled the lecture circuit for awhile, talking about Garrison's injustice. He, too, was an obscure figure when he died in 1974.

Then last year, former CIA official Victor Marchetti revealed that high-level CIA conferences in early 1969 had determined to "give help in the trial." Said Marchetti: "I sure as hell know they didn't mean Garrison." Marchetti maintained that both Shaw and David Ferrie, another of Garrison's prime suspects, had served the agency at one time.

Now the CIA has admitted as much. Memorandums on a number of the figures in Garrison's probe were prepared in 1967 and 1968 for the deputy director of plans. By the summer of 1967, the agency was very concerned about "Garrison-Inspired Publicity Regarding Classified CIA Information in Warren Commission Files." The National Archives had accidentally provided a Garrison staffer with a list of all the CIA's classified assassination documents. "While one cannot condone National Archives' action in this matter," a CIA official wrote, "nevertheless I do not feel that the publication of this list will hurt CIA in the long run. . . ."

But the truth about Clay Shaw would surely have been damaging to the agency. Garrison and Marchetti were right. The CIA verified Shaw's background in an April 6, 1967, file for the deputy chief, security research staff.

"Name checks on the subject were conducted in 1949 for the present DCS," says that report. "The undersigned contacted [deleted] and [deleted] after checking, advised that the DCS office in New Orleans had contact with Shaw until 1956. [Deleted] also advised that certain information concerning Shaw had been furnished to the general counsel of this agency at the request of the general counsel, but a copy inadvertently had not been sent to the Office of Security. . . . [Deleted] was advised that Shaw was of interest to DCS a number of years ago and that specific details would be obtained."

The next memo about Shaw is dated May 1, 1967, from Howard J. Osborn, director of security, to the deputy director for support. "The CIA staff, in a detailed staff study of the Garrison investigation, has noted past CIA contact with only two figures named in the inquiry, Clay L. Shaw, and Carlos Bringuier, in both cases the contact was limited to Domestic Contact Service activities. . . ."

When Lee Harvey Oswald was arrested, his notebook contained the name and business address of Carlos Bringuier. He was a fanatically anti-Castro Cuban whom Oswald had approached to offer his services in the summer of 1963. Then Bringuier, discovering Oswald handing out *pro*-Communist literature on the streets of New Orleans, had allegedly punched him in the nose. A few days after that, they had debated on a local right-wing radio program. By then, it might be said they were well-acquainted.

Other surprises in the CIA files are quick takes. None of them were followed up:

- George de Mohrenschildt, a petroleum engineer with possible intelligence ties who squired the Oswalds around Dallas' Russian community until

April 1963, is quoted in a July 1964 file as voicing the following sentiments in Haiti after the assassination: "De Mohrenschildt said that President Kennedy was hated by the Dallas elite, and he felt that it was very likely that certain reactionary elements in Dallas had organized a plot to get rid of Kennedy and used a disturbed person such as Oswald to achieve their ends. . . ." In two days of testimony before the Warren Commission, de Mohrenschildt was never questioned about those remarks.

- A Cuban named Ruedolo, once in a training camp for the Bay of Pigs invasion, apparently arrived in Spain without a valid visa on November 27, 1963, and landed in a Madrid jail. "Can you find out why police think he was expelled from U.S. and how he got to Spain?" a CIA memo asks. "Any ideas on how this story linking him with assassination of president may have originated?" A later memo records: "Report subject's involvement in assassination appears have originated in New York." This is the last we know of Ruedolo.

- An early report out of Mexico City describes an Arnesto Rodriguez of New Orleans as well-acquainted with Oswald. "According to Maria Rodriguez de Lopez, her son-in-law has tape-recorded conversations with Oswald." The CIA notes that the information was passed to the FBI. So much for Arnesto Rodriguez.

The final question is why the CIA turned over 500 of its 1100 classified assassination files to public scrutiny. Conceivably, they wanted to avoid a court fight. After Bernard Fensterwald, Jr., filed suit for the files last October, the matter was assigned to D.C. District Court and Judge John Sirica.

"We went to the wire on a trial, then the CIA suggested we meet instead," says Fensterwald, the Washington attorney for James McCord and James Earl Ray who also runs the "other CIA" (Committee to Investigate Assassinations). "I'd asked originally for five computer printouts on Oswald, his aliases, and Marina Oswald. I got absolute gobbledygook. One page of hieroglyphics out of their computer—just an index. So I got George O'Toole, who helped install their computer system, to go out there with me. They said, 'What you're really interested in is the stuff on the shelf. Give us a couple of months to go over the classification.'

"This has not been done at random. If the FBI was doing it, I'd conclude they didn't know what was significant. But the CIA knows what they're doing. They're putting out a lot of information and I don't know why."

Fensterwald is still working to get his hands on the CIA's last 600 files. His intention, he says, is to deliver them to John Sirica for his perusal.

So the Watergate parallels continue. Perhaps, as with the Watergate break-in, the assassination question will one day seem a side issue to the cover-up that followed.

10

A Visit to CIA Headquarters

Around the same time I was researching my story on the CIA files—and I honestly can't remember what journalistic cover I used—I somehow arranged to be given a tour of the CIA's headquarters in Langley, Virginia. My taxi driver couldn't find the place at first. It turned out that the sign to CIA points straight when you should turn left.

The Agency's guards were called the Federal Protection Agency. They met all comers at a front gate and, if your name was on a list, you were allowed to drive on through a lovely wooded area, emerging at a towering building marked by a marble colossus. Another guard just inside checked out your belongings, and then you were ushered up some stairs into a reception area, to receive a visitor's badge.

You couldn't go anywhere without being accompanied. My guide was a thin, mustached, Ivy League-looking fellow named Dennis Barron. He was an ex-reporter for the *Miami News*, now in his fourteenth year as a Company PR man. The top six floors, he explained, were strictly off-limits to visitors. Our first stop was the commemorative plaque listing 31 "war dead" (1951–72). Some names weren't included, I was told, because "they could still be traced." There was no mention of the country of demise, or of what was being performed in the line of duty.

Barron led me down a series of long corridors, past a display of paintings and some sculptures done by Agency employees. "You'd be amazed what some people do in their spare time," my guide said. One of the corridors contained portraits of all the former directors. "[William] Colby's picture will be up there soon," Barron continued, and that will bring the total to eleven. We moved on, past a bulletin board that listed a garden club, and Knitting & Crocheting, along with auto-mechanics and sailing classes. Just plain folks, I surmised, but didn't say this aloud.

We reached the CIA library. Of its four floors, I would be permitted only to see the first. I glanced at a sign that read, HID. "Are you allowed to tell me what that means?" I asked. "Historic Intelligence Documents," Barron said, and added, "No fiction here."

One corridor had a series of medals on the wall. I learned that "Extreme Heroism" is the highest, which gets voted on by governmental leaders, and only a couple of CIA agents had ever been deemed worthy of receiving it.

We sat down in Barron's office. He said he gives about 600 press briefings a year; in fact, I'm the third of four today. Sy Hersh might be ripping the CIA on

Page One of the *New York Times*, but inside on the foreign news pages, there would be four stories generated *from* the CIA. "That's been going on for years," the ex-newsman said proudly. "The Agency doesn't get much credit for good things, but that's the reality we live with."

I noticed a "burn basket" on his desk, and wondered how they ensured security within these confines. Barron said that security guards visit all the offices nightly to ensure that all materials were locked in a two-drawer cabinet or placed in a "vault" area behind it. If papers get left on the desk once, you get a warning. If it happens a few times, you're liable to be out of a job.

There was actually a CIA edict against visible waste. According to Barron, TOP SECRET papers must be shredded and liquefied. They were now developing a new machine to permit pulp to be used as fuel for boilers, a good use for the tons of paper that needed to be disposed of daily.

"Nobody likes the image of the slinking spook," Barron explained. "But this isn't Fish & Wildlife. Intelligence success discussed in public becomes an intelligence failure."

I nodded.

Barron continued, "Intelligence today is not as in former years. The most important things these days are not undercover, but available through technical means. You work toward a goal—what is the next generation of Soviet missiles going to be like in 1980? You begin now to piece things together. An analyst never gets credit, because he's a desk jockey. But he's got the brains and the know-how."

I nodded again. Then I asked whether he'd read the Senate's report on the CIA's involvement in the assassination of foreign leaders. Barron didn't blink. "I have to know what's in it," he said. "I read and practically memorize public testimony and the speeches of the director. I spend most of the day on the phone, sometimes 30 or 40 calls a day from the press."

I was in too deep to stop now. What about anything new on the Kennedy assassination? I asked.

"We've turned the agency upside down," Barron said. "Everything has been released to the investigative committee. Nothing is secret from Congress. Making it public is pretty well their decision. We decided there is no plausible, believable link between the CIA and the assassination."

I nodded one last time. We got up and walked down another corridor. Past four cafeterias and an executive dining room. Past a variety store and a newsstand that's staffed by blind personnel.

"I can tell that you, like everybody else, have an idea about spooks," Barron said. He grinned. I didn't nod this time. Playing it cool.

As he led me toward the door, he pointed to a large plaque on the front wall. It was biblical: "Ye shall know the truth and the truth shall make you free."

My guided tour of CIA headquarters was over.

11

The Village Voice, June 21, 1976

"Cubans Connected to JFK Murder—But Which Cubans?"

*T*he *Warren Report*, with its simplistic conclusions about Lee Harvey Oswald's "inability to enter into meaningful relationships," is about to become obsolete. Before this month is up, the Senate Select Committee on Intelligence will release its own 172-page study of the Kennedy assassination—its last and possibly most damaging chronicle of CIA–FBI wrongdoing, and the first step toward a congressional investigation sometime after the November election. This much is now certain: The motive, one way or the other, goes back to Cuba—either with Fidel Castro, or against him.

In the past few weeks, new information has come out. First a new book called *Betrayal*, written by an ex-CIA contract employee named Robert Morrow, who claims the assassination was engineered by a group of right-wing financiers and anti-Castro exiles in retaliation for what they considered Kennedy's sellout at the Bay of Pigs and Cuban Missile Crisis. Then came arguments from the opposite angle—copyrighted articles in the *New Republic* and *Washington Post* that made it look as if Castro had better start preparing his defense. From the looks of these, the confusion is only beginning.

If *Post* writer George Crile's hypotheses are correct, the duplicity surrounding Cuba in the early 1960s was more staggering than ever imagined. Consider "AM/LASH," the Cuban the CIA selected to use a poison pen to kill Castro in the fall of 1963. Crile identifies him as Rolando Cubela and makes a strong case for his having been a double agent for Fidel. A more unlikely Castro agent, but one Crile also suspects, was Florida Mob boss Santo Trafficante, Jr. A key figure in the CIA's liaison with the Mob in failed attempts to assassinate Fidel, Trafficante is shown receiving favored treatment from Castro in a Havana jail, working closely with Castro in a lottery racket, and in 1963 announcing to a prominent Miami Cuban that Kennedy was "going to be hit."

The theory goes, if Castro was getting advance inside information on attempts against his life, might he have decided to retaliate? Tad Szulc, in the *New Republic*, reports that Bobby Kennedy actually formed a top-secret intergovernmental committee shortly before his brother was killed to look into the possibility that Castro might organize attempts on the lives of high U.S. government officials. One of the Crile stories closes with a quote from Robert Morgan of North Carolina, a senator on the Select Committee: "There is no doubt in my mind that John F. Kennedy was assassinated by Fidel Castro or someone under his influence in retaliation for our efforts to assassinate him."

But the one man in a good position to know Castro's attitude toward the Kennedys believes the Castro motive simply doesn't make sense. He is William Attwood, former U.S. ambassador to Guinea and Kenya, current publisher of *Newsday*. In the fall of 1963, as a special adviser to. America's UN delegation, he undertook secret negotiations to normalize relations with Cuba.

Asked last week what he thought of the Castro's-revenge idea, Attwood scoffed: "Well, I think that's ridiculous. It was quite obvious to me that Castro, at that time, wanted to normalize relations with us. He had no interest whatsoever in breaking this off, he wasn't playing any game. I was on the phone at one point to Havana, setting up a possible meeting down in Varadero to discuss an agenda. In fact, I was supposed to see the president right after Dallas to discuss the kind of questions I'd be asking. Then, if Castro was agreeable, I was to go down very quietly. Not many people were aware of this undertaking."

According to Attwood, by the fall of 1963 U.S. policy toward Cuba was operating on several different tracks. Things had become so diffused that, after Attwood received an olive-branch feeler from Cuba's UN delegate and got approval from the Kennedys to pursue it, Secretary of State Dean Rusk wasn't even informed.

"The State Department had its own policy toward Cuba, which was sort of a frozen, do-nothing policy," Attwood recalled. "The CIA, what was left of the gung-ho types, might well still have been plotting something. But I think the Kennedys saw this as a chance to defuse Cuba as a political issue in 1964. They didn't want to be attacked for having loused up the Bay of Pigs. They could say, 'All right, maybe the Bay of Pigs was a mistake, but *now* we have an agreement that Castro will not subvert Latin America and also give compensation for our companies that he'd expropriated, in return for which we lift the blockade and unblock the Cuban assets in America.' These were some of the proposals. And things were moving along."

The Kennedy assassination brought a halt to all that. For one thing, Oswald was an apparent Castro sympathizer. For another, says Attwood, "We were entering a political year, and I don't think Johnson really knew what was involved. It sounded too complicated and too risky." Nonetheless, Attwood remembers, Castro did give his okay for negotiations to begin and, according to a French journalist who was with Fidel on the day of Kennedy's death, he was "shocked and dismayed at the news of the assassination."

"I've been to Cuba since and stayed in touch with Cubans here at the UN," Attwood concluded, "so I have every reason to believe they were sincere. I've always felt if there *was* any Cuban involvement, it would have been on the part of the anti-Castro Cubans, who might have had reason to be fearful that some kind of normalization was in the works and would have wanted to prevent it. That's the only conclusion I can draw from my own experience."

The rumor is that the forthcoming Senate report will confirm Attwood's suspicions, especially concerning the exile groups that conducted anti-Castro operations in 1963 from Lake Pontchartrain, Louisiana and the Florida Keys. That summer, much against the CIA's wishes, the Kennedys had cut off their funding. The Coast Guard had been ordered to watch for any new raids directed at Cuban shores; numerous exiles and Minutemen soldier-of-fortune types were arrested. And bitterness against the Kennedys was rife.

If there was anti-Castro involvement, of course, that means a conspiracy on American soil. It also suggests a good reason for a CIA-FBI cover-up, particularly if those agencies had ever made prior use of the conspirators. Most of all, in this bizarre realm of turncoats and double-turncoats, it raises the question of just who might have used—and maybe set up—Lee Harvey Oswald. . .

Robert Morrow is a forty-seven-year-old Baltimore electronics consultant who was once arrested in a CIA counterfeiting scheme and who claims in his semi-fictional autobiography *Betrayal* that he's closer than anyone to cracking the case.

"For more than a decade," Morrow writes in his introduction, "handcuffed by the secrecy agreement required of everyone directly or indirectly on the payroll of the Central Intelligence Agency, I lived with what I knew. . . . This book is based upon my experiences, on events related to me at the time and subsequently by close associates, and on evidence available in public testimony . . . some dialogue has been improvised and certain events reconstructed."

There is little doubt, according to Washington sources, that Morrow did indeed work Cuban affairs for the CIA during the early 1960s. That, at least, makes him the first ex-CIA employee to speak out publicly on this subject.

The problem with *Betrayal* (published by Henry Regnery) is sorting out the improvisations and reconstructions from what Morrow really knew. Where he uses real names, the parties concerned are dead. Where he cannot remember specifics of dates and scenes, he invents them. And his scenario for the assassination itself, as he readily admits, is nothing more than an imaginative hypothesis.

But if only some of Morrow's firsthand knowledge is accurate, he has dropped a bombshell. His initial recruitment by the CIA, he says, grew out of his confidential relationship with Cuban exile leader Mario Garcia Kohly. Until the fall of 1963, Morrow claims to have maintained fairly regular contact with former CIA Deputy Director Charles Cabell and case officer "Ed Kendricks," who bears a strong resemblance to E. Howard Hunt's onetime boss of covert operations

Tracy Barnes. Cabell and "Kendricks," according to Morrow, were the overseers of his main CIA project during those years—a scheme to manufacture and then flood the Cuban economy with $50 million in counterfeit pesos

Here, in chronological order, are Morrow's most startling revelations:

- As an engineering specialist in jamming and coding techniques, Morrow recounts his selection for a top-secret mission during the Bay of Pigs invasion. Given the code name Robert Porter, he says he was flown into Cuba's Camaguey Mountains to try to discover the source of some unusual pulse transmissions that the CIA suspected might be a signal system for ballistic missiles. His alleged pilot was David Ferrie, who died mysteriously in 1967 when New Orleans District Attorney Jim Garrison was about to indict him for conspiracy in the Kennedy assassination.

- The CIA, says Morrow, actually stepped up the Bay of Pigs invasion date without Kennedy's okay. Infuriated, Kennedy then demanded all data gathered about possible ballistic missiles turned over to his brother at the Justice Department. Not only did the CIA conclude that the Soviet Union was operating a control center in the Camaguey Mountains, Morrow continues, it also obtained photos smuggled out by the anti-Castro underground of missile launching sites under construction. But the Kennedys chose to do nothing at that time.

- On a mission to Europe, Morrow says the CIA arranged for him to make a clandestine $240,000 arms purchase for Mario Kohly's Cuban underground. The deal was consummated through a Dallas man named "Jake," who Morrow says was Jack Ruby, and a CIA front called Permindex. That front was handled out of New Orleans by CIA consultant Clay Shaw, also later accused and ultimately acquitted in Garrison's trial. Morrow says he was taken to the weapons warehouse in Athens by David Ferrie.

- During that same trip, Morrow says the CIA had him pick up an envelope in Paris from an American just returned from an extended tour of the Soviet Union. The envelope, he was told, was "the information wanted from Harvey," and had been secreted out of Minsk. A year later, Morrow asserts he was told by Cabell and "Kendricks" that "Harvey" was a CIA agent who had gone to Russia posing as a defector to participate in an internal security operation: make contact with the niece of a KGB colonel and arrange to get her out of Russia as a precondition for her uncle's defection to the West.

- After the Cuban Missile Crisis, Morrow claims he was informed by "Kendricks" of CIA reports that the missiles had not been removed but taken to hidden sites deep in the Cuban interior. Elements of the CIA believed that Kennedy and Khrushchev had reached a quid-pro-quo agreement about missiles in Cuba and Turkey. This, Morrow speculates, was Kennedy's betrayal—and his death warrant.

- By mid-October 1962, the CIA was worried about losing control of one of its anti-Castro groups operating out of New Orleans. Cabell, who was no longer deputy director but still kept vigil over numerous covert activities, reportedly wanted Morrow to find out how closely some of its own contract employees—including Cuban leader Mario Kohly—were connected to a paramilitary training camp established at Lake Pontchartrain by Clay Shaw.

- Morrow says he was informed at that same meeting that one of the leaders connected with Shaw's group—"Jake," or Jack Ruby—was running Chinese cocaine out of Cuba under CIA auspices, in exchange for running guns into Mario Kohly's underground. "Harvey," who had returned from Russia with the KGB colonel's niece when he came to feel he was under suspicion, had been assigned by the CIA to report from the Dallas-New Orleans area on Ruby's activities. "Harvey," or Oswald, had also been hired for similar purposes by the FBI.

- Early in 1963, Morrow writes, he was asked by "Kendricks" to obtain several 7.35-caliber Mannlicher-Carcano rifles for delivery to Shaw's group in New Orleans, supposedly for an assassination attempt against the leftist leader of the Dominican Republic, Juan Bosch. Three of these rifles were picked up by David Ferrie by private airplane; Morrow kept a fourth, and today it rests in a gun cabinet in his Baltimore home. The others, Morrow believes, were used against John Kennedy.

- The last straw for the New Orleans conspirators, according to Morrow, was probably the arrest in early October 1963 of Mario Kohly, himself, and two others involved in the CIA's counterfeit peso scheme. The Kennedys, Morrow says, had ordered the Secret Service to make the arrests and so bust up the CIA's last best hope at undermining Castro's Cuba.

That's about as far as Morrow claims any firsthand information. He goes on to speculate about how Oswald was used, the existence of an Oswald look-alike in the Lake Pontchartrain camp, and the roles of Ruby, Shaw, Ferrie, and others. Even what he says he was told staggers the imagination and, in most instances, there is simply no way to back it up. He points to a vast conspiracy similar to the discredited Garrison case, and an equally vast cover-up by the Kennedys themselves around the Cuban missile situation.

Still, no matter how incredible it seems, the Morrow book cannot be dismissed out of hand. Consider, for example, that the CIA's newly released assassination files mention, for the first time, that Oswald's rifle might have been a 7.35-caliber Mannlicher-Carcano. There is also this declassified document dated December 4, 1963: "Source on [deleted] said he saw [deleted]. [Deleted] reported SOVCONGEN told him 30 November that Oswald sent to USSR and married Soviet girl under CIA instructions." By the time those files were released, Morrow's book had long since gone into galleys.

The counterfeit peso story and Morrow's arrest are also documented in newspaper files and court records. Washington attorney Bernard Fensterwald, Jr., recalls investigating the incident in 1966 and concluding that the arrests were "a frame by the U.S. government," just as Morrow maintains.

Morrow has told Congress that he's now prepared to turn over the bulk of Mario Kohly's private files, once the investigation begins. Kohly, who once had 115 exile groups under his United Organizations to Liberate Cuba, was the CIA's most favored leader during that period. And his files, bequeathed to Morrow upon Kohly's death in 1975 at age 76, could prove a fountain of important new information.

These days it is instructive to recall the quaint conclusion of the Warren Commission's own Gerald Ford: "The strong evidence [is] that Lee Oswald's mind turned to murder whenever he wanted to impress Marina. . . ." It's taken 12 years to move from couch to conspiracy—and the new report may be only the beginning.

12

A Cuban Exile and a CIA Break-In

On February 19, 1971, a photo studio in suburban Fairfax County, Virginia was broken into by the CIA. The break-in was mentioned for the first time, without elaboration, in the June 1975 Rockefeller Commission report on CIA activities: ". . . three police officers from the Fairfax City Police Department accompanied [CIA] Office of Security personnel while they surreptitiously entered a business establishment in Fairfax, at night, without a warrant, to photograph some papers."

Not until early 1976 did the *Washington Post* reveal that the break-in had been personally approved by CIA Director Richard Helms. It had occurred "at a photo studio run by Deborah Fitzgerald, a former CIA employee, and Orlando Nuñez, a former middle-level official in the Castro government in Cuba. Both were under CIA surveillance for some time after Fitzgerald, while working in the records division of the CIA, tried to find out what information the CIA had in its files about Nuñez. Fitzgerald and Nuñez have since married."

Initially, it was anticipated that charges would be brought against Helms, by 1976 gone from the CIA and serving as U.S. Ambassador to Iran. A Virginia county prosecutor sought the relevant files from both the Rockefeller commission and the Justice Department, but they were never forthcoming. On February 19, 1976, the Justice Department announced its decision not to prosecute Helms.

When Washington attorney Bernard Fensterwald, Jr. suggested to me that Deborah Fitzgerald might be a daughter of former Western Hemisphere Division chief Desmond Fitzgerald, I decided to pursue the story. Orlando Nuñez's phone number in downtown Washington was listed. When I called him on a trip to the Capitol in 1976, he said, "Well, you are mistaken that Deborah is the daughter of Desmond Fitzgerald." (This was true; there is no family relation). "But," he continued, "her father *was* a CIA officer, and was involved in the break-in." I told Nuñez I was investigating the Kennedy assassination, and had simply called him on a hunch. "Would it be worth our time to get together?" I asked.

"Yes," he said, "I think it would."

I caught a cab out to a high, white wood-frame house on Kalorama Road, where I was met by a tall, stocky Cuban who lived on the first floor and kept his photo studio on the second. "So," he said, seating himself on the edge of a desk inside the studio, "you want to know what my cousin had to do with the Kennedy assassination?"

"Sure," I replied, having absolutely no idea what Nuñez could be talking about.

"Lee Harvey Oswald went to see her—Sylvia Odio, my first cousin, and Sarita, her sister. I talked to Sarita in Dallas at one point, and she told me this guy [Oswald] was very thick. But even with me, she would not go into details too much."

The Odio sisters were the only people publicly known to have linked Oswald to two Cuban exiles who called themselves "Angel" and "Leopoldo." I looked hard at Nuñez and asked, "But do you think the break-in at your studio had something to do with this?"

"Why am I being wiretapped now, you mean?" Nuñez folded his arms and gazed out the window at a tall juniper tree. Then, and when I re-contacted him in June 1992, Nuñez said he honestly had no idea what the CIA was looking to find inside his studio. Because he had once been a lieutenant in Castro's rebel army, and later fought off a CIA effort to recruit him when he was in the U.S. Army stationed at Fort Jackson in 1960, and then gone AWOL and back to Cuba until the summer of 1963, Nuñez believed they falsely suspected him of being a Cuban agent. This, coupled with his relationship with the daughter of CIA official Christopher Fitzgerald, perhaps had prompted the Agency's interest.

"I don't know," Nuñez said, "the CIA could have tried to see what I knew, or had in writing or in masked form that would connect me to Sylvia Odio and what I knew about her. Which was really very little. In 1963, Sylvia was being courted by the right-wing in Dallas, and I believe was made a target of people who needed her association. Who those people were, I have no idea. Possibly CIA, or right-wing, or adventurers, or even Castro agents pretending to fly the flag of being right-wing extremists. Any of these might have sought out my cousin because she was fashionable. She spoke languages and went to finishing school in Pennsylvania. She had connections back in Cuba because her father was in prison there at that time. But she herself had no street smarts to understand who those people were. Was she used? Yes, categorically."

Nuñez knew he had been under surveillance for some time prior to the break-in. Who the intruders were, beyond their CIA and police affiliations, has never been made public.

13

Harper's Weekly, September 6, 1976

"The Vindication of Jim Garrison"

The office lies in a seamy sector of New Orleans, amid a tableaux of hash houses and broken bottles about twenty blocks from the French Quarter. Inside, though, the second floor of 710 Carondelet is a spacious place: wood-paneled, lined with law books and pretty Southern secretaries. Here, far from the madding crowd, Jim Garrison conducts his unobtrusive law practice. And sometimes, behind closed doors, he will talk about what they did to him during his moment in the sun.

"I get the feeling a part of the CIA is interested in bringing the truth out now," the former District Attorney is saying. "The agency is a house of many mansions. It may in the long run be the only way for them to get the egg off their face."

Jim Garrison pauses, and vacantly stares across the room. At 54, almost ten years since he announced the existence of a possible conspiracy involving elements of the CIA and the military in the assassination of John F. Kennedy, he remains an imposing figure—six-foot-six and 240 pounds, his long face brimming with purpose. Yet there is something tragic about him. Something in the slump-shouldered way he moves, or that his eyes avoid you during a conversation. Perhaps Jim Garrison is the personification of those haunting final words of Fitzgerald's *The Great Gatsby*: "And so we beat on, boats against the current, borne back ceaselessly into the past."

In the handsome office, he is saying now that the right-wing has actually questioned the Warren Commission's lone-assassin conclusion far more than liberals. "It's really not that complicated," he continues. "Elements of the CIA utilizing anti-Castro adventurers and elements of the [Meyer] Lansky Mob. It all revolved around Cuba, getting Cuba back."

His voice still quavers when he talks about it, partly with bitterness and partly with a profound sadness. Then, suddenly, the voice will wane, the strength will ebb, the mind seemingly will drift. And the scars will show in whispers:

"At the Shaw trial, two alternate jurors thought he was guilty as charged. They were satisfied a conspiracy existed, but . . . but we weren't able to show them the motive."

Jim Garrison was a man far ahead of his time. Who, in 1967, could believe that the Mafia's brotherhood included the CIA? Even in the darkest days of the Vietnam War and Watergate it seemed frighteningly un-American to consider that part of our own country's military-industrial complex might have murdered a President who threatened its interests.

That prospect, of course, is still frightening. But now, at last, the modus operandi that Garrison tried and failed to show is looming clearer. Through a glass darkly, and ever so slowly, his vindication seems possible. The CIA has released documents admitting its long-denied affiliation with Clay Shaw, the main target of Garrison's investigation. In addition, *Betrayal*, a new book by former CIA contract employee Robert Morrow, links Shaw to Jack Ruby and an extremist group of Minutemen and Cuban exiles operating out of New Orleans. Finally, the onetime roommate of David Ferrie, another of Garrison's prime suspects, has revealed to this writer in an exclusive interview that Ferrie was involved in a plan to fly at least one of Kennedy's assassins out of the country on November 22, 1963.

Still, perhaps the full truth will ever elude us. Today, many of the principals— including Shaw and Ferrie—are dead. A recent spate of counter-rumors have sought to link Lee Harvey Oswald or Ruby or both to Fidel Castro. The Castro-did-it idea is really the oldest—and most convenient—of conspiracy theories, buttressed now by a reverse psychology that hypothesizes a revenge motive for the CIA-Mob attempts against the Cuban Premier's life. It's a simplistic thesis, easier on the psyche than Jim Garrison's complex bitter pill. The question is, if Garrison's theory was so wrong, why did elements of the government set out to totally destroy him?

Who, then, was Jim Garrison? What was he trying to say, and how was he silenced? And who were Clay Shaw, David Ferrie, and the others who once bore the brunt of Garrison's "J'Accuse"?

Until February 1967, the District Attorney of Orleans Parish was a relatively obscure figure. Not that he wasn't a local crusader. Since his surprising election victory in 1961, Garrison had appointed a black assistant district attorney, driven the gamblers off Bourbon Street, and warred with the city's criminal court judges over their refusal to approve funds he'd requested for an intensive investigation of New Orleans crime. One judge charged him with defamation of character and leveled a $1,000 fine, a conviction ultimately overturned in a U.S. Supreme Court decision. Later, the Supreme Court would not prove so kind.

Almost immediately following President Kennedy's assassination, one of Garrison's assistants received a suggestion from one Jack Martin, a local private detective with intelligence ties, to pick up and question a certain David Ferrie. Ferrie, a homosexual rumored to have CIA ties, was then employed as a private investigator and, probably, personal pilot by New Orleans reputed Godfather Carlos Marcello. At the moment of the assassination, he had been in a federal courtroom watching Marcello be acquitted of deportation proceedings that John and Robert Kennedy had instigated two years earlier. That same day, in "celebration" of Marcello's victory, Ferrie and two friends zoomed off on a one-thousand-mile auto trip to Texas for a little ice-skating or "duck hunting." When questioned by law enforcement officials later, Ferrie couldn't remember which, but after driving all night through a torrential downpour, his party arrived at a Galveston skating rink. There, Ferrie bypassed the fun and instead holed up for two hours in a pay telephone booth. When his call finally came, he departed as abruptly. The three immediately returned to Louisiana, where Ferrie went alone to Clay Shaw's hometown of Hammond before returning on November 25 to New Orleans and the questions of Jim Garrison. He was then turned over for further questioning to the FBI. But whatever Ferrie said, it is still locked away in the National Archives. The Secret Service questioned him, too, and posed the curious question of whether he'd ever loaned Lee Oswald his library card. Curiously, too, the Warren Commission chose not to bother with David Ferrie.

So, for a time, Garrison forgot about it. As he describes in his book, *A Heritage of Stone*, it was a visit with Senator Russell Long—who expressed grave doubts about *The Warren Report*—that stirred his interest again in 1966. Oswald, of course, had been born and raised in New Orleans, then resided there again for six months in 1963. He'd been seen in the company of Latins, passed out leftist FAIR PLAY FOR CUBA leaflets from the same building that housed an anti-Castro group, and called attention to himself with a street fight and a radio appearance. In absolute secrecy at first, Garrison began his own private investigation of Oswald's contacts and activities in the area. The hiatus lasted until February 17, 1967, when a local reporter checking court vouchers on Garrison's expenditures learned he'd spent over $8,000 on the Kennedy case—and broke the story to the world.

One of the quickest reactions was Ferrie's. Fearing for his life and seeking protective custody, he went to Garrison as the DA was finalizing plans to arrest and charge him with conspiracy. But before formal charges could be drawn, Ferrie decided to return to his apartment. Within 72 hours, he was dead. The coroner's verdict called it a heart attack. But Ferrie had left a strange suicide note and, stranger still, his door was locked from the outside.

This was enough for Garrison. After calling Ferrie "one of history's most important individuals," a week after his death he announced the arrest of one of New Orleans' most prominent citizens—Clay Shaw, founder and director of the International Trade Mart until his retirement in 1965 to write plays and restore historic French Quarter homes. Shaw, said Garrison, was the real name of "Clay Bertrand," queen of the city's homosexual community whom a local attorney had told the Warren Commission was an associate of Oswald. Then, after one witness claimed to have heard Shaw, Ferrie, and Oswald discussing the assassination and another said he'd seen Shaw pass Oswald some money on the Lake

Pontchartrain waterfront, four judges ruled there was enough evidence to hold Shaw for trial. He remained free on $10,000 bail—and then the tumult and the shouting began.

On Garrison's part, it was a case of too much too soon. "My staff and I solved the assassination weeks ago," he proclaimed. "I wouldn't say this if we didn't have the evidence beyond a shadow of a doubt. We know the key individuals, the cities involved, and how it was done."

When then Congressman Gerald Ford, a member of the Warren Commission, asked to see Garrison's information and pass it on to Lyndon Johnson, the DA responded: "I am running this investigation, not the President, not the Attorney General. We are investigating a conspiracy which appeared to have occurred in New Orleans, and they don't have a thing in the world to do with it. Now, if they want to help me, I'll welcome their help. But I'm not reporting to anybody."

Those were strong words, and probably foolish ones. Before long, the most powerful machinery of the government had been uncorked against Garrison and his sensational charges. It began with delaying tactics. Through a carefully designed series of legal maneuvers (including the improbable complaint that *The Warren Report* was binding upon all U.S. courts and thus enjoined the prosecution of Shaw), the defense lawyers managed to get an injunction against Garrison that took two years for the Supreme Court to overrule. By then, Garrison himself was under investigation by the IRS and SEC; his every effort to extradite key witnesses and subpoena vital information had been thwarted, and he trusted hardly anyone, not even his own staff.

The full story of how Garrison was hamstrung would fill a volume. It began with verbal abuse from Attorney General Ramsey Clark, who even before his own confirmation had begun defending that "perfectly fine man, Clay Shaw." Strangely, on the very day Shaw was charged with conspiracy, Clark announced that the FBI had already investigated Shaw in 1963 and found him innocent of any complicity. Later, at the request of Shaw's lawyers, the Justice Department issued a statement that Clark's remarks had been in error. They said there had been no such investigation, because none had been necessary.

"Officially," wrote *Life Magazine's* Dick Billings in a *Chicago Sun-Times* newspaper column, "the federal government won't admit he (Garrison) is worthy of concern, while in fact the FBI watches every move he makes. Agents trail him whenever he leaves New Orleans."

The most concerned agency of all was the CIA. By the spring of 1967, a Louis Harris poll revealed that 66 percent of the American people believed there had been a plot to kill Kennedy—"and a major contributor to these feelings of doubt is the assassination investigation of District Attorney Jim Garrison." The CIA's first on-the-record interest in Garrison came that April, in a series of memoranda about his main suspects. These memos, finally released earlier this year, include one particularly angry diatribe after the National Archives inadvertently gave a Garrison staffer a list of all the CIA's classified assassination titles.

According to Victor Marchetti, former CIA executive assistant to Richard Helms and author of *The CIA and the Cult of Intelligence*, the "Company's" concern probably went considerably beyond anger. Marchetti remembers a number of discussions about Garrison at the Director's morning staff meetings: "During the Clay Shaw trial, I remember the Director (Helms) on several occasions asking questions like, you know, 'Are we giving them all the help they need?' I didn't know who they or them were. I knew they didn't like Garrison because there were a lot of snotty remarks passed about him. They would talk in half sentences like is everything going all right down there . . . yeah, but talk with me about it after the meeting or 'We'll pick this up later in my office.'"

There was rumor, even then, that the CIA might be paying Shaw's lawyers. For sure, somebody in the Agency helped stymie Garrison's efforts to subpoena two vital witnesses—an alleged ex-CIA contract employee named Gordon Novel, and former CIA Director (and Warren Commission member) Allen Dulles himself. When Garrison sought to bring Dulles before a grand jury to ask if Oswald, Shaw, or Ferrie ever had any CIA association, the proper and usually routine procedure was a subpoena under the Uniform Out-of-State Witness Act. Garrison's request, however, was rejected by the District of Columbia. Another was rejected by Ohio Governor James Rhodes, after Novel fled from New Orleans to Columbus to avoid Garrison's probe. Novel, who claimed he was merely in the "electronic intelligence equipment manufacturing field," had extensive prior association with anti-Castro Cubans. In 1974, he would show up in Charles Colson's White House office with a plan to wipe out the Nixon tapes with a laser beam. And when asked in 1975 about the Garrison investigation, and particularly a suit Novel filed against Ohio Bell telephone company, this was his reply:

"It's really quite simple," Novel recalled. "I had talked by phone to Mr. Allen Dulles at length, and we discussed how I might send him documents that could be used by the CIA counsel to avoid or avert his having to go to New Orleans to testify before Mr. Garrison's grand jury. The conversation that we had, even though I was not an agent of the CIA, would have been very incriminating. Garrison could have gotten access to these tapes, played them at the Shaw trial, and used them against us. Ohio Bell admitted to having them. And I've got a tape of them admitting they have a tape."

Such Watergate-like machinations abounded in New Orleans. Before long, Garrison was seeing spies everywhere. He fired one ex-CIA man who'd joined his staff in good faith, and overlooked another who hadn't. Other staffers were induced to "defect." One, Tom Bethell, his custodian of files, gave a Xeroxed copy of virtually his entire case to Shaw's attorneys before the trial. Even elements of the media seemed intent on crippling him.

The most blatant media interference came from two NBC newsmen—Richard Townley of the local WDSU affiliate, and Walter Sheridan, executive producer of a scathing hour-long network attack on Garrison. Both men were indicted by a New Orleans grand jury for bribing witnesses, suppressing evidence, and interfering with trial proceedings. The charges centered around Garrison's key witness Perry Russo, who claimed Townley had threatened him with being discredited but offered him a chance to "cooperate" with NBC. According to Russo, Sheridan had told him it was NBC which flew Gordon Novel out of Louisiana and originally to the CIA's hometown of McLean, Virginia. Upon their arrest in July 1967, both Townley and Sheridan posted bond. Their trials never took place.

Unfortunately, Garrison often played right into his enemies hands. As the months passed, his flamboyance eroded into paranoia. "After mid-1967," remembers Richard E. Sprague, a founder of the Committee to Investigate Assassinations, "Jim stopped writing to anyone and answering phone calls. The only way to communicate with him, which is still true, was to call where you knew he was. He failed to take into account the impact of his lack of communication with certain people who had been his friends."

By the time Shaw finally came to trial in February 1969, Garrison really no longer had a case. His strongest material had been leaked and co-opted, his most important witnesses were dead or unavailable. Some he did call were lacking in character, if not credibility. One came to court in a toga and said he was a reincarnation of Julius Caesar. A "mystery witness" from New York, who said he'd heard Shaw plotting at a party and did indeed take the jury right to Shaw's house, revealed under cross-examination that he'd once fingerprinted his own daughter for fear his enemies had gotten to her. Most of the press seized upon such absurdities; the rest was lost. After five weeks of testimony, it took the jury only 50 minutes to return a verdict of not guilty for Clay Shaw.

So Garrison's crusade largely came to an end. Shortly, his wife left him and he lost his bid for a fourth term as DA. He went into the hospital with a back ailment, then claimed he'd been given an injection of staphylococcus germs in an attempt to kill him. Nobody paid much heed.

In truth, the government was not done with Jim Garrison. More than three years after his disastrous day in court, the Justice Department and the IRS consciously set out to finish him off. It is a seamy story, ignored amid the later revelations of burglary and enemies lists and financial scandal. But before considering what we've since learned about Clay Shaw and David Ferrie, it is enlightening to examine the breaking of Jim Garrison 1972.

Even by 1972, Garrison was still pursuing his nemesis. For Shaw's denial of ever having known, seen, or met Oswald or Ferrie, the DA had charged him with perjury—and the case was about to go to the Supreme Court. It was an election year for Richard Nixon; a year that, in the words of John Dean, the White

House would amply "use the available federal machinery (especially the Internal Revenue Service) to screw our political enemies."

Pershing Gervais was an old friend of Garrison's. He had served on his investigative staff. And he owed Garrison some money. Coincidentally, Gervais also happened to have some problems of his own with the IRS. He was the ideal fellow to sign a contract with John Wall, of Attorney General John Mitchell's staff, to plant fake bribe money on Garrison and bug conversations that could be made to sound as if Garrison was on the take. The idea was that Garrison was accepting bribes to permit the continuing illegal operation of pinball machines in New Orleans.

Later, seven conspirators who admitted their guilt would be granted immunity in a ploy to get Garrison.

For the initial work, though, five IRS agents participated with Pershing Gervais. One hid in the trunk of Gervais' car when it parked in front of Garrison's house. Two more parked down the street, another hid in an alley behind the house. All were equipped with radio receivers and tape recorders. The bug in Gervais' pocket was personally authorized by John Mitchell. And when Gervais came to "repay" his debt of $1,000, Garrison accepted. The taped conversation was general enough for many interpretations. The question would later be—had IRS and Justice experts altered it by putting certain words in Garrison's mouth in the right places?

Around the time Garrison's perjury case against Shaw went to the Supreme Court, Justice indicted Garrison for bribery. Arrangements were made for Gervais to leave the country. He was to settle in Vancouver with his family and assume the identity of "Paul Mason," who would then gain employment with General Motors of Canada at $18,000 annually. But when things didn't work out in Canada as pleasantly as "Mason" had hoped, he decided to grant an interview. He gave it to Rosemary James, ironically the same reporter who broke the story of Garrison's Kennedy investigation in 1967. It was broadcast over New Orleans WWL-TV on May 22 and 23, 1972.

"I guess it could be described as I'm here at the convenience of the government, whatever that really means," Gervais began. Maintaining he'd been forced to serve as a government informer, he continued: "It became clear that they were really interested in but one man, Jim Garrison, and in their minds they knew that I was the guy who could get him. . . . They wanted to silence Jim Garrison. . . . I was forced to lie for them. . . . (It was) a total complete, political frame-up. I know he wasn't guilty."

Later, in court, Justice's John Wall would say the government had offered, promised, and given nothing to Pershing Gervais. But Gervais had countered: "How in the hell did I get to Canada? They paid every goddamn nickel of it. . . . I've got the most ridiculous, the softest job in America. . . . Before I left New Orleans they guaranteed me, unequivocally, $22,000 a year, tax free."

The tax-free talk had been a shuck, said Gervais, and that was why he was talking. As for his current job, it was to "in effect, investigate, or spy on, or determine why it was that this oil company was not accorded certain privileges in Canada by the Canadian government. . . ."

The Wall Street Journal picked up the story in its May 30, 1972 edition: "General Motors Corporation confirmed that it hired briefly, at the request of the Justice Department, a former New Orleans policeman who helped the government in its case against Jim Garrison . . . The GM hiring disclosure also has brought to light a fairly widespread, but previously unpublicized, practice of some big American multinational corporations finding jobs for U.S. government informers and secret witnesses in out-of-the-way corners of their operations here or abroad."

Other documents would eventually confirm the deal—a letter contract between Justice and Gervais, a Photostat of the fake "Mason" birth certificate, the transcript of a taped phone call to Gervais in Vancouver from Gerald Shur of Justice that offered Mitchell's personal congratulations for Gervais' help. But the government denied everything, and Justice did not drop the case. Gervais next surfaced in a small town in Mississippi, claiming he'd lied to the news reporter and that Garrison had tried to buy him off.

So the Pinball Bribery Conspiracy Trial finally began on August 20, 1973. By then, the Supreme Court had rejected Garrison's last straw against Shaw.

The judge at Garrison's 5½-week trial was Herbert W. Christenberry, the same man who had stopped him in 1969 from further prosecuting Shaw in the local courts. For the most part, Garrison handled his own defense. The judge allowed the U.S. Attorney to introduce 55 tapes of conversations with Garrison and others. But Garrison was never able to use the TV interview with Gervais.

In the end it came down to a battle of tape experts questioning whether Garrison's voice had been spliced into portions to try to nail him. The jury found him innocent on its first ballot. And Garrison left the courtroom calling it an honor "to be prosecuted by the most corrupt administration in the history of our nation."

The specter of Clay Shaw, though, did not go away.

The following summer of 1974, Garrison's chances looked bright for a seat on the Louisiana State Supreme Court. On August 15, two days before the election, sixty-year-old Clay Shaw died. Garrison missed a run-off spot on the ballot by a few thousand votes.

That six-foot-four silver-haired bachelor, a former Army officer who built the $14 million International Trade Mart, was a man not without influence in New Orleans—and beyond. Indeed, Garrison could scarcely have tagged a more difficult man to prosecute than Clay Shaw. Of all the rumors about Shaw (including a set of leather whips found in his house, which Shaw claimed were for a Mardi Gras costume), the most persistent—and the hardest to prove—was his link to the CIA.

Then, early this year in response to a freedom of information suit, the CIA released a batch of documents on the Garrison investigation. One was dated April 6, 1967, addressed to "Deputy Chief, Security Research Staff." It read: "The undersigned contacted [deleted] and [deleted] after checking, advised that the DCS office in New Orleans had contact with SHAW until 1956. [Deleted] also advised that certain information concerning SHAW had been furnished to the General Counsel of this Agency at the request of the General Counsel, but a copy inadvertently had not been sent to the Office of Security . . . [Deleted] was advised that SHAW was of interest to DCS a number of years ago and that specific details would be obtained."

DCS stands for Domestic Contact Service, the branch that E. Howard Hunt served in the 1960s in covert activities. According to Victor Marchetti, when he inquired of his CIA superiors why they were so interested in the Shaw trial, he was told Shaw had been a CIA contact whose job was to monitor businessmen going behind the Iron Curtain—"to try to find out if so-and-so was going to a denied-access area." The businessmen would then be debriefed by the CIA.

This particular assignment came intriguingly close to Oswald's "defection" and return from the Soviet Union. It also gives partial corroboration to a story told this reporter by "Captain Sam," an alleged ex-CIA man now residing in Arizona. According to "Sam," who insisted his real identity remain secret, "Garrison wasn't too far off. He had a lot of people nailed. Shaw and Ruby, I was told, had been drawing the attention of the CIA for quite a few years. I'd seen material prior to the assassination that Shaw and Ruby knew each other for quite a long time.

"There was an underground in the U.S., I'll refer to it as a tunnel, where Russian agents . . . Well, say you're someone they want to defect, there are means to get you out through an underground tunnel. Ruby and Shaw had access to get people through. Ruby was a double agent, working mainly for our side. Shaw, I don't know. But another thing Shaw and Ruby could do very hastily, more so Shaw—for instance, we had two agents caught by Nigeria during the Biafran conflict, facing a firing squad at daylight, and we wanted to work a trade with them. Our State Department is so slow there's no way of setting anybody up in that short time. But Clay Shaw could get you a yes or no within 1½ hours."

The story strains credibility, until one examines Shaw's remarkable—and well-documented—connection with a worldwide trade network called Centro Mondiale Commerciale (CMC). The fact that Shaw was a member of the CMC's exclusive Council Committee broke in April, 1967 in the Italian newspaper *Paese Sera*. The CMC had been expelled from Rome in 1962 for failure to pay its $160,000 monthly rent, and was rumored to have moved its headquarters to Johannesburg. Before that, according to the Italian paper, Shaw had come to Rome on a number of occasions to fraternize with such other Council members as L. M. Bloomfield, former OSS major and Montreal banker;

Swiss Minister Ernest Feisst; Sicilian Prince Gutierez di Spadafora; and Ferenc Nagy, the ex-President of Hungary. They were an international, often reactionary, cadre—and Shaw was the lone American representative. Their parent organization was the "Permanent Industrial Exhibition," or Permindex, of Basel, Switzerland, which had financed the French OAS against de Gaulle and been openly accused of criminal activities by the Swiss press. Permindex, wrote *Paese Sera*, was really little more than a subsidiary of the CIA.

Such speculation was totally ignored by the American press. The story made the rounds of Europe, and *Life Magazine* knew about it but said nothing. Yet when Paris Flammonde, an American author doing a book about Garrison's case, called the Italian Consul General in New York to inquire about the Rome activities of the CMC, he was finally told: "Why don't you contact the American Embassy in Rome?"

There the mystery might have rested, except for the new book, *Betrayal*. Robert Morrow writes in *Betrayal* that he worked for the CIA during the early 1960s, and remembers being told about Shaw by his agency contact; that Shaw was a contract consultant for the CIA, associated with a number of companies used by "covert operations" as a cover in South America. It had been arranged for Morrow to buy some machine guns in Athens for the anti-Castro underground, through a Shaw associate named "Jake." Jake, who was really Jack Ruby, had assisted with weapons purchases for the Bay of Pigs, brokered through a Canadian firm with the source in Greece. David Ferrie, who worked closely with both Shaw and Ruby, would meet Morrow in Athens, where they would pick up the machine guns for transfer to the U.S. through Central America.

In Athens, Morrow says Ferrie met him late in 1961 and took him to a building on the Piraeus waterfront. It was filled with tiers of crates marked as machine parts, all with U.S. company names. The weapons were embedded inside. The building, according to Morrow, was marked "Permindex S.A." on one side and "Centro Mondiale Commerciale S.A." on the other.

On the way back to the U.S., Morrow continues, he received a telex from the CIA at the Permindex office in Madrid. He was instructed to meet a man named "Hampshire" in Paris, who was just returned from an extended tour of the Soviet Union and would give him an envelope of papers: "the information wanted from Harvey." Harvey, Morrow surmises, was the code name for Lee Harvey Oswald.

Morrow goes on to describe Shaw as the brains behind a group of fanatic Minutemen and anti-Castro Cubans training in paramilitary teams around Lake Pontchartrain. Morrow believes it was this group that carried out the assassination of John Kennedy, and that Shaw, along with Oswald, Ruby, Ferrie, and others, was the one who set the terrible wheel in motion.

David Ferrie was an expert pilot and a gun-runner. He did private investigative work both for Carlos Marcello and Guy Bannister, who ran local anti-Castro operations. Most likely, he had once tutored a youthful Lee Oswald in the New Orleans' Civil Air Patrol.

There were numerous references to his probable association with Clay Shaw. A whole slew of people from Clinton, Louisiana were sure they'd seen Shaw, Ferrie, and Oswald together there that fall. Another witness claimed to know of Shaw and Ferrie flying to Montreal in the summer of 1963. And the name of a wealthy Shreveport man appeared in both Shaw's and Ferrie's personal notebooks.

But the Warren Commission's Counsel Wesley Liebeler recalled Ferrie like this: "I remember specifically going through a substantial stack of FBI reports on Ferrie that we received in order to make our determination. It was perfectly clear that he was not involved in any way." Indeed, Jack Martin, who first came forward with the story that Ferrie had instructed Oswald in the use of a tele-scopic site, eventually would say he'd made it all up. Perhaps there was method in Martin's change of heart. His close associates—Ferrie, Bannister, Maurice Gatlin, and Hugh Ward—by early 1967 were all dead.

Robert Morrow, in *Betrayal*, says he and Ferrie flew on a clandestine CIA mission into Cuba during the Bay of Pigs to try to detect the presence of Soviet missiles. If true, this would substantiate Ferrie's CIA connection. Assuredly, he was an excellent pilot. He was also not against illegal "intelligence" type activities, such as a 1961 burglary of a Houma, Louisiana arms bunker in which Ferrie, Gordon Novel, and two others were caught and arrested. It was no secret that Ferrie loathed Kennedy for refusing to provide air cover for the Bay of Pigs. According to one unclassified FBI report, he "might have used an off-hand or colloquial expression, 'He (Kennedy) ought to be shot.'"

It remained for Ferrie's former roommate, a gay activist named Raymond Broshears, to shed further light on his probable involvement in a conspiracy. In the heart of San Francisco's Tenderloin district, the Reverend Broshears maintains an office called HELPING HANDS, a place for the city's gays to come when troubled by the law, the straights, or other gays. Broshears is a large man with a neatly trimmed, downturned mustache and sad brown eyes. He dresses in black, with white clerical collar and a handsome cross around his neck. At the end of a long day, he sits behind his desk and, hesitantly, nervously, remembers his time with David Ferrie.

"He called me here in San Francisco shortly before his death. He said he was going to be killed. I said, oh sure, what are you drinking. No, he says, really. I said, why don't you come out here? He said, 'I can't really leave the South. I don't want to come out there with all those Communists.' That was it. The next thing I knew, he was dead. They said he killed himself. But he didn't. You know it, and I know it."

Broshears is silent for a long moment, then: "He believed Kennedy was a Com-munist, or being controlled by the Communists. David wasn't a red-baiter; he really believed this. He had a deep love for his country. And he believed we were in danger of being invaded, that the missiles had never been removed from Cuba and there was going to be an all-out atomic holocaust in the U.S. When you can understand that, and his religious part—he would wear priest robes and perform a mass, you see—well. . ."

There is another long silence as Broshears considers the question about Ferrie's sudden trip to Texas through a driving rainstorm on November 22, 1963.

"David was to meet a plane. He was going to fly them on to Mexico, and eventually to South Africa. They had left from some little airfield between Dallas and Fort Worth, and David had a twin-engine plane ready for them, and that was the purpose of his mad dash through a driving rainstorm from New Orleans. But the plane crashed off the coast of Texas near Corpus Christi. That was what David was told in the telephone booth that day. Apparently, they had decided to try to make it to Mexico on their own. They did not."

Had Ferrie ever told Broshears who was on that plane?

"They had code names. The only one I remember was García."

Another pause. "He told me Lee Harvey Oswald did *not* kill the president. He was very adamant about it, and I believed him. All the things he told me about Oswald, I doubt he could have shot a rabbit 50 feet away. He said four people were going to shoot. It was a very patriotic thing to David. I don't think it was any great long drawn-out conspiracy. It was a conglomerate of different right-wing ideologies pushing on a few people, and it all came together at the same time. I think they were manipulated very cleverly—by somebody pulling the strings."

Inside the law office on Carondelet, Jim Garrison reclines in his chair and contemplates quietly. He has recently withdrawn from the Criminal District Court judgeship race when he failed to gain the support of the incumbent. He has been spending his leisure hours finishing a novel, *The Star Spangled Contract*. In fiction, he says, you can say a lot of things they don't allow you to say in real life.

I show him an article about one of his former staff, a man he's convinced was an infiltrator from the CIA. As he reads down the lines, all the old wounds seem to surface again across his face, and he says bitterly: "So fucking clever, laying down false leads like this. He tore the shit out of us. He was 100 percent Agency!" But as he reads on, he begins shaking his head. The knockout punch, the slam he's come to expect against himself, is not there.

"Surprisingly objective," he says at last. "Not vicious at all. Maybe he's more complex than I thought."

Twelve years after, it has all become more complex than anyone thought.

14

Memories of an FBI Informant

My instructions were to wait in the parking lot of an outdoor diner called The Hat in the L.A. suburb of Alhambra. A few moments ago, a fellow had sat down across from me at a picnic table and stared suspiciously at my double-cheese whopper. "Mr. Dean?" I semi-whispered. The man shook his head no. I folded up my burger and walked over to stand beside the '55 Chevy that a friend had loaned me. In this situation, I figured, it was best to be conspicuous.

Ten more minutes passed. It felt like everybody was eyeing me from behind their French fries. Suddenly, I was *sure* someone was coming up behind me. As I turned, a shutter clicked. "Sorry about that," said Harry Dean as we shook hands, "but you might be a hit man." We walked across the street for coffee.

Harry Dean, alias Dean Fallon, was a short, balding man with a very round face and a constant nervous fidget. A few months earlier, in the summer of 1975, he'd worn a mask and called himself "Mr. X" in taping a *Tomorrow Show* with NBC's Tom Snyder. The word was that NBC considered the program too hot— or too something—to air. Then the *National Tattler* had blown Dean's cover and named him as one of the four individuals who held the keys to cracking the Kennedy case. And he'd come home to California to work on a manuscript about his days as an FBI informant.

Ever since the *Tattler* story, he was saying between sips of black coffee, the threats had been coming. The last was only a few days ago. Anonymous phone call, advice to keep his trap shut. He paused. "If you're with the John Birch Society," Harry Dean said finally, "I feel sorry for you."

I took a big bite of coconut cream pie. "Well, I'm not," I replied, but he was already probing into a stack of papers that he'd secured in our booth beneath his Pentax camera. He brought forth a single sheet. It was a mimeographed poem in blank verse, titled "Waiting Justice Sleeps." My eyes moved quickly to its concluding stanza:

> In the southeast U.S. was a federal spy
> Oswald by name, in the same job as I
> In a network hemispheric and vast
> And all knew the others as the dye was cast.

It was signed "code name 'JR'." "That stands for Junior," Dean said. Another of his *noms de guerre*. It was also the name by which he sent flowers—and a special poem—each year on November 24 to Marguerite Oswald, who in turn placed them on the grave of her son Lee. "I've been doing this since 1964," Dean continued, "always with a poem indicating his innocence. I know it aggravates the agencies which I quit shortly thereafter. Mrs. Oswald always sends me back a picture of the grave, with my flowers around it. I don't know why."

Before we could go further, he explained that if I want to tape-record him, he'll have to first go home and get his machine, too. It was a long-standing policy. We agreed to rendezvous again at a quieter coffee shop a few blocks away. As we parted company, Dean told me he'd noticed that in profile I myself looked strikingly like Oswald.

I was waiting at a new corner table, casting wary glances out the picture window, when he showed up again twenty minutes late. We aligned our tape recorders side by side. I ordered another round of black coffee and coconut cream pie.

"My background is that of a misguided missile," Dean began. "Bizarre, even not too bright. I've endeavored and undertaken many things—learning to fly, being a Bible student, various things at which I was never successful for any length of time. Then I got involved in the revolutionary anti-Batista, or pro-Castro, revolution. I saw this as an opportunity to really do something in life. The turning point came after I returned from Cuba in 1960 and was made to see things in light of our foreign policy. The insinuation was strong that these people were communists, enemies of the U.S. I became convinced that what was coming would obviously put me in one helluva spot. I'd be on the other side, where I didn't want or deserve to be. So I began working against Castro as an undercover operative, to inform the FBI as to certain activities."

His first assignment was as an FBI penetrator of the Fair Play for Cuba Committee in Chicago—the same group that Oswald later founded a chapter of in New Orleans. As the Chicago group's secretary, Dean "blew the whistle on everything that came down the road" and got rewarded with a new mission in L.A. of keeping tabs on Castro agents infiltrating into the U.S. through Mexico. Then, late in 1962, the Bureau had him shift gears. He joined the John Birch Society.

"That," said Dean, inhaling deeply, "is where I fell in with various people that planned to kill Mr. Kennedy."

His instructions were to convince the Bircher fanatics that he was so ashamed of his work for Castro that he'd now do anything to rectify himself in the eyes of God, Mom, Country, Apple Pie, and so on. He was not, he added, terribly successful. The Birchers never really trusted him. Eventually, he'd gotten the boot. But not before he'd figured out some curious things.

"Oswald was working in the same areas I did, because he had a fantastically good background for infiltrating. He could suddenly become an anti-communist and infiltrate the right, or remain a communist and infiltrate Cuban intelligence. He was just another of our very own agents, doing a helluva job to the last week of his life, it seems. And Oswald was all over the place—just like the Bureau had Harry Dean all over the place."

His voice grew whispery, subliminal, as if Lee Oswald had once caused Harry Dean an identity crisis. He mentioned something about Oswald being a patsy, and the theory of an Oswald look-alike, then said: "Very simply, one of my associates in the John Birch Society said to me once: 'Hey, Dean, I know a guy who looks exactly like you.' I said, 'Gee, that's too damn bad, I feel sorry for the guy.' He kept harping on that subject really heavy. I let it go. Later they were trying to get me an office here in L.A. It's *possible* they didn't know what they were doing when they asked me to be sure my office was on a higher floor, otherwise the Castro-ites might bust it up. I never did confirm whether Mr. Kennedy was planning to come here in a political parade. But it became obvious they were planning to set me up—for *something*."

They, according to Dean, were the then-Western director of the Birch Society (later a Republican Congressman), a controversial former Army general, and a friend of John Wayne's who led the charge at Saipan in World War II and was featured in the film, *Hell to Eternity*. The earliest plot to eliminate Kennedy, Dean continued, was scheduled for Mexico City at the end of June 1962. "The idea was for someone to assassinate him while running alongside his car, when he came to visit on June 30. But the sympathy for Mr. Kennedy [among Mexicans] made it impossible for any assassin to escape, and that plan fell through."

Later, in Dean's scenario, the hero of Saipan brought together a crew of anti-Castro guerrilla raiders and used Birch Society influence to keep them well funded. The raiders traveled back and forth between L.A. and the Florida Keys. They stopped off in Dallas to meet the former Army general, who had his own crew of brown-shirt types staying at his mansion. Bigger plans got laid. The only monkey wrench was Dean, who saw money change hands.

"[Name deleted] had a Drive-Against-Communist-Aggression office in Mexico City. He was going back and forth all the time. It was August '63 when arrangements were made to get $10,000 for a 'new' kind of Mexican operation. When I found out about it, they were madder than blazes. I didn't put two and two together for a considerable time. But then along comes Oswald a month or so later on the Mexico scene. It's what they call laundering funds."

Dean refused to elaborate concerning his knowledge about actual contact between Oswald, the congressman, the general and the hero of Saipan. His documentation, he said, would all come out in his book.

"Aren't you ever in fear for your life?" I asked, taking my last bite of my second round of pie.

"I guess I'm not at all," Dean replied. "No use being in fear. Nothing I can do about it, so to hell with it. I carry a weapon most of the time, that's true. But I wouldn't have a chance to use it anyway, might as well face it. Just an added weight is all it is."

He cast a long, John Wayne-like glance out the picture window. It was twilight time in Alhambra. He began to talk about breaking away from the FBI in 1965.

"I was tired of it. I wanted them to drop me and forget about me. My wife had left me—I came home one day to an empty house, including the wallpaper and the carpets were gone. That was heart-breaking right there. But it's probably common with everyone that dabbles in the life of intelligence. Secrecy, lies, deception. Take old Oswald's wife Marina, a beautiful Russian broad, she was on his goddamn back all the time. You've got all these obligations and guys walking around trying to put a knife in your stomach or knock your teeth out, he had to get her off him any way he could. I had the same problem. A life of deception. Today I just do more or less confidential investigations, I mean *very* confidential, just for certain people that I make little runs for, look into things and all that."

Harry Dean sighed loudly. Across the empty coffee cups in the gathering darkness, he handed me a photograph. It had come air-mail from Marguerite Oswald. It showed a bouquet of yellow mums placed slightly to the left of Lee's concrete slab. There was a postcard Dean had attached to her missive, with the following typed inscription:

> Lee Harvey Oswald
> Did he assassinate the President?
> Was he truthfully accused?
> Guilty, yes? Or was he innocent?
> He has left all the world confused.
>
> — Jr.

15

Harper's Weekly, July 21, 1976

"Assassination Assignation: Captain Sam on the Death of a President"

About six months ago, bitten with the bug of the Great Assassination Revival, this mild-mannered reporter set forth on an odyssey in search of Poe's "mystery all insoluble," tracking the mysterious collection of men whose names have long been whispered among assassination buffs: mobsters and mercenaries, dictators and diabolists, priests and perverts, spiers, and liars.

This is the story of one of them, a former CIA contract employee who claims not only to have known Lee Oswald, but his double, and who has threatened my safety should I reveal his real name.

Here, then, is the way life is when a mild-mannered reporter elects to cross the border into the realm of cloak-and-dagger. Whether there is substance to these tales, only time and a new investigation will tell. For now, you may be the judge.

PHOENIX—"I've kept quiet 15 years." The words escape in a husky, Andy Devine–like whisper from the man behind the desk. He even looks somewhat like Devine: a chinless, beguilingly soft face, and upwards of 250 pounds on a five-by-nine-foot frame. By his own admission, he's gained almost 100 pounds since his days as a contract employee of the Central Intelligence Agency. Now, as I ask him to recall those days, his voice cracks with apprehension and his hands tremble.

I shall call him "Captain Sam." That's the name he says he used while training anti-Castro exiles in Florida for another invasion attempt of Cuba. If I use his real name, "payback is a bitch," to borrow his favorite phrase. If anyone ever asks, he will deny meeting me.

We are sitting behind the closed doors of an Arizona lawyer's office whom he serves as a licensed private investigator. My visit had come as a surprise. He was aware of only one assassination researcher—an ex-newspaperman in Texas—who knew how to contact him. He's reluctant to say anything. The only compelling reason to go public with his story, he says, is that people are still dying for what they know about the events of November 22, 1963. And Captain Sam would like to know who's eliminating them.

"There's only one reason I'm alive," he says, lighting a cigarette to steady his nerves. "Because I've squirreled away enough sensitive information about intelligence activities for immediate release if anything strange happened to me. But there's no way I'd ever testify about any of this. No way. Payback's a bitch."

What if you and I flew to Washington tonight and had the Senate grant you immunity? I suggest. Captain Sam shakes his head. "There are many ways to discredit someone," he says.

From everything I'd been able to learn about him, Captain Sam's CIA connections seemed real. He had a long history of association with Cuban exiles in Florida, including the notoriously violent CIA-backed group called Alpha 66. From 1961 to 1964, while rumored to be in South Africa, he had actually worked quietly in Florida using a variety of code names. One of his assignments, it's been said, concerned Lee Harvey Oswald.

"Look, if I talk to you," he is saying, "there's one thing you should know from the start. Half of what I'll tell you might be truth, and the other half bullshit. But all of it is what I was told. That's part of the game in the intelligence business. You confuse your own operatives with false information; maybe *nobody* knows the full truth about a particular assignment. Okay?"

I nod.

"Okay," says Captain Sam, "come with me."

We pass through the doors of the outer office toward his waiting car. It's a ninety-degree scorcher in Phoenix. "We're having some problems," he says, "with some process servers trying to get to a couple of clients of ours from Kansas City. They're watching this office, but don't know where their hotel is. So we're probably going to be followed. I'm on my way downtown, acting as a kind of decoy. Later, we'll pick these people up at their hotel. We won't be able to talk when they're with us. But we can talk now, and you can take notes but I don't want any tape recorders. Is that understood?"

Through the mid-afternoon traffic on the outskirts of the city, he begins to weave his tale. "I know Lee Harvey Oswald was employed by the CIA, and I know there were two Oswalds. It gets confusing even to me; you'd figure it's something that would come out of a movie. Because I've spent many a sleepless night trying to figure this shit out, and I'm not certain which Oswald was which. Tom Kane of New York City was picked as his double, although that may not have been his real name. He was almost a dead-ringer, except a little taller and there was more meat on him. Oswald had no chest. Tom lost a lot of weight trying to make up for it, but he never could do it in the chest area."

But why was it necessary? I ask. Why two Oswalds?

"We'd been plagued with an intelligence leak. The agency, including probably the State Department and Military Intelligence, was just getting killed with a high-level intelligence leak. With Cuban affairs, everybody knew who we were and what we were doing almost before we did. They got our *orders* before we did. So Oswald and Tom Kane were part of a penetration team directed against Castro's intelligence to find out where that leak was coming from. It was coordinated somehow so that if one of the two disappeared, we'd have something to go on. It really had nothing to do with a plot to assassinate the President. Not at first. I was part of that penetration."

"There were five of Castro's people at an initial meeting, waiting for Oswald to return from Russia, in an apartment building on West Ninety-Ninth Street in New York. He'd already managed to connect up with Castro's intelligence. The group believed I was working for Castro's intelligence. I fed them a lot of good information. I was told to, and it probably cost a lot of lives. I met with Oswald alone in New York—except I don't know if it was really him or Tom Kane—and I made a report to the FBI in New York City. They claim there are no copies of that report, but that's a lie. I talked on two occasions to an FBI expert on Latin-American countries."

We are parked across the street from a Phoenix skyscraper. Captain Sam scrutinizes the double doors. "I'm going to have to go inside here for a minute," he says. "Need to make a phone call." Almost immediately upon his return we pull out again. "We should lose them now. Can you drive?" I nod. "When we get to this hotel, I'll go inside for my clients. You take the car and just keep circling around the block, okay?"

Circling, circling. Everything seems to be going in circles.

At last, after a half-dozen tries, he emerges with a middle-aged man and his teenaged son. I turn my notepad face down on the seat. Captain Sam introduces me as his partner. The clients from Kansas City are involved with an Arizona Indian tribe in a squabble over property rights and Captain Sam doesn't think it's safe for them to return to their hotel. After dinner we drive them to the home of a friend of his, where they will spend the night on the couch.

"I'd like to hope the agency had a major fuck-up, but I don't know," he is saying now. We are driving again through the darkened streets, aimlessly driving as I scrawl his words into my notepad. "I do not really feel in my heart that the agency assassinated Kennedy or had anything to do with it. With some of the evidence, I've really thought of it as a probability, but in my heart I refuse to believe it."

The key part of the Oswalds' penetration effort, he emphasizes, was to discover the source of an intelligence leak. The possibility that Castro would assassinate Kennedy seemed remote. It was discussed, but never taken seriously.

"I mean, we had that one group infiltrated by four or five different agents. I actually had several meetings with the Cubans where an assassination was discussed. That was in 1962, with Oswald. Nobody really took an interest in it, other than the people involved. Everybody else's report was—nothing to worry about. I reviewed quite a few of these reports personally. We felt Castro was using this kind of talk as a screening operation for something else."

Captain Sam pauses for a long moment at a stop sign. There is no traffic in sight. He is looking down, looking through the steering wheel, staring at nothing. I try to read his features, but cannot. Suddenly, he looks up and again begins to drive.

"Oswald called me the night before the assassination took place. At least it sounded like his voice. I was in Tipton, Indiana, with my family. I'd dropped out of things for a while, because I was catching too much heat from the FBI. I'd still see reports, but that was about it. The FBI really did a severe surveillance of our people, believe it or not. It really messed us up. But anyway, he called me and he was in a frenzy. He said, 'I can't get hold of anybody, can't contact anybody, they're going to kill him tomorrow.' I said, 'Don't worry, it's all taken care of.' Everybody else thought it was a bullshit deal. The agency had known the hit date 10 or 12 days beforehand, but nobody believed it. I guess I was like everyone else. I figured he had to be wrong. But Oswald was the only one who nailed it to the head. Maybe that's why he was killed."

His voice sounds distant, almost hollow. I am thinking there must be a sign, a hint, a change in intonation, something that might reveal whether this strange and remarkable story is true. But it doesn't come.

"I'll drop you off at your hotel," says Captain Sam.

He agrees to meet me once more. The next day we have lunch in a shopping center near his office. We sit at a corner table eating hamburgers. He is drinking bloody Marys.

"Under Oswald's report—and there's nothing to indicate he was wrong— there were three gunmen. I don't know their positions, other than the fact that I remember seeing the word *snapscope*. That would indicate a below-ground-level placement for one of the gunmen."

But why didn't the CIA simply get rid of them? I ask.

"Dead men tell you nothing. You're always after the guy above until you reach the top. You stop them, you give the game away. The CIA is not a law enforcement agency, it's not interested in busting people. It's intelligence."

Those words seem a contradiction to the revelations of recent days, but I say nothing. He sighs. "Look, it's like this. Even if a CIA man is standing next to the guy who actually shoots John Kennedy, he would not be in a position to do anything. It would depend on the individual whether he'd try to stop it. We lose men in the field every day. In the eyes of the CIA, a president is no better and no worse. It was a bad deal, everybody's sorry, but when you get right down to it, we didn't lose a great man, we lost another American.

"It really gets confusing. A lot of the stuff I saw, I don't know which Oswald they're referring to. But I know it didn't end with Kennedy's death. A lot of people started getting killed. Maybe Castro hit Kennedy, and this is something else. Whoever and whatever it is, it's a very effective method."

Suddenly, my head seems to spin. I stare at him—the Andy Devine face, the burly frame—but he looks out of focus. Everything seems to be going in circles.

"I don't think I have any more questions," I say.

"As you go along, you'll find a lot of people nobody knew about," says Captain Sam. "A lot are dead, a lot in insane asylums, a lot won't talk. But there are lots of people more interesting than me around. I'm just a small fish."

16

Who Was 'Captain Sam'?

After all these years, I feel no compunction about revealing his identity. His real name was Ronald Lee Augustinovich. The Garrison files contained enough information about him to convince me that he was worth tracking down. I got his address through Texas researcher Penn Jones. After our two days together in Phoenix, I never saw the man again. That he worked in some capacity for the CIA seems likely. Like he said, perhaps half his story is true. Verifying which half, I knew at the time, would be all but impossible.

Sometimes, as I wound my way through the maze, the unexpected happened. That was certainly the case the day I interviewed Frank Ellsworth, a federal agent with the Alcohol, Tobacco, and Firearms Agency, at his office in Dallas. I went to see Ellsworth because he'd been one of the first on-the-scene inside the Texas School Book Depository, and also one of the few to actually question Oswald. I was completely unprepared for his suddenly saying:

"Now why this has never come out anywhere, I've often wondered. There was an individual in this town who was an absolute dead ringer for Oswald. I happened to arrest him personally shortly before [the assassination]."

The article I wrote about this for *The Village Voice* attracted more attention, at the time, than anything else I'd come across.

17

The Village Voice, August 23, 1976

"Is the 'Second Oswald' Alive in Dallas?"

DALLAS—In mid-November 1963, shortly before the assassination of John F. Kennedy, a curious arrest occurred in Dallas. It did not seem so curious at the time—simply a young man, allied with local right-wing Minutemen and charged with a violation of the National Firearms Act. When the fellow managed to raise bond, his release received a routine okay from his arresting federal agent, Frank Ellsworth of Treasury's Alcohol, Tobacco and Firearms (ATF) division.

But a few days later, when Frank Ellsworth was called to a police interrogation room to question Lee Harvey Oswald about the rifle found in his alleged assassin's nest, the agent was certain that he'd made one of history's most tragic mistakes.

"Oswald was sitting in a chair about 10 feet from the doorway," Ellsworth would remember. "And all I could see was headlines that I'd just turned loose the man who killed the President."

He hadn't. However, the man Ellsworth had arrested and released was, in his words, "an absolute dead-ringer for Oswald—identical build, weight, coloring, facial features, hair. They were like identical twins; they could've passed for each other."

Of all the mysteries that still surround the Kennedy assassination, few have proved more intriguing than the possibility of a "second Oswald." Almost from the moment of Oswald's arrest, perfectly credible witnesses claimed to have seen him driving a car (though Oswald didn't drive). They had seen him in a gun shop, at a rifle range and cashing a check in a grocery store. The problem was, especially in the month of November 1963, wherever "Oswald" was supposed to have been seen, he was really somewhere else.

Of course, it is hardly uncommon for false reports of identification to arise during a much publicized investigation. Apparently for this reason, the Warren Commission dismissed even its most reliable witnesses as cases of mistaken identity. It remained for the commission's critics to speculate that an Oswald look-alike might have been used by someone in a conspiracy. One scholar, Professor Richard Popkin, even devoted a whole book to that question (*The Second Oswald*, 1966).

The notion of an Oswald "double" being involved in a conspiracy takes several forms. Obviously, Oswald being seen in two places at once would serve to confuse detectives forever. Besides this, Popkin and others hypothesize, a look-alike could have helped blaze a trail of misleading evidence to implicate Oswald as an assassin—even if Oswald never really fired a shot.

The two most famous "double Oswald" incidents make a conspiracy theory feasible, at least. One involved a "Leon Oswald" who came with two Latin companions to the door of a Cuban woman, according to police and FBI reports, and who apparently had voiced the opinion that the President ought to be killed. When this occurred in Dallas in late September 1963, Oswald was supposedly on his way to Mexico. The other incident was the repeated sighting by several witnesses of "Oswald" target-practicing at a Dallas rifle range shortly before the assassination—almost always at times when the Warren Commission concluded he'd really been somewhere else.

It is even possible, say the critics, that a look-alike could have fired some shots himself. As dubious as that may sound, a Dallas deputy sheriff named Roger Craig did give chase to a man who ran from the Texas School Book Depository and climbed into a light-colored Rambler station wagon a few minutes after the assassination. Later that day, Craig positively identified the man as Oswald. But, according to police sources cited in *The Warren Report*, Oswald was already far away from the building and riding a bus toward his home.

Last week, in the Dallas office where he now serves as a regional public affairs officer for ATF, Frank Ellsworth broke a twelve-year official silence to confirm a look-alike's existence. While refusing to divulge his name and passing off the incident as "sheer coincidence," Ellsworth admitted that the man is still alive, well, and living in Dallas; that he had been interrogated by federal authorities shortly after the assassination and found to have been "nowhere near downtown Dallas;" and that in several instances where witnesses believed they'd seen Oswald, notably including his constant practice in November at a Dallas rifle range, they were actually seeing his "twin."

If not for several other revelations about this mysterious personage, his existence might be dismissed as a curiosity of history. But, strangely enough, while the real Oswald was supposedly a fanatic leftist and member of the Fair Play for Cuba Committee, his "twin" was an equally fanatic right-winger and member of the Minutemen. Like Oswald, he seems to have traveled in and out of Mexico. Like Oswald, he apparently associated with Cuban exiles. If his presence in Dallas was indeed "sheer coincidence," then why didn't the Warren Commission reveal it and clear up the rumors?

"Quite a number of officials—state, federal and local—were aware of this situation, because we talked about it," says Ellsworth. "We laid it to rest, and satisfied ourselves it was merely coincidence. I have a vague recollection that this man was questioned about the assassination, but not by me. Possibly nobody paid much attention because we had Oswald in custody. We weren't looking for a fugitive.

"I'd tracked this other fellow undercover through another man for several months before I actually met him. I think this began sometime in the summer of 1963. When I finally made contact with him, I led him to believe I was a crook. He claimed to have done some arms smuggling in and out of Mexico, but not when I was dealing with him. I didn't have the impression he'd ever been into Mexico that much. And yes, there were rumors that he had some connection with the family of (Texas billionaire oilman) H. L. Hunt. I personally didn't place a great deal of credence in those rumors.

"But I do remember two instances where Oswald was supposed to have been at someone's house in North Dallas, and I was able to ascertain after the assassination that it was actually the look-alike. I wasn't keeping notes of where he was minute by minute, but these were instances where witnesses thought they saw Oswald in the company of several Minutemen. One of these times did involve a group of Minutemen at a rifle range. The look-alike knew all those people. Several of their names came up in my conversations with him, and I'd noted at the time that he was out shooting with them."

The Oswald look-alike was eventually convicted on "one of the gun violations," but Ellsworth says he cannot remember the sentence. Subsequently, the man gained his release and Ellsworth remained in occasional contact with him over the years.

Despite considerable prodding, Ellsworth refused to name him. He would say only that "He's straightened out and has a right to privacy." But there is already on record, in two recently declassified Warren Commission documents, at least a hint of who he might be. Here, the plot begins to thicken.

One document is a Warren Commission interview with Ellsworth, dated April 16, 1964. There is no mention of the Oswald "twin." The interview deals with Ellsworth's knowledge of Texas arms traffic and lists Ellsworth's three revelations "of value":

1. At the time of the assassination of the president, there was almost no information available to the government concerning the activities of Dallas Cubans and other groups in illegal armaments.
2. An organization knows as the Minutemen is the right-wing group in Dallas most likely to have been associated with any effort to assassinate the president.
3. The Minutemen are closely tied to General (Edwin) Walker and H. L. Hunt.

"Mr. Ellsworth described in some detail his undercover efforts in procuring the arrest of a local gun shop owner who is an ardent member of the Minutemen. As a result of these undercover activities Agent Ellsworth learned that Manuel O. Rodriguez, apparently a Cuban survivor of the Bay of Pigs episode, was attempting to purchase arms in Dallas for Alpha 66. Rodriguez is also a member of the DRE."

Alpha 66, one of the most notoriously violent of the anti-Castro Cuban groups, maintained its Dallas headquarters on Hollandale Street, where an early sheriff's report supposedly had Oswald paying a visit. The DRE, or Cuban Student Directorate, was in Oswald's notebook; again, he is said to have attended a meeting where General Walker spoke in the fall of 1963.

A Secret Service memorandum dated April 24, 1964, is devoted entirely to Manuel Rodriguez, whom the Secret Service at one time had considered a potential danger to the President. On Page 2, it reads: "On 1-16-64 Agent Ellsworth, alcohol and tobacco tax unit, was interviewed relative to any knowledge he might have on the subject. Agent Ellsworth had recently worked in an undercover capacity while gathering evidence against *John Thomas Masen* (my italics) . . . for violation of National Firearms Act. Agent Ellsworth states that during his association with Masen, Masen had mentioned Rodriguez as being a Cuban who was attempting to buy arms—machine guns, bazookas, and other heavy equipment—from Masen. . . ."

John Thomas Masen. Was this the Minutemen gun shop owner? And possibly the Oswald look-alike? For *this* answer, one must probe still deeper into the cryptic Warren Commission files. Sure enough, buried away in the National Archives is an FBI report dated March 27, 1964. It begins:

"Mr. John Thomas Masen, Owner, Masen's Gun Shop . . . advised he purchased about ten boxes of 6.5-millimeter Mannlicher-Carcano, Western Cartridge Company, ammunition from Johnny Brinegar in early 1963 and that he sold these 10 boxes to individuals. He stated he was not able to recall the identity of any persons to whom he sold this ammunition. . . ."

Strangely, the various government reports on Masen's activities don't overlap. The FBI was seemingly interested in finding the source of ammunition for Oswald's 6.5-millimeter Mannlicher-Carcano rifle. The Secret Service was curious about Masen's anti-Castro associates. The Warren Commission privately noted his connection with the Minutemen, but published nothing about him.

Putting all this information together, a pattern emerges. Ellsworth's Oswald look-alike was arrested shortly before the assassination; so was Masen. Ellsworth's look-alike had Minutemen connections, traveled in Mexico, and been nabbed on a firearms charge; so had Masen. If Masen was *not* the Oswald double, he must have had a pretty good idea who was. The question then becomes—were all these connections, including those with anti-Castro groups, merely "sheer coincidence?"

When subsequently questioned about the information he gave the Warren Commission and Secret Service on John Thomas Masen, Frank Ellsworth did a double take.

At first, when I asked if Masen might be the Oswald look-alike, Ellsworth issued a hesitant denial. Then at the very end of the interview, suddenly he became confidential: "Look, you've got me boxed in," he said. "You're trying to get me to tell you something I'm not at liberty to tell without grossly jeopardizing myself and my agency. But if you can find Masen, the answer to what you've been trying to worm out of me will become immediately apparent."

John Thomas Masen is not listed in the Dallas phone book. He does, however, still work here; he is a gunsmith, apparently one of the best in town, operating in the back room of a sporting goods store in a North Dallas shopping center.

According to Frank Ellsworth, the Oswald look-alike had put on about 30 pounds over the years. So, it seemed, had Masen. He was about the same height as Oswald, a stocky, brown-haired, thirty-six-year-old. And the moment we shook hands, an uneasy feeling settled over me. If you looked closely, you could still see a resemblance. There was no way to be sure, and yet. . . .

"If I saw a picture of Lee Harvey Oswald, I'd probably pick it out," he is saying, carefully smoothing some oil along the sight of a rifle. "But I can't really visualize his face. There was one man who used to come into the store—we see all the kooky ones—extremely weird, but . . . but no, I don't think he resembled Lee Harvey Oswald."

It is early evening, but Masen is working late. He talks while he works, adjusting and cleaning one rifle part, then another. When he hears the name of Frank Ellsworth, his eyes flash and his reply is acrid.

"I got set up on that situation. There was an agent from New Mexico who represented himself as a buyer for the Cuban revolution against Castro. I sold him a couple automatic arms. They entrapped me into buying some parts. They finally dropped all charges except failure to keep proper records. I paid a $200 fine, but they took my firearms license away. And this has cost me an enormous amount of money, not being able to deal in firearms. I recently applied for a presidential pardon, and was turned down."

Had he ever associated with the Minutemen? "I'd been to a couple parties. I knew some of the group. I realized they were gonna try to help take Cuba back and I was very sympathetic to the cause."

What about General Walker? "I met him back there. When things are unpleasant, you block them out. You try to forget. This has cost me $20,000 or $30,000 over the past 12 or 13 years. I don't know if I did any business with his people."

And H. L. Hunt? "Mr. Hunt was a fine man. One of my dear friends lived next door to them. But did I ever work for him? No. Did I ever receive money from him? No. Although I might have said I did at one time. You see, one of my dearest friends was in a sorority with a daughter. I met a good deal of the Hunts. I have some friends who were under the impression that the Hunts poured a lot of money in their coffers."

For a moment, Masen pauses. He gives me a long probing look, as if he knows precisely what I'm driving at. "Look, as I told them back then, *if* there was a Minutemen situation I'd been connected with, I couldn't have told 'em anyway. My life wouldn't be worth a penny. Realistically, that's what it amounted to."

"You know," he goes on, "I wouldn't be in your shoes. Going around asking people about the Cubans, the Kennedy assassination. Why should people talk to you? There's no way they can do anything but lose.

"One thing you should remember," says John Thomas Masen, "what may be a living to you"—there is another pause, another long look—"can be a life to them."

"But if you want my opinion, to think the assassination was the act of one man, well, it'd be a very hard thing to do. I've got some friends who are top marksmen who say it couldn't have happened like they said. I really don't believe this was the brainstorm of one deranged man. I think it was the sophisticated work of someone with a great deal of money, who could buy a life."

18

The Lingering "Double Oswald" Mystery

In the years since my article about the "Second Oswald" appeared, the mystery has only grown more bizarre and elusive. One researcher, John Armstrong, has even published an epic-length book, *Harvey and Lee*, postulating that there may in fact have been an intelligence operation that utilized two look-alike Oswalds since their early years. My own further investigation into the anomalies led me to wonder whether that seemingly most far-fetched of theories might indeed have basis in reality.

In 1975, a memorandum from J. Edgar Hoover was discovered by a researcher in the National Archives. It had been withheld from the Warren Commission. The memo was addressed to the State Department and dated June 3, 1960, nine months after Oswald had supposedly defected to the Soviet Union.

"Since there is a possibility that an impostor is using Oswald's birth certificate," Hoover wrote, "any current information the Department of State may have concerning Oswald will be appreciated."[39]

The Hoover memo came as an apparent reaction to a report he had received on May 12, 1960, from John Malone, Special-Agent-in-Charge of the FBI's New York office. Malone quoted from an interview with Oswald's mother, Marguerite, that "Lee Oswald had taken his birth certificate with him when he left home . . . since Oswald had his birth certificate in his possession, another individual may have assumed his identity."

After Hoover wrote to the State Department, it sent warnings to various offices asking they be on the lookout for an Oswald impostor. Then, on March 13, 1961, the deputy chief of the U.S. Passport Office wrote to the Consular Section of the State Department concerning Oswald. Supposedly he had left his passport at the American Embassy in Moscow after he arrived in September 1959. Early in 1961, he had just begun making inquiries at the Embassy about repatriating to the U.S.

The passport office's letter stated: ". . . this file contains information first, which indicates that mail from the mother of this boy is not being delivered to him and second, that it has been stated that there is an impostor using Oswald's

---

[39] Hoover letter: FBI File No. 105-82555, addressed to: Office of Security, Department of State.

identification data and that no doubt the Soviets would love to get hold of his valid passport, it is my opinion that the passport should be delivered to him only on a personal basis and after the Embassy is assured to its complete satisfaction that he is returning to the United States."

There followed another State Department communication to the embassy in Moscow on July 11, 1961: "The Embassy's careful attention to the involved case of Mr. Oswald is appreciated. It is assumed that there is no doubt that the person who has been in communication with the Embassy is the person who was issued a passport in the name of Lee Harvey Oswald."

After all this began surfacing in 1975, Warren Commission investigator W. David Slawson was asked about it by the *New York Times*. He responded: "I don't know where the impostor notion would have led us, perhaps nowhere, like a lot of other leads. But the point is, we didn't know about it. And why not? It conceivably could have been something related to the CIA. I can only speculate now, but a general CIA effort to take out everything that reflected on them may have covered this up."[40]

Before his death in 1998, I had two extensive telephone conversations with Colonel Philip J. Corso, a retired Army Intelligence officer who had served for four years on the staff of the National Security Council under President Eisenhower. He had later been an investigator for Senator Strom Thurmond and, after the Kennedy assassination, been asked by Warren Commission member and Senator Richard Russell to look into some unresolved questions about Oswald. Corso was named as the source of a rumor that Oswald had been a paid informant for the FBI. Corso recalled informing Senator Russell that the Mannlicher-Carcano assassination weapon lacked the effective range and accuracy to have done the shooting attributed to it; another accurate, high-velocity weapon had to have been fired.[41]

Corso also believed that all the sightings of Oswald "look-alikes" appeared very suspicious. That was the subject I pursued with him late in 1994 and early 1995. So had Anthony Summers for a *Frontline* special that aired in 1993, although Corso's revelations did not make the cut. "My whole operation with Senator Russell was all verbal," Corso told me. "There was no paper trail. This idea of two Oswalds, I never bothered to make that public. But I came to the conclusion that there *were* two Oswalds. Maybe even two families."[42]

Corso said he'd first discussed this *before the assassination* with William Sullivan, an Assistant Director of the FBI under Hoover and "a close friend of mine from my White House days. He told me that a phony defector named Oswald had gone

---

[40] Slawson quote: *New York Times*, February 23, 1975.
[41] Corso background: *The Third Decade*, Volume 9 (2), "Introducing: Lieutenant Colonel Philip J. Corso, Army Intelligence" by James L. Cypher.
[42] Colonel Corso: Author's telephone interviews, December 24, 1994 and January 3, 1995.

to Russia, as part of an operation being run by our Office of Naval Intelligence. And that now his birth certificate was possibly in the hands of the Soviets, or someone impersonating him in the United States. I also talked about this with a Mr. Frank Hand, who was liaison between the White House, CIA, and State Department. He told me that the CIA had put a control agent on the Oswalds to monitor their activities, after they came back to Dallas-Fort Worth."

While conducting his post-assassination investigation for Senator Russell, Corso said he'd had "many discussions" about this with Robert Johnson, Deputy Director of the U.S. Passport division. "We found out that there was a fake passport circulating also, which matched up with the birth certificate of a Lee Harvey Oswald who was in the Soviet Union. Now fake passports are often used in intelligence. I used them in Rome, putting International Red Cross passports in the hands of my informants. I'd take the identity of a man who was missing or dead. The Soviets had perfected this system much more than we had, in a very sophisticated way. The KGB were experts at faking documents like passports and birth certificates, make them look so authentic that you couldn't tell the difference. We knew the Soviets 'played back' people whose identity they'd taken, with look-alikes in countries all over the world.

"So because of certain discrepancies that our Military Intelligence was picking up, the story was that there'd been an Oswald circulating in the Texas area, carrying a fake passport and birth certificate, but he was really a Soviet look-alike. In our opinion, the look-alike was over here trying to penetrate the Alpha 66 and other operations of the anti-Castro operations. Then the real Lee Harvey Oswald himself showed up on the scene—so there were two of them. It was a big mystery to us why the Russians let him and his wife come back, because they should have known the pros back here would get suspicious. These things were just not done by them, unless there was a motive."

Corso added, "But I don't think the Soviets killed President Kennedy. They were alarmed, though, because they had a look-alike defector operating in the area, and they knew we knew it. So they were afraid it might be pinned on him. But no, I would look into the renegade CIA people, along with the anti-Castro Cubans. This thing took a lot of planning."

And what was Senator Russell's reaction to all this? I asked. "He told me, 'Phil, I believe everything you've said, but we can't publish this. They [the other Warren Commission members] will never believe it and they'll never put it in print.' But he said, 'At least I know,' and as a result he initially refused to sign *The Warren Report*, until Lyndon Johnson did some arm-twisting."

Might the intelligence agencies have used variations on Oswald's first and middle names to try to keep track of which was which? Consider that there are nearly 50 separate instances of U.S. government files—emanating from the CIA, FBI, Secret Service, Military Intelligence, Dallas Police, and Warren Commission testimony—where "Lee" and "Harvey" are transposed. In a number of these cases, the original file identifying a "Harvey Lee Oswald" was altered after the assassination to read "Lee Harvey Oswald."

One esteemed researcher into the assassination's many mysteries, Peter Dale Scott, believes that the maintenance of government files under each of those names were part of an effort to hide some kind of intelligence operation involving a single individual. Perhaps so. But what if there was in fact an intelligence operation involving an Oswald who identified himself as Lee, and another who called himself Harvey?

When Robert Oswald showed up at the Dallas Police station not long after being informed of his brother's arrest on November 22, 1963, the very first question posed to him by the FBI was this: "Is your brother's name Lee Harvey Oswald or Harvey Lee Oswald? . . . We have it here as Harvey Lee." Robert replied, "No, it's Lee Harvey Oswald."

When the first Dallas police memo was generated on Oswald that day, it also listed him as "Harvey Lee Oswald." Over at Fort Sam Houston, Texas, when a U.S. Army cable was dispatched to the U.S. Strike Command at McDill Air Force Base in Florida, it began: "Following is additional information on Oswald, Harvey Lee."

By November 25, 1963, when the Secret Service interviewed Oswald's widow, Marina, her husband's first name was known throughout the world. But the question put to Marina nonetheless was: "After you married Harvey, where did you and Harvey maintain your address or residence?"

A few days after that, the Secret Service spoke to William Stout Oswald, who "stated that although Harvey Lee Oswald is said to be his second cousin, he had never met him nor had he known Harvey was also employed by the William B. Reily Coffee Company."

This pattern had been manifesting for a long time. When Oswald was living in the Soviet Union, a March 2, 1961, memo from the U.S. Passport Office to the State Department Security Office "requested that the recipients advise if the FBI is receiving info about Harvey on a continuing basis."

A CIA document generated three days after the assassination records: "It was partly out of curiosity to learn if Oswald's wife would actually accompany him to our country, partly out of interest in Oswald's own experiences in the USSR, that we showed intelligence interest in the Harvey story."

We find the same anomaly in certain records kept by Soviet officials during Oswald's two-and-a-half years over there. He is known to have used the nickname "Alik" with friends and associates in the USSR. Oswald's hospital records for the period he lived in Minsk carry several names: "Harvey Alik Oswald," "Harvey A. Oswald," and "H. A. Oswald." The name "Lee" does not appear on any of them.

Back in Texas on Thanksgiving Day 1962, Oswald entered his name as "Harvey" in his half-brother John Pic's address book. Yet, when Oswald was earlier stationed with the Marines in Japan, a J. E. Pitts who served with him remembered: "Oswald . . . had an intense hate for anyone that called him by the nickname of 'Harve' or by his middle name of 'Harvey' and he wanted to fight anyone that did it."

A 1977 book, *The Oswald File*, by British solicitor Michael Eddowes, first raised the notion that the Soviet Union had slipped a well-trained operator into the U.S. in the summer of 1962 using Oswald's identity.[43] The discrepancies that Eddowes raised could not be easily dismissed. They began with that most basic of human measurements, Oswald's height.

The Warren Report listed Oswald as standing five-feet-nine inches tall, the height recorded by the Dallas police after his arrest and during the autopsy on his body after he was slain by Jack Ruby two days later. The commission's twenty-six volumes of testimony and exhibits contained twelve different documents denoting the same height. These all pertain to Oswald in the United States after his return from the Soviet Union. The five-foot-nine height appears on all of his employment applications, including the one at the Texas School Book Depository, as well as his measurement by the New Orleans police after being arrested following a street confrontation with anti-Castro Cubans on August 9, 1963.

Back on December 28, 1956, Oswald had also been recorded as five-foot-nine, upon completion of his initial Marine training. But *The Warren Report* fails to mention that, when Oswald was released from the service in September 1959, a doctor and two other Marine officials recorded his height as five-feet-eleven-inches on three separate occasions over an eleven-day period. That same height is shown on the passport Oswald used to travel to the Soviet Union, as well as an application that he made for admission to Switzerland's Albert Schweitzer College on March 4, 1959. Eight documents in the Warren volumes list a height two inches taller than the man who was brought into custody on November 22, 1963. All of the five-foot-eleven heights appear on documents relating to his Marine discharge and subsequent overseas travel.[44]

When Oswald's wallet was examined by the police on the afternoon of the assassination, they found both a 1959 Marine Selective Service System Registration card and a Department of Defense Identification Card listing his height as five-feet-eleven inches. In the same wallet was a counterfeit Selective Service System Registration card under the fictitious name of "Alek James Hidell." Hidell's height was listed as five-feet-nine inches.

Late on November 24, 1963, the Dallas police released Oswald's body and the Secret Service took it to the Miller's Funeral Home morgue in Fort Worth some

---

[43] Eddowes: *Dallas Morning News*, November 23, 1975, "New Book Alleges Body of Assassin Not Oswald" by Earl Golz.

[44] Height discrepancies: *Khrushchev Killed Kennedy* by Michael H. B. Eddowes (Dallas, TX, self-published: 1975), pp. 18, 96–97.

35 miles away. The next morning, before a 4 PM scheduled burial, the body was unattended when "an FBI team with a camera and crime lab kit arrived," according to an article in the *Fort Worth Press*. They were said to have spent considerable time checking over the body and taking another set of fingerprints.

Then, on December 3, an FBI agent went to look up Oswald's early medical history at the Harris Hospital in Fort Worth. There it was recorded that, at age six in February 1946, Lee Harvey Oswald was operated on after being diagnosed with acute mastoiditis of the left ear. The mastoidectomy and operative scar were both noted on Oswald's Marine Corps health records. But neither the scar, nor any bone removal, were listed in the post-mortem report on November 24, 1963.[45]

The funeral director who buried Oswald, Paul Groody, years later told journalist Jim Marrs a strange story. About three weeks after the burial, a couple of Secret Service agents came to Groody asking questions about some marks on Oswald's body. "They told me, 'We don't know who we have in that grave,'" Groody remembered.

On February 18, 1964, Richard Helms, then in charge of the CIA's clandestine operations, sent a memo to the FBI. He was interested in a scar that Oswald was supposed to have had on his left wrist, after he allegedly attempted suicide in Moscow in 1959. Helms requested any FBI information, "including the undertakers, copies of any reports, such as autopsy or other, which may contain information pertinent to this point. . . . The best evidence of a scar or scars on the left wrist would of course be direct examination by a competent authority and we recommend that this be done and that a photograph of the inner and outer surfaces of the left wrist be made if there has been no other evidence acceptable to the [Warren] Commission that he did in fact attempt suicide by cutting his wrist."

A week later, two Dallas FBI agents contacted C. J. Price, the Administrator at the Parkland Memorial Hospital where Oswald's autopsy took place. Their report said: "He advised he was unable to recall seeing any report or observation on the part of any person who attended LEE HARVEY OSWALD after his fatal shooting by JACK RUBY on November 24, 1963, that commented on a scar on OSWALD's inner left wrist. He said he observed LEE HARVEY OSWALD while he was in the Trauma Room and during the time he was sent to surgery at Parkland Memorial Hospital on the day of the shooting and he failed to observe any scar on Oswald's wrist."

Price suggested that the agents follow up with Dr. Earl Rose, one of the two Medical Examiners who had performed the actual autopsy. One of those agents was Manning Clements, the same FBI man who had gone to the police station to obtain a physical description after Oswald's arrest. Oswald had told Clements

---

[45] Mastoidectomy: Eddowes, pp. 19, 94–95.

that he stood five foot nine and had no permanent scars. Clements had also recorded the contents of Oswald's wallet, and is likely to have noticed the discrepancy with the two ID cards listing him as five foot eleven. Accompanying Clements to see Dr. Rose was Tom Carter, the senior of two agents who had interrogated Oswald after he returned to Dallas-Fort Worth from the Soviet Union. The physical description "obtained from observation and interrogation" listed in Carter's report at that time was five foot eleven—one of only two instances where the taller height shows up on an Oswald record after he came back. (The other was on his June 25, 1963, passport renewal form, matching the height on his 1959 passport.)

During the FBI's interview with Dr. Rose, the agents are noted as having asked about a one-and-three-quarter inch transverse scar on Oswald's inner left wrist. They queried the doctor about whether this scar could actually have resulted from a suicide attempt, and Dr. Rose replied it "might possibly be associated" with such. The agents also asked about two scars on Oswald's left upper arm identified in the post-mortem report. They should have been aware that an earlier Marine record showed not two, but three, scars. The doctor replied that color slides he had taken were over-exposed, and so the existence of any arm scars could not be further identified.[46]

Dr. Rose was not asked to confirm whether there was evidence on Oswald's corpse of the childhood mastoidectomy. When the *Dallas Morning News* asked the doctor about this in 1975, he responded: "I won't say that we couldn't have overlooked a mastoidectomy. That is a possibility and I certainly won't deny it ... [But] we went into very careful details to note as many of the abrasions or scars or any type of skin blemish to help in identification in case this question arose."[47]

The Warren Commission document that was declassified in 1975, and led to the Dallas newspaper's interview with Dr. Rose, is a memorandum of March 13, 1964, by commission investigator W. David Slawson. Referring to a letter from FBI Director Hoover—written the day after the two FBI men visited Dr. Rose—the Slawson memo states: "The CIA is interested in the scar on Oswald's left wrist ... The FBI is reluctant to exhume Oswald's body as requested by the CIA."

Around Easter of 1964, Marina Oswald received a visitor asking her to sign some papers. These were to authorize the installation of an electronic alarm system at the Oswald gravesite. As she told the *Dallas Morning News* in 1980, "I signed lots of papers and they were never translated or explained to me. I just did what I was told. They said it was very expensive to upkeep the grave, very

---

[46] Scars: Eddowes, pp. 96–97.
[47] Rose quote: *Dallas Morning News*, November 24, 1975, "Scar, Height Raise Oswald Queries" by Earl Golz.

inconvenient to have a guard for 24 hours and an electronic device would be much cheaper and more convenient for them."[48]

After Marina signed whatever the papers specified, the CIA and FBI's interest in ascertaining whether the buried body was really Oswald suddenly ceased. On Good Friday of 1964, someone tampered with the gravesite. Oswald's tombstone disappeared, only to turn up a year later in a garage in Oklahoma.

Eventually, at the impetus of author Eddowes and Oswald's widow, Dallas authorities agreed to exhume Oswald's body. His brother Robert fought to prevent it, and Marina said she suspected that the grave had already been opened with Robert's complicity. Finally, in October 1981, Robert gave up his opposition. A team of four forensic pathologists examined the remains. "Beyond any doubt, and I mean any doubt," said team leader Dr. Linda Norton, "the individual buried under the name Lee Harvey Oswald in Rose Hill Cemetery is in fact Lee Harvey Oswald."[49]

This would seem to have settled the matter. But it didn't. The two funeral home directors who had prepared Oswald's body for burial in 1963—Paul Groody and Alan Baumgartner—were also present at the exhumation and deeply troubled about what they saw. Oswald's body showed absence of any signs of a craniotomy, a customary autopsy procedure where the skin is drawn off the skull and a V-shaped cut is made permitting forensic pathologists to see the brain. Since the autopsy report on Oswald recorded the weight of his brain, there is no doubt that a craniotomy was performed in 1963. In fact, both Groody and Baumgartner had observed it, because they'd put the skull back together and sewed up the scalp in getting the body ready for burial.

Since the two morticians now saw no indication of a craniotomy, they concluded that the body exhumed in 1981 was *not* the same one they had buried in 1963. Groody told reporters that Oswald had been embalmed very carefully, with the body placed in an airtight coffin inside an airtight cement vault. But when workers opened the grave in 1981, the cement vault was in pieces and the coffin's seal was broken. The water and air that had seeped into the coffin resulted in the body being deteriorated to a skeleton.

In February 1984, Marina Oswald filed suit seeking copies of a videotape that recorded the exhumation and subsequent examination. But she was never able to obtain it.

---

[48] Marina Oswald quote: *Dallas Morning News*, November 23, 1980, "Marina Suspects Grave Empty" by Dan Carmichael.
[49] Body exhumation: *Dallas Morning News*, October 5, 1981, "Doctors Identify Body as Oswald" by Earl Golz.

19

New Times Magazine, June 24, 1977

"Three Witnesses"

*F*or more than two years, New Times *has explored the mysteries surrounding the assassination of John F. Kennedy. At first our articles pointed out the holes in the Warren Commission's theory that Lee Harvey Oswald acted alone in Dallas on November 22, 1963. After the House of Representatives voted—in the wake of Watergate and the exposure of FBI and CIA abuses—to investigate the assassination anew, we reported extensively on the Committee's progress. Now, of course, that investigation has been crippled by the forced resignation of Chief Counsel Richard Sprague* (New Times, *May 13).*

What we present here is an intriguing series of tales surrounding the assassination. It is the story of three men: a baron, a gunrunner, and a Cuban refugee. One was a close acquaintance of Lee Oswald; the others say they met him before the assassination. One killed himself the very day a House investigator planned to interview him; another will not let his name be used, because he fears for his life. All three talked at length to Dick Russell, the author of a forthcoming book on the Kennedy assassination. Taken alone, their stories are scenes from Raymond Chandler, snapshots of a once-incredible netherworld that has become increasingly familiar. As a whole, they may form the framework to the answer to what really happened in Dallas.

The Baron

Like Fitzgerald's Gatsby, Baron George Sergei de Mohrenschildt was borne back ceaselessly into the past. In June 1976, a sultry day in Dallas, he had stood gazing out the picture window of his second-story apartment, talking casually about a young man who used to curl up on the couch with the Baron's Great Danes.

"No matter what they say, Lee Harvey Oswald was a delightful guy," de Mohrenschildt was saying. "They make a moron out of him, but he was smart as hell. Ahead of his time really, a kind of hippie of those days. In fact, he was the most honest man I knew. And I will tell you this—I am sure he did *not* shoot the president."

Nine months later, on March 29, one hour after an investigator for the House Assassinations Committee left a calling-card with his daughter, the Baron apparently put a shotgun to his head in Palm Beach, Florida. In his absence came forward a Dutch journalist and longtime acquaintance, Willem Oltmans, with the sensational allegation that de Mohrenschildt had admitted serving as a middleman between Oswald and H. L. Hunt in an assassination plot involving other Texas oilmen, anti-Castro Cubans, and elements of the FBI and CIA.

But how credible was de Mohrenschildt? As an old friend in Dallas' Russian community, George Bouhe, once put it: "He's better equipped than anybody to talk. But we have an old Russian proverb that will always apply to George de Mohrenschildt: 'The soul of the other person is in the darkness.'"

Intrigue and oil were the two constants in the Baron's life. He was an emigrant son of the Czarist nobility who spoke five languages fluently and who, during the Second World War, was rumored to have spied for the French, Germans, Soviets and Latin Americans (the CIA's predecessor, the OSS, turned down his application). After the war, he went on to perform geological surveys for major U.S. oil companies all over South America, Europe and parts of Africa. He became acquainted with certain of Texas' more influential citizens—oilman John Mecom, construction magnates George and Herman Brown. In Mexico, he gained audience in 1960 with Soviet First Deputy Premier Anastas Mikoyan. In 1961 he was present in Guatemala City—by his account, on a "walking tour"—when the Bay of Pigs troops set out for Cuba.

Finally, when Lee and Marina Oswald returned to Texas from the Soviet Union in June 1962, the Baron soon became their closest friend. Why? Why would a member of the exclusive Dallas Petroleum Club take under his wing a Trotsky-talking sheet-metal worker some 30 years his junior?

The Warren Commission took 118 pages of his testimony to satisfy itself of de Mohrenschildt's benign intent, but among critics the question persisted: Was the Baron really "baby-sitting" Oswald for the CIA? While de Mohrenschildt told the commission he'd never served as any government's agent "in any respect whatsoever," a CIA file for the commission, declassified in 1976, admits having used him as a source. In the course of several meetings with a man from its Dallas office upon de Mohrenschildt's return from Yugoslavia late in 1957, "the CIA representative obtained foreign intelligence which was promptly disseminated to other federal agencies in ten separate reports." The Dallas official, according to the file, maintained "informal occasional contact" with the Baron until the fall of 1961.

The Warren Commission volumes, however, contain only passing reference in de Mohrenschildt's testimony to a government man named "G. Walter Moore." His true name was J. Walton Moore, and he had served the CIA in Dallas since its inception in 1947.

In two brief, cryptic interviews with me in the 18 months before his death, de Mohrenschildt claimed he would not have struck up his relationship with Oswald "if Jim Moore hadn't told me Oswald was safe." The Baron wouldn't elaborate on that statement, except to hint that it constituted some kind of clearance.

J. Walton Moore is now a tall, white-haired man in his middle sixties, who continues to operate out of Dallas' small CIA office. Questioned at his home one summer evening in 1976 about de Mohrenschildt's remarks, he conceded knowing the Baron as a "pleasant sort of fellow" who provided "some decent information" after a trip to Yugoslavia. "To the best of my recollection, I hadn't seen de Mohrenschildt for a couple of years before the assassination," Moore added. "I don't know where George got the idea that I cleared Oswald for him. I never met Oswald. I never heard his name before the assassination."

For sure, the CIA did maintain an interest in de Mohrenschildt at least through April 1963. That month, Oswald left Texas for New Orleans and de Mohrenschildt prepared to depart for a lucrative geological survey contract in Haiti. On April 29, according to a CIA Office of Security file, also declassified in 1976, "[Deleted] Case Officer had requested an expedite check of George DE MOHRENSCHILDT for reasons unknown to Security."

There is one alleged ex-CIA contract employee, now working for an oil company in Los Angeles, prepared to testify that de Mohrenschildt was the overseer of an aborted CIA plot to overthrow Haitian President Francois ("Papa Doc") Duvalier in June 1963. The existence of such a plot was examined, but apparently couldn't be substantiated, by the Church Committee. Herb Atkin is sure the plot did exist.

"I knew de Mohrenschildt as Philip Harbin," Atkin said when contacted by telephone a few days after the Baron's suicide. "A lot of people in Washington have claimed that Harbin did not exist. But he's the one that ran me from the late fifties onward. I'm certain that de Mohrenschildt was my case officer's real name."

If so, the Harbin alias may have a readily identifiable origin. De Mohrenschildt's fourth wife, Jeanna, was born in Harbin, China.

One summer day in 1976, still in her bathrobe, she sat at a dining room table cluttered with plants and dishes and watched her husband begin to pace the floor. "Of course, the truth of the assassination has not come out," she said. "It will *never* come out. But we know it was a vast conspiracy."

The Baron turned to face her. "Oswald," he said, "was a harmless lunatic."

At our first interview, I had asked de Mohrenschildt what he knew about the recurring reports of Oswald in the presence of Cubans. He had nodded agreement. "Oswald probably did not know himself who they were," he replied. "I myself was in a little bit of danger from those Cubans, but I don't know who they are. Criminal lunatics." When I broached the subject now in the presence of his wife, de Mohrenschildt said something to her in Russian. She then answered for him: "That's a different story. But one must examine the anti-Castro motive of the time. After the Bay of Pigs."

A few months later, de Mohrenschildt was committed by his wife to the psychiatric unit of Parkland Memorial Hospital. There were rumors of a book naming CIA names in connection with Oswald, squirreled away with his wife's attorney. According to journalist Oltmans, upon leaving the hospital de Mohrenschildt told him: "They're going to kill me or put me away forever. You've got to get me out of the country." In March, the Baron took a leave-of-absence from his French professorship at Dallas' virtually all-black Bishop College. He flew with Oltmans to Belgium, wandered away during lunch, and wound up in Florida at his daughter's home. There, a tape machine being used to transcribe a television program is said to have recorded his suicide.

The Gunrunner

Robert Ray McKeown lives with his only daughter in a little wooden house in south Miami. There is a pane of glass missing from the front door so that, from the rocking chair where he sits inscrutably behind his sunglasses, he always knows who's knocking. At 65, the same age George de Mohrenschildt was, Robert McKeown hasn't worked in five years because of lung trouble. Now, he says, he's going to write a book about some people he once knew. Two of them—de Mohrenschildt and ex-Cuban President Carlos Prío Socarrás—apparently committed suicides within a week of each other. Two more died some time ago. Their names were Jack Ruby and Lee Harvey Oswald.

In the fall of 1975, McKeown surfaced briefly on a CBS special about the Kennedy case, telling Dan Rather about Oswald and a Latin man coming to see him concerning the purchase of four high-powered automatic rifles in the fall of 1963. CBS didn't ask about McKeown's earlier association with Jack Ruby, as documented by the Warren Commission. Indeed, according to McKeown, there was plenty he didn't say to CBS.

"One thing is," he says, "I knew that Cuban with Oswald from before. Knew him from Cuba. 'Cept he didn't know I knew. His name was Hernandez."

The intricate chain tying McKeown to the dramatis personae of the Kennedy assassination begins in Cuba in the mid-1950s. A mechanical engineer, McKeown had designed a new coffee-cleaning machine and opened offices in Havana under Fulgencio Batista. But when the dictator demanded his own five-thousand-dollar-a-month cut and McKeown refused, Batista confiscated the business. So McKeown came to Miami—and to the patronage of Dr. Carlos Prío Socarrás.

The "Cuban Democracy" tenure of Carlos Prío (1948–1952) has often been described as the most corrupt in the island's history, a time when political gangs (and some American counterparts) ran rampant. In the end, Batista ousted him. But, as McKeown puts it, "Prío got out of Cuba with a helluva lotta money, and he didn't give a damn how he spent it either. I carried $100,000 in cash in my goddamn inside coat pocket a lotta times."

The two of them became comrades in arms, shipping them from Houston to Fidel Castro's revolutionary band in Mexico City. After the revolution, according to McKeown, Prío had a promise from Castro to resume the presidency. Besides McKeown, Prío enlisted a young mercenary named Frank Sturgis, other Cuban exiles and occasional aid from Teamster-Mafia interests. Then, in 1958, the FBI cracked down.

For his part in supplying illegal weapons, McKeown got six months in jail and a $500 fine. Then, having done his time, he says he says he began receiving a stream of unusual visitors: Someone from Mexican intelligence, a CIA man who wanted him to check out a certain Mexican, two Miami "intelligence officers" who wanted him to work closer with the Cubans on "something to do with cocaine." On January 3, 1959, as Castro marched into Havana, a Houston newspaper headlined: GUNRUNNER HAILS CASTRO VICTORY. A week later, a deputy sheriff dropped by. A man in Dallas was desperate to reach McKeown, "in a case of life and death."

The man was Jack Ruby. "He told me his people were willing to give me $15,000 to help get five people outta Cuba. He mentioned some Jewish-sounding names, and a fella in Las Vegas. And his people, he said, were the Mafia. That's what he called it, the Mafia, but he never did mention no names. Later he says he's gonna give me $25,000 for a letter of introduction to Castro, but he never did come up with the money."

Four-and-a-half years passed before Lee Oswald made a similar visit to McKeown's door. "I was married to a schoolteacher," McKeown remembers. "I'd divorced my wife right after all my trouble. Lived right on the water in a little town called Bay Cliff, right between Houston and Dallas. One Saturday morning—it was either August or the first of September, because my wife was gettin' ready to go back to school—about 11 o'clock, somebody knocked on the door. I'd heard this car stop out there, station wagon, and I seen these two guys get out. Real light color car, kinda pinkish. This guy driving it, the one I knew before, his name was Hernandez. This other guy said, 'My name's Oswald. Just call me Lee.' Then he says, 'I can see I got the right man.' I said, 'Whataya mean?' He says, 'Well, your name is McKeown, isn't it?' So I invited him in with this Spanish man, who was well-dressed, with a tie and everything, and Oswald he was in shirtsleeves. And Oswald commenced telling me, after he sat down, he said, 'Might as well get to the point. I want to know if you'd be interested in furnishing some arms. My contacts have a big opportunity to take over Salvador.'"

Salvador?

"Down in Central America. San Salvador. And I told him, I said, 'Now listen man, lemmee tell you something. I'm on five years probation and I don't want no part of no kinda arms.' So Oswald kept talkin', kept talkin', says, 'Well, I know I got the right man and I know you can get me anything I want, can't you?'"

McKeown says he was adamant in his refusal, and the two departed. About a half-hour later, they returned. This time, Oswald offered $10,000 for four .300 Savage semiautomatic rifles with telescopic sights.

"Oswald said, 'You're the man that run all the guns to Castro and got caught with the cache here in Houston, aren't you?' 'Yeah,' I says, 'but that's all in the past.' I told him I didn't want no part of this kinda business."

Still, says McKeown, Oswald persisted by telephone. "My wife was home alone and she tells me, 'Who in the hell was it calling you wantin' to know if you changed your mind yet?' I says, 'I don't know who it is.' I was tryin' to keep her from findin' out about my past. Then the FBI come to see me, same day as the assassination. Hell, I was scared. I didn't tell 'em nothin' about Oswald. But I knew that was the little sonovabitch ..."

Before he agreed to go on CBS, Robert McKeown consulted with his old friend, Carlos Prío. After Castro's takeover, Prío had gone back to Cuba. But when Castro did not welcome him back into the echelons of power, Prío returned to exile in 1961 and became a spokesman for anti-Castro forces in Miami. Last April 5, Prío was found in his Miami Beach garage with a .38-caliber bullet in his chest. McKeown, contacted by telephone, had no comment.

He did, however, have something to say about George de Mohrenschildt. "He came to me one time. Long time ago." Why? "Well, that's something else. Just to ask me a few questions, that's all." Concerning Cuba? "No, Oswald." After or before the assassination? "Oh, before. No, after. No, before—goddamn, after. It's been so long." And what did he want to know? "Well, none of your business. I don't want to get all messed up in this."

Author's note: The last section of this article, on Cuban refugee "Carlos," is not included. His story appears later in this volume, where he is identified as Antonio Veciana.

20

"Loran Hall and the Politics of Assassination"

Loran Hall was scared. He sat in his Long Beach, California, real estate office on a Saturday afternoon late in May—10 days before he would invoke the Fifth Amendment at a hearing of the House assassinations committee. Every time the bell rang, he took a revolver from beneath a pile of papers and tucked it under his belt.

The day before, Hall had received a phone call. There had been several calls since May 19, when two congressional investigators served him with a subpoena to testify about the assassination of President Kennedy. Someone had left a dead cat in his front yard and a dead pigeon, with a Kennedy half-dollar in its bill, outside his office. Someone had threatened one of his kids at school.

Most of that Hall had attributed to "nuts and weirdoes." But not yesterday's call. This one was explicit: "Santo is taking a yacht trip in the Bahamas on the sixth. He would like to return on the eighth."

Hall, who was scheduled to testify on June 7, said he had replied: "As far as I'm concerned, he can." The caller hung up. Hall believed the message concerned Santo Trafficante, Jr., alleged Mafia don of southern Florida and reputedly one of the most powerful mobsters in the country.

According to congressional sources, the House committee wanted to question Hall about his association with Trafficante—an association that apparently began in 1959, when Hall and Trafficante spent five months together in a Havana jail, and continued during the early '60s, when Hall was soliciting anti-Castro funds from wealthy Americans.

The committee was also interested in a taped interview given to investigators by Dutch journalist Willem Oltmans. In this interview Hall reportedly claimed that he had attended a meeting in Dallas during the summer of 1963; there, he said, he had been offered $50,000 to kill Kennedy.

And House investigators wanted to ask Hall about his possible relationship with Lee Harvey Oswald. FBI reports had raised the possibility that Hall may have been seen with Oswald in Dallas two months before Kennedy's death—a time the Warren Commission had placed Oswald elsewhere.

Hall refused to answer all questions when he appeared before the committee on June 7; although he was scheduled to testify again, on September 14, his subpoena was continued, pending a new date. It has been rumored that the committee is trying to gather more evidence against Hall. The committee's chief investigator reportedly suggested that Hall might be granted immunity if he were to testify. But Hall has said that he's not inclined to trust the committee.

Early this summer, he agreed to an interview with me—provided no tape recording was made. (A conversation between us in October 1976 was taped by mutual agreement.)

During our interviews, Hall spoke of Trafficante and of a plot, apparently funded by organized crime, to assassinate Fidel Castro in 1963. Hall said he participated in the plot, along with Trafficante and two other reputed organized-crime figures, Sam Giancana and John Roselli.

Hall repeated his account of the $50,000 offer—made, he said, at a meeting in a Dallas oilman's office a few months before Kennedy was killed.

He also told me that shortly before the assassination he had heard Lee Harvey Oswald's name mentioned by a Cuban exile, but he denied that he and Oswald ever met. Hall spoke of efforts to implicate him in the president's death, in which he claims to have played no role. He said he believes some of these efforts may involve federal authorities.

Hall, 47, was raised in Wichita, Kansas. He quit high school to join the army, served in Germany as a sergeant, and went to Havana in 1959. He was working in Santo Trafficante's Hotel Capri casino when Castro seized power and began evicting the American gangsters who had thrived under Batista. In April 1959, Hall was sent to a Quonset-hut prison in which Trafficante was being held.

"There were six huts altogether, and the rest were packed with wall-to-wall people," Hall says. "In ours, there was Santo, his son-in-law, and one of his dealers. I was the fourth. When you walked in, you saw like a living room in the front. There were four barrels, all with ice in them—water, fruit, wines and champagne, Coke and Pepsi. Santo had his meals catered. The food came out every night in a Cadillac."

Hall's story is corroborated by a CIA/Warren Commission report ["Memo to the Director, 27 Nov. '63"] declassified in 1976, which tells of John Wilson, a British journalist who had learned in Cuba of "a gangster-gambler named Santo who could not return to the USA because there were several indictments outstanding against him. Santo opted therefore to remain in prison for a period of time, paying Castro for his rather luxurious and definitely non-prisonlike accommodations. . . . While Santo was in prison, [he] was visited by an American gangster-type named Ruby."

According to *The Warren Report*, Jack Ruby visited Cuba in September 1959—the month Hall was released from prison. Hall says he never met Ruby.

He does not deny, however, that he met "American gangster types" while in prison. One of them, according to Hall, was Johnny Roselli, who has been described as a recruiter for CIA-Mafia plots to assassinate Castro. Hall says he met Roselli again in the spring of 1963.

At that time, Hall was the leader of a group of anti-Castro Cubans who were working with other exiles to plan a second Bay of Pigs. He recalls that he got in touch with the Trafficante organization early in 1963. Then, about April, he says he was invited to a meeting in a Miami Beach hotel, where John Martino, reputedly a fringe Mob figure, introduced him and Cuban exile leader Eddie Bayo to Roselli and Giancana.

Hall describes the meeting: "Out of the other room came Santo Trafficante. Giancana looked at me and said, 'Is this the one?' Santo said, 'Yes,' and walked out. The only reason he was there was to verify me. We discussed money and whether Martino [an electronics expert] could make the necessary equipment."

Meetings continued, Hall says, until late May; as a cover, a story was circulated that two Soviet colonels were prepared to defect and testify that Russian missiles were still on Cuban soil. This story apparently convinced William D. Pawley—a retired U.S. Ambassador to Cuba and former assistant secretary of both State and Defense—that he should lend his yacht to spirit the colonels into the United States. The cover may have also convinced *Life Magazine*, which reportedly prepared to send a writer and photographer along on the rescue mission.

This basic story—without mention of Hall or an assassination plot—appeared in a 1975 copyrighted article in *Soldier of Fortune Magazine*. The article called the mission Operation Red Cross and reported that John Martino, the electronics expert, had helped to enlist Pawley's yacht and acquire $15,000 in front money from *Life Magazine*.

Richard Billings was the *Life* reporter assigned to cover Operation Red Cross. Billings is reluctant to discuss his involvement, except to say that he then believed the plan centered on the Soviet colonels' defection.

"I'm trying to find out some more things about the mission, things I didn't know before," Billings told me. "I'm still very curious about what else may have surrounded it. But at the time of the operation, I did not know of any involvement by Loran Hall."

Billings says *Life* never gave the mission financial backing. Hall agrees. "Time-Life didn't put up a dime," he says. "The money came from Sam Giancana. I saw Giancana give $30,000 to John Martino to buy supplies."

Hall says he left Miami for New York in May 1963 because he believed he was under FBI surveillance. Before he could return, the mission—including his own group of anti-Castro raiders—took off for Cuba.

On the night of June 9, Eddie Bayo and nine others apparently left Pawley's yacht by speedboat and headed for the southeast coast of Cuba; they were not seen again. According to *Soldier of Fortune*, Pawley arranged for a CIA search party, but Bayo and his men weren't found.

Hall, who returned to Miami a few weeks after missing the boat, says he was first informed that Bayo's team was safe in the mountains of Cuba. Then, in September, he was told Bayo had died.

The team's fate may remain a mystery. Early this year Trafficante took the Fifth Amendment when he was subpoenaed by the House assassinations committee. John Martino, according to *Soldier of Fortune*, was "afraid of something" and never discussed the mission; he died of a heart attack in 1975. Giancana also died in 1975, after being shot. William Pawley committed suicide last January. And Johnny Roselli's body was found in an oil drum in Biscayne Bay last year.

Shortly after Roselli's death, columnist Jack Anderson reported that Roselli had told him he was convinced the last Mafia hit team sent to Cuba had been captured and persuaded to work with Castro. Roselli purportedly told Anderson that members of this team, who might have been Cubans from the old Trafficante organization, later returned to the U.S. to assassinate JFK and set up Oswald.

Could Roselli have been referring to the missing crew of Operation Red Cross? Hall wouldn't speculate but told me: "You gotta know that Santo Trafficante had Cuba locked up prior to Castro—the narcotics, the gambling, everything. When he got kicked out, he still had his connections. It might've been a thing where Santo says to himself. 'I can still insure my shipments of dope from Cuba to here. All I gotta do is put the word to Fidel that these guys are comin' over to put a hit on him.'"

This theory was first published in a 1976 *Washington Post* article by George Crile. In it, Crile quoted a Federal Bureau of Narcotics report that said Trafficante was "allegedly Castro's outlet for illegal contraband in this country." The article also quoted a Miami Cuban, José Aleman, who recalled Trafficante's telling him late in 1962: "Mark my words, this man Kennedy is in trouble, and he will get what is coming to him. . . . He is going to be hit."

Hall says he had no contact with Trafficante after the meeting in April 1963. Others aren't sure. Gerry Patrick Hemming, who had worked with Hall on anti-Castro activities, says Hall left Miami for Dallas shortly before November 22, 1963, "with plans to see Trafficante in St. Petersburg on the way."

Hall claims that he didn't see Trafficante and that he was not in Dallas on the day of the assassination. "I was in Monterey Park, California, shaving, when the news came on TV," he says. "I'd just taken my wife to her job and I was getting ready to go out and apply for work."

A few months before the assassination, Hall says he attended the portentous meeting in Dallas at which he was offered $50,000. The meeting began as a fund-raiser for his anti-Castro cause, Hall says, but then "a man who owned a trucking company in Dallas jumped up and offered me $50,000 to blow Kennedy away." Hall says that oilman Lester Logue, in whose office the meeting allegedly occurred, immediately disassociated himself from the offer: "Logue said he'd have nothing to do with it and broke the meeting up."

When I telephoned Logue, he denied that any such meeting took place. "Sure, I knew Loran," Logue said. "I helped him when he and a group of Cubans were ostensibly making raids into Cuba. It had nothing to do with Kennedy. There's no point in my answering Hall's charge because of course, it's a fabrication."

Hall says, "I've volunteered to take a voice analysis and a lie-detector test concerning the meeting we had in Dallas. And I would welcome Lester Logue and his attorney to the session. If he'd like to, he can take the test with me."

The day Kennedy was shot, a Cuban refugee named Sylvia Odio fainted when Lee Harvey Oswald's face appeared on her TV screen. Odio later told the Warren Commission that Oswald and two Latins, who called themselves Angel and Leopoldo, had solicited funds at her Dallas apartment on the night of September 26, 1963. When Leopoldo telephoned her the next day, she told the commission, he said Oswald was an "expert shots-man" who felt Kennedy "should have been assassinated after the Bay of Pigs" and who was soon to be introduced "to the underground in Cuba."

After hearing Odio's testimony, the Warren Commission asked the FBI to investigate. On September 16, 1964, FBI agents visited Loran Hall in California. The FBI's report said Hall had admitted visiting Odio with a Mexican-American named Lawrence Howard and a man named William Seymour, who looked slightly like Oswald.

The Warren Commission concluded that Odio had been mistaken when she identified Oswald as one of her visitors. Then, just after the report went to press, Odio examined photographs of Hall, Howard, and Seymour—and said she was certain they were not the men who had visited her. She again told FBI investigators that she could identify Oswald as one of those who came to her apartment on September 16.

Odio's testimony is considered significant because the Warren Commission had concluded that Oswald was on a bus trip between New Orleans and Mexico City on the night Odio says she was visited by him. Hall, like Odio, disagrees with the commission.

Hall says, "When I read in *The Warren Report* what I supposedly told the FBI, not one statement resembled what I really said. I *never* told the FBI I'd seen Mrs. Odio. I told the agent Mrs. Odio's name and picture didn't strike a note with me. He said, 'Well, could there be a possibility you've ever met her?' I said, sure, I'd met hundreds of people in Dallas, Texas."

The reasons for the FBI's first visit to Hall remain unclear. Hall says he believes it was part of a conscious effort to use him as the scapegoat in an assassination cover up.

Hall says he also believes that the Kennedy assassination and the plan to kill Castro are related. "I think [the Castro mission] has an absolutely direct bearing on the assassination." he told me. "I'd go so far as to say I probably sat as close as I'm sitting to you now to some people who had a part in it. But I really can't be sure who they are."

Hall told me that he had been willing to talk to the House committee until investigators Clifford Fenton and Ken Klein duped him at a meeting in Los Angeles. Hall said he had set up ground rules by which he would give an informal deposition in the presence of radio newsman Art Kevin, whom he trusted.

Kevin, who acted as an intermediary between Hall and the committee, says, "Hall wanted me there as a back-up, to make sure his words wouldn't be twisted. The committee agreed, then turned around, ordered me to leave, and subpoenaed him. They made a willing witness into a hostile witness."

Fenton, the committee's chief JFK investigator, says no such agreement was made. "Hall's name has come up enough times with other witnesses that we feel he might have evidence that's really material to this case. But there's no way we could have a reporter present while we interviewed."

To which Hall replies: "At first I really thought Congress was gonna try to find the truth. But they apparently don't want me to clear myself. For 14 years, it seems every agency in the world has kept me from getting my story out. Why should it be any different now?"

21

Discovering Antonio Veciana

My interest in talking to Antonio Veciana was based on an article in the *Saturday Evening Post*, "Dallas: The Cuban Connection," that appeared in March 1976. It described him as one of the founders of the militant Cuban exile group, Alpha 66, who had been involved in a plot to assassinate Fidel Castro in 1961. After Castro's secret police found out about it, Veciana's partner, Reinaldo González, had been tracked to a farm outside Havana owned by a wealthy Cuban businessman. For their part in the plot, Amador Odio-Padron and Sara del Toro were arrested and sentenced to prison. They were the parents of Sylvia Odio, whom "Leon" Oswald and two Cuban exiles would pay a visit to in Dallas in late September 1963. The article concluded that Veciana might "shed some light on the Odio incident."

I was staying in Miami at the home of Gaeton Fonzi, then an investigator for Senator Schweiker's subcommittee, when I mentioned my interest in Veciana. "Well, I'd say the possibility that he was at Odio's door is a false association," Fonzi replied. "He *is* here in Miami, but he's just out of prison on a narcotics charge. I'm sure he won't talk to you."

There seemed something curious about Fonzi's reaction. I found Veciana's phone number listed in the city directory and, after asking in halting English how I got his name—"The *Saturday Evening Post*," I said—agreed to meet me at the side of the post office facing the Trailways bus station in downtown Miami.

Shortly after 2 PM, a blue Maverick pulled to the curb. From the passenger side emerged a stocky Cuban, about six feet tall, wearing sunglasses. The driver got out, too, and stood by the car door as the passenger approached me. I walked down the steps and extended my hand. "Antonio Veciana?" I asked. "Yes. Mr. Russell?" I sensed a nervousness in his voice. He was dressed in an open-collar black silk shirt and black slacks. "Can we go to your hotel?" he asked.

"To tell you the truth, I haven't eaten all day and I'm starving," I said. "Would you mind going inside the restaurant there in the bus station and I'll buy you a hamburger?"

He nodded. He gave some kind of signal to his driver, who got back in the Maverick and drove off. When we reached the restaurant, Veciana said he wasn't hungry but asked that I take a table and wait for him, then disappeared. Five minutes passed. When he returned, I could see his driver lingering around the newsstand outside the cafeteria entrance.

We sat down in a booth. He spoke first. "Would you show me your card, please?" He removed his sunglasses.

"Well, I . . . I have no card, I. . . ."

"Your government card," he persisted.

"Look, if you think I'm with the FBI or the CIA, you're mistaken. I'm exactly what I told you, a writer from New York. I do have a letter of assignment to do a story about all the murders taking place lately in Little Havana, from *New Times Magazine*, if you want to see it."

Veciana nodded silently. I brought the letter from my briefcase and handed it to him. "Okay," he said. I brought out my notebook.

The story that Veciana gradually unfolded was one he had already been confiding to Fonzi and the Senate subcommittee. That was the reason, I realized, that Fonzi had tried to steer me off the trail. No journalist had interviewed Veciana yet and, because he was to prove one of the most critical witnesses toward establishing a CIA connection to Oswald, Fonzi wanted to keep it that way.

I found myself in a bind. Veciana insisted that I not tell Fonzi that he was talking to me. He also pleaded with me to use him only as a source, because if his real name was revealed in this context, he feared for his life.

I agreed, and I honored it. Then, about six months later, on January 19, 1977, my heart stopped when I read the headline of a syndicated column by Jack Anderson in the *New York Post*: A MR. X ENTERS THE JFK MYSTERY. Although the article did not identify Veciana, it contained enough details that anyone even slightly "in the know" would be able to. Someone on the congressional investigating committee must have leaked Anderson the story. I called Fonzi. He was furious.

Even then, in the first article I wrote that spring outlining what Veciana had said ("Three Witnesses" in *New Times*), I called him "Carlos." Not until the following summer of 1978 did I use his true name, in the article that follows, from *The Village Voice*. Given that Anderson had blown Veciana's cover long before, I no longer felt compelled to protect him.

He went on to testify in executive session before the House Assassinations Committee. Several weeks before its report was schedule to be released, he was driving home from work when someone fired four shots at Veciana's car in Little Havana. One ricocheting bullet struck him in the side of the head. He survived the attempt to kill him, but has remained largely silent on this subject in the years since.

22

"This Man Is a Missing Link"

Early last week, the House Select Committee on Assassinations released photographs of four men, one a man named "Maurice Bishop." The committee, which is about to begin open hearings into the possibility that President John F. Kennedy and Martin Luther King, Jr., were victims of conspiracies, asked if anyone could identify either Bishop or the other three mystery figures it sought for questioning in the probe. I do not know Maurice Bishop, but I know someone who does.

Though the committee gave no public details about its interest in these men, sources close to the investigation reveal the following:

- Two photographs of a young man with blond hair, allegedly taken in Mexico City in 1963, have been identified to the committee as being the same fellow who entered the Cuban embassy that fall, claiming to be Lee Harvey Oswald. Eusebio Azcue, the former Cuban consul in Mexico City, is said to have provided this startling information last spring in Havana to a team of visiting investigators that included Congressmen Richardson Preyer and Carl Stokes. There has long been speculation that someone pretending to be Oswald may have called at the Cuban and Soviet embassies, blazing a false trail.
- The photograph of a man on the curb in Dealey Plaza is known among assassination researchers as "the umbrella man." In films taken as the president was shot, the same man is depicted raising and then lowering a black umbrella as JFK's limousine passes. Some researchers have speculated that the umbrella might actually have been an exotic weapon that fired the fatal shot.

Maurice Bishop is a more proved story. My knowledge of him began in the summer of 1976 when, in the course of researching a book on the assassination, I spent a week in Miami's Cuban exile community. One of the men I hoped to interview was Antonio Veciana, a founder of an anti-Castro group called Alpha 66. In the early 1960s—before Kennedys curtailed commando raids

Cuba—Veciana had helped raise $100,000 to support such paramilitary attacks. Reportedly, he had also been involved in at least one assassination plot against Fidel Castro.

I found Veciana's name in the telephone book and called him. He spoke halting English but agreed to meet me down-town across from the Trailways bus station. He was a stocky Cuban, about six feet tall, and he looked to be about 40. After an hour of small talk in a nearby grill, we drove to one of the big hotels along Miami Beach and found an isolated corner in the lobby. There, I learned that Schweiker's staff was protecting him as its key witness. There, I learned too about Maurice Bishop.

Veciana had been president of a Havana accounting firm when Castro took over Cuba. Embittered by Castro's turn toward Communism, he began to secretly raise funds for an anti-Castro uprising. Shortly thereafter, in 1960, he received a visit from the gentleman who called himself Maurice Bishop. It was to be the first of more than 100 meetings, in a relationship that would last 12 years.

Bishop, who stood about 6'2" and appeared about 45, dressed expensively and had sunspots below his eyes. He told Veciana he was part of an American intelligence service, but instructed him not to ask which one. He wanted to train Veciana to lead a group of anti-Castro Cubans in sabotage and psychological warfare inside Cuba. Another American, whom Veciana knew only as "Melton," assisted with his instruction.

The initial strategy was to spread false rumors among the population about the economic instability of Castro's regime—a CIA tactic later used against Salvador Allende in Chile. When this failed to create a stir, Bishop used Veciana to coordinate an assassination attempt. The first was scheduled as Castro prepared to introduce the Soviet cosmonaut Yuri Gagarin, but was cancelled when Bishop feared a violent Soviet reaction.

The next was planned for October 1961 during a Castro speech, using a bazooka fired from a nearby rooftop. But Castro got wind of the plot and Veciana was forced to flee Cuba by boat. Bishop, who spoke French and possessed a fake passport from Belgium, stayed on undetected.

A month later in Miami, Bishop contacted Veciana again. Together they laid plans to form the group Alpha 66. Veciana traveled to New York, where he worked on another plan to eliminate Castro should he come to speak at the United Nations. Then, after the Cuban Missile Crisis, Veciana says that Bishop organized a series of commando attacks on Russian merchant ships in Cuban harbors. Bishop's plan, he adds, was to force another confrontation.

"Bishop kept saying Kennedy would have to be forced to make a decision," he remembers. "The only way was to put him up against the wall. Three ships were attacked in different ports of Cuba. The first one was a mistake in identity; it was a British ship. The other two were Russian. To further make Kennedy reach a point, we held a press conference in Washington to let him know about the commando groups. That was when Kennedy ordered that I be confined to Dade County, Florida."

In response to the terrorist raids, the Justice Department restricted a number of Cuban exiles to Dade County in the spring of 1963. But that summer, Veciana's meetings with Bishop resumed. In August, Bishop had him fly to Dallas.

"When I arrived there," says Veciana, "Bishop had given me the address to a building, a bank or insurance company. Bishop was waiting there with a young guy, an American, and the three of us walked to a cafeteria. The young guy did not say one word. He was very quiet, very strange. When I take a cup of coffee, Bishop says to him: 'I'll meet you in two or three hours.' Bishop and I then talked about the movement and our plans, but not when this guy was there. This was Lee Oswald. I didn't know until November when I saw his picture. But this means Oswald was working with Bishop."

"After the Kennedy assassination," Veciana continues, "the FBI contacted me to ask several questions. At first I was worried but the agent who interviewed me said that it was a matter of routine, nothing important. I didn't tell the agent anything, because I thought it would harm the movement."

After the assassination, Veciana says he waited a year before going back to Dallas. "I never asked Bishop about Oswald," he says, "because Bishop always told me that in this type of work, you just do things, you don't ask." Then, early in 1964, Bishop himself raised the subject. Veciana's cousin was then a leading official in Castro's intelligence service. Many times, Bishop had beseeched Veciana to try to glean information from the cousin.

"Now Bishop asked me if I thought that by getting my cousin a considerable amount of money, would he say he'd talked to Oswald to make it appear that Oswald was working for Castro? Because of this, I asked Bishop if it was true that Oswald had been talking with Castro agents. Bishop said it did not matter if it was true, what was important was to get my cousin to make that statement.

"I always thought that getting Cuban agents to say Oswald was working for them was a cover for Bishop himself," adds Veciana. "I always believed Bishop was working with Oswald during the assassination. About five months later, I brought up the topic about giving money to my cousin. Bishop said there was no need to talk about that plan any longer. He never brought up the topic again, and I never asked."

Over a year passed. With Kennedy's death, the anti-Castro commando raids began to wind down too. Veciana worked to slowly infiltrate some of his people into Cuba and set up internal guerrilla warfare. He was in Los Angeles when Bishop asked for a rendezvous in Las Vegas.

Veciana then moved to Puerto Rico where, using the cover of a sports promoter, he worked for Bishop training people to infiltrate the local Communist movement. In 1968, he went on to Bolivia as a thirty-thousand-dollar-a-year banking specialist for the State Department. His other job was to destroy the image of the recently murdered Cuban leader Che Guevara. According to Veciana, three Cuban CIA agents had been involved in Guevara's murder.

While in Bolivia, Veciana also sought to undermine the leftist government of Juan Torres. "I secretly started a campaign to inform the public that the coins would be devalued. There turned out to be a military coup (August 21, 1971). Torres fled to Argentina and was killed." Veciana also maintains that Bishop twice tried to kill Bolivia's Minister of the Interior, a Communist, but the man fled to Cuba.

Veciana's next project centered around Castro's 1971 visit to the Marxist Allende government in Chile. "Once Allende was voted in, we knew Castro would go to Chile. A lot of the officers of the Chilean Army were very cooperative with me and Bishop. They knew everything, when Castro would arrive and where he was going to be. The plan was to have TV cameras with machine guns inside them. We had two agents ID'd as pressmen. All this was planned directly by Bishop.

"Perhaps it was very similar to the Kennedy assassination. Because the person that Bishop assigned to kill Castro was going to get planted with papers to make it appear that he was a Moscow Castro agent and then he would himself be killed. So he would have been seen to be a traitor to Castro.

"It never got off the ground. One of the agents had an appendicitis attack, and had to be rushed to a hospital. The other said he wouldn't do it alone. We had all gone to Chile as diplomats, by car through Peru."

After this, says Veciana, "A lot of differences began to come up. I was tired of waiting so long. So many lives being lost, and Castro still alive. On July 24, 1973, the DEA (Drug Enforcement Administration) arrested me and accused me of trafficking in cocaine. Two days after the accusation, *I was given my money.* At the end of 15 years, they paid me. All Bishop had ever paid was traveling expenses; he said this was cumulative salary. Before I went to the Atlanta prison, I told Bishop what my family needed. After that Bishop never contacted me again. I do not know where he is now. But I am sure the trial was a set-up because of my previous activities. I was sentenced to seven years, paroled in 17 months—out very, very quickly. There the Senate started its investigating."

A few months after our meeting, Schweiker's people brought Veciana to Washington. He was taken secretly to a monthly meeting of the CIA's Association of Retired Intelligence Officers, where it was hoped he might provide a positive identification of Maurice Bishop. Apparently, the House has now ruled out that possibility. Curiously, sources close to the committee say that Veciana is not expected to be called to testify when the JFK hearings begin on September 6.

At last report, Antonio Veciana still lives in Miami. Although I originally agreed not to use his name, he has since appeared on a TV documentary with a portion of his story. If Maurice Bishop can be found, perhaps the tangled web that still surrounds the Kennedy assassination and related events of the '60s may yet find its way into the history books.

23

The Man Who Knew Too Much

The story of my relationship with Richard Case Nagell is the primary subject of my first book on the Kennedy assassination. I wrote about it for the first time in 1982, in an article for *Gallery Magazine*, a decision I made at the time after a letter from Nagell saying he had "closed up shop."

I have often been asked whether I ever had reason to be frightened in the course of knowing Nagell. I do know that, one night in Los Angeles, someone had been tailing us as Nagell dropped me off at my driveway. Another time, he told me over the phone, "You'd be surprised at how many people in Los Angeles know who Dick Russell is." He paused and then said, "Including some Cubans."

I asked, "Well, am I in any danger?"

"No," he replied evenly, "I would have alerted you if you were."

He then asked whether I'd ever tape recorded any of our conversations.

Although I'd often wished I had, I truthfully told him that I hadn't. "I didn't think so," he said. "These two guys who said you did were so adamant about it, that I finally didn't believe them."

"What two guys?" I asked.

"They said they were sitting next to us in the bar. They were CIA."

That much I was certain of: there were those who were not pleased about Nagell's ongoing relationship with a journalist who then worked for a prominent magazine (*TV Guide*).

24

Gallery Magazine, March 1981

"The Man Who Had a Contract to Kill Lee Harvey Oswald Before the Assassination of President John F. Kennedy"

Why didn't the Warren Commission or the House Select Committee on Assassinations call on ex-intelligence officer Richard Case Nagell to testify before them? Were they afraid of the devastating story he had to tell, a story that would not only have challenged their findings but most likely would have destroyed most of their conclusions?

"Richard Nagell is a name which is totally unknown to the American public. Yet, a few years hence, it may be very familiar to any schoolchild as *the* person who 'broke' the JFK case. Despite the fact that he was ignored by both the Warren Commission and the House Assassination Committee, Nagell is probably the key witness who knew the details of the genesis of the assassination and who is still alive. To stay healthy, Richard Nagell must tread very softly."
—BERNARD FENSTERWALD, Jr., Washington attorney

Late on the afternoon of September 20, 1963, a man described in the next day's newspapers as a thirty-three-year-old "battle-scarred Korean war hero" walked into the State National Bank of El Paso, Texas, and approached a teller for one hundred dollars in traveler's checks. Suddenly, he reached inside his sport jacket, drew a Colt .45 pistol from his belt, turned, and aimed two shots into a plaster wall just below the bank's ceiling. Then, as casually as he had entered, he moved out the door toward his car in a nearby alleyway. By the time a young policeman closed in to arrest him, he had backed the car onto the sidewalk and was calmly motioning for a pedestrian to pass. "I guess you've got me now. I surrender," the man said, and raised his hands.

Because a firearm had been discharged on federal property, the El Paso FBI was alerted. It sent two agents to the scene. In the apprehended man's wallet, the agents found a U.S. military certificate. In one of his pants pockets was a mimeographed newsletter from a Los Angeles chapter of the Fair Play for Cuba

Committee. "Why don't you check my car and get that machine gun out of my trunk?" he was reported to have remarked. There was no machine gun; what the FBI found were two briefcases.

On the way to the El Paso Federal Building for further questioning, the man issued only one statement to the FBI: "I would rather be arrested than commit murder and treason."

I first heard the name Richard Case Nagell in the summer of 1975. I was researching a possible book on the assassination of President Kennedy, wading through the voluminous reports of the Warren Commission, following many torturous trails of conspiracy evidence, and running into as many dead ends. Early that summer a California philosophy professor and Warren Commission critic named Richard Popkin began announcing to anyone who would listen that he had "solved the Kennedy assassination." Like a number of other journalists, I flew to San Diego to see what, if anything, Popkin had discovered.

It quickly became difficult for me to separate fact from fantasy; most other journalists there had given up trying. Popkin had *two* complete scenarios on the assassination. The main one, supported by hundreds of pages of transcripts from a Filipino hypnotist, involved a young Puerto Rican who'd allegedly confessed to being a "robot gunman" or "zombie killer."

The professor's alternate scenario, concerning an American spy named Nagell who'd been connected with the President's accused assassin Lee Harvey Oswald and who came in from the cold by getting himself arrested, was dismissed at the time as the flip side of Popkin's mystifying "solution."

It was several months before I paid much notice to a pile of Xeroxed material I had carted home from San Diego. Included was a photocopy of the pages of a small brown spiral notebook, which according to Popkin had belonged to Richard Nagell. I turned the pages and scanned the names. The pages were filled with locker numbers, lists of theaters and restaurants alongside specific dates and times in a variety of locations in the U.S. and Mexico. I had read that such notations are often used to indicate intelligence rendezvous points, either for the drop and pick-up of information or for clandestine contacts.

The notebook contained names of congressmen, attorneys, American leftists, officials in Far East governments, a Soviet military attaché, six names under the heading "CIA," and two listings for the "Fair Play for Cuba Committee." I began becoming more interested in this aspect of Popkin's theories, as well as in the man who'd kept the notebook. As Professor Popkin had related the story, the notebook had been among the effects taken from Richard Nagell's trunk that September afternoon in El Paso, 1963, and held for 11 years by the FBI.

One entry in particular rang a bell:

C.E. MEXICO D.F.

PHONE:

11-28-47

I played with the initials "C.E." Were they a person's name? Perhaps "Cuban Embassy." The entry went on:

MEET

JUFER REST

CALLE VERSALLE

LAREDO, TEXAS

Two months and two days after this notebook was seized from Richard Nagell, remarkably similar listings had been found in the address book of Lee Oswald: names of American leftists, a Soviet Embassy official, and Cubans. Even the number of the Cuban Embassy in Mexico City, which Oswald listed atop one page:

Mexico City

Consulada de Cuba

Zamora Y F Marquez

11-28-47

Sylvia Duran

One week after Nagell was arrested, Oswald had, according to the Warren Commission, tried and failed to obtain a visa to Cuba at the Cuban Embassy in Mexico City. He had, said the Commission, traveled into Mexico by bus from Laredo, Texas.

Perhaps the similarities were coincidence. But I went through more of Popkin's material and found two sets of FBI reports, both filed in the National Archives under "Lee Harvey Oswald: Internal Security—Russia." The first series was dated December 20, 1963:

RICHARD NAGELL incarcerated in the El Paso County Jail on a complaint charging him with Bank Robbery advised that for the record he would like to say that his association with OSWALD was "purely social" and that he had met him in Mexico City and in Texas. . . .

Although questioned as to where and when his contacts with OSWALD were made, he refused to comment further and said he had nothing more to say.

An FBI report bearing a date of January 30, 1964 contained two statements. One came from an El Paso Secret Service agent named Oscar G. Weisheit, Jr., who advised that a Dallas Secret Serviceman had shown a mug shot of Nagell to Oswald's wife on January 18. Marina Oswald responded that she had never seen him, nor did she know anyone by his name or aliases.

The second segment of this FBI report read:

On January 27, 1964, the El Paso Times *contained an article entitled: "Suspect Says Agents Asked Him About Oswald, Activities Link."*

According to the Times *article, "RICHARD NAGELL, charged with attempted bank robbery, said he had been questioned by the FBI and the U.S. Secret Service regarding alleged subversive activities and also LEE HARVEY OSWALD, the alleged assassin of President Kennedy."*

The article contained information regarding the appearance of NAGELL before U.S. District Judge HOMER THORNBERRY in El Paso in connection with the bank robbery charge filed against him and stated:

"Instead of asking for a plea, FRED MORTON, assistant U.S. District Attorney made a motion to put NAGELL in a federal institution in Springfield, Missouri, for psychiatric observation. The motion was granted over NAGELL's vigorous objections."

The FBI had obviously shown some interest in Nagell and his alleged connections with Oswald, yet I found that there was no mention of Richard Nagell in *The Warren Report* or even in the 26 volumes of Warren Commission documents. Nor is there any indication that the Commission was ever made aware of the existence or contents of Nagell's notebook.

Nagell had tried, in a letter dated March 20, 1964, and written by him from the El Paso County Jail to the Warren Commission's Chief Counsel:

"Dear Mr. Rankin,

Has the Commission been advised that I informed the Federal Bureau of Investigation in September 1963 that an attempt might be made to assassinate President Kennedy?"

On April 16, 1964, Nagell made another attempt. This time, he wrote to J. Edgar Hoover:

"My responsibility concerning the then prospective action of Lee H. Oswald [alias] (Albert Hidell) terminated with the dispatch of the registered letter from Richard Nagell to the FBI in September 1963.

Since the information disclosed in that letter was judged to be mendacious by the FBI, as is quite evident, then with whom the responsibility lies for what subsequently happened in Dallas is rather obvious. . . ."

I had seen enough. Nagell was making strong allegations that seemed to have basis for investigation. And apparently no other journalist had delved much into this new angle on the assassination. I flew to El Paso in early October 1975, to sift his clues at their point of origin.

My first stop was the newspaper morgue of the *El Paso Times*, where the faded clip files on the mysterious stranger and his bizarre "attempted robbery" began with a banner headline in a morning edition of Saturday, September 21, 1963: Veteran Tries Daring Bank Holdup. The article stated that detectives and FBI agents going through Nagell's suitcase had found records showing an eleven-year career in the Army, highlighted by three Purple Hearts and a Bronze Star in Korea, and an honorable discharge in 1959 with the rank of captain. Nagell had told the agents he'd entered the Army as a buck private and was in line for promotion to major when he was discharged, and that he was fluent in Russian, Japanese, and Spanish. The article continued:

His army papers disclosed Nagell had graduated with honors from the Army Military Intelligence School, from a special leaders course, and had served in the counterintelligence corps (CIC). He has records showing he had been given top security clearance on September 22, 1950.

In one of his commendation certificates was a notation that Nagell was a "perennial calm and levelheaded officer of superior intelligence."

I found more biographical material in Nagell's trial records. Raised in an orphanage and foster homes, he had joined the Army in 1948 at age 18. During the Korean War, he had been the youngest American to receive a battlefield promotion to captain. By 1958, according to his lawyer's summation, he had been "loaned" by Military Intelligence to "another intelligence agency" for assignments in Hong Kong, Formosa, Korea, and Japan. Then, at the American Embassy in Tokyo, he had married a Japanese woman. Late in 1959, at his wife's urging, he had resigned his commission and returned to the United States to work for the State of California. In 1962, amid marital troubles, he had suddenly left his job, wife, and two children behind and traveled to Mexico City. That was as far as the court chose to trace his history, until his appearance in September 1963 in the El Paso bank.

I interviewed Nagell's arresting officer, his jailer, his defense attorney, and the man who'd prosecuted him.

Officer Jim Bundren recalled going through the trunk of Nagell's car with an FBI agent and finding a tiny Minolta camera, "pictures of top security places in Korea," and a couple of small spiral notebooks. "The names in them were government officials that didn't mean anything to me," Bundren told me. "The FBI kept the notebooks, but they shut that up pretty quick. Washington or where, I don't know."

Nagell told Bundren that he'd wanted to get caught and be put in federal custody.

"Did he ever mention the name of Lee Harvey Oswald to you?" I asked.

"It's hard to correlate everything now. Oswald's name came up. I honestly can't tell you whether he mentioned Oswald before or after the assassination, but it came up."

I next asked Fred Morton, the former Assistant U.S. Attorney who had called for recurring "sanity tests" for Richard Nagell, about the notebook.

"Yeah, he had a notebook with him, in his belongings. I don't know if it was offered in evidence. The only thing I remember about specifics is that it had the address of that Fair Play for Cuba Committee that Oswald was associated with. I don't know whether they wanted free rum or what."

"Did you ever see that notebook?" I asked.

"I think I did, but I don't remember for sure. I don't know if anybody gave a damn."

Then Morton began to laugh. "When we got to trial, his own lawyer asked him if he was a Communist. [Nagell's court-appointed lawyer] Joe Calamia's tactic was to make a wreck out of the guy in the courtroom, try to show that he was crazy. That was his defense. Nagell didn't want to assert that defense, Joe did it in spite of him; Joe and I kidded about it since. The guy was really as calm as tea and crumpets. But when Joe got asking him this stuff, he objected at least twice to his own lawyer's questions. Finally he broke down, and Judge Thornberry had to call a recess.

"But Joe got him off. It took a long time, but he got him off."

"A long time" was an understatement. In January 1964, Nagell had been transferred to the United States Medical Center at Springfield, Missouri for psychiatric evaluation. In March he was reported competent to stand trial and sent back to El Paso. *USA vs. Richard Nagell* began on May 4, 1964. Two days later, after brief deliberation, the jury returned a guilty verdict on two counts of entering a bank with intent to rob. Judge Homer Thornberry handed down a maximum term of 10 years.

A month after Nagell's conviction, attorney Calamia entered an appeal based on "crucial evidence newly discovered": alleged brain damage suffered by Nagell in the 1954 crash of a B-25 bomber near Baltimore's Friendship Airport, a crash which he alone had survived. In January 1966, Nagell's conviction was overturned and a new trial began the following September. Again Nagell was found guilty and given the same sentence. Finally, on April 4, 1968, the U.S. Court of Appeals reversed the conviction once again, "in view of strong evidence that defendant was insane at time of offense." After 4½ years behind bars, Nagell was set free.

It didn't add up. Despite considerable evidence to the contrary, there seemed to have been an effort to discredit Nagell as either a would-be bank robber or a madman. Somehow I would have to speak with him directly. All I had to go on was a Los Angeles address scrawled across a page of Popkin's notes. Assuming it was Nagell's, and that he still lived there, would he allow me to interview him?

It was an autumn Sunday morning when I eased a rented car onto the south freeway and toward the outskirts of Los Angeles, through the little towns that line the Pacific seacoast. In one such town, not far from the ocean, I hoped to have tracked him down.

As I rang the bell a third time at a modest wood-frame house, the handle turned and the front door opened slightly. Half of a man's face formed a silhouette against the darkness within.

"Mr. Nagell?"

"Yes."

"I'm sorry to show up unannounced like this, but I didn't know how to reach you by phone. I'm a writer from New York, and I've come a long way to see you. I'm looking to set the record straight about a certain historical event and . . ." I felt foolish, and only silence answered me. "I know you've been screwed around by a lot of people over the years. All I can assure you is, I'm looking for the truth."

"I don't know. I'm very busy today. . . . Well, all right, come in."

The door opened to reveal a lean man—perhaps six-foot-two—with light brown eyes and close-cropped, reddish brown hair. He would be 45, I calculated.

Nagell told me I'd come at an opportune time; his son was out bike riding, and we could talk until he got back. He preferred that I didn't tape-record the conversation ("I've had some bad experiences with that"), but he began adjusting some dials on an audio sound system beside the front window. "I hope you don't mind," he said, "but I've made a practice of recording all my conversations about this subject. A lot of things have been distorted over the years. And I've learned that this is one means of protecting myself." His bearing was sad, almost stoic.

"May I assume that your action in the bank on September 20, 1963 was somehow related to the assassination of President Kennedy?"

"Well, it had nothing to do with any *alibi*, as some people seem to believe. I didn't have to establish an alibi. I was on my way out of the country, and I did not plan to return. Instead, I walked into a bank and busted two caps."

Nagell said his life had been threatened periodically but that he had "life insurance"—certain documents and photographs being kept in a foreign country. "The material that would be released in the event of my death would prove quite embarrassing to certain people." He said he didn't fear the CIA or FBI so much as somebody on his own deciding to "pull a Jack Ruby."

Nagell disappeared into a bedroom and returned with two letters, which he handed to me without a word. The first was dated January 3, 1967, the day that Oswald's slayer Jack Ruby died in prison. It was addressed to Senator Richard Russell of Georgia, then Chairman of the Committee on Armed Services and a member of the Warren Commission:

". . . I would urge rather than attempting to learn more about Mr. Oswald's stay in the USSR and his dealings with a pro-Castro committee, that any future inquiry be directed along more productive lines. Further, I suggest that any field investigation deemed necessary be conducted by an agency that has no private ax to grind. Mr. Oswald and his activities came under my scrutiny during 1962 and 1963."

The letter goes on to say that Oswald had no significant connection with the Fair Play for Cuba Committee, pro-Castro elements, any Marxist or racist group, or any investigative, police or intelligence agency, domestic or foreign:

". . . He was involved in a conspiracy to murder the former Chief Executive during the latter part of September 1963. This conspiracy was neither Communist inspired nor was it instigated by any foreign government or organization or individual representative of any foreign government."

"In the summer of 1963 I received instructions to initiate certain action against Mr. Oswald, who was the indispensable tool in the conspiracy, and thereafter depart the United States, legally. Although I did neither, I did, subsequent to obtaining a valid passport and prior to my arrest, dispatch a letter via registered mail, to the Director, Federal Bureau of Investigation, advising in sufficient detail of the aforesaid conspiracy and the identity of Mr. Oswald."

"After the tragedy at Dallas, when I became convinced that the FBI was more concerned with keeping me in custody (and with cleaning its dirty linen) than it was in resolving facts which would have shed light on the assassination, I clammed up completely. Later, however, when I felt I was going to be rail-roaded into either a prison or a mental institution, I made every reasonable effort under the existing circumstances to testify before the Warren Commission. I even sent letters to the Chief, Secret Service Division and Mr. J. L. Rankin, then General Counsel for the Commission."

"For what little it is apparently worth now, my opinion is that the death of President Kennedy was indirectly, if not directly, resultant from a conspiracy and also due in great part to the stupidity or negligence of the FBI. . . ."

Attached was Senator Russell's reply, dated 17 days later: "Permit me to acknowledge and thank you for your letter and the information it contains. With every good wish, I am—Sincerely, Dick Russell." (In 1970, shortly before his death, Senator Russell was quoted in the Washington press as believing that "someone else worked with him [Oswald] on the planning.")

The second letter that Nagell handed to me was dated January 8, 1967 and addressed to Senator Robert Kennedy. It contained a carbon copy of the letter to Senator Russell:

"Whether the tragedy at Dallas was indirectly or directly resultant from a conspiracy, only time and an unbiased, thorough inquiry will tell. But in either event the matter is now academic. The deed was done; and it could have been prevented. . . ."

We talked for a while longer before Nagell stood up to shake hands. "I don't really think I have anything more to say today. If you feel the need to contact me again, I'll give you the number of a friend here in Los Angeles. He will always know how to get in touch with me."

I did contact Richard Nagell again. We corresponded (via a post-office box) for six months after I went back to New York. In 1977 I got a job writing for *TV Guide Magazine* in Los Angeles; we met several times. Through these conversations, the files maintained by two of his ex-lawyers to which he granted me access, and other research, I have pieced together what I could of Richard Nagell's story.

Perhaps the best place to begin is the mid-1950s, after Nagell's graduation from Military Intelligence School. He then returned to the Far East, scene of his military exploits, as part of a clandestine spy unit called Field Operations Intelligence (FOI). As Senior Intelligence Adviser in South Korea, Nagell admits having participated in political assassinations, kidnapping, blackmail, and counterfeiting operations. Early in 1957, after telling his superiors that he was "fed up" with committing crimes in the interest of national security, he was reassigned to counterintelligence duties in Japan. In Tokyo he first met a young Marine stationed at the Atsugi Naval Air Base, Lee Oswald.

"We had a casual but purposeful acquaintance in Japan," says Nagell. "My relationship with Oswald there, and later in the United States, was strictly with an objective."

From Tokyo, Nagell's path led to Los Angeles and, on August 20, 1962, into Mexico. Taking up residence at Mexico City's Hotel Luma, Nagell reestablished contact with a CIA official he'd known previously in Japan. He signed a contract with the CIA and received an assignment as a "double agent." He would seem to work for the Soviet KGB, but his actual duties would serve the CIA. The Soviets had attempted to recruit Nagell before through a Japanese professor, after Nagell had made no secret of his disenchantment with various U.S. intelligence tasks in the Far East. Now Nagell established liaison with a high-ranking KGB officer in Mexico. His initial CIA mission, he says, revolved around the gathering Cuban missile crisis. He was to feed "disinformation" to the Soviets.

At about the same time, Nagell was given an assignment by the Soviets. Part of the missile crisis agreement was a promise by Kennedy not to seek the overthrow of Fidel Castro. This infuriated the anti-Castro Cuban exiles in America, particularly a CIA-financed group called "Alpha 66." This group was rumored to be plotting the assassination of Kennedy, a deed they would try to pin on Castro. The KGB wanted Nagell to return to the U.S., to begin surveillance of the Cuban exile community and find out more. On October 21, 1962, he left Mexico City for Dallas.

In his briefcase, Nagell was carrying a photograph given him by the KGB: a picture of Lee Harvey Oswald. While he was in Dallas, the Soviets wanted Nagell to keep tabs on Oswald, who had defected to Russia in 1959 and returned to the USA in 1962 with his Russian bride.

"When he was in the Soviet Union," says Nagell, "they had suspected him as a spy and considered him emotionally unstable, prone to commit some act that could bring embarrassment to them." Since Nagell had known Oswald before, it was felt he could establish contact and surveillance. Nagell is cryptic as to what he found out about Oswald that fall. "He was just being used—by a lot of people, for their own reasons."

Meanwhile, Nagell followed a Cuban exile plot to assassinate the President when he addressed the released Bay of Pigs prisoners in late December in Miami. This plot never got beyond the talking stage, but it was followed by another, to take the President's life when he went to Beverly Hills for the premiere of the movie *PT-109* in June 1963. Again, the plot fizzled, but Nagell continued his surveillance of two Cuban exiles involved, whose "war names" were "Angel" and "Leopoldo."

"Leopoldo" was an ex-CIA operative trained by the U.S. military at Fort Jackson, South Carolina. Though Nagell will not identify him further, he says that his alias was derived from "a now-defunct Mexican restaurant, a sometimes contact point, once located at 3675 Beverly Boulevard in Los Angeles." The other, Angel, "also used the pseudonym 'Rangel' as a surname on at least one occasion." Besides their connection with the Alpha 66 group, according to Nagell they had ties with the anti-Castro organizations MRP in Miami and JURE in Puerto Rico.

Their next attempt to kill Kennedy, originally scheduled for late September in the Washington, D.C. area, involved a third figure: Oswald. The exiles had met Oswald in New Orleans, where he was passing out leaflets for the Fair Play for Cuba Committee. According to Nagell, Angel and Leopoldo convinced Oswald they were "agents for Castro's G-2 intelligence service, operating undercover." They then solicited Oswald's help in assassinating President Kennedy, as supposed retaliation by Castro for assassination attempts against his own life.

Nagell says he was close enough to this conspiracy to participate in a planning meeting on either August 23 or 27 in New Orleans. He maintains that he secretly recorded a conversation about the assassination among Oswald, Angel, Leopoldo, and himself, and that he gave the cassette to a friend in Los Angeles for safekeeping the following month.

Nagell's next instructions regarding Oswald came from his KGB contact. He was to "try to persuade Oswald that the deal was phony and if this didn't work, and if it looked like things were going to progress beyond the talking stage, to get rid of him."

The Soviets, according to Nagell, were "the last people that wanted Kennedy dead." The nuclear test-ban treaty had just been signed in August. *Rapprochement* between the U.S. and Castro seemed in the offing. An assassination plot seeking to pin the blame on Castro, and utilizing a young man who'd spent nearly three years in the Soviet Union, might conceivably bring the world again to the brink of war.

So, sometime in early September, Nagell met privately with Oswald at Jackson Square in New Orleans. Displaying photos of Angel and Leopoldo, Nagell informed him that they were not Castro agents as they claimed, but "counter-revolutionaries known to be connected with a violence-prone faction of a CIA-financed group."

"He was informed," Nagell wrote later, "that he was being 'used' by fascist elements in an attempt to disrupt the Cuban revolution, and probably to incite the U.S. government to severe retaliatory measures against Cuba (in the form of invasion) etc. He denied that there had been any serious discussion to kill President Kennedy. He seemed genuinely upset and visibly shaken.... He stated he was a friend of the Cuban revolution."

Nagell's next action was to dispatch a registered letter to J. Edgar Hoover, revealing the whereabouts and identity of Oswald and his role in a plan "to murder the Chief Executive of the United States . . . during the latter part of September." Nagell says he revealed enough details to warrant the arrests of Oswald, Angel, and Leopoldo.

After dispatching this letter, Nagell says he then met again with Oswald. Oswald was told that a Soviet agent code-named "Oaxaca" wanted to speak to him in Mexico City. He was asked to depart the U.S. before September 26 and register at a certain Mexican hotel. He would be contacted there by "Laredo" (Nagell) and introduced to "Oaxaca" the same day.

"He was instructed not to go near the Cuban or USSR embassies," says Nagell. "Oswald agreed to do so when he was advised that he would be provided with more than sufficient funds to make the trip to and from Mexico City by plane. He was told where and how he was to pick up the money on 9/24/63, his expected date of departure from New Orleans."

On September 17, Oswald picked up a Mexican tourist card in New Orleans. Nagell had already left the city, carrying a .45-caliber Colt pistol—intended for use on Lee Harvey Oswald in Mexico.

But Nagell was having second thoughts about his orders to eliminate Oswald and then depart the U.S., apparently to take up permanent residence in the Soviet Union. He was no longer certain as to the boundaries of his "double agent" role, and whether his actions were truly for the CIA or the KGB. On September 20, he drove his 1957 Ford into the West Texas town of El Paso. There, at the post office, he mailed three letters. One contained five $100 bills, the expense money for Oswald's Mexican journey. Then, while President Kennedy was addressing the United Nations about an "atmosphere of rising hope" engendered by the nuclear test-ban treaty, Nagell walked into the El Paso bank and brandished the pistol—which he says he used "consciously as a message to somebody awaiting me across the border in Juarez."

He had decided he could not go through with the KGB's assignment. Doubtful about which master he was really serving, unable to kill a man and then face life abroad without his children, he chose instead to get himself placed in federal custody. The letter to Hoover had been sent. He had done his duty. Or so he believed. Now the FBI would find the evidence in his trunk which would surely indicate he had another motive besides "attempted bank robbery."

While Nagell sat in federal custody, waiting for the FBI to discover the conspiracy, Oswald was on the move. He was last seen in New Orleans on the night of September 24. A Cuban refugee named Sylvia Odio told the Warren Commission that he came to her home in Dallas the next night, accompanied by two Latins. Their names: Angel and Leopoldo. (The FBI later "identified" these men to the Commission, and said there was no evidence that they had known Oswald. In fact, the men the FBI "identified"—Loran Hall and Lawrence Howard—had never used those particular "war names.")

On September 26, according to *The Warren Report*, Oswald crossed into Mexico alone by bus at Nuevo Laredo, Texas. He reportedly told a fellow passenger he was "en route to Cuba" by way of Mexico City "to see Castro, if I could." The next day Oswald (or someone using his identity) showed up at the Cuban and Soviet embassies in Mexico City, carrying evidence of pro-Castro activities and seeking visas. Cuban intelligence reports say he told Embassy personnel: "Someone ought to shoot that President Kennedy. . . . Maybe I'll try to do it."

Oswald returned to Dallas, for the final time, after a week in Mexico, telling his wife that the trip had been unproductive. The Oswalds were questioned by the FBI about their Russian connections and Lee's activities with the Fair Play for Cuba Committee, but the investigation apparently didn't delve any deeper.

Back in El Paso, Nagell was asking in early November for a court hearing "to show cause why I [am] being held in jail without having been arraigned or indicted by the federal grand jury." Then, on November 19, while President Kennedy was preparing for his fateful visit to Texas, two FBI agents came to visit Nagell in the County Jail. Nagell's jailer, Juan Medina, recalls the FBI and later the Secret Service coming often to see his prisoner. According to a chronological account of his imprisonment drawn up by Nagell, one-half hour after JFK's assassination on November 22 Nagell handed a note to his jailer requesting to see the Secret Service as soon as possible. Instead, the FBI came again. Nagell says he then told Agent Thomas B. White, Jr. about the registered letter to J. Edgar Hoover. (FBI headquarters in Washington denies ever having received this letter.) That night, Nagell says he wrote a letter concerning the conspiracy to Secret Service Chief James Rowley in Washington, but never received a reply.

By the time he was released from Leavenworth Penitentiary in April 1968, Richard Nagell had given up trying to tell his story to authorities.

On May 24, 1968, Nagell was issued an American passport (unusual for a convicted felon) and left the country six days later. It was some time before he surfaced again. On October 24, the following Associated Press dispatch came out of Berlin:

East Germany has released a former U.S. Army Captain it held for four months. Informed sources said Richard Nagell, 38, was delivered at a border crossing point between East and West Berlin yesterday in the presence of East Berlin attorney Wolfgang Vogel, attorney Ricey S. New of Washington, and an official from the U.S. Mission in West Berlin. . . .

Informed sources said Nagell was taken off a train by the East Germans four months ago while he was on his way from West Germany to West Berlin through East Germany. . . . The U.S. Mission had not disclosed that Nagell was being held. He was not brought to trial and apparently no specific charges were brought against him, the sources added. . . .

What was Nagell doing in East Germany? According to his story, he had been taken to the Ministry of State Security prison, accused of "criminal intelligence activities." From there, he was taken to the Soviet Union, where he authored what he says is the only copy of his full story of the events surrounding the Kennedy assassination.

Nagell returned to the U.S. in November 1968. Three months later he again met with Garrison, and deemed it inadvisable to testify at Garrison's Clay Shaw trial. Nagell then flew to Mexico City, and again to Europe. He says several attempts were made on his life during this period.

Since that time Nagell had rarely surfaced in the public eye. In 1974, while living in Los Angeles, he hired attorney Bernard Fensterwald, Jr., to help him get a disability compensation from the Army. Fensterwald, whose client James McCord had broken the ice about the Watergate burglary, hoped through Nagell's case to bring the JFK story to light. But Nagell dismissed the attorney before this could happen.

Nagell says that to his knowledge, Oswald's slayer Jack Ruby was not involved in any conspiracy to assassinate Kennedy. As for Oswald, Nagell believes that he probably did fire the shots attributed to him, but doubts Oswald's expertise as a marksman:

"I don't know how much he improved between September and then. Maybe, if he spent a lot of time on a rifle range. . . . But I do know that things did not change so drastically from the time of my arrest. There's no doubt in my mind that he pulled a trigger. Later on, everyone was trying to protect their own incompetence or inefficiency in not doing anything to stop him."

A man is sitting at a corner table in a bar called the Blarney Castle, his back to the other customers. It is a hot day in Los Angeles. The man is wearing a light tan suit with a necktie. His long hands move in quick, furtive gestures, reaching to shake a cigarette from a pack of Salems.

One beer passes in small talk. At the mention of his children, he shakes his head sadly. For almost a year, the children have been living with their mother. For a time before that, the man had tried raising them on his own, but the burden had proved too great. It was largely because of them he'd stayed silent all these years, carrying inside himself the terrible secret of what he knew about certain events of the autumn of 1963. At one time, this man might have changed the course of history.

"I don't think about it much, to tell the truth," he says unconvincingly. A second beer, a fourth cigarette is passing. "Sometimes, though, I get to thinking and I can't go to sleep. Thinking of what I could have done, the mistakes that could have been handled differently. I was young. So idealistic! How could I have been like that? But I was realistic, too. I didn't believe in Utopias. I had my own beliefs, my own feelings."

It is late on a Friday afternoon, a time referred to as "the happy hour" by those seeking to unwind from the working day, and the bar is growing crowded. Always my recent rendezvous with the man have been in places like this. Though I know he still lives in Los Angeles, I have no idea where. As for his current livelihood, all he will say is that he keeps very busy. He changes his unlisted phone number every few months.

Yet, in a strange way, I have become his confidant. Our meetings are few and far between, perhaps twice a year. But I believe he has said more to me than to anyone else in the country concerning what he's called "my own weird little secret." Perhaps it is not so much that he trusts me as simply his need to periodically talk to someone who already realizes the intricacies of the subject matter. For three years of my life, I have probed the murky catacombs that still surround the assassination of John F. Kennedy. Dozens of theories, and almost as many tales of supposed firsthand knowledge, have been spun for me across many a long, dark night of the American landscape. Finally, it has all come down to one man—this man who now sits across from me, methodically savoring the last dregs of a third bottle of beer—one man whose story (as much as I know of it) I believe.

My association with Richard Nagell ended in September 1978. He had determined that he no longer wished to discuss the assassination subject, that there had been pressure put on him from "certain sources," and that it seemed in both our interests for our periodic meetings to cease. I have not seen him since.

25

The Paisley Puzzle

Aﬆer my article about him appeared in *Gallery*, Nagell sent the publisher a disclaimer. "As author Dick Russell knows very well," he wrote, "following my acquittal in 1968 on what can only be called trumped-up charges, I have never had any 'story' to tell anyone (let alone to tell a journalist or a Congressional committee) about my past intelligence activities, Lee Oswald, or any events which may have led to the assassination of the President. And, after what happened to me at the hands of a corrupt judicial system and a two-faced Administration, I couldn't care less about such matters."

Maybe he had to say that, I thought. Two years later, Nagell agreed to meet with me again. And we spoke intermittently by phone and exchanged further correspondence.

One envelope from Nagell, that had shown up in my mailbox at *TV Guide* in October 1978, was a Xerox of a newspaper clipping. CIA MYSTERY DEATH: EX-DEPUTY DIRECTOR'S BODY FOUND FLOATING IN BAY, it was headlined. The body was that of a man named John Paisley. Nagell typed in these words above the article: "10/3/78 Re: Richard Case Nagell's Letter to Director of Central Intelligence, Certified Mail Receipt No. 293838, dated May 17, 1976."

I did not know what that letter had contained, but Nagell's tip was enough to put me on the trail of John Paisley. The article, also for *Gallery Magazine*, appeared in the summer of 1981.

Richard A. Sprague, first director of the House Committee on Assassinations, 1976–77.

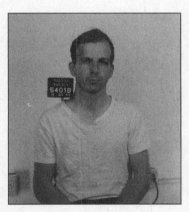

Lee Harvey Oswald in custody after the assassination.

New Orleans D.A. Jim Garrison, who mounted the first independent investigation
into the assassination.

Soldier-of-fortune Gerry Patrick Hemming.

Lawrence Howard, anti-Castro "freedom fighter."

Three men the FBI claimed visited Sylvia Odio: Lawrence Howard (left), Loran Hall (pointing), unidentified man, and Oswald look-alike William Seymour (right).

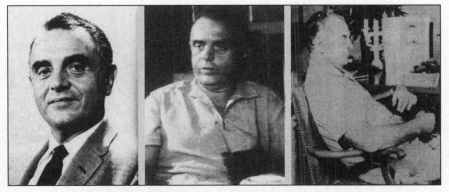

Oswald's "friend" in Dallas, George deMohrenschildt.

Cuban exile leader Antonio Veciana (left) with Armando Fleites.

David Atlee Phillips, likely Veciana's CIA case officer "Maurice Bishop."

The many faces of Lee Harvey Oswald.

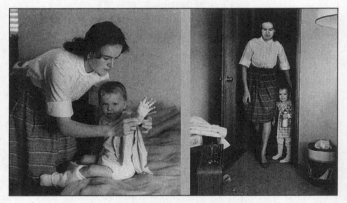

Marina Oswald in the early 1960s.

Richard Case Nagell.

Nagell's yearbook photo from Albany High School.

Desmond FitzGerald, who ran the CIA's Cuban Task Force in 1963.

Henry Hecksher of CIA, Nagell's possible case officer.

Manuel Artime (center), Cuban exile leader under Hecksher, next to JFK at Miami's Orange Bowl, December 1962.

The CIA's Sidney Gottlieb, who ran MKULTRA.

MKULTRA field operative Ike Feldman.

Oswald (far right) at sixteen, at meeting of David Ferrie's (second from left) Civil Air Patrol in New Orleans, mid-1950s.

Douglas Horne, who investigated the president's autopsy for the Assassination Records Review Board.

The president's casket being loaded onto Air Force One.

The autopsy doctors (left to right): "J" Thornton Boswell, James J. Humes, Pierre A. Finck.

26

Gallery Magazine, May 1981

"The Spy at the Bottom of the Bay"

Some say John Paisley was a top Russian spy planted in the CIA. Some say he was both. Some say John Paisley was a brilliant CIA operative looking for a master Russian spy planted in the CIA. Was his "strange" suicide actually murder?

For almost 20 years, a quiet but ominous fear has haunted the corridors of the Central Intelligence Agency. It is the specter of a "mole"—an American official somewhere in the upper echelons of the CIA who is really a Soviet agent planted by its own spy network, the KGB.

In the words of a CIA insider: "If there is a mole inside the CIA hierarchy, this means that every particle of our intelligence is suspect and possibly contaminated. It means the Soviets have detailed knowledge of our verification capability and can circumvent it. It changes the world power balance."

Three years ago, a widespread CIA search intensified for a mole who might conceivably be operating his own spy ring within the Agency. This followed a series of arrests of several former CIA employees who admitted having passed intelligence secrets to the Soviets. Many of these secrets concerned clandestine electronic and satellite surveillance systems the U.S. was using to monitor Russian strategic weapons developments. Loss of those secrets was termed by the CIA "the most serious espionage disaster in 20 years."

Then, in late September 1978 a CIA official who specialized in those very secrets disappeared from his sailboat one calm Sunday on the Chesapeake Bay. A week later the body of John Arthur Paisley, a former Deputy Director in the CIA's Office of Strategic Research, washed ashore.

At first, the CIA issued statements claiming Paisley was a "low-level analyst," who didn't work on any "sensitive" matters; the Agency said he was simply a part-time consultant, working on "routine administrative matters, with a very limited access to classified information" at the time of his disappearance.

The cover-up did not take long to unravel. John Paisley had, in fact, retained unlimited access to CIA Headquarters and its most closely guarded information.

On the day he vanished, he was working, while sailing, on a top secret report about Soviet weapons capabilities.

The CIA finally conceded that Paisley was a "brilliant analyst." But, the Agency continued to stress, he had never been involved in any "clandestine intelligence activities," and no credible evidence existed to suspect that his death was "other than a suicide." The FBI agreed. So did the Maryland State Police—but it kept its investigation open.

But Paisley's widow Maryann, a onetime CIA employee herself, expressed doubts that the body was actually that of her husband. If it indeed was, she was convinced he'd been murdered. The Senate Select Committee on Intelligence, finding enough *potential* evidence to back up her beliefs—and furious at the CIA's "lack of candor"—then launched its own investigation into Paisley's death.

The Committee's final report was classified Secret in April 1980. The results of an investigation by the White House's Intelligence Oversight Board have not been made public, either. But, according to an FBI memorandum released under the Freedom of Information Act, the White House group was looking into allegations "such as CIA may have murdered Paisley to conceal the identity of a 'mole'; that CIA has failed to furnish all materials in their possession to the FBI; and that Paisley was in some way connected to the Nixon 'Plumbers'" (the Nixon crew whose "dirty tricks" came to light during the Watergate investigation).

Maryann Paisley retained a prominent Washington attorney, Bernard Fensterwald, Jr., to, as she says, "find out what really happened to my husband." Fensterwald, whose clients have included James McCord (the Watergate burglar who broke that scandal in 1973) and James Earl Ray, is no stranger to conspiracy investigations. Fensterwald believes the body was Paisley's, but he, too, is convinced that the fifty-five-year-old CIA official was murdered.

This *Gallery* investigation is based on exclusive access to several thousand pages of FBI and CIA documents released to Fensterwald under the Freedom of Information Act; a number of depositions taken by the attorney from Paisley's acquaintances; and on extensive interviews with Fensterwald, Mrs. Paisley, CIA officials, and others. It probes a number of new questions about John Paisley. For if, as the CIA maintains, he did *not* engage in undercover espionage, but was merely an analyst serving on the overt—or "white"—side of the Agency, then:

- What was the purpose of Paisley's relationship with Soviet defector Yuri Nosenko—and why did they meet three times in the year before Paisley's disappearance?
- What was the nature of an approach made to Paisley by the KGB at the 1971 SALT negotiations in Helsinki?
- What was Paisley's role in preparing the KH-11 electronic surveillance manual that found its way into Soviet hands in February 1978?

- What was a classified CIA phone book doing in Paisley's Washington apartment—and why did he share the eighth floor of that building with eight employees of the Soviet Embassy?
- Finally, was John Paisley looking for the CIA mole? Had he uncovered the mole's identity? Or was he, perhaps, a mole himself?

It was nearing dusk on the Sunday evening of September 24, 1978. Ray Wescott, an engineer for the Goddard Space Research Center, was standing, with his family, peering out across Chesapeake Bay through some high-powered telescopes at the Calvert Cliffs, Maryland nuclear power plant. They watched with curiosity as a sailboat moved to almost within boarding distance of a tugboat and barge going in the opposite direction. But darkness was falling, the plant was closed, and it was time to start heading home.

As the family neared their car—the only one left in a large parking lot—another car suddenly pulled in and stopped right next to theirs, at such an angle that it would be hidden from the guard at the entrance. Three men in business suits and a well-dressed woman got out of the car. One of the men was carrying a large aluminum case. They walked rapidly toward the telescopes. "Let's get out of here," Ray Wescott whispered to his family.

A week would pass before Wescott saw the newspaper story about an abandoned sailboat having washed ashore the next morning, just around the bend from the telescopes on Calvert Cliffs. And about a body that surfaced later, apparently that of a CIA official named John Paisley.

Wescott went to the Maryland State Police. Had he seen the man on the sailboat go aboard the passing barge? the police asked him. No, replied Wescott, he hadn't. Well, said a policeman, someone else did.

Wescott also told his story to the CIA and the FBI. He and his family then made a vow never to discuss what they'd seen that Sunday evening. He was stunned when, two years later, the CIA released a document with his name on it. Stunned and frightened.

"The Paisley case is a very complicated thing," said Wescott. "I'm very uncertain in my own mind what happened there. I'm sure these agencies could get to the bottom of things a lot better than someone who happened to have been in a certain spot at a certain time. But when you give very specific information out and it isn't acted upon, you tend to wonder, Why not?"

There is, of course, no way of knowing whether the sailboat was Paisley's or whether the arrival of the four mysterious individuals was connected to his death. In Paisley's last known radio contact—which his friends say occurred at dusk—he told them he was still anchored and working on some papers near Hooper's Island Lighthouse—a considerable distance from the Wescott family outing. But later, when the body came ashore several nautical miles beyond the range of the Coast Guard's search, the lighthouse location became questionable. Maryann Paisley has believed from the beginning that her husband's reference to being anchored there was really a signal of some kind, because he had once told her the CIA maintained a "safe house" in that area, an estate where the Agency sometimes held secluded rendezvous.

It was 10:25 AM on Monday, September 25, when a ranger at Point Lookout State Park received a call about "a boat apparently adrift in the Chesapeake Bay." Gerald Sword drove quickly down to Hays Beach, where he found a thirty-one-foot sailing sloop listing in a few feet of water. The ranger waded aboard. The boat was abandoned. Scanning the top page of a neatly stacked pile of papers on a cabin table, Sword noticed something about nuclear missiles.

Across the table lay an open briefcase. Its lid, Sword noticed, was up and facing the pile of papers, so that anyone working at the table would've had to have walked around to the other side of the table to use the briefcase. Other papers inside the briefcase were in disarray. One bore the name and address of a Mr. John Paisley. Sword jotted the information down, drove to a nearby farmhouse, and called the Coast Guard.

Information found on board, he told them, indicated that the missing owner was "either a government agent or a person doing an in-depth study on military-type strengths." Would the Coast Guard like Sword to go back and secure it from any passersby? No, the Coast Guard replied, Wait there 15 minutes. Sword felt this a strange request, but complied. When he did return to the sailboat, the Coast Guard was on board. "We no longer have any need for you," they told Sword.

Later, one of these Coast Guardsmen would remember seeing a partially mapped sailing course beside the sloop's wheel, and an open package of luncheon meat and mustard-smeared knife on a sink counter. "It looked like he'd filled in part of the chart and decided to get something to eat," recalled the Coast Guardsman, "and then been interrupted."

But the Coast Guard does not officially admit seeing any "neatly stacked pile of papers." By the time Maryann Paisley arrived on the scene late that night—supposedly the next person to go aboard—those papers were gone. And the briefcase was no longer lying on the table, but on the bed.

According to ranger Sword, later that week a Coast Guard man informed him that "two CIA agents and a lieutenant colonel from the Pentagon had gone aboard. Apparently the information was of a higher classification than the agents were permitted to handle, so the colonel took possession of the papers."

Indeed, considerable time elapsed that first day before anyone bothered to contact Maryann Paisley. That afternoon, the Coast Guard had phoned the Washington-based international accounting firm of Coopers & Lybrand, where Paisley had gone to work a few months earlier as a thirty-six-thousand-dollar-a-year "special assistant" to the president, K. Wayne Smith.

Smith immediately took two measures. First he called the CIA's Office of Strategic Research, then he dispatched an accounting employee to Paisley's nearby apartment. Recently separated from his wife, Paisley had moved to 1500 Massachusetts Avenue when he joined the accounting firm. Oddly enough, he was the only American living on the eighth floor. The building was located not far from the Soviet Embassy, and Paisley's new neighbors were eight Russian nationals. The accounting employee was allowed inside the apartment to remove one item, Paisley's telephone Rolodex. According to Smith, this was done in order to see "if there were other numbers that we could call to try to locate him." But the Rolodex did not stay long at Coopers & Lybrand. A company secretary remembers the FBI coming shortly thereafter to pick it up.

Meanwhile, although her office number was known to Paisley's associates, nobody tried to reach Maryann Paisley at her job at a Washington nursing home. After work that Monday, she drove to a writing course that she was taking at a nearby university, then stopped for dinner with a friend. It was after midnight when she arrived at her split-level suburban home in McLean, Virginia, and noticed that the back gate was unlocked. "Someone's inside," she thought.

"I decided to make a lot of noise in hopes that whoever was there would leave," she remembers. "I had many exits. I went upstairs, started turning all the lights on, and began working my way down. Then the phone rang." It was Phil Wagener, Paisley's former deputy at the CIA. He told her of the boat's discovery, then agreed to drive Maryann and her twenty-year-old daughter the eighty miles to Chesapeake Bay.

If anyone had been in the Paisley home, he vanished in the course of the phone call.

It was 2 AM when Wagener and the Paisleys stopped at tiny Solomons Island to pick up Colonel Norman Wilson. Paisley used Wilson's dock facilities. Wilson, himself a retired intelligence official, had spoken to Paisley the previous afternoon. "Leave the lights on at the pier. I'll be back after dark," Paisley had said. "The only unusual thing," Wilson would remember later, "was it took him quite a while to answer the call. Normally he keeps his set within arm's reach of wherever he is on the boat."

When they reached the site of the abandoned *Brillig* (a name selected by Paisley from the Lewis Carroll nonsense poem "Jabberwocky"), Colonel Wilson went aboard with Mrs. Paisley. "I didn't see anything that looked classified," he told the CIA's Wagener. But he didn't report any "neatly stacked pile of papers," either.

Back in Washington, the Paisleys' twenty-two-year-old son, Eddie, had gone to his father's apartment but was refused admittance. This seems odd, in light of the accounting firm's easy access. But even stranger was what Eddie Paisley saw when he did get in on Tuesday morning: his father's papers were strewn everywhere; a camera, tape recorder, and several hours of tapes detailing the Paisley family history were missing; and several nine-millimeter bullets were scattered on the floor of a closet.

For a week, while the Coast Guard made a helicopter and boat search near Hooper's Island, Paisley's disappearance went publicly unreported. Fearing another burglary, the family went to Paisley's apartment again and brought all his remaining effects home. Then, on October 1, several miles from where the *Brillig* had run aground, a bloated and decomposed body was pulled from the bay. Despite being laden with two belts containing 38 pounds of diving weights, it had floated to the surface. The victim had been shot once behind the left ear with a nine-millimeter bullet.

The body's location, however, Maryann Paisley was told by the Coast Guard, suggested that it probably wasn't her husband. Her first suspicion had been that he might have been kidnapped by the KGB. The weekend of his disappearance, two Soviets connected with the United Nations had been found guilty of espionage in New York. "I thought it could be quick revenge," Mrs. Paisley says. "A message from the Russians."

For a long time, that identification was in doubt. There were sizable discrepancies in height and weight between the corpse and Paisley, although decomposition can cause such changes. Nobody from the family ever identified the body, which, because of its condition, was cremated. "They encouraged cremation without identification, which seems odd," says attorney Fensterwald.

Now, in his Washington office, the lean, bespectacled attorney sits pondering "some other things in this case that defy any explanation. One is the CIA's insistence that they didn't have the fingerprints of their employees, which they claimed for weeks until finally somebody came up with Paisley's prints, supposedly through the FBI. The CIA has since—I think by mistake or accident—released a dispatch dated October 1, 1978, which clearly indicates they had the prints all along. So they were lying about it. What motivated them?"

Originally, the CIA said that a set of prints they'd sent the FBI when Paisley joined the Agency in 1953 had somehow been lost. Eventually the FBI came up with prints that had been voluntarily submitted by a "Jack" Paisley in 1940. The age, hometown, and parents' names all matched up. So did the prints, which the FBI had taken from the body before cremation. Fensterwald says that the fingerprint evidence "no longer gives us ground to argue" whether the body was Paisley's. But Fensterwald still has doubts. As for the official verdict of suicide, Fensterwald is certain it is nonsense.

"There's no sign that anybody fired a shot aboard that vessel," he says. "No gun was ever found. There wasn't any suicide note. He apparently was in the process of eating a meal when whatever happened occurred. He had talked to a number of people that day, in person and by radio, and certainly didn't seem depressed or like anything was wrong with him. According to the official theory, he jumped in the water with the gun and then blew his head off, having put two diving weights on to begin with."

Nine months after the body's discovery, Calvert County Coroner Dr. George Weems came forward at a press conference to reveal that he'd been the first to examine it and had seen markings on the neck indicating it had been "squeezed, or had a rope around it—the type of things you see when people are strangled."

To probe the mystery of John Arthur Paisley, we must first go back and trace the known record of his life. Born in Sand Springs, Oklahoma in 1923, John was two when his mother walked out on his alcoholic father and moved her three children to Phoenix, Arizona. There, young John became a radio buff, working with homemade crystal sets. Later he put that knowledge to work in World War II as a radio operator in the Merchant Marine. Then, in the late 1940s, he worked in Palestine for a while, operating the communications network for the United Nations' Bernadotte Mission.

He met Maryann McLeavy when she was working in New York for Tom Yawkey, the late millionaire owner of the Boston Red Sox. The Paisleys were married in March 1949 and John, while working part-time as a Marine Radio Operator for various steamship companies, spent four years attending the University of Chicago.

He took a degree in International Relations, specializing in Soviet affairs, then traveled to Washington with 15 other graduates in search of jobs.

One of John's former professors had gone to work for the CIA. It was a young agency then, chartered in 1947 to analyze Cold War problems and not yet the "rogue elephant"—as Senator Frank Church would later come to characterize it. Paisley was at sea on a steamship when word came that he alone—among all his classmates—had gained employment in the nation's capital. His old professor admired his radio background and helped secure him a CIA position in 1953, in a branch that kept track of Soviet electronics.

Paisley rose rapidly at the CIA during the Eisenhower years. He went on loan to the National Security Agency, which monitors worldwide electronic communications, for a couple of years. Returning to the CIA in 1957, he studied the Russian language in order to probe Soviet technical journals and intercepted intelligence.

It is a very neat, self-contained picture: the anonymous analyst burrowing between the lines of *Pravda*, ferreting out economic anomalies. But after his disappearance, Maryann Paisley came across quite another picture of John in private talks with several undercover CIA agents. A tall woman in her early fifties, she too had worked briefly for the CIA, as a computer programmer on the clandestine side. She and John rarely talked together about their intelligence activities; that was the nature of the beast. Yet it still came as a surprise when she asked the two agents whether John had done clandestine work. "Yes, he loved it," they replied.

What *kind* of undercover work? The agents would not be more specific with Maryann. But she believes it must have had to do, at least in part, with the CIA's interrogations of a number of Soviet officials who, over the past 20 years, had defected to the West with vital secrets.

"I do know that John interviewed most of the major defectors," she says. "A lot of times. From time to time, he would talk about whether you could believe a defector's material. But he never mentioned anybody by name."

My own interest in the Paisley case had begun not long after the discovery of the body, when I received a newspaper clipping about the "CIA Mystery Death" from a man I knew who had specialized in undercover counterintelligence work. He had once served as a double agent in the CIA–KGB spy wars, and he had told me about a word that the Russians use in identifying their intelligence sources. The term was *nash*, the Russian word for "ours." "When the KGB says 'He is *nash*,' they mean 'He is ours,'" my source had said.

Now, in this newspaper clipping, he had drawn a circle around a paragraph identifying Paisley's job in the Office of Strategic Research. At the top of the clipping, he had typed: "Was he '*nash*'? He was '*nash*'!"

However my source had come across this information, I had come to trust his insider's tips on the intelligence business. Long before it was publicly acknowledged as possible, he had also told me of a number of KGB penetrations into the CIA's Soviet affairs area—including, he indicated, a mole near the top. Now he seemed to say John Paisley had been such a mole.

Some officials in the CIA apparently had similar suspicions, at least after Paisley's disappearance. A CIA memo of September 28, 1978, discusses a review of Paisley's file that "brought to light several items which in themselves are fairly innocuous but taken as a whole can be somewhat troublesome."

Indeed, says Maryann Paisley, as a student in Chicago, John kept a huge ham set in the center of their living room and sizable antenna on the roof. "He talked to a lot of people. He played chess by radio with somebody in Russia, I remember. It was all in code, not verbal. John was a Morse Code man." Paisley was a student of electronics and the Soviet Union, two fascinations which would put him in good stead at the CIA. But might these fascinations have been less innocent than they seemed?

To look deeper at this question, we must turn now to the Kennedy years. The early 1960s appeared to be a time of several counterintelligence coups for the CIA. First came a defector named Anatoli Golitsin. But in addition to the Soviet secrets that Golitsin brought with him, he carried a dire warning. The CIA, he said, had been penetrated near the top by a KGB mole. "The mole," Golitsin added, "was activated in 1958."

Then, in the immediate aftermath of President Kennedy's assassination, came another Soviet defector. This was Yuri Nosenko, a KGB counterintelligence official. He came bearing news that the KGB had never even talked to the

President's alleged assassin, Lee Harvey Oswald, during his 32 months in the USSR Nosenko also said that there was *no* Soviet mole inside the CIA.

Golitsin insisted Nosenko was a fake who was sent by the Russians to mislead the CIA. For more than three years, the CIA then kept Nosenko in isolation in a windowless cell and subjected him to often brutal interrogation. CIA sources say it was Paisley who wrote out questions seeking to establish whether or not Nosenko was legitimate; then he analyzed the defector's responses.

While a number of inconsistencies turned up in his other information, Nosenko held firm on the key questions about Oswald and the potential mole. In 1968, although a bitter CIA internal dispute continued to rage over Nosenko, he was officially deemed bona fide, given a large sum of money, and set up with a new identity and home in North Carolina. Paisley was apparently a key figure in clearing him.

Back in the mid-1960s, Maryann Paisley remembers John's getting furious when the CIA refused to publish some of a defector's data in its intelligence newsletter. "This would have been Nosenko," she says. The defector's information corroborated her husband's own analysis of Soviet missile strengths. "What are we here for if we don't do something with this kind of information?" she remembers him saying. He even resigned from the CIA and accepted a job at the Defense Department, only to reconsider when the CIA published the material.

Why was Paisley so intent on deeming Nosenko legitimate? If anyone at the CIA wondered about this, it didn't seem to stand in the way of Paisley's continuing advancement. A workaholic, his seventy-hour weeks saw him rise to division chief and then, in October 1969, to become Deputy Director of Strategic Research. This gave him a "supergrade" government clearance of GS-17, the second highest grade possible at the CIA.

Following a year's sabbatical at London's Imperial Defense College—a period when Maryann says she doesn't know what John was really doing there, but remembers him using an assumed name—Paisley came back to Washington in 1971. CIA appointment logs reveal that he was interested in just about every major foreign policy area during those final Nixon years: cables with Saigon; the India-Pakistan War of 1971; Chinese missiles; ocean surveillance; Soviet options in the Yom Kippur War of 1973; and monitoring of the Strategic Arms Limitation Talks (SALT).

This last item found Paisley going abroad again in 1971, where he served for a time in Helsinki as a CIA adviser at the sensitive SALT talks.

According to CIA sources who do not wish to be identified, something else happened to Paisley in Helsinki. One day he reported to his CIA superiors that an approach had been made to him by the KGB. The Russians had offered him a substantial sum in exchange for information about the U.S. negotiating position. The CIA advised Paisley to go ahead and "take the pitch." It would be a means of learning more about what the Soviets knew, or wanted to know, as well as of feeding them some misleading information. Paisley is said to have gone ahead. How much accurate information he passed on is not known.

Back in Washington, there had been press leaks on several sensitive subjects, including the SALT talks. According to his wife, "John was assigned to find out where the leaks from within the intelligence community might be coming from." Uncovering sources of leaks was also one of the early duties of the White House "Plumbers" unit. At least on this subject, Paisley served as the CIA's liaison with the Plumbers. This is verified by several internal meetings concerning Paisley and Watergate, recorded in the CIA's appointment logs.

"18 August 1971—John Paisley came up re: . . . that Ehrlichman [Nixon's aide, John] may call the Director and request more on 'leaks.'"

"23 May 1973—Session with Paisley re: 'Plumbers.'"

"25 April 1974—Paisley returned call re: memo to IG [CIA Inspector General] on Watergate."

When shown these appointment logs, Phil Wagener could only shake his head in wonder. "This is the first I've heard about this," said Paisley's former deputy. "It stuns me, frankly. The job John had was so demanding, and this is a totally different area. It is like there'd be two John Paisleys."

Paisley's assignment to look for leaks paralleled an even more sensitive probe within the CIA: the ongoing search for the mole. During the early 1970s, this involved the CIA's seeking to learn who was in regular contact with four Soviet defectors, and why. One of these was Yuri Nosenko. Another was an ex-Soviet Navy captain, Nicholas Shadrin. As the CIA had done with Paisley himself at the SALT talks, the Agency was using Shadrin in a "double" role. The defector was continuing to feed selected information back to the KGB. It was Paisley who had the task of collecting the data provided Shadrin, then analyzing the KGB response.

The CIA hoped Shadrin's role might somehow lead them to the mole. The mole probe was primarily the responsibility of the CIA's counterintelligence branch, but, as ex-CIA official Victor Marchetti notes, "To try to track him down, you would need somebody to evaluate the information. Paisley may have been made the contact man on this matter with Counterintelligence."

Yet in June 1974, at the age of 50, John Paisley abruptly retired. His wife says he was in line for another promotion, but instead he decided to quit the Agency and "just live on his sailboat for a year." He was given the Distinguished Medal of Honor for his 21 years of service.

However, according to *Time*, the CIA's mole search had taken an interesting turn at the time of Paisley's departure. It was focusing on his own department, the Office of Strategic Research. Could the very man the CIA had trusted not only to analyze KGB data but to feed duplicitous data to the Soviets really have been deceiving the CIA?

Nobody ever had a chance to find out. For, soon after Paisley's retirement, a major shake-up occurred inside the CIA. James Angleton, the longtime head of Counterintelligence and the most fanatic prober in search of the mole, was fired in a power struggle with a new director, William Colby. Colby didn't believe in Angleton's mole theory. Soon, amid revelations about CIA domestic spying, drug experiments, and even assassination plots against foreign leaders, the Agency was in a near shambles. Several hundred operators lost jobs.

Almost overlooked in this shifting tide of events was the mysterious disappearance of Nicholas Shadrin, late in 1975. The defector vanished in Vienna, when he left his hotel for a rendezvous with his KGB contacts. The lingering Angleton faction of the CIA was convinced that Shadrin had been betrayed by the mole and murdered by the KGB. But the Agency's mole quest had come to a halt with Angleton's dismissal.

Perhaps it was coincidence, then, that Shadrin's own sailboat had been moored near John Paisley's boat on Solomon's Island. Perhaps it was also coincidence that, shortly after his retirement, Paisley bought a new sailboat (the *Brillig*) in North Carolina and anchored for several months not far from Yuri Nosenko's secret residence there. The CIA, in a seemingly hedged statement issued in 1979, said: "There is no official, recorded basis for the allegation of a relationship between Paisley and Nosenko." Other Agency people insist that the American and the Russian became friends after Paisley officially left the CIA.

But when Paisley returned from his year of sailing in mid-1975, any CIA suspicions about him seemed to have been swallowed up during the Agency shake-up. Bringing some of his former CIA aides along, Paisley worked for a while under an Agency contract at the MITRE Corporation, researching improvements in the U.S. spy satellite program.

Then, in August 1976, he accepted a CIA offer to coordinate a top secret reevaluation of Soviet strategic capabilities and intentions. He became the go-between for an "A team" of intelligence community specialists, and a "B team" of civilian experts (such as Paul Nitze, who had been the chief U.S. negotiator at the SALT talks). Basically, Paisley's job was to provide the B team with classified documents. He thus had access to the highest classified materials on the USSR—perhaps even more access than when he'd worked full time at the CIA.

Soon, though, the two teams were feuding over how hard a line to take on the Soviets. Paisley was considered a dove, and a B team academician who disagreed with his views leaked Paisley's name to the *New York Times*. Paisley was furious. "The fact that I'm on this project is not supposed to be known," he said. Maryann remembers George Bush, then the CIA Director, followed up by sending John a sweatshirt with "A team" on the front and "B team" on the back. An insider's joke, it was an attempt to humor John's ill feelings.

But a sudden, simultaneous loss of CIA secrets to the Soviets was no joke at all. The first revelation about this came on December 22, 1976 when retired CIA man Edwin G. Moore was arrested after leaving a package of classified documents at a Soviet residence (he was later convicted of selling classified documents to the Soviet Union, and given a life sentence). Moore had been smuggling material on mapmaking and logistics out of CIA Headquarters. Ironically, he and Paisley were acquainted. "They came into the Agency at the same time," says Maryann, "and went through a training program together."

Three weeks after Moore's arrest, two young California men, Christopher Boyce and Andrew Lee, were picked up for passing thousands of CIA documents to KGB agents over a two-year period (convicted, they were given long prison terms; Boyce, however, later escaped, and is at large). Some of these concerned secret satellite systems the U.S. planned to use to verify the SALT treaty.

Then came the loss of a top secret manual detailing the operations of America's most important and complex surveillance satellite. It was known as the KH-11 system, a new means of gathering information on Russian strategic developments. Using at least three complicated sensing systems, and lenses so accurate they could distinguish between civilians and military men from an altitude of 200 to 300 miles, the satellite was even equipped with a side-looking radar device that could "see" through over-cast. CIA memos record that Paisley had been in the study group that created the KH-11. Other CIA sources say Paisley helped write the KH-11 Manual, and instructed operators which sites in Israel, China, and the USSR should be kept under surveillance. The KH-11 was going to be used to verify Soviet compliance with the SALT treaty.

But in March 1978—a few months after the CIA admits giving Paisley a briefing on the KH-11—this manual found its way into Soviet hands. William Kampiles, a twenty-three-year-old former CIA employee, was arrested and charged with the theft of a number of copies (Kampiles received a forty-year sentence for selling the manual to the Soviets). The CIA believes it is possible the KGB had Kampiles write a letter that led to his arrest. The CIA feared the KGB sacrificed Kampiles to provide the U.S. with a plausible explanation for the manual's loss—and to protect the mole.

After this intelligence disaster, President Carter personally went to CIA Headquarters to demand that the Agency close its security breaches. Now the CIA began a desperate, renewed search for a mole. A former CIA station chief named Cleveland Cram was brought out of retirement to review all cases of Soviet defectors. In April 1978, Cram determined that at least four defectors "probably" were double agents, deliberately planted by the Soviets to undermine the CIA. A watchful eye was again being kept on all the contacts of Yuri Nosenko.

During that same April, John Paisley moved into the apartment complex whose floor he would share with eight employees of the Soviet Embassy. Up until then—after separating from Maryann—he had lived around for a few months, sometimes with a girlfriend, sometimes at the homes of his CIA associates. But when he went to work for Coopers & Lybrand, according to president K. Wayne Smith, "John said he would like to have an apartment within walking distance of the office, and I said that makes good sense."

"John laughed about it," Maryann remembers. "He said, 'I'm across the street from the National Rifle Association and down the block from the Russian Embassy—what could go wrong?'" But, she adds, her husband's interest in the CIA's mole theories were continuing, too. "The CIA was doing a lot of work in evaluating what these defectors had to say, because they were all trying to implicate one another at that time. I know John was still working on this very late in the game."

At the same time—as CIA memorandums attest—Paisley maintained his "continuing unescorted access to Headquarters," and to "a multitude of compart-mented programs." He also met on a periodic basis with Carter's CIA Director, Admiral Stansfield Turner. Their talks included Paisley's analysis about what the loss of a "highly sensitive listening station" in Iran would mean to U.S. satellite overflights of Russia.

According to his CIA acquaintances, a change came over John Paisley in his last months. Phil Wagener says, "He suddenly seemed to become calm and serene, and some friends later interpreted that he'd already made up his mind to commit suicide and didn't have any more conflict." Colonel Norman Wilson remembers Paisley watching a *Mission: Impossible* episode on TV. "He laughingly used the word 'self-destruct' a couple of times," says Wilson. Shortly before Paisley turned 55, Wilson recalls him saying that he "didn't plan to exceed the speed limit."

Betty Myers, a girlfriend that Paisley had been seeing for several years, also believes it was a suicide. John was often depressed, she says, and enjoyed quoting her melancholy poems such as "Richard Cory." She says she told him she was leaving him shortly before his last sail.

But Maryann Paisley, who remained in touch with John, takes a different view. "He was more himself than he'd been in a long time. He'd gotten his sense of humor back. He'd attended a session of Lifespring [a group-encounter movement] and loved it. We'd sat down together and gone back over our marriage. He felt bad because he'd always taught the kids that to withdraw, and not show how you feel, is a good thing. He had long discussions with them about how mistaken he'd been.

"I always said that John would never be an invalid. He would choose suicide. But he wasn't in ill health, he didn't have money problems like the CIA has said, he didn't have any motive. We were in touch. I'd seen him that Thursday before he sailed, talked to him on Friday. I would have known if something was wrong."

So let us turn again to those last days of September 1978. The day before Paisley's last voyage, ex-CIA Director Richard Helms was testifying before the

House Assassinations Committee about Yuri Nosenko. Helms said he did not consider Nosenko "a bona fide defector."

On Sunday, September 25, Paisley showed up at Solomon's Island in a rented car; he told friends his van was in for repairs. At that same hour, a notification that he was due for a CIA security check arrived in his Washington office. It had been since June 1967, that he'd been asked to take part in the Agency's "Reinvestigation Program." His CIA contract and "Visitor No Escort Badge" were to expire on September 30. Whether or not Paisley had any advance knowledge of the check is unknown.

It was a portentous weekend: the Camp David Summit accords between Egypt and Israel were taking place. On the Chesapeake Bay, a thin, bearded man anchored his beloved *Brillig* early on a warm Sunday afternoon, then set to work on his final report for the CIA about the secret A team/B team project. He radioed his friends he'd be in late.

Then a curious pattern of events occurred. A CIA document dated September 28, 1978 reports: "Lieutenant Cook of the Portsmouth, Virginia, Coast Guard Station advised that on the night of Mr. Paisley's disappearance, a Soviet vessel was proceeding up Chesapeake Bay, and on the same night there was an unusual amount of communications traffic from the Soviet summer residence on the eastern shore of Chesapeake Bay."

The CIA conducted its own investigation, determining not that a Soviet ship had been in the area, but indeed that two Polish vessels had. The CIA had no explanation for the "unusual amount of communications traffic from the Soviet summer residence," which, according to one of the covert agents Maryann Paisley spoke to, is "really a Soviet safe house, where the KGB has kept people." It is located not far from the CIA's *own* safe house, which the Agency admits is some 15 miles north of the lighthouse where Paisley supposedly anchored. Such are the incongruities in the jabberwocky world of the CIA and KGB, where houses are never very safe places to be.

A sailboat is its own "safe house." There, a man may work on private papers without interruption, and be secure from outside influences. There, a man's world is at his fingertips. At least that's the way it must have seemed to John Paisley, who also found considerable freedom to indulge his lifelong passion for ham radio. Possibly too much freedom.

Although the CIA says it found nothing unusual about the four pieces of sophisticated radio gear found on the *Brillig* there is the likelihood that someone may have removed another item: a classified device known as a "burst transceiver." Basically, this is a scrambler for secret communications.

The *New York Times*, basing its story on a Senate Intelligence Committee source, reported Paisley's ownership of a burst transceiver early in 1979. The CIA went to some lengths to deny this, for, if Paisley had used such a device on the *Brillig*, it seems doubtful Paisley would have been transmitting to the CIA—what necessity would there have been in that? It is far more likely that any such communication would have been aimed somewhere else—perhaps toward a certain "summer residence on the eastern shore of Chesapeake Bay."

Maryann Paisley did find it odd that her husband's sailboat antennas were permanently tuned to one station. Then there was his radio schedule. "With his ham friends, he had a morning schedule," she says. "But he had another schedule at five o'clock almost every night. And that is the time that we can't find out who he talked to."

Remember the missing papers that ranger Sword had seen stacked neatly on the *Brillig*'s cabin table? A CIA memo says only: "Coast Guard personnel found some papers dealing with the Cuban crisis, but Lieutenant Murray was not sure if they were classified or not." Other CIA sources say Paisley had removed a number of classified documents from Headquarters. These included a top secret report of U.S. surveillance capacities and—a more frightening possibility—detailed inventories of the American nuclear arsenal.

A few months after Paisley's disappearance, Maryann Paisley had a meeting with James Angleton, the departed CIA official whose career passion had been the search for an Agency mole.

"*He* interviewed *me*, it wasn't the other way around," she says. "He asked me if John always wore a beard, because people used so many names. He didn't memorize names but looks, and he didn't recognize pictures of John with a beard.

"I told him that I questioned the identity of the body. The only thing he said was that, if it wasn't John's body, he would be able to find out and he would let me know. I've never heard from him."

James Angleton, even in retirement, was obviously still on the case—looking for where the bodies were buried.

So what really happened to John Paisley? His girlfriend and many CIA acquaintances maintain he was simply a middle-aged man who'd left his family and could no longer cope with life. His widow is convinced that he was killed—"I just don't know if it was murder or execution"—but refuses to believe John was anything but a loyal CIA man.

But it seems increasingly likely that the truth lies buried somewhere in these questions: Was Paisley a mole who feared he was about to be exposed? Was he murdered—or spirited away—by Soviet agents before he could be found out? Or did the CIA arrange his murder—or disappearance—to avoid the humiliation of admitting it had been deceived, for more than 25 years, by a Soviet double agent?

The answers, shrouded in the mist that surrounds the CIA–KGB spy wars, may never be known. It must be noted, though, that while the murky waters may have claimed John Paisley, the electronics genius who loved to communicate on the radio, after his disappearance, no further satellite secrets are believed to have been passed to the Soviets. Perhaps, after all, there is light at the end of the tunnel of a mole.

27

A Visit to the KGB's Inner Sanctum

On the Ides of March in 1991, during the last months of the Communist Soviet Union, I traveled to Moscow to write a magazine story on the first grassroots conference between Russian and American environmentalists. It was the era of Gorbachev, *glasnost*, and *perestroika*. The Berlin Wall had already come down. The Cold War was ending, and it seemed as appropriate a moment as any to do something else while I was in the vicinity—approach the KGB about opening certain of its files on the Kennedy assassination.

On its face, my quest might have seemed quixotic, if not downright mad. After all, the *Komitet Gosudarstvennoi Bezopasnosti* (KGB) had a reputation as perhaps the most ruthless intelligence operation in the world. In the past, foreigners had been arrested, even executed, for messing around with its spies. And I was in search of secret knowledge about a historical event that still had a capacity to raise a dagger from behind the cloak.

Still, this might be my one and only chance. Somewhere in the KGB's archives, the "confession" of Richard Case Nagell surely still existed. And, I thought, there was a way to make a case that revealing it at this point in history could be a good thing, in terms of the American attitude toward the Russians. According to Nagell, their intelligence agency, after all, had tried to prevent Kennedy's assassination.

So, on the third day of the environmental conference, I approached a young American woman who worked for the Natural Resources Defense Council and was fluent in Russian, and asked if she would be my interpreter on this curious mission. I told her I knew there could be some risk involved, given the sensitivity of the subject matter, and would certainly understand if she declined. Somewhat to my surprise, she agreed to accompany me.

We were on a bus heading into the center of Moscow when another young American woman came over and plopped down beside me. She was with the Environmental Research Foundation: short, bespectacled, cute, and full of enthusiasm. She had gotten wind that I was going to try to get inside KGB headquarters (apparently, it hadn't taken long for word to get out at the conference). She'd been reading spy novels ever since she was a little girl at her father's knee, and please, please could she come along too, it would be a dream come true. Let's call her June. "Well, June," I said, "I don't know, the KGB isn't exactly your typical tourist destination. This could even be dangerous." But she was insistent, and I gave in.

So, accompanied by not one but two American women, I hailed a cab at Red Square and had my interpreter ask the driver if he'd take us to Dzerzhinsky Square. "Kay Gay Bay?" he responded incredulously, and shook his head no. The second taxi contained an apparently more adventurous sort, and he beckoned us inside. He immediately began offering me tins of black caviar at ten bucks a pop, hard currency only please. Buy two, get the ride for free. I did, and dropped the pair of tins into my briefcase.

The driver grew philosophical as, about a mile away from Red Square, we neared an imposing stone building that sprawled the length of an entire city block. "On this street," he said, "people never stop, they just keep on walking." Not to worry, he continued, there were actually four KGB buildings in this area, and he would take us to one that customarily received visitors. Pointing again at the main KGB headquarters as we turned the corner, he added, "In that one, there are as many floors below"—he paused briefly—"as there are floors above." He was referring, my interpreter added with a weak smile, to the old section of the KGB known as Lubyanka Prison—corridors of terror and torture under Stalin. "I see," I said coolly.

A couple of blocks further, the taxi dropped us off at a nondescript building with an unmarked red door. A young uniformed soldier responded to our knock. As I had instructed her, my interpreter explained that I was an American journalist and had written a letter—which was true, except it was in my briefcase—and that we had now come for my scheduled appointment with Major General Alexander Karbainov. That was, of course, not true, but Karbainov *was* a real name. I'd read in a recent issue of *National Geographic* that he was chief of Public Relations for the "new" KGB.

The soldier looked a bit nonplussed, but ushered the three of us into a small waiting area with six chairs and a little statue of Lenin with fake flowers at his feet. A mother and her child were sitting next to a door with a combination lock that you could only enter by punching a code. I observed a woman do so, and emerge again carrying a stack of files. A couple more people wearing fur coats soon joined the waiting group. Twice the soldier returned to say that someone would be with us shortly.

After about twenty minutes, a stocky, mustached man wearing a tweed sport coat and a scarf strode into the room. He did not offer his name, or ask for ours. Nor was there any request for identification. He merely asked our purpose in being here, and my interpreter repeated what she'd told the soldier. He said he would be back, and passed through the coded door. In another few minutes, he returned and informed us that the name Alexander Karbainov was not familiar, could it be Yevgeny? No, I assured him, it was Alexander. Then he disappeared again.

This time when he came back, the man said, "I spoke to someone who will see you. But we must go to another building." So our trio trundled out onto the street. He and my interpreter took the lead, talking about the weather: "This is the time of year when winter fights with spring," he told her poetically. Turning onto the street where our taxi driver had said people "just keep on walking," we stopped at an entryway halfway down—and walked up a few steps and into the notorious Lubyanka.

We were immediately surrounded by three soldiers who it seemed had not been told to expect us. They were extremely suspicious despite our accompanying guide. One walked briskly to pick up a telephone. The other two backed off but stood a short distance away glaring at us. I noticed an elevator at the top of a flight of marble stairs. The phone rang and, after a brief conversation, our guide was motioned over. He returned to tell us that we'd gotten there too quickly, the person we were to see had yet to arrive.

"As soon he comes down, I will leave you in his hands," he said. He smiled and asked what I liked best about Moscow. "Oh, Saint Basil's Cathedral in Red Square," I responded exuberantly and then, realizing I was in the presence of The Party, hastened to add: "And, of course, Lenin's tomb. We were very impressed with Lenin's tomb!"

Then, for the first time, he asked pointedly what my interest was in paying this little visit to the KGB. I really didn't want to say, especially with the three soldiers clearly bending their ears in our direction. And I never had to answer because, suddenly, the elevator door at the top of the marble staircase opened. And a man simply stood there, staring down at our incongruous party.

He, too, wore a tweed jacket, with a tie and checkered pants that didn't go with the outfit, and he sported a furry brown mustache. He looked to be in his early fifties. After what seemed like an eternity, but was probably no more than thirty seconds, he came to the edge of the staircase and beckoned us up with his hand. Along with our guide, we followed him into the waiting elevator. He had pocked skin and a mole on his right cheekbone, I noticed, feeling very much like James Bond sizing up Dr. No. A mirror was affixed to the back of the elevator. Fairly obviously, we were being watched.

To my considerable relief, the elevator went up instead of down into the bowels of old Lubyanka. It came to a jarring halt at the third floor. As we walked out into a hallway, the first object to greet us was a coat-rack. The two KGB gentlemen helped us all off with ours, ladies first. Our guide then bid us farewell. I asked if he smoked and, when he said yes, offered him a pack of Marlboros—"the thing to do," I'd been told—but he politely declined and vanished around a corner.

We turned left down one hallway, then left again. The winding corridors felt like something out of Kafka. Every door we passed was closed. Not a sign of habitation. The walls and floor were fashioned from cheap wood paneling.

We walked along on a red runner rug with pastel flowers. Finally we came to a room with a sign in English that said: PRESS BAR. Our mustached host opened the door and motioned us in. The room was vast, with white curtains on the far wall behind a bar and a considerable number of glasses. Another man was waiting here, a short, pudgy fellow with oily, slicked-back hair and wearing a blue serge three-piece suit. His expression was stern. He did not offer to shake hands.

The two men pulled some large green-cushioned chairs around a small coffee table and the three of us sank into them—my translator nearest the furry mustache, me to her right, June across from us and the blue suit next to the lady who loved spy tales. I glanced up to see a camera focused on me from the wall across the room.

Once again, no names or credentials were requested, though my interpreter did explain that we were all here on an environmental exchange. Mustache turned to face me and began by asking politely, "So ... what brings you to KGB? What can we do for you?" I explained that I was writing a book about the Kennedy assassination, and interested in learning whether they could help me. Mustache sat back a bit in his chair and proffered a little smile. I went on that I had the names, from other books, of two KGB officers named Kostikov and Nechiporenko who had served in Mexico in 1963 and I would like to interview them if they were available. I thought I detected a spark of recognition to the names.

Trying to pack as much as I could into my introductory remarks, I added that my book contained new information—about a right-wing American conspiracy to kill Kennedy, and about the KGB learning of this ahead of time and trying to prevent it, while U.S. intelligence agencies also knew but did not lift a finger. I raised a finger of my own, the index, for emphasis.

Mustache nodded several times before hearing the translation, as if he understood my English but wasn't saying so. Then he said he remembered very well the day Kennedy was assassinated. He had been a schoolboy at the time. Kennedy was a remarkable man, he continued, and it was a very sad day for America. "Yet there have been many books written about the assassination," my interpreter translated, and to my surprise the man began to list off several, starting with Manchester's *Death of a President*.

Blue suit stood up and closed the doors to the room. When he sat down again, he spoke for the first time. "He says he really does not understand," said my interpreter. "Specifically, what new information do I have? Would I repeat this please, and clarify?"

So I did. Then mustache piped up again. "He says he has not seen anything about this in any of the books."

"I know," I replied, "that's because this is new information."

"Well, this is very interesting, very interesting," he added. "But what is your source for this information?"

"A man," I said evenly, "who worked for the CIA—*and* the KGB."

Neither man seemed thrilled to hear about a double agent. Or at least that I *knew* about a double agent.

Blue suit leaned forward in his chair. "And what is the *name* of your source?" he demanded.

Mustache was more level-headed about it. "Can you tell us his name, or is it a secret source?" he asked after a pause.

"If I tell you," I said, "is it likely you can help me?"

"It is very difficult in any case, very complex." Then he added something to the effect that he doubted the KGB knew of any assassination plans in advance, he'd never heard this before.

"I am not looking to put the KGB in a bad light with my investigation," I told him. "In fact, I believe in this era of openness, the fact that your agency sought to stop Kennedy's assassination would be helpful to the relations between our two countries. The story needs to be told."

"If it is true, it should be told," mustache said. He did not push further for the name.

I said I was certain the KGB had a file about this, since my source had been in Moscow in 1968 and had written down everything he knew for the KGB. Mustache shifted in his chair.

Blue suit spoke again. "What you need to do," he said, "is to lay all this out in a letter, with specific questions."

"And drop it in a box at Kuznetsky Most 22," mustache added.

"You must be specific, official, tell us who your publisher is," said blue suit. "And you should be sure to include the name of your source."

I mentioned that I had a letter in my briefcase which spelled out much of this information. But they expressed no interest whatsoever in seeing it. They had issued my instructions, and I needed to follow them, that was all there was to it.

"Well, is there someone I should address my letter to?" I asked.

"No," mustache said, "simply to KGB of USSR."

"Well, I will only be in Moscow for another week."

"That is all right, we can get in touch with you in the United States," said blue suit.

"That is, if we can help you at all," added mustache.

When I asked if they would seek to find any and all files on my source, he responded: "We will look, and if we have the information we'll find out about it. And we would then help you."

"All right," I said. "Fair enough."

The two men rose. Our twenty-five-minute meeting inside the KGB's inner sanctum seemed to have reached a conclusion. Back by the elevator, they insisted on helping both women put on their overcoats once more. I asked them each if they smoked. Blue suit nodded yes, but mustache became flustered and said a quick *"nyet"* to my offer of cigarettes.

As we descended toward the street, I asked whether they received many foreign visitors like ourselves these days. "In the past, never!" mustache said. "Today, not so many. Mostly journalists and ... *serious* authors." His emphasis on the word hinted that he might not consider me in that category. I asked whether the CIA would photograph us as we walked out the door. But my interpreter thought better of translating my question.

Back outside in the crisp late afternoon air, I noticed a long line of people queued up across Dzerzhinsky Square. It turned out to be for the largest toy store in all of Moscow.

I had thought it discrete to take no notes during the meeting, but now was intent on jotting down everything I could recall while it was still fresh. So we headed straight for the nearby Intourist Hotel—a place I vaguely recalled Lee Harvey Oswald frequenting when he first came to Moscow—and walked toward the bar. I spied a young fellow reading a paperback of a John le Carré novel, and thought it appropriate to take a table next to his.

"What's the book?" I asked.

"Smiley's People," the dark-haired American replied, but rather brusquely.

So, with my two female companions, I launched into putting our heads together to recollect our strange journey. June, I noticed, was an especially good observer. She had a wonderful eye for details—what the men were wearing, what the décor of the rooms looked like—and for this I expressed my gratitude, because I'd been too intent upon the conversation to notice these things.

After about five minutes, the American reading the spy novel abruptly rose and made a beeline for the exit.

Back at our hotel on the outskirts of Moscow that night, a kid who roamed the halls peddling various wares in exchange for hard currency came running up to me. In English, he said: "Want to buy KGB T-shirt?" I cracked up laughing. "Kid, you don't know how funny that is!" I said and, of course, bought one.

I told the whole story to my conference roommate, a scientist for EarthWatch named David Silverberg. He was going into town the next day to visit a couple of old friends from Princeton. When he returned that following evening, he took me aside immediately.

"This is rich," David said. "When I went to see my friend Richard, who's over here studying the Soviet economy, he was extremely nervous. The first words out of his mouth were, 'You're not going to believe what happened to me yesterday! I was sitting in the Intourist, when this guy came up and asked me about the book I was reading. He had these two women assistants with him. They sat down next to me and started talking about what entrance they went into at the KGB! It was all *very* weird. I thought, this is one place I *don't* want to be! David—I think I'm being set up!'"

I began to laugh. "So what did you tell him?" I asked.

"I said, 'Well, Richard—that was my roommate!'"

When I accompanied David to meet Richard a couple of days later, I introduced myself by saying: "Hi. I'm from the KGB." Well, he turned out to have a good sense of humor. He also thought he knew where Kuznetsky Most 22 was. I'd mulled it over, and decided to follow through on the KGB men's request. I drafted a letter. And I did name my source, at the last minute inserting a photograph of Nagell and an article from the *Washington Post* that described his being arrested behind the Iron Curtain and then released four months later at Berlin's Checkpoint Charlie in the autumn of 1968.

It wasn't easy to find the address, though. We got badly lost upon emerging from the metro, wandering off in the wrong direction. Eventually, someone directed us to Kuznetsky Most, where at Number 22 there was a sign identifying this as the hiring headquarters for State Security. After passing through a couple of glass doors, sure enough, there was the "drop box." Richard explained to the soldiers who stood nearby, eyeing us suspiciously, that I had been told to come here. And I slipped the envelope through the slot.

I'd made an appointment to meet another person that someone at the conference had suggested I see. His name was Sergei Kharlamov, and he was a correspondent for Spain's *El País* newspaper who had co-authored a biography of Gorbachev. He was said to be well-connected, and possibly able to help in my quest to get at the KGB archives. He spoke no English, so I asked Richard to accompany me to our rendezvous back at the Intourist, and David came along as well.

Sergei was a short, bespectacled, red-haired fellow in a three-piece suit, who seemed like a cross between Truman Capote and Peter Lorre. At a corner table, I began telling him about my research into the Kennedy assassination and my visit to KGB headquarters. Sergei spoke of having recently given a speech at Moscow University, where he taught a course on "Democratization in the USSR," to a group of KGB officers. They were very clannish, a world unto themselves, almost like a monastic order, he said. But they were curious about the burgeoning democracy movement and wanted his point of view.

Sergei's advice was that I follow up with a telephone call, to let the KGB know that I had dropped off the letter. Otherwise, it might just get lost in the Party bureaucracy. But whether or not they would then contact me, he added, depended very much on what occurred in politics in the near future. There had already been attempts to ostracize Boris Yeltsin because of the support he had among the Russian people and, if these succeeded, I could probably forget it. Sergei did not believe there would be a civil war, but felt a catastrophe could well be around the corner, depending upon what happened with the economy.

We all went to dinner together, along with two other Americans from the conference and several of Sergei's Russian friends. It was a Georgian restaurant, where you had to pass through two sets of doors—rather like an old American speakeasy—and where a very large lady counted heads and made sure that payment would be in dollars. The vodka toasts were many, and the food incredible, and the price was definitely right: about eight dollars total for a five-course meal.

At the end of dinner, I gave Sergei a list of names I had of KGB officers I'd like to interview about the events surrounding November 22, 1963, in Dallas, along with the information about Nagell that I'd already given the KGB. Sergei said he would see what he could do.

He'd been talking loudly in the restaurant, and again outside as he stood near a long limousine that obviously belonged to Party higher-ups. As David, Richard and I got into a taxi, David told me that he saw Sergei laughing and walking in the direction of a police car. When a backfire occurred next to us, David thought for a moment that we were being shot at!

We rode in silence back to Richard's apartment building. Before we entered, he instructed us that he never speaks English once inside until reaching his residence on the top floor.

Whether or not Sergei was more than a journalist, I never found out. But that July, I received a letter from Richard, who had just returned from the Soviet Union. It contained a second letter, from a mutual acquaintance, who wrote in English: "I spoke recently with Sergei Kharlamov about your inquiries into the Kennedy assassination. Unfortunately, Kharlamov reports that since the political situation continues to worsen, it is practically impossible for a Western journalist to conduct interviews with KGB agents, past or present. He doubts that you will receive a response to your letter and he does not think it worth your time, at present, to continue trying to investigate the KGB's knowledge of the assassination."

I followed up with a phone call to Richard a few weeks later, who said: "Sergei checked with his contacts. The KGB has really cracked down on its agents in recent months, especially the retired ones. First they raise their pensions. Then a current member visits them, and reminds them of how they were better treated than anyone else in Soviet society. Those retired agents who talk lose all their benefits."

It was not long after that when Gorbachev ceded power to Yeltsin, and the Soviet Union began quickly to crumble into separate nation-states.

I never heard from anyone connected to the KGB. That December, ABC-TV's *Nightline* aired a program about having gained entrée to what the KGB claimed were supposedly all its files on the Kennedy assassination. There was nothing in there to indicate that Oswald was of more than casual interest to the KGB after his defection to the USSR in 1959 and during his two-and-a-half year stay, before returning with a Russian wife to Dallas-Fort Worth. There was certainly nothing revealed about any foreknowledge of the assassination on the KGB's part, or about Richard Nagell.

When the news show ended, I flipped off the channel in disgust. And decided to set down what I knew, incomplete as it might be, in a book that became *The Man Who Knew Too Much*.

There is a postscript to the story of my visit to the KGB. A couple of years later, I was in Washington, D.C., and paid a visit to my old friend, Lois Gibbs, at her office in the Virginia suburbs. Lois, who became famous in fighting to expose the story of the environmental disaster that happened to her community of Love Canal, New York, had gone on to form the Citizen's Clearinghouse for Hazardous Wastes. Over time, her organization had become the most successful of the grassroots environmental coalitions, causing considerable aggravation to polluting corporations.

As we talked that morning, Lois told me that she'd been having some problems. A young woman with seemingly strong credentials had been hired to work in the office. Suddenly, she began making accusations against various other employees, turning them against one another. She had even claimed that Lois was embezzling money from the organization and using it for her personal ends. Lois had dismissed her after making some follow-up calls, and discovering that the woman had a history of doing this kind of thing with another environmental group. She'd caused such dissension that the group, having formerly won a number of legal cases against big companies, was forced to disband.

"That's terrible," I said. "She sounds like an agent provocateur."

"Yes, I'm sure that's true," Lois said.

"Can you tell me who it was?" I asked.

"Her name was June," Lois said, and added her last name as well.

My heart began to pound. It all came rushing back at me in a flash: The won't-take-no-for-an-answer means by which she'd talked her way into joining me. The uncanny observational quality she possessed. I'd been accompanied into the KGB's inner sanctum by an American spy!

"Lois," I said, "you're not going to believe what happened to me."

28

Los Angeles Times Book Review, February 7, 1993

"Confessions of a Conspiracy Theorist"

Anyone who has delved into the Kennedy assassination literature knows that this is a stranger-than-fiction realm. Not only do we encounter double and triple agents, but double and triple Oswalds. Why, according to official government records, is the Lee Harvey who defected to the Soviet Union taller than the one who came back? Later, in New Orleans and Dallas, the soon-to-be-accused assassin was seen *here* when he was really *there* because all these other guys were running around, by design or not, who looked very much like him.

I'm glad I grew up in Kansas City and not in Dallas. When I started conducting interviews for what (17 years later) became the book, *The Man Who Knew Too Much*, Oswald's older friend, George de Mohrenschildt, told me that I bore a striking resemblance to Lee. So is there something I don't know about the roots of my obsession? For I cannot exclude myself from the legion of private-citizen detectives who pursue new clues about the tragedy of Dallas with indefatigable perseverance (or, some observers might say, with a monomania that makes Captain Ahab look like a well-rounded man).

I did not intend for the assassination to preoccupy me for almost two decades. I was basically an apolitical, teenage sports fanatic on November 22, 1963. Only as the years passed did I look back in rising anger and realize that the country's fabric, if not its future, was torn apart that day. When more than two-thirds of the people surveyed believe that the truth has been deliberately withheld about the murder of one of America's most popular leaders, it says something profound about the gaping wound in our national psyche. For many, the attempt to resolve the riddles of the assassination has become akin to a quest for the Grail; no accident the demise of Camelot, all seekers agree.

As a freelance journalist, I roamed across the country for two solid years in the late 1970s, interviewing Cuban exiles, soldiers-of-fortune and acquaintances of Oswald. Two of these (including George de Mohrenschildt) shortly after we met ended up dead; another survived a gunshot to the head. It was, to say the least, an unsettling pursuit. No less so when the anonymous phone call came: "Stay out of our business—or you're dead!" When it turned out that the *Godfather*-styled voice was a friend playing a trick, I was hopping mad. Didn't he realize what it was like to spend several hours with retired (fired?) CIA counterintelligence chief James Angleton, then go sit in a Washington movie theater and watch *Three Days of the Condor*?

It became, by the spring of 1978, a curious kind of journalistic double life. The day passed inside my then-office at *TV Guide*'s Hollywood bureau, writing about taking a road trip with Bob Hope. At twilight, I found myself in a dimly lit Irish bar, sitting across from a tall, scarred man who kept a wary eye on the other patrons. Once, he had been an agent of the CIA—and the KGB.

When I first showed up unannounced on Richard Case Nagell's doorstep in suburban L.A., following up on a fellow researcher's tip, it was 1975. That was the year the dam broke on many of the CIA's dark secrets: plots to assassinate foreign leaders, domestic spying, mind-control programs. Richard Nagell, I came to believe, held a big key toward unlocking the darkest of all.

His ultimate revelation bespoke one of history's greatest ironies. According to Nagell, the KGB tried to prevent the assassination—while the CIA and FBI, also aware of a plot, allowed it to proceed. The intent of a group of domestic conspirators was to falsely cast the blame upon Castro's Cuba. Instead of obeying a KGB order that he, Nagell, kill the "patsy," Oswald, in September, 1963, in Mexico, Nagell alerted the FBI before shooting two holes into the wall of an El Paso bank—intentionally getting himself placed in federal custody two months before that fateful day in Dallas. After being railroaded through prison for 4½ years, Nagell ended up being arrested again in 1968—by the East Germans!

In introducing a brand-new cast of characters, I also faced the daunting realization that whole sects have already formed within the greater assassination culture. Are you with the David Lifton or the Harrison Livingston School on how far the tampering went with the President's autopsy? How many gunmen fired from (a) the grassy knoll, (b) the book depository window(s), (c) the Daltex rooftop, (d) the sewer opening, (e) the next limousine? What were *all* those bad people doing in Dealey Plaza—driving in from Florida, tramping away from boxcars, radio transmitters strapped to their belts, phony Secret Service credentials hanging from their lapels—while, as the shots rang out, somebody who looked a helluva lot like the accused assassin was photographed standing in the Depository doorway watching the parade pass by?

I decided to avoid the technical difficulties and focus upon the whodunit: (1) CIA, (2) FBI, (3) Pentagon, (4) Mob, (5) Cuba, (6) Cuban exiles, (7) USSR, (8) ultra-right extremists. But in starting to assemble my addition to the six-hundred-odd volumes printed since Dallas, the more I studied all the possible equations, the more diffuse the scheme became. Besides, over the years, every time I found myself getting too immersed in probing the subject, my personal life would fall apart. Wasn't I better off concentrating on writing about contemporary problems like the environment? Yet there I was, in the wake of Oliver Stone's *JFK*, plunging into the maze again.

This time my wife accompanied me. One afternoon Susan was studying an article by the late Mae Brussell—a researcher I had always considered a bit "fringy"—about the so-called "Nazi connection." Susan kept insisting I reread it and, secretly smug that she was off on a tangent, I put her off as long as I could.

"Read *carefully* the section on General Willoughby," she instructed.

Reluctantly, I did. Charles Willoughby, the onetime chief of intelligence for General Douglas MacArthur (1941–51), turned out to have been born in Heidelberg, Germany, as Adolf Tscheppe-Weidenbach. "Hmmmmm," I said, "that sounds familiar." Scavenging through my files, I retrieved an anonymous letter, received in response to my first published piece on the assassination back in 1975. The letter-writer, who called himself "the Brooklyn waiter," pointed to an acquaintance named "Tscheppe-Weidenbach" as the possible "mastermind" of the JFK conspiracy. The name had seemed like gobbledygook to me at the time.

"Honey," I said 17 years later, holding aloft the letter, "I think we're onto something." We? her eyes said. OK, we.

Thus, when I was supposed to be entering the homestretch, we embarked together on a whole new course of research. It led to a host of connections—Tscheppe-Weidenbach, Willoughby and Allen Dulles, ex-Nazis, the Hunt oil family, Cuban exiles. Nagell, my central character, was becoming but one crucial part of a much broader tapestry. Sifting through interviews old and new, having no idea how all the disparate pieces might fit together, gradually we saw a pattern emerge.

The Man Who Knew Too Much, friends joked, became "the book that grew too much." Yet there seemed little I could do about it. In describing a hall of mirrors, I had to accept that my book would raise more questions than it answered. In the end came the realization that, as a great friend once said: "You don't solve a mystery, you partake of the mysterious."

29

Boston Magazine, November 1993

"From Dallas to Eternity"

The assassination of John F. Kennedy 30 years ago altered history. And for a few local men, that horrible moment has meant a lifetime obsession with the mystery of it.

In the world of those who study assassination, it was a star-studded cast that went to Chicago last spring for the second annual Midwest Symposium on Assassination Politics. There were Judge Burt Griffin of the Warren Commission staff and a trio of investigators from the House Select Committee on Assassinations (1977–79). Oliver Stone's research director for the film *JFK*, Jane Rusconi, was on hand, as well as other writers and investigators. Even Stone himself, in Chicago on other business, dropped by one evening.

Outside the auditorium where he had just delivered the keynote speech, Cambridge's Carl Oglesby stood at one of the souvenir tables, laying out a few bucks for some buttons: "Hoover Knew," "Oswald Was a Patsy," "The CIA Did It."

President of Students for a Democratic Society (SDS) at the height of the Vietnam War, author of three well-received books on the Kennedy assassination, Oglesby at 57 still bore many trademarks of a sixties refugee: lean, bearded, bespectacled, intense, with a Red Sox ball cap tilted back on his head.

Why, a full generation since that terrible day in Dallas, was he still passionately calling for a new investigation into the murder of the nation's thirty-fifth president?

Oglesby grew thoughtful after I, a brother buff from Boston, posed the question. "I didn't ask for this," he said finally, "and I don't really like it. It seems to me that this preoccupation has screwed up my life, kept me from having the normal range of writers' interests. If there hadn't been a Kennedy assassination, I'd probably be writing literary criticism at a beautiful cottage on a lake somewhere."

Instead, Oglesby works out of a cramped second-floor office midway between Central and Harvard squares, his walls lined with all 26 volumes of the Warren Commission Report and dozens of the six-hundred-some books written on the JFK case. Parked near them is the bicycle that is his primary means of transport into the nineties beyond.

Oglesby is not alone in being locked into a time and place—12:31 PM, November 22, 1963, Dealey Plaza—nor in questioning the Warren Commission's conclusions. Philip Melanson, 49, professor of political science at the University of Massachusetts/Dartmouth, recalls a time when his family accused him of being more interested in David Ferrie (an Oswald associate) than he was in them. Matthew Coogan, 46, under secretary of transportation in the Dukakis administration, spent two years laboring nights and weekends on a monumental manuscript, *Thirty Years of Deception*, which he says now stays under the bed, where the cats can play with it.

And I, after 17 years of on-again, off-again fixation, finally saw my 824-page tome, *The Man Who Knew Too Much*, arrive on bookstore shelves last year, when I was 45 years old. Friends have called it "The Book That Grew Too Much."

What can I reply? Well ... But did you read the part about the Oswald double or the possibility that Lee himself might have been a triple agent or that maybe some CIA Dr. Strangelove messed with his mind? And what about the Nazi/Mob/Big Oil connection trying to make it look as if Fidel and the KGB did it?

I do not mean to make light of the subject. We buffs do not know who conspired to assassinate John F. Kennedy, but we believe it's still vital that we find out. Judging by the 15 million people who went to see *JFK* in theaters, and by the 20 new conspiracy books plus 17 reissues that followed in the movie's wake last year, the assassination remains more than just our biggest unsolved mystery; it is an open wound in our national psyche, an axis on which our recent history turns.

It seems fitting that some of the most vital scholarship to probe the assassination's many open questions should emanate from Massachusetts. Professor Melanson, also the author of critical books on the Martin Luther King and Robert Kennedy cases, is acknowledged by assassination researchers as having assembled the most cogent analysis of Oswald's likely intelligence connections (*Spy Saga*, 1990).

Oglesby's 1976 *The Yankee and Cowboy War* is still considered a pioneering study of how the battle between the eastern establishment and the West's "new money" forces may have led to JFK's death and then to Watergate. And Coogan's under-the-bed manuscript was described in 1991 by the late attorney Bernard Fensterwald, Jr., founder of the Assassination Archives Research Center, in Washington, as the most interesting, complex, and important document that he had seen in a quarter century.

So what are we all after? What is the mind-set that pursues clues toward a cathartic justice that will probably never be served? And upon what evidence do we base our mutual conviction of a cloaked "secret government" with its dagger aimed at our very system of representative democracy? To answer these and other questions, I sat down for a series of long, soul-searching talks with my three local compatriots.

Carl Oglesby, son of a tire builder from the former rubber capital of Akron, was working in the defense industry on November 22, 1963. As the man in charge of technical publications for the Bendix Aerospace Systems Division, in Ann Arbor, Michigan, one of the little corporate secrets to which he was privy concerned a communications relay device designed for fighting against an elusive insurgent foe—specifically, in the jungles of Vietnam and Laos.

Listening to the shocking news from Dallas over a radio in the art department, Oglesby glanced out a window and realized that the flag waving on the pole outside should properly be placed at half-mast. He went up the Bendix chain of command with his request. Despite the personnel director's advice—"This is not your call"—Oglesby finally arrived outside the swank offices of the general manager.

"First I heard chuckling," he recalls. "I could just see around the corner, and there was the GM standing with a wineglass. I had never seen any kind of alcohol at Bendix; it was strictly illegal on the premises. With that much to clue me in as to the mood of the front office, I turned around, walked back, and worked. Worked overtime."

The Bendix flag was not lowered that day, he recalls. But something had happened to Oglesby. It did not surface when the official lone-assassin conclusion came out in 1964. ("I thought, Sure, Oswald did it, why would the Warren Commission lie?") Nor even when Oglesby quit Bendix, in 1965, and made the great leap from aerospace promoter to antiwar protester. Only as he later came to study the short life of the accused assassin did he realize that "Lee Harvey Oswald was me, at a certain age—an honest, patriotic working-class kid who had no idea of the ways he was being put to use."

From his youthful years when his favorite TV program was *I Led Three Lives*, Oswald's background had spy versus spy written all over it. A teen marine who avidly studied the words of Karl Marx. An apparent defector to the Soviet Union who came back to Texas with a Russian wife and found work at a photo shop that did classified work for the Army Map Service. A Castro supporter who was often seen in the company of rabid right-wingers. Hoover's FBI, which staked its reputation on uncovering the slightest trace of subversion, did not even see fit to include Oswald among the some 32,000 individuals on what Hoover called its "Security Index." Clearly, something was wrong with this picture.

Oglesby didn't take up the Oswald enigma in earnest until 1974, when Bob Katz read one of his columns in the *Phoenix* and invited him to become part of a small group that soon became the Assassination Information Bureau (AIB). Katz, today the president of a national lecture agency (the Cambridge-based K & S Speakers), recalls that "what Carl brought to the movement to solve President Kennedy's murder was a particularly keen appreciation of how the assassination was part and parcel of an immense rightward political shift. He was able to assure people like myself that our fascination was not prurient, that it had a larger importance."

Although he refers to himself today as a sort of conservative liberal, Oglesby was by the mid-sixties among the leading figures on the political left. SDS, which invited him into its ranks after members at the University of Michigan saw one of his three professionally produced plays, ended up electing Oglesby its national president a few days shy of his thirtieth birthday.

After having invented the antiwar teach-in, Oglesby eventually split away from a new, violence-prone SDS faction known as the Weathermen. He had a brief side career as a folk singer/guitarist, cutting two albums on the Vanguard label. His first book was *Containment and Change*, published in 1967, an analysis of America's plunge into Vietnam and other third-world countries. In 1971 he moved to Cambridge to teach a course at MIT called Through Politics, and he has lived there ever since except for a year in Washington, D.C., with the AIB.

In Washington that year, 1977, Oglesby found himself approached by a Soviet embassy official, a close encounter he later chronicled in *Playboy* as "My Dinners with Andrey." The fellow, clearly KGB, also "clearly wanted a relationship," Oglesby recalls. "I got wined and dined and thought, Well, what to do here? Is this maybe an opportunity to make a point? I had been irritated no end at all those years of hearing I was supposedly on the other side, not a proper American. So I mentioned Andrey to an acquaintance who I thought would put me in touch with someone in the CIA. I got approached by an FBI guy instead. Yep, Oglesby informs to the FBI! Well, I actually felt Gus [the FBI guy] and Andrey were both wonderful people and kept thinking, Why can't they just have a beer, kick off their shoes together, and get real?"

Now that the cold war is over and presumably the United States and Russia can get real about the past, is Oglesby optimistic that the truth about the assassination will out? Not really, although he figures that the Russians could probably add considerably to our knowledge about Oswald and may even have conducted their own investigation into who killed JFK. "It's a very heavy catch-22," he notes. "As long as they were enemies of the United States, they wouldn't have been believed, and now that they're the docile home companions, they don't want to make any waves."

Unless an insider comes forward, Oglesby doubts the mystery will ever be resolved. He remains convinced that a "big, very big" homegrown conspiracy resulted in JFK's death. "Kennedy was killed in order that the Vietnam War be escalated. I think you can boil it down to that."

While crediting JFK with moving toward a much more responsible foreign policy during his final days, Oglesby is not at all enamored of him as a moral leader. But he staunchly believes that the "secret government" residing within the military, the CIA, and the FBI must be exposed.

Two years ago, he even briefly flirted with the idea of taking on Joe Kennedy as the Libertarian candidate for Congress, strictly in order to provide a forum to challenge the Kennedy family's unwillingness to pursue all this. It was Norman Mailer who talked Oglesby out of it over a drink one night at the Ritz-Carlton. Politics, as the onetime unsuccessful candidate for mayor of New York put it, was not a suitable endeavor for a writer.

Philip Melanson has written three books that, he wryly concedes, "can't even be read by family members with dictionaries." They bear such titles as *Political Science and Political Knowledge: An Epistemological Analysis of Methodology in the Profession.* He has also made a highly reasoned argument that Sirhan Sirhan, slayer of Robert Kennedy, was a hypnotically controlled gunman.

As a Ph.D. whose specialty is studying transfers of power and the health of governments, Melanson sees no contradiction. "What happened to the Kennedys," he believes, "were not only watershed political events that affected our lives directly as we lived through them; they are also the Rosetta stone of what kind of democracy we were and subsequently became."

Raised in Stoneham, where his father worked for the phone company, Melanson became only the second member of his large family to get a college degree. "It was almost impossible to grow up in Massachusetts in that era without being fixated on the Kennedys," he recalls.

Of Melanson's 30 mentors at the University of Connecticut, 28 were part-time functionaries for the State Department or the CIA. He was a freshman there when the assassination happened, and he recalls hearing, two days afterward, "all this cheering and yelling in the dorm—because Ruby had shot Oswald. Great, somebody got the guy who got the president! I remember thinking, Yeah, so what, all right. Never knowing how long it would take me to figure out that (a) Oswald wasn't the guy who killed the president, and (b) he was being killed for an entirely different set of reasons that were part of a plot."

Sometime in the mid-seventies, Oglesby's AIB came to make a presentation at Melanson's school, UMass-Dartmouth, known at the time as Southeastern Massachusetts University. Melanson's students in Introduction to American Government sparked his own interest and, on a research trip to Washington, he began poring through some Warren Commission files in the National Archives. Today, Melanson estimates he has put a fingerprint on every one of the six-hundred-thousand-odd pages in the Oswald, Ruby, and main-case files that have so far been released by the FBI. He teaches an entire course called Political Assassinations in America, and his university houses the world's largest collection on the murder of Robert Kennedy.

As one of the few conspiracy theorists with academic credentials, Melanson has found himself courted by tabloid TV. Interestingly, the mainstream network-news programs have largely ignored him, which Melanson views as part of an establishmentarian response that continues to support the Warren Commission.

"I think the assassination is a Rorschach test: if you're a defender of the political system, you defend the lone-nut ideology."

Sitting in the downstairs den of his gray wood-frame Cape Cod–style home in Marion, about a ninety-minute drive from Boston, Melanson mused: "Just by [their] putting Oswald out there as the centerpiece, you could almost predict this self-perpetuating momentum for cover-up. Say the CIA is innocent of involvement, but they can't expose their Cuban operations and the assassination attempts against Castro. The FBI cannot afford to expose the fact that they monitored Oswald and maybe used him as an informant. You didn't have to be a real genius to know that. But what this tells us, I think, is that the plotters were not ordinary citizens but people who knew how the CIA and FBI would react."

Unlike Oglesby, Melanson sees Oswald as a likely participant in the conspiracy, although probably not the shooter. But Oglesby and Melanson agree that the assassination was essentially a *coup d'état*. And the professor finds a higher percentage of truth in the best literature of the critical community "than in all the official documents put together," even though he concedes that there is also "a lot of junk and wild theories out there."

In the course of preparing his book *The Martin Luther King Assassination*, Melanson managed to track down a Toronto man who he is convinced brought James Earl Ray his initial getaway money. (Ray was captured in London two months after the King shooting and later convicted of the crime.) For *The Robert Kennedy Assassination*, Melanson broke considerable new ground in uncovering how Sirhan may have been hypnotically "programmed" to shoot on that June 1968 night after RFK won the California primary.

Seeing the fingerprints of the intelligence community in all three cases, Melanson finds it a "very real possibility" that the assassinations were somehow linked. "The sixties were the most politically violent, psychologically paranoid decade in modern history. At the time of their deaths, both Kennedys and King were taking what I would describe as radical issue stands, in terms of being diametrically opposed to very powerful interests. I think King's death was sealed not in the fight for integration but in his taking on the Vietnam War. With Bobby Kennedy, again, taking on the war, and going back to his hounding the gangsters when he was attorney general. To this day, I'm amazed to talk to intelligence officers and find, when they open up about their fears and perceptions of these three political leaders, that it's like George Bush talking about Saddam Hussein."

Melanson's hope is that study of the sixties assassinations may someday achieve the same level of respectability as historical analyses of, say, Pearl Harbor.

For Matthew A. Coogan, then the Dukakis administration's under secretary of transportation, the quest began six years ago with a book he was reading. It was not about the assassination but a Peter Maas biography of convicted arms dealer Edwin Wilson (*Manhunt*). Finishing a paragraph about how casually

Wilson hired hit men, Coogan says he dropped the book and said to himself: I didn't know our government used people like that. I wonder how this relates to November 22, 1963.

Coogan, whose father was a prominent lawyer and a law professor at Harvard, Yale, and elsewhere, was a student at Newton High when JFK was assassinated: "I've never seen grief as united as that day, ever." He went on to study social relations at Harvard, hiring on as a research assistant for the MBTA upon graduation in 1969. Within a year, he was advising Governor Frank Sargent on highway policy.

At age 40, when he stumbled upon *Manhunt*, Coogan seemed the quintessential establishmentarian. By then he was directly responsible for the design of the six-billion-dollar Central Artery/Third Harbor Tunnel project. After Dukakis' gubernatorial departure, Coogan stayed on for six months and then became a vice president of Rackemann Environmental Services, specializing in international transportation consultations. This past summer, he moved on to solo consulting and into a Vermont country home with his family.

When we first sat down together, Coogan was living in a North End townhouse, where the wall of his home office was lined with some four hundred volumes on various aspects of the intelligence community. His own manuscript, bound in black leather with *Thirty Years of Deception* peering through a cover square, contains four-hundred-plus pages and thirty chapters covering the years 1954 through 1986. It begins:

"John F. Kennedy was murdered as part of a major political *deception*, in an attempt to force the United States into a major land war with Cuba. He was murdered in a *coup d'état* in which a small disloyal clique of government employees had determined that he was not going to carry out the foreign policy toward the Caribbean that they wanted. And so he had to die. To carry this out, the clique formed a bond with organized crime and exploited the passions of exiled Cubans who longed to retain their homeland. The pattern of the intelligence operatives combining with the managers of organized crime, and the passions of the Cuban exiles would influence the course of American politics for the three decades that followed."

Coogan's "black book" is an amazing compilation, tracing patterns and players from the CIA's 1954 overthrow of the Guatemalan government all the way through the Iran-contra scandal. Sometimes he refers to the process as "sort of Hegelian—you know, hypothesis, reaction, synthesis." Other times he draws analogies to Plato's cave, where what is taken for truth is merely shadows.

Coogan notes that his wife, Patricia, was remarkably understanding of the complexities of the pursuit. "Her interest was my sanity, not my politics. If she saw me at the typewriter at three in the morning, knowing I had to go to work at seven, she would call me insane."

Using a yellow highlighter to mark his reference texts, Coogan took no notes and ended up working entirely from memory. In his first draft, he had Oswald up there with the saints as a totally virtuous person who walked into a situation and got framed. "I don't believe that anymore at all," Coogan now says. Today, he views Oswald as a low-level intelligence operative—who was carrying out orders he believed to be legitimate, or had no method of cross-checking if he didn't—set up to take the rap in a classic deception scheme.

But the intellectually challenging question, as Coogan sees it, is not really whodunit but who caused the facts to be suppressed and why. "What I've decided is, the men and women who believed our nation needed a secret government for the cold war were probably right. The way nations interact with one another is far worse than my visits to the United Nations ever told me as a kid. So the people around Eisenhower created one government that we can look at, touch, vote for and against—and another that we can't even ask about.

"At each step, the secrecy was consistent with their vision of a barbarian world of communism and the need to defend the virtuous world of democracy. I think these were rational men. The question for us, as citizens, is whether, in our trust and belief in these men, we sanctioned the creation of institutions that we—and they—lost control of. It sure looks like it. This is not a conspiracy theory; I would argue it's a historical examination of a trend. And if those of us who are trying to understand this phenomenon are right, it has become a grave and overwhelming threat to democracy."

Coogan, however, insists he is not the least bit interested in having his assemblings made public. He wrote his book simply because of a personal need to separate out some thoughts in his mind. And the manuscript is serving that purpose right where it is, under the bed.

30

High Times Magazine, January 1994

" 'Case Closed': A Fraud on the American People"

The latest, much-ballyhooed book on the Kennedy assassination, Gerald Posner's *Case Closed* (Random House, $25), appears patently incestuous before a careful reader even opens it. On the back cover, renowned novelist William Styron "cannot believe that any rational reader" could finish it and still fantasize about a conspiracy. On the inside cover, espionage expert David Wise informs us that this is "at last the voice of sanity."

What is not said is that Wise, Styron, and Posner all share the same publisher (Random House) and even the same editor (Bob Loomis).

But since its publication last September, *Case Closed* has also drawn raves from the *New York Times* and most other major media. Posner has appeared on numerous national TV shows, assuring us that Lee Harvey Oswald was indeed the lone, unaided assassin of President Kennedy, and the author has seen his book climb onto the bestseller lists.

Not bad for a book that opens with a mistake in its first sentence. "More than two thousand books have been written about the assassination...." Posner writes. In fact, there have been only some 660, of which *Case Closed* may rank as the slickest—and most fraudulent—yet to come down the pike.

I must admit that I am one of the many authors ("buffs," as we're referred to) whose work is shamelessly discarded by Posner. My 1992 book, *The Man Who Knew Too Much*, about two-thirds of which examines the life of counterspy Richard Case Nagell, is twice dismissed out-of-hand by Posner—although it is not even listed in his bibliography and clearly he did not bother to read it. Posner's remarks about Nagell's alleged "insanity" are fraught with so many inaccuracies that this alone would force me to question the validity of his other analyses.

To refute Posner's claims point-by-point would take a book in itself. This ex-Wall Street lawyer's prosecutorial brief bends evidence to fit his theory, omits critical evidence which runs counter to it, and relies heavily on speculation to make his case. Any impartial jury would surely send Posner packing.

Take his "incontrovertible evidence" that the Warren Commission's much-maligned single-bullet theory is correct. This "magic bullet" is said to have hit Kennedy and Governor John Connally simultaneously, inflicted seven nonfatal wounds, and emerged from this assault on flesh and bone in virtually pristine condition. It was supposedly found when it rolled out from under a mat on an unidentified stretcher in a Parkland Hospital hallway some 45 minutes after the assassination. Many prudent researchers wonder whether the "magic bullet" was planted there.

Posner claims enhanced computer simulation as his supporting proof. He bases it upon an entry wound in the base of the President's neck, and a lower exit wound in his throat. However, Kennedy's doctors and nurses at Parkland Hospital, who observed the throat wound before it was altered by a tracheotomy, have described it as an entry wound. Posner's location of the wound in the President's back is also vigorously disputed. And, of course, his simulation is worthless if data fed into the computer is in error.

This is but one of dozens of examples of the outrageousness of *Case Closed*. In assessing the alleged emotional derangement of Oswald's slayer Jack Ruby, Posner relies almost exclusively on Warren Commission testimony. His lone fresh source material consists of interviews with Ruby's brother and ex-Dallas D.A. Bill Alexander—the latter admittedly having once helped "invent" a story that Oswald served as a confidential informant for the FBI.

So just who is Gerald Posner anyway? A reviewer as cavalier as Posner himself in assessing research colleagues might describe him as rather obsessed with Nazis, drugs and spies. Random House publicity describes him as the author of four previous books. *Hitler's Children* (1991) consists of interviews with some of the Nazi leadership's off-spring. *The Bio-Assassins* (1989) is a novel about the KGB invading a CIA laboratory and making off with a lethal bacteria that invades the central nervous system. *Warlords of Crime* (1988) is a nonfiction saga about the Chinese drug trade.

But perhaps the most intriguing Posner tale is the story of his introduction to the writing genre, as co-author of *Mengele: The Complete Story* (1986). Josef Mengele, the notorious "Angel of Death" at the Auschwitz concentration camp, was one of many Hitler henchmen who managed to escape from Germany and resettle in Latin America after the war—often with the help of U.S. intelligence agencies. Posner, two years out of law school, purports to have been drawn into a five-year-long fascination with Mengele in 1981, during a pro bono legal effort to obtain compensation for surviving twins who had been subjects of the Nazi's experiments. Posner and co-author John Ware, a London-based TV producer, ended up being granted "exclusive and unrestricted access to the Mengele family papers and diaries."

Posner also ended up testifying before the U.S. Senate on an important question: "whether Mengele had been held by American forces" after the war.

The biography finds it "incontestable" that after U.S. military authorities "mistakenly released Mengele from custody in mid-1945," no further involvement took place. French government documents, maintaining that American officials detained and then released Mengele again in 1947, are dismissed by Posner as "unsupported by any evidence in any (U.S.) government file."

Thus, in the midst of a worldwide hunt for Mengele (or his remains) in the 1980s, Posner played a curious role, basically "clearing" U.S. intelligence of any untoward conduct in letting the "Angel of Death" roam free. For an expert on the narcotics trade, Posner was noticeably quiet on the subject of Mengele's suspected drug dealings from his Paraguayan hideaway—trafficking that found him in liaison with the Corsican mob, which was long utilized by the CIA and, ironically enough, recently linked in a BBC documentary to the Kennedy assassination.

The timing of the publication of this latest Posner book—the same day the National Archives opened thousands of pages of long-classified JFK-assassination government files to public scrutiny—raised at least this writer's eyebrows. Could it be that *Case Closed* was an effort to defuse any new revelations that might occur as the thirtieth anniversary of the assassination approached?

There was, in fact, no similar wave of publicity accompanying the declassification of the House Assassinations Committee's report on Oswald's activities in Mexico City. Yet this long-awaited study confirms that the CIA did take photographs of Oswald entering both the Soviet and Cuban embassies two months before the assassination—while officially denying the existence of such pictures for 30 years. The report also raises the question of why a pre-assassination CIA file on Oswald was closely held by James Angleton's elite Counter Intelligence Special Investigations Group.

But the corporate media are not rushing to send a team of reporters probing these thousands of pages of fresh files. They would prefer to let Posner spare them the time, the only casualty being the truth of what really happened on November 22, 1963. In reality, there may be no better case for reopening the JFK investigation than the sham called *Case Closed*.

31

The Reflections of
Marina Oswald Porter

A few months after *The Man Who Knew Too Much* was published, I returned from a conference in Chicago to a message on my answering machine. Marina Oswald Porter, whom I'd spoken with a couple of times while finishing my research, had called. When I rang her back, she began: "I've been chewing on your book—and I've got a bone to pick with you."

It was never quite clear what that "bone" was. Marina said that she was willing to give Richard Nagell the benefit of the doubt. "Maybe Lee was in the same kind of predicament—a double or triple agent—and he did not know who he was really serving." She went on to say, "I got upset at first—because I did not know where you stand. I figured out for myself how Lee fit into it. I'm not going to tell you, because it would be misleading."

When she was in protective custody after the assassination, Marina remembered, "Nobody ever counseled me. The government lawyer told me, 'Don't elaborate, just say yes or no.' Later, I did not recognize my own testimony to the Warren Commission. The way it was translated, I don't talk like that at all. They made it look like I did not even finish the fifth grade."

Then she continued, "You are on the right track if you think Lee is innocent. He was not just a plain Joe from the street, of course not. He was manipulated and he got caught. He tried to play with the big boys. But a frame-up could also happen to you, your children, or your neighbors."

Bill Clinton had been elected to his first term a few months earlier, and Marina wondered, "Does a president have the power to reverse something like the Warren Commission? If he wants to do something for future generations, then reopening the investigation is the place to start. But the longer Clinton is in office, the more his hands will be tied."

Was it still possible to bring legal action, Marina asked, based on the fact that her husband had been shot while in the hands of the police? "I am at the end of my rope," she confessed. "I'm fifty-two years old, and I don't want to live anymore sometimes. I think of my grandson and go into a deep depression.

"Even if Lee was in the Texas School Book Depository, that does not necessarily mean he was on the sixth floor. Because he loved President Kennedy. At the time, yes, I wondered, how did he snap? What did *I* do? Strong guilt. I have to live with myself.

"Well," Marina concluded our call, "maybe we will talk again."

It was a strong conversation but one that left many questions unanswered, and I hoped she might be willing to elaborate in the future. That August, there was another voice-mail message; Marina said she had a question she needed to ask me. I had just watched her on TV, fielding tough questions from Tom Brokaw, and began by telling her that I thought she'd held her ground beautifully.

"Well, that won't get me anywhere," Marina replied. Later, she added, "I made a fool out of myself. I am angry not just because Lee was wrongly accused. I did not have time to talk about the deeper reasons."

Her question for me revolved around an Oswald Uniformed Services ID card that had been in Nagell's possession—though with a different photograph of Oswald, a different signature, and a lack of Department of Defense overstamp that appeared on the same ID card that the Dallas police seized after the assassination. Marina wondered if I knew any more about that card than I'd written in the book. I didn't. She also wondered whether Nagell had been in touch with me, and whether there was any way she could communicate with him. At that point, Nagell was nowhere to be found.

She spoke of the new book, *Case Closed*, by Gerald Posner, which purported to be the last word on the assassination and proclaimed the Warren Commission's findings correct. "I would like to believe that, too," Marina said, "I could live a more peaceful life . . . I think Lee was the perfect patsy. I can't tell you how much he admired John F. Kennedy. My motive is not to reclaim his [Lee's] name for the sake of it. But so many things don't make sense—like why did they destroy his military records in 1973?" (The Army claimed this had been part of a "routine" cleansing.)

"I am completely helpless," Marina said. "Look at the big machine behind that phony baloney Posner—compared to books like yours, which have a hard time seeing the light. I spoke briefly to Posner when he was writing his book. That gave him the power to say, 'I did interview Marina,' so he is off the hook legally.

"But I don't know where to go from here. Is there anything in those files that has not been sanitized yet?"

She went on to reveal that the pictures she had taken of her husband in April 1963, holding the Mannlicher-Carcano rifle he allegedly used to shoot the president, had been "tampered with." In the original photos, she thought that "the rifle was different. There should be more pictures, with different poses," Marina recalled. "The stairs are in the wrong place."

There was a pause before Marina spoke again. "Why am I calling you? It is probably therapy, because I have run out of people to talk to. Can *you* walk away from it?"

I told her I'd hoped I could, but it didn't seem to be possible.

"That is the trouble with it," she added, "you go so far and you cannot stop. It is not important to me who did the shooting, but the reasons behind it and the cover-up. This is not good for the nation. America is dying because this was allowed thirty years ago. I cannot understand the apathy."

History changed irrevocably that day, I said.

"No, history went back to where it was supposed to be," she said. "Because Kennedy would have changed it."

As our latest conversation drew to a close, Marina said, "If I was an idiot at twenty-two, I hope I am a little bit wiser now. I wish I did not know these things."

Then she made a full circle back to the military ID card. "That card with the privileges, there is something there. I *know*."

I explained to a wealthy friend who lived in Cambridge, Massachusetts—and was a longtime supporter of efforts to uncover the truth about the assassination—that Marina wanted to find some way to re-open the investigation. The idea we came up with was this: why not bring together as many topflight lawyers as we knew, and introduce Marina to them for a brainstorming session?

I called Marina to tell her. She thought a moment, then responded, "I am at a dead end. I forgot how to smile, to laugh. Well, maybe it can be arranged. I have to give something back."

We spoke again in a couple of days, when she definitely agreed to come. "I've run out of options. Maybe something will come out of it." She would agree to answer questions at a teach-in, but would offer no formal presentation, just "homemade philosophy." Nor did she want any advance publicity about her visit.

On October 5, I called again to go over travel arrangements. "Sometimes I want to put a fence up around my house and never see anyone," she said. "It's just constant pain." She planned to wear slacks and a sweater. "I hope nobody will be insulted," she said.

Shortly before her scheduled flight from Dallas, we had one last phone call. "I am scared to death," Marina said. "The clown is tired . . . I don't trust my own shadow. I am grasping for straws. We'll hope for the best."

It was November 12, ten days before the thirtieth anniversary marking the assassination. I remember my wife and I taking Marina out to dinner that night, and her painful recollection of being taken advantage of by an FBI agent during the course of her post-assassination confinement. "I was a walking zombie in those days," she reflected.

On a Sunday afternoon, in front of a crackling fireplace in my living room, we assembled. Jim Lesar and Dan Alcorn, attorneys from Washington, were on hand. Gaeton Fonzi, former investigator for Senator Schweiker and the House Assassinations Committee, had flown up from Florida. Harvey Silverglate, a prominent civil liberties lawyer in Cambridge, was there with his wife, as was another attorney friend, Joan Stanley. Marina sat in a comfortable leather-backed chair.

Marina began the conversation. "If there is no law on the books, create one, please," she implored the room.

Lesar, who also oversaw the Assassination Archives Research Center in the nation's capitol, responded that it was difficult to get a foot in the door on legal action because the statute of limitations had expired in most instances. Still, he felt we had a unique opportunity over the next several years to get a new investigation moving. The Assassination Records Review Board appointed by President Clinton to examine and release most of the still-classified files also had the power to subpoena witnesses.

"There is a mechanism here to enable us to keep the issue upfront and demand more of Congress," Lesar said.

"Is there a King Solomon nowhere in the lawyer community to come up with some clever thing?" Marina asked.

Lesar then suggested a report compiled by distinguished private citizens could be presented to an official investigative body.

Marina turned to face Fonzi. "Forget me, this is not a personal vendetta," she said, "this is just healing wounds."

Fonzi said, "I'd like to figure out a more radical approach from the legal point of view."

Marina wondered about holding a trial in Texas. Lesar said, "But you could only try someone if you have a suspect in a conspiracy." The prosecutor Alcorn added, would be the Dallas District Attorney, but that office's response had always been that "the FBI came and took all the evidence away." Alcorn had looked at all the federal statutes and seen no possibilities, so Texas was realistically the only place something could happen. "But we don't have a suspect right now," and it was ineffective to bring a legal action that was not going to proceed.

Joan Stanley asked Marina what her ultimate goal was. "I would like to establish the fact that Lee Harvey Oswald was innocent of the crime he was accused of," Marina said. "What if I sue the city of Dallas?"

The question then arose as to whether a case might be based around negligence with Oswald's security. However, negligence is a civil matter, and the statute of limitations had expired. Silverglate noted that an investigative grand jury might be possible. However, Lesar said, "the problem is that you'd need to convince Texas to do it."

Silverglate went on that the federal government hides behinds its "supremacy clause." In other words, Congress can override a state constitutional provision. He described having tried to subpoena in Massachusetts a federal agent who helped in an investigation, but the man simply did not show up. If a state grand jury subpoenas federal records, it doesn't mean that the feds have to comply.

"There's maybe another possibility," Stanley said. "The murder of [police officer J.D.] Tippitt has never been solved officially. This would keep things within the confines of Texas law."

Again, the problem was that the records weren't there, but in custody of the FBI. On what grounds could a grand jury be convened? Were there any suspects beside Oswald, who purportedly committed the Tippitt murder?

"The best evidence on a state prosecutorial level," said Lesar, "revolves around concealment and obstruction of justice. But you would need a change in federal legislation on this, in order to get the statute changed.

"Is there a statute on suing the city?" Marina asked.

"Three years after it happened," Lesar said, and soon after asked, "When was the first time you voiced suspicion that the official version [of what happened] was not correct?"

"Twenty-five years later," said Marina.

The Attorney General of Texas had authority to convene a grand jury. Alcorn believed that a case could be brought, based upon the physical evidence of the president's wounds failing to support Oswald having been the only shooter.

Lesar recalled a tort known as "negligent maintenance of government records." This had come up in a lawsuit involving Scientology, where Washington's District Court did concede the existence of such a tort. But, Silverglate asked, who would issue the subpoena for discovery in Marina's case? "You run up against obdurate agencies who might not give up the records."

Alcorn suggested asking President Clinton to appoint another commission. But Marina wondered if this would simply again be a case of the fox guarding the chicken coop.

Lesar described a new interpretation of the president's wounds by Dr. Randolph Robertson, revealing that the second shot had to have come from the grassy knoll. He said he was trying to arrange a meeting with people in the Justice Department about this.

Elsa Dorfman, Silverglate's wife, wondered whether Marina and Mrs. Tippitt might do a joint action to try to bring the case of the murdered policeman into court.

Lesar, though, was ultimately forced to conclude that he did not see the legal route as feasible. A Texas grand jury was the best possibility, but its outcome was problematical at best. Joan Stanley added that there are many problems with a grand jury—all the publicity around this particular case, and the evidence being so hard to come by.

"Well, I learned the hard way," Fonzi said, "that Congress is not the body to conduct this investigation. Because it all turns into economics, budgets, and so on. You've got to move toward a presidential commission."

But a special prosecutor was a danger, Lesar pointed out, because it depended upon who got appointed. The whole issue was a political football.

And so, basically, after several hours our discussion ended not much further along than when it began. Some of the finest legal minds in the country had come together, with the widow of the accused assassin, in hopes of finding some way—*any* way—to reopen the case. Thirty years after the fact, it seemed pretty hopeless, short of someone's deathbed confession.

That night, a violinist friend played for Marina. One composition he performed was called "Song of the Lark." More than one of us had tears in our eyes.

32

High Times Magazine, March 1996

"Oswald and the CIA"

At 9 PM last November 1, the landlord of a house in the Echo Park section of Los Angeles unsuccessfully tried the locks, then pried open a window and forced his way inside. Joe Motyka had been alerted by a neighbor that his tenant, sixty-five-year-old Richard Case Nagell, had not been seen for several days. Motyka discovered the already-decomposing body of Nagell in the bathroom, and immediately alerted the police.

Only the morning before, in Washington, the Assassination Records Review Board (ARRB)—mandated by Congress under the JFK Records Act of 1992 to review for public release all still-secret files on the John F. Kennedy assassination—had mailed Richard Nagell a letter. The board was seeking access to documentation he claimed to possess about a conspiracy to murder the thirty-fifth president of the United States.

Although an autopsy performed by the L.A. County Coroner's office determined that Nagell had died of a heart attack, the timing triggered alarm inside the ARRB. More than a month earlier, based upon testimony of this writer at a public hearing in Boston, ARRB executives had decided to pursue Nagell's private files and use their subpoena power to call him to testify. Upon hearing of his sudden death, the ARRB issued a subpoena for any records he may have kept in his house and flew an investigator to Los Angeles.

What may surface next remains an open and very provocative question. As outlined in my 1992 book about Nagell, *The Man Who Knew Too Much* (Carroll & Graf Publishers, New York), the ex-military intelligence and CIA operative said he had made arrangements for certain "smoking guns" to be divulged in the event of his death. These are likely to include a tape recording done surreptitiously by Nagell in the late summer of 1963, where at least four individuals—himself, Lee Harvey Oswald and two Cuban exiles—plotted the assassination of President Kennedy. A photograph of Nagell and Oswald, which Nagell had a vendor take in New Orleans' Jackson Square, was said to be stashed in a bank vault in Zurich, Switzerland.

In summary, what Nagell has chosen to reveal about his role in the conspiracy goes like this: Under contract to the CIA, he undertook an assignment as a "double agent" who would cooperate with Soviet intelligence beginning in the autumn of 1962. Under KGB instructions from Mexico City, for a year he monitored discussions among a group of embittered Cuban exiles who were seeking to assassinate Kennedy and make it look as though Fidel Castro's Cuba was behind it. He was simultaneously asked to keep an eye on Lee Harvey Oswald, recently returned to America after his alleged "defection" to the USSR.

Oswald was brought into the conspiracy in July 1963, deceived into thinking he was working for Castro. Soviet intelligence ordered Nagell either to convince Oswald he was being set up to take the rap—or to kill him in Mexico City before the assassination could transpire. While both U.S. and Soviet intelligence agencies were aware of the conspiracy, it was the KGB—not the CIA or FBI—that attempted to prevent it. The Soviets, who had reached a growing accommodation with Kennedy after the 1962 Cuban missile crisis, were also afraid that the assassination would falsely be blamed upon them or the Cubans.

Nagell, instead of carrying out his assignment, sent a registered letter to the FBI (which he also served as a confidential informant) Director J. Edgar Hoover more than two months before the tragedy in Dallas, providing enough information to warrant the arrest of Oswald and two Cuban exiles. While the bureau says it cannot locate any such letter in its files, it is likely that Nagell kept a copy and the registered-mail receipt among his effects.

Also alerting CIA officials of the plot, Nagell then walked into a bank in El Paso, Texas, on September 20, 1963, fired two shots into the wall and intentionally had himself placed in federal custody. He hinted to me in a series of meetings that right-wing extremists, including wealthy Texas oil interests and CIA renegades, were ultimately behind the assassination.

Considerable documentation, including a notebook seized by the FBI upon Nagell's arrest that contained listings remarkably similar to Oswald's own notebook, already lends credibility to his story. Yet he was ignored by both the Warren Commission and the House Select Committee on Assassinations. The new ARRB thus became the first official government body to express an interest in what he might be able to reveal. And, like Oswald's friend George de Mohrenschildt—who allegedly committed suicide hours before a House Select Committee investigator was to see him in 1977—suddenly, Nagell was dead.

Previously unavailable files released so far through the ARRB's process have already raised more questions about a high-level cover-up surrounding Nagell. After his arrest in El Paso, he was held without a trial for nine months in a county jail, where the FBI and Secret Service visited him on several occasions after the assassination. Although no mention is made of Nagell in the Warren Commission's 26 volumes, FBI reports from December 1963 clearly state that he talked of having known Oswald in Texas and Mexico City.

Transcripts of assassination-related telephone conversations with President Lyndon Johnson show that his friend Homer Thornberry, a federal judge who had been a Texas Congressman, was in touch with LBJ twice in the weeks following the assassination. Then, late in January 1964, Thornberry suddenly stepped in as the new judge in the Nagell case—where court transcripts indicated a concerted effort to suppress Nagell's efforts to describe his true motive for his alleged "attempted bank robbery." Thornberry handed down the maximum sentence upon Nagell's conviction in June 1964, a conviction that was later overturned on appeal. Nagell was released from prison in the spring of 1968, flying to Europe shortly thereafter, where he was arrested on a train by East German authorities and held for four months behind the then "Iron Curtain" before being released to U.S. authorities at the Berlin border.

Long before this, according to a just-declassified March 20, 1964 CIA file, the agency was pursuing the significance of six names of CIA employees found in the Nagell notebook taken by the FBI in September 1963. Another CIA memorandum, dated July 20, 1963 out of its Mexico City station, tells of an American using the name Eldon Hensen who wanted to establish contact with the Cuban Embassy there. Having picked up this information via a telephone tap, the CIA then dispatched someone posing as a Cuban Embassy officer to lure Hensen to a hotel restaurant. The file describes Hensen's expressed willingness to "help Castro government in U.S., willing travel, has many good contacts in States, can 'move things from one place to another'"—which carries overtones of Nagell's own "double" role.

Author John Newman, in *Oswald and the CIA*, his 1995 book based on the recently released files, uses this incident to highlight the CIA's capability "to enter surreptitiously into someone's life to control or manipulate it," a scenario Newman cites as a precursor to the agency's shenanigans when Oswald paid visits to the Soviet and Cuban embassies in Mexico City two months later. What Newman fails to mention is the significance of the CIA file's stating that Hensen "agreed accept phone call with key word 'Laredo' as call from [deleted] contact."

In one of my interviews with Nagell in 1978, he discussed his own use of the same code name, "Laredo," when making contact with Soviet intelligence. When I last spoke with Nagell in April 1994 and gave him Hensen's physical description, he said only: "That fits somebody I'd run into at the time."

Asked why he chose not to mention Nagell in his book, Newman responded: "My methodology made that impossible. If it wasn't in the new documents, it didn't make it into my manuscript. I wanted to keep everything focused on the CIA's internal paper trail. I still don't know what to make of the Nagell story; if it's true, it's dynamite."

What Newman sets down about the CIA's "paper trail" does, in fact, add credence to the Nagell revelations. Here, for example, is the author's summary analysis of the three months preceding the assassination:

"The CIA was far more interested in Oswald than they have ever admitted to publicly. At some time before the Kennedy assassination, the Cuban Affairs offices at the CIA developed a keen operational interest in him. Oswald's visit to Mexico City may have had some connection to the FBI or CIA. It appears that the Mexico City station wrapped its own operation around Oswald's consular visits there. Whether or not Oswald understood what was going on is less clear than the probability that something operational was happening in conjunction with his visit."

Noting the possibility of a CIA "renegade faction" manipulating Oswald, Newman concludes: "We can finally say with some authority that the CIA was spinning a web of deception about Oswald weeks before the President's murder," based upon an exhaustive survey of now-visible files that were denied to previous official investigations.

This dovetails with Nagell's earlier statements that the CIA's Cuban Task Force, then run by Desmond FitzGerald, as well as the agency's Mexico City station, were deeply embroiled in the Oswald affair. It also backs up his claim that Oswald did not know who was pulling his strings.

Newman devotes considerable attention, too, to Gerry Patrick Hemming, whose CIA files bear curious parallels to Oswald's. A former Marine who filed reports to the agency, Hemming claimed to have met with Oswald near the Cuban consulate in Los Angeles early in 1959. Hemming's trail into the Cuban exile community seems to have been followed by two CIA employees in Los Angeles, Joseph DaVanon and Ernest Liebacher. Both of their names appear in the notebook seized from Nagell by the FBI in September 1963, under the heading "CIA."

Also pertinent is Newman's tracing of earlier CIA interest in Oswald, from the moment the ex-Marine showed up at the American Embassy in Moscow trying to renounce his citizenship in October 1959. "I was particularly interested," Newman says, "in trying to marshal evidence for Oswald having been a counterintelligence dangle. In other words, the CIA would have been using him to ferret out a 'mole,' who was first thought to be in the U2 program before the focus very quickly changed to their own Soviet Russia Division." (A "mole" is a hidden asset of the KGB, such as Aldrich Ames; observing the then top-secret U2 spy-plane program was part of Oswald's mission while a Marine in Japan.)

Newman observes that the "most pronounced fingerprints" on Oswald emanated from the CIA's mole-hunting unit, CI/SIG, run by the late superspook James Jesus Angleton. The existence of Soviet moles inside the CIA was among Nagell's key points about the assassination. He indicated that John Paisley, who was in charge of a CIA unit overseeing Soviet electronics at the time Oswald was employed in a radio-electronics factory in Minsk—and who died mysteriously in 1978—was one such mole. Nagell also hinted that his own case officer inside the Mexico City station had nefarious ties to Soviet intelligence, which he himself did not discover until the late summer of 1963.

This is not to say that the Soviets were behind the assassination, a theory that Nagell adamantly repudiated, but rather that the CIA hierarchy's cover-up of its relations with Oswald related to its ultra-secret mole hunt.

Norman Mailer, whose 1995 book *Oswald's Tale* offers fresh insights into Oswald's time in the USSR, conducted numerous interviews with ex-KGB agents there. After reading Newman's book, Mailer says:

"I redid a little of my thinking on what the KGB told us. They were very consistent, which made me suspicious as it made me confident. They said over and over they were not interested in Oswald because they had better information on the U2. 'What is he, some kind of exotic dangle?' they wondered. 'Did the CIA send him over here as just someone who they [CIA] could observe what's done to him? So we don't do anything to him, we won't debrief him overtly, we don't want to tip our hand.'

"I accepted that, when I got to know the KGB and how conservative they were, how terrified of making a mistake. The KGB is seen in America as a tremendous evil, adventurers. Yeah, they had a wing of 100 guys who were daredevils, like the CIA, but generally the outfit was exceptionally conservative. But reading Newman, I began to think they were afraid that the CIA was after a mole who was telling the KGB about the U2. This is something I didn't think of while we were over there, I wish we had. We didn't see all the KGB files, no question. They didn't reveal a lot to us, saying they were protecting their sources, and there's no question we received an edited version of their files."

Taking up residence for three months in Russia, Mailer was granted access to much information gathered by the KGB during Oswald's tenure in the USSR, which his book quotes at length, and proves that Soviet intelligence bugged Oswald's Minsk apartment and maintained constant surveillance of his activities. Mailer believes the KGB "never would have used Oswald. They had too much petty stuff on him. Once you've seen a man losing arguments and being stupid with his wife, it's very hard to pick him to go out and kill a President. In fact, their first fear was that the assassination was a provocation by the United States to start a nuclear war. But I used to quiz the KGB very hard about whether they didn't keep up with Oswald when he came back to the USA. Finally what they confessed was, they didn't have the resources. It was very difficult because their every move here was being watched."

This, of course, does not take into account whether the KGB could have utilized an American "double agent," like Nagell, to keep tabs on Oswald. On the U.S. side, Mailer thinks the CIA/FBI cover-up was "to protect other things. They had a lot more relations with Oswald than they have allowed. This may have gone as far as [the FBI's] COINTELPRO, and even people inside the [CIA's anti-Castro] JM/WAVE operation knowing of his potential as a killer."

Mailer's book has been taken to task by conspiracy theorists as a sellout, as his research led him to offer a 75 percent conclusion that Oswald probably acted alone. "But I'm not totally convinced [of that]." Mailer says. "If somebody came along with exciting evidence, I'd be willing to chase down another direction. I don't feel the case is closed for me at all."

Mailer and Newman were scheduled for a debate at the Coalition for Political Assassinations conference in Washington last October, until certain preconditions set by Mailer were turned down by the coalition's chief organizer. This led Newman, a retired military-intelligence analyst, to take Mailer to task at the conference, especially over his failure to study the latest batches of CIA files. For his part, Mailer says he figured, "What's the point? We could only do a slipshod job on the new files and they'll be digestible for years to come."

As for Newman's work, Mailer adds: "I think the service he performed was to lay out what the intelligence agencies had *not* been wanting to give us. It's almost as if they were providing the outer husk of the onion, and we're going to have to keep fighting to get layer after layer after layer. But I'd have been much happier if Newman had used his knowledge of intelligence to give us a fighting chance at some idea of how the routing [of CIA/FBI internal information] really works."

While each of these latest books on the assassination unearths some new ground—particularly Newman's sometimes ponderous, but meticulous, scrutiny of the CIA's all-too-evident operational interest in Oswald long before November 22, 1963—the real breakthroughs are likely to follow in the coming months from the Assassination Records Review Board. The ARRB ran up against FBI stonewalling last August, after voting for full release of 15 records which the bureau then appealed directly to President Clinton to continue to withhold on "national security" grounds. The ARRB has come under fire from some assassination researchers for complying with FBI and CIA requests to keep back certain files "relating to sensitive intelligence sources and methods."

Still, what's been publicly released so far—with the promise of much more to come before the ARRB mandate expires late in 1997—has given additional fuel to conspiracy researchers. We now know, for example, that David Phillips, the CIA's covert-action chief in Mexico City, was in Washington on October 1, 1963, waiting to pick up "bulk materials." These probably included transcripts of conversations between Oswald and Moscow's Soviet Embassy, some of which appear to have involved an Oswald impostor.

We also know that, as early as February 1961, Phillips was supervising a CIA operation against the Fair Play for Cuba Committee, a one-man chapter of which Oswald established in New Orleans in the summer of 1963. Phillips was working in tandem with James McCord, a CIA agent later involved in the Watergate scandal. As far back as 1976, both Phillips and McCord were cited in cryptic comments by Richard Nagell as having played some role in the CIA's relationship with Oswald.

Until a CIA file release by the ARRB last September, the CIA had always refused to acknowledge its use of double agents against the Soviets. However, a November 29, 1963 cable relating to its Mexico City operations states that CIA "double agents have not had meetings with Sovs [Soviets] since assassination." This is further substantiation for the agency's utilization of operatives like Nagell.

According to Noel Twyman, a San Diego researcher who was able to speak to Nagell twice over the telephone in the months before his death, he expressed renewed fear for his life but said his private files were in safekeeping. Nagell added that there are individuals still alive who would be greatly "embarrassed" in the event his materials should come to light.

Two police officers entering Nagell's residence after his body was discovered found no evidence of anything having been disturbed. A number of weapons were inventoried and the house was sealed off by the L.A. Coroner's office, pending the arrival of an executor named by Nagell for his estate. An LAPD officer was said to be watching the house to make sure that nobody broke in. Meantime, a curious message went from the coroner's office to the L.A. Public Administrator, which is in charge of estate arrangements. "When entering the house, beware of traps or pitfalls, due to deceased's CIA background connections," it said. Clearly, L.A. officials realized this was no ordinary case.

Richard Case Nagell died as he lived, alone and holding his cards close to his vest. The Assassination Records Review Board did make contact with his executor, but what transpired next is being held closely by Washington. Will the world soon know the full story of "the man who knew too much?" For now, it is a waiting game.

33

High Times Magazine, August 1996

"JFK & the Cuban Connection: Havana's Spies Spill the Beans"

*L*ike Korea's DMZ, the ninety-mile strait that separates Havana from Miami *is a place where the Cold War survives. This particular Cold War hotspot may have been the matrix for the conspiracy on the life of John F. Kennedy. But even as the JFK whodunit became a Hollywood craze and national obsession in the USA, stateside conspiracy-heads had no contact with those in Cuba who were investigating the cataclysmic 1963 assassination. Now, for the first time, top figures from Fidel Castro's intelligence apparatus have come forward with their own pieces to the puzzle. Their story was recently unveiled at a watershed summit meeting between Cuban and U.S. assassination researchers at Nassau, the Bahamas. Dick Russell, one of America's foremost researchers attending the conference, offers this ground-breaking report to* High Times.

On a full moon early last December, a select group of around 25 people from Cuba and the USA converged in the Bahamas for a historic gathering. Wayne Smith, former head of the U.S. diplomatic mission to Cuba and today a supporter of improved U.S.-Cuban relations at Washington's Center for International Policy, worked for two years to arrange this first-ever meeting between Cuban officials and U.S. researchers of the assassination of President John F. Kennedy. The Assassination Records Review Board (ARRB), an official body in Washington established to review all documents related to the assassination for public release, also sent a representative.

Before now, the information contained in Cuban files on events leading to the tragedy in Dallas on November 22, 1963 had remained secret. But the Havana delegation to the conference included General Fabian Escalante, former chief of Cuba's G-2 intelligence agency, and his lifelong assistant, Arturo Rodriguez. Also on hand was Carlos Lechuga, Cuba's ambassador to the United Nations in 1963—with whom the Kennedy Administration had been quietly working towards an accommodation between the USA and the island nation 90 miles off the Florida coast.

General Escalante, as director of Havana's Institute for National Security Studies, has headed an investigation into the JFK case since 1992. Escalante remains a close associate of Premier Fidel Castro, so clearly his project has the highest sanction. He promised a sneak preview of a new book on the assassination, authored by himself and Arturo Rodriguez, to be published by Ocean Press later this year.

Portents were in the air from the outset. The road to the Nassau conference site was called John F. Kennedy Drive. The hotel bartender's name turned out to be Oswald. And it became clear that the Cubans had definitely come with a point of view.

"We believe Kennedy became an obstacle to U.S. military aggression against Cuba," Escalante put it. "There were two objectives to the plot—to kill Kennedy and to blame Cuba for the crime."

The Miami Puzzle

The Cubans backed up their claim with new evidence linking right-wing Cuban exiles, renegade CIA officials, organized-crime figures and possibly wealthy Texans to the conspiracy—a complex scenario in which accused assassin Lee Harvey Oswald was set up as (in his own words) a "patsy" whose history would implicate Havana and its Soviet allies.

After the October 1962 Cuban Missile Crisis brought the USA and USSR to the brink of nuclear war, Kennedy's agreement with the Soviets officially barred further U.S. attempts to overthrow Castro or invade Cuba, and U.S.-Soviet relations began to thaw. Even though the CIA continued to plot Castro's assassination, the Kennedy Administration quietly began seeking a rapprochement with Cuba, says Escalante. But before long, wind of the President's efforts got to the CIA and its Miami-based Cuban-exile minions.

Exile militant Felipe Vidal Santiago, arrested on a 1964 sabotage mission into Cuba, told his captors that in Washington, D.C. in December 1962 he'd met with a lawyer/lobbyist connected to a "Citizen's Committee to Free Cuba." This lawyer informed Vidal Santiago of a conversation he'd had with Republican Henry Cabot Lodge, soon to be U.S. ambassador to South Vietnam, who said he'd heard from Kennedy aide Walt Rostow of "a plan to open a dialogue with Cuba."

"Vidal told us he was very surprised," says Escalante. In fact Vidal, infuriated and betrayed, had alerted his exile cohorts, as well as a CIA contact, Colonel William Bishop. "It was almost like a bomb, an intentional message against Kennedy." Vidal was also an information conduit for General Edwin Walker, the ultra-right Texan paramilitary leader at whom Oswald had allegedly taken a shot in April 1963. And FBI files call Vidal a "very close friend" of Miami mobster John Martino, who intimated to family and associates that he had foreknowledge of the JFK assassination.

Then in April 1963, Lee Harvey Oswald—only nine months back from a two-and-a-half year "defection" to the Soviet Union—moved to New Orleans and set up a one-man chapter of the Fair Play for Cuba Committee. By this time, the Kennedy Administration was clamping down on CIA-backed exile raids against Cuba, and the exiles were publicly accusing Kennedy of betraying their cause.

"By mid-1963, we had infiltrated a special group of exiles working with the CIA," says Escalante. "A CIA official came to a safe-house in Miami and said to a group of Cuban exiles, 'You must eliminate Kennedy.'"

The Cubans did not know this CIA man's name, but they knew plenty about David Atlee Phillips, who was running the CIA's covert operations out of its Mexico City station. It has long been speculated that Phillips was really "Maurice Bishop," who was identified by exile leader Antonio Veciana, speaking to Congressional investigators in 1978, as his CIA case officer, involved in numerous assassination plots against Castro.

Veciana claimed "Bishop" introduced him to Oswald at a meeting in Dallas in September 1963.

Although Phillips' physical description was a near-match for that provided by Veciana, the exile would never positively identify Phillips as "Bishop." Phillips, who died in 1988, denied using the alias or working with Veciana.

Now the Cubans say they have evidence that "Bishop" was indeed Phillips. "In 1979, Veciana told one of our informants in Miami he had been pushed to identify the CIA officer by the House Select Committee on Assassinations and had given a fake name, but that it was David Phillips," says Escalante. "A close friend of Veciana also told us Phillips had threatened Veciana so he would not reveal his true identity." Further corroboration came from another informant to the Cuban government who had delivered a written message from Phillips to Veciana in 1959, when he was still in Havana.

One of Phillips' close associates was a Miami-based CIA officer named David Morales. Escalante says Morales was identified by Rolando Cubela as "one of the officials" who spoke with him in Paris in September 1963 about assassinating Castro. Cubela, a Cuban official who was really a double agent code-named AM/LASH by the CIA, was in Paris picking up his weaponry—a pen containing lethal poison—to kill Castro at the very moment of JFK's assassination. In the aftermath of the JFK assassination, his mission to assassinate Castro was scotched. Cubela, a crony of top Miami mobster Santo Trafficante, was finally arrested in Cuba in 1966.

Trafficante was one of several gangsters hired by the CIA to recruit Cuban exiles into assassination plots against Castro. His Havana casino operations had been shut down by Castro when the Revolution took power in 1959, and he was briefly imprisoned; Rolando Cubela is believed to have helped negotiate his release. Upon arriving in Miami in 1960, Traficante found himself among the top targets of U.S. Attorney General Robert Kennedy—the president's kid brother.

Mob Lawyer, a recent book by the late Trafficante's attorney, Frank Ragano, contains allegations that the mobster worked with New Orleans mob boss Carlos Marcello and Teamsters Union leader Jimmy Hoffa—both targets of Robert Kennedy's far-reaching corruption probes—in helping plan the JFK assassination. New information released at the Nassau conference supports these allegations.

Havana's Missing Pieces

The Cubans' information comes from Tony Cuesta, a Cuban exile leader taken prisoner in a 1966 raid. "Cuesta was blinded in an explosion and spent most of his time in the hospital," Escalante recalls. In 1978, he was among a group of imprisoned exiles released through a deal with the Carter Administration. "A few days before he was to leave," continues Escalante, "I had several conversations with him, and he wrote up a declaration. Cuesta volunteered, 'I want to tell you something very important, but I do not want to make this public—because I am returning to my family in Miami, and this could be very dangerous.' I think this was a little bit of thanks on his part for the medical care he received." Cuesta died in 1994.

In his written statement, Tony Cuesta named two other exiles involved in the JFK assassination, Eladio del Valle and Herminio Díaz García. "We asked, but he did not want to be questioned further about this," Escalante says.

Eladio Del Valle was murdered in Miami in 1967, on the same night that David Ferrie—Carlos Marcello's personal pilot, and an associate of both del Valle and Oswald—supposedly committed suicide in New Orleans, hours before he was to be questioned by District Attorney Jim Garrison about the assassination. According to Escalante, del Valle served in both military intelligence and the judicial police in the regime of Fulgencio Batista, the Cuban dictator ousted by Castro. "Del Valle was in charge of narcotics in a town south of Havana, where he had business dealings with Santo Trafficante," Escalante's Cuban files show. After Castro's triumph, del Valle fled to Miami and formed the anti-Communist Cuban Liberation Movement.

"We managed to penetrate this organization," reveals Escalante. "We came to know a lot of plans for exile invasions, secret overflights to provide arms to internal rebel groups. David Ferrie was the pilot for some of these flights. One of our agents talked on many occasions with del Valle, who in 1962 told him that Kennedy must be killed to solve the Cuban problem."

(Herminio Díaz García died in Cuba during the same 1966 raid in which Tony Cuesta was arrested.)

Further substantiation was also provided this writer by Richard Case Nagell, a CIA/KGB double agent whose body was found last November 1 in Los Angeles—just as the ARRB was attempting to reach him for an interview. I interviewed Nagell extensively for my book, *The Man Who Knew Too Much*, in which he recounts penetrating several plans to assassinate Kennedy, all involving embittered Cuban exiles, during the 1962–63 period. Nagell would never reveal the identity of two exiles he claimed deceived Oswald into believing they were Castro operatives. But he did say that del Valle was in touch with one of the Oswald-linked exiles. And every time I probed him, Nagell always steered the conversation to Tony Cuesta—the man who, according to the Cubans, knew the answer to my question.

Havana–Washington Shadow Play

In September 1963, just two months before the assassination, Cuban UN Ambassador Lechuga was contacted by one of Kennedy's trusted UN delegates. William Attwood. "He told me this was a private interview," Lechuga recalls. "We spoke on three occasions, trying to break the ice between our countries. Attwood said we should begin a dialogue. He said the idea came from Kennedy, but that we should keep the conversations secret because if the Republicans found out there would be a huge scandal in Congress."

Lechuga says he was surprised by the American's approach, because exile raids and efforts to destabilize Cuba were continuing. Adds Escalante: "There was a double track happening. One path was continued sabotage and isolation of Cuba, to force us to sit down at the negotiating table under very disadvantageous conditions. So the Cuban government took its time to deeply study Attwood's proposal. In our view, one strategy was coming from the Administration and another from the CIA, the exiles and the Mafia." The Cubans are convinced that word about the secret talks leaked out, and sparked a conspiracy to kill the American President and invade Cuba.

In September 1963. Rolando Cubela traveled to Brazil to meet with CIA contacts about killing Castro. Simultaneously, an American journalist, Daniel Harker, interviewed Castro at a gathering inside Havana's Brazilian Embassy. Harker's article quoted Castro saying: "United States leaders should think that if they assist in terrorist plans to eliminate Cuban leaders, they themselves will not be safe." The story, widely disseminated in the U.S. press, would be used by right-wing elements as evidence that Cuba was behind the assassination.

But Escalante says the article was a distortion. He says what Castro really stated was: "American leaders should be careful because the anti-Castro operations were something nobody could control." He was not threatening JFK, but *warning* him.

In late September that year, Oswald left New Orleans for Mexico City. On the way, he showed up in Dallas at the door of Cuban exile Silvia Odio, in the company of two Latins who identified themselves as "Angel" and "Leopoldo," who told Odio they were soliciting funds for the *Junta Revolucionaria* (JURE). Odio's exile organization. After the visit, according to Odio, "Leopoldo" telephoned her and described their U.S. companion as "kind of loco. He could go either way. He could do anything—like getting underground in Cuba, like killing Castro. He says we should have shot President Kennedy after the Bay of Pigs."

The Cuban hypothesis is that the Odio incident had a dual design. JURE was run by Manuel Ray, a moderate exile leader opposed by the CIA but in close touch with the Kennedy Administration. But the Cubans say "Angel" and "Leopoldo" were agents from the right-wing exile group Revolutionary Student Directorate (DRE), which operated under the CIA's direction. It was the DRE's propagandists who actively sought to tie Oswald to Cuba immediately after the assassination. Escalante offered a possible identification of "Angel" as DRE leader Isidro Borja, who closely resembled a man seen standing behind Oswald in a famous photo, helping him pass out FAIR PLAY FOR CUBA leaflets in New Orleans.

Then on September 27, 1963, Oswald showed up three times at the Cuban consulate in Mexico City, seeking an immediate visa to visit the island. He also visited the Soviet embassy on the same day. (Some researchers believe this could have been an impostor "Oswald," but the Cubans say it was the real Oswald.)

Oswald's request was turned down. He angrily stormed out, and shortly returned to Dallas. Says Escalante: "We believe Oswald was acting according to plan—to travel to Cuba for a few days, in order to appear as a Cuban agent after the assassination."

Escalante further claims that when that plan failed, the CIA's David Phillips arranged to have letters addressed to Oswald from Havana. On the final day of the 1995 Nassau conference, a slide-show depicted five letters addressed to Oswald from Cuba; two dated before the assassination, three immediately after. One of these letters, intercepted by Cuban authorities, was dated November 14, 1963 and addressed to "Lee Harvey Oswald, Royalton Hotel Miami" (where Oswald had never, in fact, stayed). It was signed "Jorge." According to Arturo Rodriguez, "The text was of a conspiratorial character. It was written on the same kind of typewriter as the two others, which the FBI has concluded were composed on the same machine. We think all these letters were written by the same person—as part of a plan to blame our country for the assassination."

Felipe Vidal Santiago told Cuban intelligence that on the weekend before the assassination, he was invited to a meeting in Dallas by the CIA's Colonel

William Bishop. "It was supposed to be a meeting with a few wealthy people to talk about financing anti-Castro operations," says Escalante. Bishop left on his own "for interviews" numerous times during their stay in Dallas. After approximately four days they returned to Miami.

Not long before his death in 1993, Colonel Bishop confirmed to this writer that he'd had knowledge of the JFK plot. The Cubans indicate that the Vidal-Bishop Dallas trip concerned plans for re-taking the island once Castro's people had been implicated in the assassination.

Escalante surmises: "Oswald was an intelligence agent of the U.S.—CIA, FBI, military, or all of these, we don't know. He was manipulated, told he was penetrating a group of Cuban agents that wanted to kill Kennedy. But from the very beginning, he was to be the element to blame Cuba."

"Not less than 15 persons took part in the assassination," Escalante theorizes. "At the same time, knowing a little about CIA operations, we see how they used the principle of decentralized operations—independent parties with a specific role, to guarantee compartmentalization and to keep it simple."

The Nassau gathering marked the inception of what is anticipated will be an ongoing exchange between Cuban and U.S. researchers into the assassination. The hope is that access to Cuban documentation might be provided in the future—such as Tony Cuesta's written "declaration." The fact that former Cuban intelligence officials are willing to share their knowledge signifies a momentous watershed in the ongoing effort to unravel the haunting mystery of who really killed JFK.

34

A Man Named "Bob":
New Clues in the Nagell Saga

S ince Nagell's sudden death in 1995, and even since the revised edition
of my book came out in 2003, a number of new clues have continued to
surface that verify portions of his story—and offer fresh leads for investigators.

1. In terms of "back-up" for Nagell's story, a significant piece of new information appears in a book published in 2007, written by Ion Mihai Pacepa,
   a former chief of the Romanian intelligence service. It pertains to what
   Nagell wrote Senator Richard Russell in 1967 from prison: "In the summer of 1963, I received instructions to initiate certain action against Mr.
   Oswald, who was the indispensable tool in the conspiracy, and thereafter
   depart the United States, legally."[50]

As he wrote elsewhere, Nagell was to try to persuade Oswald "that the deal was
phony and if this didn't work, and if it looked like things were going to progress beyond the talking stage, to get rid of him." Several time in our interviews,
Nagell emphasized: "If anybody wanted to stop the assassination, it would be the
KGB. But they didn't do enough."

The book by Pacepa, who was granted political asylum in the U.S. in 1978, is
titled *Programmed to Kill: Lee Harvey Oswald, the Soviet KGB, and the Kennedy
Assassination*. Its claim, based on alleged inside information, is that Oswald was
originally recruited by the Soviets but then went "out of control." So, Pacepa
writes, "In the spring of 1963, the chief of the PGU's Thirteenth Department
[KGB assassination unit], General Ivan Fadeykin, began searching for an agent
to 'neutralize' Oswald."[51]

It seems that Nagell may have been the agent assigned to that task.

---

[50] Unless otherwise specified, all the Nagell quotations are taken from my book, *The Man Who
Knew Too Much* (New York.: Carroll & Graf Publishers, 1992).
[51] Pacepa quote: *Programmed to Kill* by Ion Mihai Pacepa (Chicago: Ivan R. Dee, 2007),
p. 255.

2. The public record on where Oswald was during late August and the first two weeks of September 1963 is virtually nonexistent, although he—or someone looking like him—did show up in Clinton, Louisiana. In a letter to attorney Fensterwald, Nagell described a meeting he had with Oswald—also apparently in September—in Jackson Square, New Orleans. There Nagell attempted to persuade him that he was being set up as a fall guy, in an assassination plot then scheduled for the latter part of that month in the Washington area. "He was asked some subtle questions relating to his discussions with Leopoldo and Angel," Nagell wrote, "about his pending move to Baltimore, Md., why he was going there without his wife and child, etc."

A recently discovered FBI memorandum describes a letter from the U.S. Civil Service Commission, dated October 15, 1964, concerning one of its investigators, Patrick F. Tallaro, who'd been conducting a neighborhood investigation at an apartment house at 915 Saint Paul Street in Baltimore. The landlady informed Tallaro "that her housekeeper, Mrs. [Georgia] Ward, had seen Lee Harvey Oswald on television at the time of President Kennedy's assassination and recognized him as the man who had stayed in a room at their place for about two weeks in August 1963." When the investigator then asked the housekeeper how she could be certain, "Mrs. Ward stated that she recognized Oswald so quickly because she had seen him frequently during the two week period, as he rarely left his room and seemed to have no particular activity or job. . . . Both Mrs. Ward and Mrs. Tarsia [the landlady] stated that Oswald apparently used an alias instead of his own name. The Investigator did not ask to examine the ledger for names listed in August 1963."[52]

3. When Nagell took himself out of the picture by shooting two holes in the ceiling of the El Paso bank on September 20, he said that all his actions were intended as a signal to someone waiting for him across the Mexican border in Juarez. When he asked teller Patsy Gordon for $100 in *American Express* traveler's checks, the specific reference was by design. At our last meeting, Nagell suggested that I examine his trial transcript and think about why the prosecution raised such an objection to his mention of American Express. And, in a letter he wrote Art Greenstein, Nagell indicated it was through American Express that he was supposed to receive payment for his intelligence work in 1962–63.

The letters "Am Ex" appear at least six times in Oswald's address book as well. Author Joan Mellen revealed, in her 2005 book *A Farewell to Justice*, that when

---

[52] Baltimore: FBI files 100-10461-8453 (October 15, 1964); 100-10461-8455 (October 29, 1964).

Oswald was arrested for a street altercation with anti-Castro Cuban exiles in New Orleans that August, on the margin of a note he handed to police lieutenant Francis Martello was the espionage number for Michael Jelisavcic, a CIA asset at American Express. (When the CIA declassified the document in recent years, the number was inadvertently non-redacted.) Jelisavcic was the manager of American Express in Moscow at the time of Oswald's defection, according to FBI files. As late as January 1965, FBI Director Hoover wrote in a memo to his Special-Agent-in-Charge in New York about an investigation of Jelisavcic and added: "During the course of any interview of subject, you should closely question him concerning the circumstances surrounding his name and phone number being in the address book of Lee Harvey Oswald."[53]

4. Robert Clayton Buick, in a new book called *Reflection: Behind the Rain*, goes into further detail about his being tasked by the CIA to spy on certain people at Mexico City's Hotel Luma, which a paper trail shows both Buick and Nagell to have frequented in 1962–63. A bullfighter in Mexico at the time, Buick's book now identifies his CIA handlers, who used false names, as David Phillips and E. Howard Hunt. (Phillips called himself "Maurice Bishop," according to Buick.)

It was September 1963. "You'll be looking for any subversive activity, strong anti-American sentiments," Buick says Hunt instructed him. Hunt later called and requested specific information on the Hotel Luma's cocktail waiter, Franz Waehauf, a Czech national whom Nagell had earlier been assigned to keep an eye on. Buick claims he told Phillips and Hunt about a "little weasel face dude talking to Waehauf" one night in late September. Asked to keep watching, Buick then made a point to run into "Alek Hidell," who bragged that he wanted to get to Cuba and was planning to go by boat. "Hidell" also told Buick he was first going to "hit" President Kennedy: "It's all set, the machinery is already in gear." Curiously, Phillips and Hunt wanted to be assured that he'd identified himself as "Alek," not "Alex." Buick assured them that it was 'Alek." Had he seen the fellow in the Luma before? Phillips asked. Buick flashed back to having observed him once before, about two months earlier, sitting in a booth with a tall man who had a scar across his face. That would have been Nagell, and Oswald, summer 1963—a time when Nagell once told me Oswald made his *first* trip to Mexico City.[54]

When assessing the credibility of Nagell, it is crucial to keep a time-line in mind. Only in recent years through declassified documents have we learned that

---

[53] Hoover memo on Jelisavcic: FBI file, January 18, 1965, "Michael Jelisavcic, Espionage-R."
[54] Buick story: *Reflection: Behind the Rain* by Robert Claytor Buick (Bloomington, IN: Author House, 2007).

David Phillips, in charge of CIA anti-Castro operations in Mexico in 1963, was also the CIA's main man in charge of penetrating the Fair Play for Cuba Committee (FPCC). We have known since 1975, when Nagell's notebook seized by the FBI in September 1963 was finally released to attorney Bernard Fensterwald, Jr., that it contained listings for the FPCC as well as for the Cuban Embassy in Mexico City—listings that a notebook maintained by Oswald also contained.

In the mid-1970s, Nagell wrote in one of his "cryptograms" to his friend Art Greenstein: "What's this? Dave Phillips, titular head of Latin American operations (a position once held by Dizzy Fits: Desmond FitzGerald), organizing former U.S. Intelligence officers to defend the CIA against those who attack it? Why the advertisement that he had been station chief in la República Dominicana, Brazil, Venezuela? Why nothing said about his capers in Mexico? Was he a mere accomplice in the N-matter?" (It seemed clear to me that the "N-matter" referred to Nagell himself.)

We also have learned only recently that information about Oswald's activities was closely held in the fall of 1963 by Desmond FitzGerald's Special Affairs Staff inside the CIA.[55] Many years earlier, Nagell had written that he "did [FitzGerald] some favors in Mexico, in the 1962–63 period, when he was ramrod for dirty tricks in Latin America." Nagell also said that, on August 27, 1963, through CIA channels he had alerted FitzGerald about an assassination plot against Kennedy involving Oswald.

We have learned, again only recently, that Cuban exile leader Manuel Artime was a key figure in the CIA's AMWORLD operation, an attempt in 1963 to assemble a military force of Cuban exiles who might produce a coup against Castro, and thus bring about conditions for the U.S. to come to their aid. Also, that Artime had a strong relationship with Robert Kennedy and that FitzGerald (according to David Talbot's 2007 book, *Brothers*) "raged against the way the president's brother was micromanaging Cuba policy and running his own secret game with the exile leaders he favored. . . . The more affiliated Artime became with Bobby, the less the CIA trusted him." Recently declassified CIA files reveal that FitzGerald ordered surveillance placed on Artime for the first two weeks of July 1963, even as the exile leader was billeted in a CIA safe house in Maryland.

Back in 1970, Nagell wrote that, while in Miami in January 1963, "I conducted surveillance on a man, said to have been an ex-CIA employee, observed talking to [exile] leader Manuel Artime and former Cuban senator/racketeer Rolando Masferrer." In 1974, in a document he filed with the U.S. Court of Claims in Washington, Nagell elaborated that his ongoing 1963 investigation into Artime was one of the reasons he became convinced by September that he "may have performed services for a foreign nation." Nagell hinted that Artime

---

[55] SAS and Oswald: Summers, *Not in Your Lifetime*, p. 384.

might in fact have been a Cuban intelligence agent, after being captured at the Bay of Pigs and then released from jail by Castro late in 1962. While Artime was, according to Nagell, not directly involved in the Kennedy assassination, he "may have been in meetings with certain people."

Central to the Nagell story was another CIA man whom he identified only by the pseudonym of "Bob." They had known each other in Japan, and run into each other again in Mexico City in September 1962, shortly before the onset of the Cuban Missile Crisis. For the next year, "Bob" then became Nagell's point-of-contact with the CIA, initially assigning him to participate "in a 'disinformation' project directed against the Soviet Embassy at Mexico City." Nagell also revealed that "Bob" was a "subordinate" CIA officer whose ultimate reporting was to Desmond FitzGerald.

Thanks to newly released CIA files, we now have a candidate for who "Bob" really was. His name is Henry Hecksher. He was the senior political officer for the CIA's AMWORLD project, and a special assistant to FitzGerald. Hecksher was also the case officer for Manuel Artime. In Mexico City, the only officer designated for involvement in AMWORLD was David Phillips. Hecksher and Phillips, it turns out, went way back.

A small obituary appeared in the *New York Times* on March 29, 1990: HENRY HECKSHER, 79; SERVED OSS IN WAR AND LATER THE CIA, it was headlined. The obituary mentioned his service in Laos, Indonesia, Japan, and Chile—but said nothing about operations against Cuba. It did elaborate: "He was the CIA station chief in Santiago, Chile, during the time the CIA spent more than $8 million in an unsuccessful effort to prevent the election of Salvador Allende Gossens and later sought to make it impossible for him to govern once he was elected. President Allende did not survive a military uprising against him in 1973."

Through a relative of Hecksher's, I was able to obtain copies of résumés he'd filled out over the course of his career, as well as a letter he wrote outlining some highlights of his life in intelligence. I also conducted interviews with several of his associates. The picture that emerged was an intriguing one.

Hecksher had been born in Hamburg, Germany, in 1910, where his father was a member of the German Parliament and Managing Director of the Hamburg America Line. Henry attended private schools as a youth, then went on to study law and economics at universities in Berlin, Freiburg, and Hamburg, graduating from the latter with a degree in International and Criminal Law in 1937.

Tom Polgar, a longtime friend who worked closely with Hecksher in the CIA, recalled: "His was a very distinguished family. I don't know if there was any Jewish blood, but he left Germany on his own, for political reasons."[56] Hecksher went first to London, "with a view to extending my banking experience," studying

---

[56] Polgar quotes: Author's telephone interview, March 24, 2008.

the foundations of England's money markets while aiding in the resettlement of Eastern European refugees. He then entered the U.S. on an immigration visa in March 1939, initially employed by the Princeton Bank & Trust Company.

Joining the Army before Pearl Harbor, the thirty-one-year-old Hecksher rose rapidly through the ranks. He saw action in five major battles during World War II, including participating in the D-Day invasion. By war's end First Lieutenant Hecksher, an Order of Battle specialist with the Third Army, decided to apply to the OSS. Polgar, then an investigator with the OSS's Office of Security, was assigned to look into Hecksher's background. "I got very, very favorable results," he recalled. "Everybody spoke very highly of him. And the next thing I know, he shows up in Berlin in 1946 as my superior!"

Hecksher became chief of the OSS's counterintelligence branch in post-war Berlin. Fluent in German, it was he who first interrogated a number of prominent Nazis prior to the Nuremberg Trials. An "Interrogation Picture Book" that Hecksher took at the time included Admiral Wilhelm Canaris, Walter Schellenberg, Julius Streicher, Fritz Thyssen, and Adolf Hitler's step-sister.

After the American occupation of Berlin, Hecksher moved via the OSS to a long career with the CIA. "His main interest was Soviet communism, that was a passion for Henry," according to his sister-in-law. He was multi-lingual (speaking, besides German and English, Dutch, French, Russian and Spanish), and traveled widely. Through the mid-1950s, Hecksher's primary station remained "BOB"—Berlin Operating Base. During the 1953 Berlin riots after Stalin died, Hecksher unsuccessfully sought permission to arm the rioters with rifles and stun guns.

"Henry was my officer who dealt with counterespionage, and also senior German officials," recalled Peter Sichel, who was his boss at BOB.[57] "He was extremely bright and imaginative, and an extremely good liaison with people like the police and security services, and the legal bureaucracy in any country."

In 1954, Hecksher was detached to Turkey to assist in modernizing their counterintelligence service. "During the second half of 1954, I served under deep cover in Guatemala to assist in the overthrow of President Arbenz," he would write years later.[58] That was Hecksher's first foray into Latin American affairs. Hecksher used the cover of being a coffee buyer. David Phillips, in his autobiography, calls him "Peter," and remembers Hecksher taking him on a fact-finding trip to gather content for Phillips' broadcast radio propaganda.

"From 1956 till 1957," Hecksher later wrote, "I was chief of operations of Tokyo station. I was in direct liaison with the Japanese intelligence services to work jointly on Soviet and mainland Chinese targets."[59] This was, however,

---

[57] Sichel quotes: Author's telephone interview, March 24, 2008.
[58] Hecksher in Guatemala: Letter supplied by family, November 19, 1982.
[59] Hecksher in Japan: Ibid.

apparently not an assignment that Hecksher spoke much about, even to his friends. The way Tom Polgar remembered it, "Henry, I think, was considered for a position of chief of intelligence in Tokyo, and then it was decided that he would be switched to Laos, and Peter Sichel would take his place in Tokyo."

Asked about this, Sichel said, "As a matter of fact, I never went to Japan, I went to Hong Kong. You see, I was going to be sent to Japan and then it turned out that the military attaché there was a man who had told the FBI that I was a Soviet agent. He had been a colonel in military intelligence in Berlin when I was there—and I found out that all his agents were being run by the Soviets! Well, he really didn't like that. So the only thing he could do was send a letter to the FBI saying that *I* was a Soviet spy! The FBI investigated me and found out I wasn't. Not that I thought they were able to do that sophisticated a job, but that's beside the point. Anyway, in Japan I would have had some problems with inter-agency coordination, so I was sent to Hong Kong. From 1956 to 1959. Henry Hecksher was chief of station in Laos at the same time."

But hadn't Hecksher been based in Japan before Laos? I asked. "No, no, never," Sichel said. When I suggested to him that Hecksher's résumé stated that he had, Sichel replied, "That I did not know. My memory is in pretty good shape, why didn't I know that?"

One of Hecksher's résumés reports that he was in Japan until late August 1957, when he moved on to Laos. This would mean that his service there overlapped with Nagell's, who arrived in Tokyo in February 1957 after also making several trips from Korea the previous year when he was with the Army's then-top-secret Field Operations Intelligence. There Nagell worked closely with the Japanese police, and says he was enlisted by the CIA to try to entice the defection of a Soviet Colonel, Nikolai Eroshkin, who was the military attaché at its embassy in Tokyo. Nagell maintained that FitzGerald, then the CIA's Far Eastern Division chief, was involved in the plan—and it would seem logical that Hecksher, as the Tokyo chief of operations working "on political affairs in Japan with specific reference to relations between Japan and the Communist Orbit," would have been privy to it as well. (After Oswald arrived with his Marine unit that September, according to Nagell, Oswald, too, later met with Eroshkin.)

While stationed next in Laos, Hecksher is said to have had some problems with American neutrality policies. The U.S. Ambassador reportedly requested his early removal as station chief, but CIA Director Allen Dulles permitted Hecksher to remain. At one point, he moved down to Thailand, where he supervised covert trans-border activities in the so-called "Golden Triangle."

Sometime in 1960, Hecksher left Laos and began operating under State Department cover in Washington. In 1982, he wrote a letter to a colleague listing some "snippets [that] may enable someone better organized than I happen to be, to piece together my life history." One such "snippet" stated: "From 1960 till 1963, I was one of the branch chiefs of the Far East Division. . . . Under my supervision the [Djakarta] Station's program was re-oriented toward penetrating the Indonesian military in anticipation of military intervention in the deposition of President Sukarno."

Nothing was said in the letter about any activities revolving around Cuba. However, Hecksher's résumé dated August 24, 1964, records: "From 1960 to Present—in charge of desk in ARA. Supervises the collection of data and the writing of scheduled and spot reports on Latin America." (ARA was the State Department's Bureau of Inter-American Affairs.)

During this same period, recently declassified CIA files have Hecksher's signature or initials on numerous reports relating to Project AM/WORLD, Manuel Artime, and anti-Castro operations. Why was it that, after his retirement from the CIA, he seemed intent on obfuscating this fact?

Constantine Broutsas, another CIA official who'd been a close friend of Hecksher's ever since they met in Berlin in the early 1950s, expressed ignorance that Henry had ever been involved with the Agency's Cuba project. "Now that I didn't know, anything about that," Broutsas said. "When I think of Cuba, I think of Bill Harvey and Ted Shackley, both of whom I knew well. But I didn't know Henry was involved in that particular phase at all. You know, our relationship in Berlin was operational, but from that point on, our friendship was personal and we didn't cross paths operationally."

Hecksher's CIA superior at BOB in Germany, Peter Sichel, would recall: "Unfortunately Henry became, as he got older, extremely right-wing. He became an absolutist and I think he got retired a little too late. That should have happened a little early, before he got involved in this whole mess in Cuba and what-have-you."

Asked to elaborate, Sichel said only: "I knew very little about it, because it was after I left the agency. I only knew it because some of my old buddies got ensnared in it. They ended up with a lot of the old German hands in the Cuba thing. Like William Harvey, who'd been Henry's boss for a while in Berlin. Harvey was an alcoholic. He was very bright, very able, but he destroyed himself."

Tom Polgar did recall that Hecksher "came into Latin American Division, I think about the same time that Desmond FitzGerald took over the division. But I was overseas for eight years then, so the period of Henry's life between '57 and '65, I really had no firsthand knowledge of."

In his written reflections on his career, Hecksher said: "My intelligence specialty is political action, but not to the exclusion of related pursuits, such as counterintelligence. The dominant focus of my professional interests has at all times been the Soviet Union, its satellites and its surrogates.... I always considered myself targeted against the KGB (active measures) and the International Department of the Central Committee of the CPSU."[60]

---

[60] Hecksher reflections: Ibid.

This, of course, would have made Hecksher an ideal candidate to oversee a counterintelligence mission against Cuba, out of Mexico City, during the time of the Missile Crisis. He spoke Spanish, and no one based there with the CIA—not Phillips, not even Station Chief Winston Scott—had the same broad range of experience against the Soviets. (According to Polgar, Hecksher had risen to become chief of the foreign intelligence staff for Western Europe in the mid-1950s.) If he had indeed worked with Nagell in Japan, he could easily have resumed the relationship in Mexico—and dispatched Nagell on his "double agent" mission.

What we do know, beyond a doubt, is that Hecksher soon became FitzGerald's main deputy charged with AMWORLD and Artime's case officer.[61] Nagell related that, almost simultaneously, he was given a list of Cuban exiles whose activities he proceeded to monitor in various locations, including those of Artime.

According to the 2008 book, *Our Man in Mexico: Winston Scott and the Secret History of the CIA*, "Win delegated AMWORLD to Dave Phillips. When Artime passed through Mexico City on his way to the exiles' military bases in Nicaragua, Phillips arranged a safe house and kept his profile low. When Artime started getting bad press as an American agent, headquarters called on Phillips to plant stories in the Mexican press casting his offshore crusade against Castro in a more positive light."[62]

In a CIA memo written by Hecksher in October 1963, he describes plans "to activate our media capabilities in Mexico City on promoting a more acceptable image for AMBIDDY-1 [the code name for Artime]. This was briefly discussed with Michael CHOEDEN [aka David Phillips] on 4 October." Phillips, according to another CIA document, was slated to arrive at the CIA's JMWAVE station in Miami "for consultation" on October 4. So Miami appears to be where Hecksher met with Phillips. (Oswald, according to the Warren Commission, had left Mexico City by bus two days earlier, bound back to Texas.)

In the course of interviews I conducted in 1976 with Antonio Veciana—the exile leader who placed Oswald at a meeting with "Maurice Bishop" (likely David Phillips) and himself in the summer of 1963—Veciana also said: "After the Kennedy assassination, I was in a hotel in Las Vegas. Bishop left to do something. In his briefcase, I saw a memo with the initials—'To HH'—plans they were doing, movements to contact, about the activities of commando groups in Cuba, counter-revolution, like a report." At the time, I could only speculate that

---

[61] Hecksher, Artime, AMWORLD: *Someone Would Have Talked* by Larry Hancock (Southlake, TX: JFK Lancer Productions & Publications, 2006), p. 111. See also Appendix B, pp. 405–11.

[62] Scott/Phillips quote: *Our Man in Mexico* by Jefferson Morley (Lawrence, KS: University Press of Kansas, 2008), p. 161.

"HH" might have referred to E. Howard Hunt, or perhaps Texas oilman H. L. Hunt or even Howard Hughes. The name of Henry Hecksher would not surface for years to come, with his trademark "HH" appearing on numerous CIA memos.

Timing-wise, there was assuredly a connection between the AMWORLD plans targeting Cuba and the build-up to Dallas. "ARTIME is preparing three (3) mother-craft and 30 to 35 attack launches in Miami to be used for daily commando raids on Cuba to begin in the fall of 1963," according to one memo. He was receiving considerable sums of money—$170,000 during August and $47,000 the first part of September, according to a State Department memorandum.[63]

Another memo, generated by Hecksher, described a meeting on the Artime project that took place between November 7 and 10, 1963, where one of Artime's leading advisors took the firm position that, while President Kennedy remained in power, it would be impossible to defeat Castro. Rafael "Chi Chi" Quintero, who worked closely with Artime, was quoted in a book by Don Bohning to the effect that Hecksher did not believe the AMWORLD effort was going to work.

Another curious parallel to events surrounding the assassination relates to a "Memorandum for the Record" that Hecksher wrote on July 10, 1963, regarding a meeting he had with Artime in Washington, concerning Artime's relationship with another exile leader named Manuel Ray. There Artime described at some length "the irreparability of his break with Manuel RAY. . . . Since, at a later stage, this relationship may become a pivotal factor in determining the political complexion of a successorship [to Castro], the facts as recorded by A-1 [Artime] have been set down below."[64]

A CIA dispatch of July 22, 1963 quoted Ray, who was the leader of a group called *Junta Revolucionaria* (JURE): "Manolo Ray himself was personally critical of the CIA and told one JURE associate that he thought CIA agents 'were more dangerous than the Kennedy administration.' He maintained that 'the Kennedy administration would end but CIA agents always stayed and their memory was longer than the memory of elephants and they never forgot or forgave.'"

An astonishing document from February 1964, signed by Hecksher, described an AMWORLD meeting in New York, where it was noted that JURE was being kept under surveillance and that Hecksher had authorized Artime's boats to fire on Ray's boats should they encounter them.[65]

---

[63] For more on Artime and AMWORLD, see *Ultimate Sacrifice* by Lamar Waldron with Thom Hartmann (N.Y.: Carroll & Graf Publishers, 2005).

[64] Artime/Ray: www.maryferrell.org/mffweb/archive, RIF 104-10308-10091.

[65] "JURE Versus AMWORLD," www.maryferrell.org/mffweb/archive.

Six months earlier, on the night of September 25, 1963, three visitors had shown up unexpectedly at the apartment of Silvia Odio in Dallas. She had arrived recently from Puerto Rico, where she'd helped establish a chapter of JURE. Her visitors introduced themselves as Leopoldo, Angel, and Leon Oswald. They said they were raising funds for anti-Castro operations, and passed themselves off as affiliates of JURE. Forty-eight hours later, Leopoldo phoned Odio again and asked what she thought of the American. Leopoldo added, "He could do any-thing—like getting underground in Cuba, like killing Castro. . . . He says we should have shot President Kennedy after the Bay of Pigs. He says we should do something like that."[66] One theory raised in later years was whether the incident may have been staged, as a subtle means of later implicating Manuel Ray's JURE group in the assassination. (Nagell told me that Angel and Leopoldo, whom he knew to be setting up Oswald, had associations with JURE in Puerto Rico.)

None of the AMWORLD operational reports have yet been released by the CIA. The next Hecksher recounted of his personal biography was that, "From 1965 to 1967, I served as the Caracas station chief," during which time he helped the Venezuela security services "to break the backbone of an urban guerrilla movement." He then became the station chief in Santiago, Chile, from 1967 until the end of 1970. "My services culminated in an abortive attempt at pre-venting the election of Salvador Allende," Hecksher wrote.[67] In charge of that particular task force was David Phillips, by then running the CIA's Western Hemisphere Division.

Upon his retirement in 1971, Hecksher received the CIA's Distinguished Intelligence Medal from Director Richard Helms. He then continued working for the Agency under contract to its Bonn station through 1977, where he writes that he kept gathering political intelligence "with particular relevance to covert action operations as conducted by Russia's clandestine services."[68]

Constantine Broutsas said, "I remember something Henry quoted to me a couple of times: 'In matters controversial, my judgment is quite sound. I always see both points of view—the one that's wrong, and mine.'"[69]

Hecksher never married. As his friend Polgar explained, he occasionally had romances, but "CIA is a very demanding master. Henry was not only a worka-holic, but he brought a spiritual devotion to his tasks and to the requirements of the CIA." And, as Hecksher's brother William once put it, "On the whole he kept his professional details under heavy iron curtains."

---

[66] Odio incident quotes: *The Man Who Knew Too Much*, p. 479.
[67] Hecksher quotes: 1982 letter.
[68] Hecksher quote: Ibid.
[69] Broutsas' quotes: Author's telephone interview, March 24, 2008.

35

Oswald—A "Manchurian Candidate"?

In the first edition of *The Man Who Knew Too Much*, I had explored the ominous possibility that Oswald could have been part of the behavior-control experiments being conducted by the CIA and branches of the military (as well as the Soviet Union) during the 1950s and early 1960s.

My interest had begun with the Luis Castillo saga that first led me into the assassination labyrinth. But later, the more I learned about Oswald, the more a peculiar pattern emerged in his life as well. The Atsugi naval air base where he'd been stationed in Japan (1957–58), it turned out, had been one of the locations where the CIA's use of LSD on unsuspecting service personnel occurred.[70] Nagell told me that hypnosis was used in intelligence for "compartmentalization of information," and sometimes a "courier" might be targeted for hypnosis.

He added, in one of his cryptic memorandums, that he'd discovered Oswald "undergoing hypnotherapy" from David Ferrie in New Orleans in 1963. Oswald had been a teenaged cadet in Ferrie's Civil Air Patrol in the mid-fifties, when Ferrie "frequently practiced" using hypnosis on his young associates, according to the House Assassinations Committee.

Edward G. Gillin, an assistant district attorney in Orleans Parish, recounted a visit from Oswald in "July or early August, 1963" to his office. There Oswald came inquiring about "whether or not a particular drug was legal or illegal," a drug that would allow someone "to see into the future." Gillin added that Oswald spoke extremely rapidly, "demonstrating a super-imposed indoctrination in which he had no great self-identification. He was spouting words, phrases, and clichés without true comprehension. . . ."[71]

Mexico City, where Oswald went on at least one occasion that summer, was a primary place where the CIA implemented a Counterintelligence program with three goals: "(1) to induce hypnosis very rapidly in unwitting subjects; (2) to create durable amnesia; and (3) to implant durable and operationally useful posthypnotic suggestions."

---

[70] Atsugi: CIA document, December 1, 1953, Memorandum for: Inspector general, Subject: Use of LSD: "Only Two (2) Field Stations, Manila and Atsugi, Have LSD Material."

[71] Gillin on Oswald: Garrison investigation files. Gillin confirmed the basic details in the author's telephone interview, 1992.

It was also summer 1963 when the CIA later maintained it put a stop to the MKULTRA program, after Inspector General Lyman Kirkpatrick warned clandestine affairs chief Richard Helms: "Research in the manipulation of human behavior is considered by many authorities in medicine and related fields to be professionally unethical, therefore the reputations of professional participants in the MKULTRA program are, on occasion, in jeopardy." Kirkpatrick recommended eliminating all testing on unwitting subjects. In 1963, the Army also ordered that all interrogations using LSD be terminated.[72]

After the assassination, when FBI Director Hoover hinted to the Warren Commission that Oswald could have been a "sleeper" agent sent back by the Russians,[73] commission counsel J. Lee Rankin requested from the CIA all "materials relative to Soviet techniques in mind conditioning and brainwashing." Helms responded with a memo that remained classified until 1974. It stated: "Soviet research on the pharmacological agents producing behavioral effects has consistently lagged about five years behind Western research. They have been interested in such research, however, and are now pursuing research on such chemicals as LSD-25, amphetamines, tranquilizers, hypnotics, and similar materials."[74]

All this was enough to make me want to pursue the subject further. In 1993, thirty years after MKULTRA ended, I managed to track down the man who'd been its supervisor. As far as I am aware, mine was the last interview he ever gave.

---

[72] Kirkpatrick memorandum: *Foreign and Military Intelligence*, Book I, Final Report of the Select Committee to Study Governmental Operations with Respect to Intelligence Activities, U.S. Senate (April 26, 1976), p. 390.

[73] Hoover on "sleeper": Warren Commission, Volume V, p. 105.

[74] CIA memo: Warren Commission Document 1131, declassified July 30, 1974.

36

Encountering the CIA's
"Black Sorcerer"

In the autumn of 1993, I traveled to the country estate of Dr. Sidney Gottlieb in Rappahannock County, Virginia. For 22 years until his retirement from the CIA in 1973, Gottlieb had spent most of his time overseeing the Agency's "behavioral studies" programs within the Technical Service Staff (TSS). That included a decade in charge of MKULTRA, top-secret experiments to determine whether LSD, hypnosis, and other methods could control the will and minds of human beings.

Gottlieb almost never granted interviews and, as I made the three-hour drive west out of Washington, D.C. in a rental car, I didn't really know why he had agreed to see me. Nor did I have any idea that I would encounter a charming septuagenarian who maintained an organic vegetable garden, a large energy-efficient home heated predominantly by solar power, and who periodically held Zen Buddhist meditation sessions in a timber-beamed living room. Nestled among fifty acres of rolling pastures and lush woodland near the Blue Ridge Mountains, Gottlieb called his retreat Blackwater Homestead.

Greeting me at the side porch door of his home, he was wearing a light-blue shirt and tan slacks. Gottlieb stood about five-feet-nine, with a round face and a stocky frame that appeared to be in good shape. He had thinning white hair, and his eyes struck me as a curious combination of gentleness and pugnaciousness. He ushered me to a comfortable velvet couch across from a fireplace with a stone hearth.

"To lower your expectations a little bit," Gottlieb began our several-hour-long interview into my tape recorder, "in the first place it's a long time ago and a lot of details are no longer in my mind. I made a conscious effort once I left CIA to go off in another direction and almost purposely had nothing more to do with the Agency. I have been really absorbed in other things."

On the coffee table beside me rested *The Tibetan Book of the Living and Dead*, *Chinese Herbal Medicine*, and other esoteric books. It soon became evident that Gottlieb had undergone quite a personal metamorphosis. "I follow a Buddhist practice now," he would say as the day wore on, "and the sort of things you're talking about is what led me to it." He also had no love lost for his former employers. "If the CIA never existed, or if you abolished them today," he said, "I'm not so sure that wouldn't be a good thing for this country. Of course there should be an analytical side, but I'm talking about the clandestine services. I look upon that as being no different than the Atom bomb scientists. Hell, they let something loose."

His wife Margaret, an attractive white-haired woman in her late sixties, remained in the background, soon fixing us a lunch of lentil soup and homemade bread, while Gottlieb began reminiscing about his recruitment into the CIA in the summer of 1951. He'd already been working in Washington for seven years, "with somewhat of a public service halo that was driving me," taking a Ph.D. in biochemistry to the Department of Agriculture, the National Research Council, the Food and Drug Administration, and finally the University of Maryland as a research chemist. Gottlieb had long been frustrated that a congenital defect, being born with club feet, kept him out of World War II. "I came from an orthodox Jewish background, and I tried to get in. Later, with the Cold War at its height, I guess I was attracted when one day a couple of people came into the lab while I was manipulating something and said, 'Your country needs you and we want you to work for us.'"

Gottlieb paused and his next words came slowly, almost painfully it seemed. "The Agency was very much in a state of growth and turmoil. They were in the middle of what I realized later was the biggest wind-up in history, to try to stimulate the Eastern Bloc to revolt and break away from the Soviets. They really just bumbled around. They had a great lack of experience and got a lot of people killed, to no purpose. This program had a cryptonym of OPC, the Office of Policy Coordination, to make it obscure. Frank Wisner ran it. He finally came to an end that somehow was appropriate—he shot himself. I don't say that with any satisfaction because I knew him personally and bear no animosity towards him. But when you live by the sword, that's what happens."

Shortly after he joined the TSS branch of the CIA, Gottlieb read a report that came in from a military attaché in Switzerland. It said that the Soviet Union had purchased 35 grams of LSD from Sandoz Laboratories, the company which had discovered the drug.

"When this was carefully looked into ten or twelve years later," Gottlieb continued, "it turned out that such a thing never happened. But we didn't know that at the time. Practically nothing was known about LSD in those days, except at Edgewood Arsenal. A man named Wilson Green, working in the Chemical Warfare Service over there, had spotted this material and was touting it as a potential chemical warfare agent. That later turned out to be nonsense, too. But I trotted up to Edgewood to find out what the Army was planning to do. Then I went to see Allen Dulles, who was running the CIA's clandestine services before he became Director under Eisenhower. We decided we needed to find out a lot about LSD in a hurry. And that's what led to MKULTRA.

"One of the problems, if you want to call it that—I was basically unsupervised. I tend to be sort of an activist. This got written up originally as a $300,000 project. We wanted to do several things. One, some in-house experiments, which meant a group of us taking LSD ourselves under some medical supervision. And two, to move quickly to some reputable people on the outside, establish a mechanism where they could do apparently overt research that they would publish. But like most government programs, it took off and then it was hard to stop it."

Gottlieb estimated he probably took forty or fifty LSD trips himself in 1953–54, "at ten to twenty times the amount you would take now to get a high from it. Of course that led to a lot of ludicrous situations, and we were lucky we didn't get into more trouble than we did. I'd get a feeling of being wrapped in a shimmering cocoon that protected me and allowed me to feel as good as I possibly could."

Others in his circle were not so fortunate. One psychologist wandered off across the Memorial Bridge, wondering if he could race the passing cars. Another man, TSS assistant Harold Bortner, suffered a mysterious early death. "It was some sort of internal problem, but I can't help but think that the crazy doses he took weren't good for him."

Then there was Frank Olson, a germ warfare researcher for the Army Chemical Corps. On November 28, 1953, a CIA scientist—on orders from Gottlieb—slipped LSD into Olson's after-dinner drink at a Maryland retreat. Two weeks later, Olson jumped thirteen stories to his death—some say he was pushed—through a hotel window in New York. When this tale finally came to light in 1975, the CIA paid $750,000 to the Olson family to settle their claim that the Agency was responsible.[75] Gottlieb told me he remained unconvinced that the LSD had anything to do with what he believes was Olson's suicide. But, he added, "there's no question that if we had known then what we discovered later about his neurotic history, we would never have given him the drug."

Gottlieb's work was enveloped in "ultimate secrecy." Not until sometime after 1960 did he finally tell his wife about the LSD research. "I wasn't supposed to know, and I was busy anyway," Margaret said, standing at the kitchen entryway. "She's a superb seamstress," Gottlieb told me confidingly. "She makes most of my clothes, including this shirt I'm wearing." He added that Margaret, after years teaching pre-school, continued to work with inmates at a local jail on a literacy program. The couple had just celebrated their fiftieth wedding anniversary.

At the CIA, far more than drug testing was included in Gottlieb's bailiwick. Indeed, he recalled the drug program as being a small exotic corner of his domain, at its peak taking a million dollars a year from the TSS's annual $30 million budget. The TSS worked on materiel for the clandestine branch such as invisible ink, as well as everything from exploding tie clips to false mustaches to poison darts.

---

[75] Olson case: Much is available on the Internet. See also *The Search for the 'Manchurian Candidate'* by John Marks (N.Y.: W.W. Norton, 1991).

"Things like electronic eavesdropping and false documentation, to a much lesser extent things around a person's identity—these were the guts. Every spy handler had to know a great deal about this, and every spy would get equipped with whatever he needed. I mean, things like microdots, which came to be an unbelievably sophisticated technology. They were the backbone of the way we would get information from places that we really needed. So it wasn't fun and games, you see."

My mind flashed back to the address book confiscated from Lee Harvey Oswald after the assassination, where authorities found the notation "microdots" written alongside the name of his employer between October 1962 and April 1963, the Jaggars-Chiles-Stovall photo-lithography firm that did classified work for the U.S. Army Map Service.[76] Developed by Army intelligence during World War Two, microdots are a means to send data by photographically reducing documents to a size that can be hidden under a postage stamp. I also thought of Oswald's use, during that same time-frame and afterwards, of false identity cards in the name of Alek J. Hidell. But I decided it would be perhaps imprudent to raise these subjects with Gottlieb. Instead, I soon steered our conversation to another MKULTRA field of study—hypnosis.

"Well, we went into it," Gottlieb replied. "If you've got a project that is looking at the covert alteration of human behavior, you have to look into hypnosis. And even into more esoteric matters like ESP. We had a close contact with Stanford Research Institute and people there who worked on extrasensory things. We didn't give them a lot of money but, with hypnosis, we did fund a few researchers with maybe $40,000 to $50,000 a year. I think we finally decided that, like LSD, hypnosis had no reliable or predictable place that we could see it applied to the spying business. In spite of *The Manchurian Candidate*."

Gottlieb was referring to the 1959 novel by Richard Condon—made into a popular movie four years later—where a soldier "brainwashed" by Communists during the Korean War is later "programmed" by American handlers to commit the unwitting assassination of an American presidential contender. Since Gottlieb had broached the subject, I brought from my briefcase a CIA report labeled ARTICHOKE, released in 1978 under the Freedom-of-Information Act. I handed it to him and waited as he scanned its contents. The document read:

"The ARTICHOKE Team visited [deleted] during period 8 January to 15 January 1954. The purpose of the visit was to give an evaluation of a hypothetical problem, namely: Can an individual of ***** descent be made to perform an act of attempted assassination involuntarily under the influence of ARTICHOKE? . . ."

The report went on that, "as a 'trigger mechanism' for a bigger project," this individual "approximately 35 years old, well educated, proficient in English and

---

[76] "Microdots": Warren Commission, Volume XVI, p. 53.

well established socially and politically in the ******* Government," be induced to carry out this assassination attempt "against a ****** politician or if necessary, against an American official. . . .

"Because the SUBJECT is a heavy drinker, it was proposed that the individual could be surreptitiously drugged through the medium of an alcoholic cocktail at a social party, ARTICHOKE applied and the SUBJECT induced to perform the act of attempted assassination at some later date." After this happened, "it was assumed that the SUBJECT would be taken into custody by the *** Government and thereby 'disposed of.'"

A follow-up memo, dated January 22, 1954, stated: "Herewith report of ARTICHOKE team on first assignment. Considering the speed with which we had to operate, I believe it went extremely well. We were ready when called upon for support, even though the operation did not materialize."[77]

Putting down the pages, Gottlieb looked across at me and said: "Now you need to know that there's some very complicated bureaucracy involved there. The ARTICHOKE project was not TSS's. We didn't start it. ULTRA came out of ARTICHOKE and BLUEBIRD. With those other things, I'm sure there was lots I didn't know. But sure, the word hypnosis and the kind of thing a 'Manchurian candidate'"—here he cut himself off in mid-sentence before resuming—"I'm strictly talking about what I know in MKULTRA. I don't blame people for trying to put all this under one umbrella, what can you expect through all this secrecy?"

There was an edge to his voice and, when I opined that it seemed novelist Condon might have had some intelligence sources, Gottlieb's reply was punctuated by a stuttering problem he had occasionally been plagued with since childhood. "Well, I'll be frank with you, yes I did read that book years ago. I thought it was a good book. But if anybody asked me, in an expert witness kind of milieu, whether I think that sort of thing has anything to do with the intelligence business, I would say unequivocally, absolutely not. Events that have transpired in the last twenty or thirty years could prove me wrong maybe, but I would doubt it very much."

So he didn't think it was possible that some evil scientist could really create a "Manchurian candidate"? Gottlieb shook his head no. But I continued to press him on the subject of hypnosis.

"The only thing we had directly to do with hypnosis, there was a weird kind of Fundamentalist Christian who was interested," he replied. "I don't know how we got involved with him, but we simply wanted him to hypnotize some people experimentally. Not covertly. And he worked on some of us, just like with the LSD."

---

[77] ARTICHOKE: *New York Times*, February 9, 1978, "CIA Documents Tell of 1954 Project to Create Involuntary Assassins" by Nicholas M. Horrock.

"Was he able to hypnotize you?" I asked.

"Oh, yeah. See, depending upon who it is, people walk around just begging to be hypnotized. It's a little touch with unreality that, in a subconscious way, they've been seeking all their lives I think, to get away from this terrible responsibility that life means. My God, I used to kid around with my family. The kids would sit around a table and I would tell them to put their right hand down. Then I would just say, 'There are balloons attached to your hand, and your hand is getting lighter.' I'd just begin and, with one of my daughters, her hand would go right up! Some people are built that way."

I brought up a statement attributed to Dr. Milton Kline, a prominent New York hypnotherapist who once did some consultancy work for the CIA. It appeared in John Marks' book about the CIA's behavior experiments, *The Search for the "Manchurian Candidate."* Marks had postulated a "programmed 'patsy' whom a hypnotist could walk through a series of seemingly unrelated events," being "amnesic only for the fact the hypnotist ordered him to do these things. . . . The purpose of this exercise is to leave a circumstantial trail that will make the authorities think the patsy committed a particular crime." Hypnosis expert Kline, according to Marks, "says he could create a patsy in three months; an assassin would take him six."[78]

Gottlieb sat quietly in his chair, then said: "There are a couple of relevant things I think you're after that I want to say about hypnosis. It was never, ever seriously researched by us. We were just keeping in touch with these people, sort of a light brush, in case our instincts were wrong. Now I will say there are people who want to be spies and do terrible things, and they're just looking for a framework to do that.

"I know this very well personally, because for a couple of years I ran agents out of Munich. I gave them communications systems, debriefed them. I used to muse—boy, this is the only place you can do illegal things legally, isn't this great? You've got license and the whole blessing of this powerful government on you. Translate that to some little guy who is itching to do something like Marks wrote about. Well, Martin Orne, the famous Philadelphia hypnotherapist, was trying to figure out a way to differentiate between the [actual] state of hypnosis and feigning hypnosis. So are you really hypnotizing such a person? I doubt it very much."

I believed I caught the drift of what Gottlieb was implying: that someone with a predisposition to do "terrible things" might himself utilize a hypnosis "framework" to accentuate such propensities. This led to my next question, following an increasingly delicate thread.

---

[78] Kline quote: Marks, p. 204.

"Does it trouble you, or do you think about the possibility, that a lot of the work you thought you were doing for the good of the country might have been usurped, picked up by unscrupulous people for unsavory ends?" I asked.

"Sure, that's entered my mind. In fact, it was one of the great sighs of relief when I left the outfit, and I would never recommend any relative of mine to join it."

I felt I could journey now into new territory—the eventual crossover between MKULTRA and the CIA's use of poisonous substances in attempts to assassinate foreign leaders. The program was known as "Executive Action" or by the cryptonym ZR/RIFLE and, like the behavior experiments, it did not become public knowledge until the mid-1970s. My raising of this subject clearly made Gottlieb uneasy.

"Well, that's quite a different kind of thing," he said, and repeated the phrase again. "To draw that line, you've gotta go way back to the Chemical Warfare Service and Fort Dietrich. See, there was an outfit there that predated my joining the Agency. It was called the Special Operations Division and it was the side of the germ warfare effort that the Army ran, to study our own vulnerability. And that happened to be an aggressive, imaginative unit. So they'd mount experiments with supposedly harmless organisms—like to contaminate the New York subway system. We did get together with them, and it was in that framework that Olson was slipped the LSD. Out of all that came a capability that no one else in the government had, and we just marched into a vacuum I guess, where they agreed to keep a supply of biological warfare agents for covert use in case the USA ever needed them."

I interjected, "And out of that emanated your trip to the . . ."

Gottlieb didn't let me finish the sentence. "To the Congo, absolutely." It happened in 1960, when Gottlieb was dispatched by the CIA's Clandestine Services chief Richard Bissell to carry a deadly bacteria to the then-Belgian Congo—and eliminate Premier Patrice Lumumba. He traveled under the cover of the Society for Human Ecology. "I was convinced this had been cleared right to the top of our government, and was something that had to be done." Gottlieb says Bissell told him, however, when he left: "Look, Sid, if this thing doesn't look kosher to you, just knock it off."

Upon his arrival in the tumultuous African nation which was seeking to throw off its colonial ties, Gottlieb became convinced that the truth would come out. "It's a very dramatic moment in my life. I had a way of disinfecting what I had with me—I think it was this anthrax organism—you could just unscrew something and Clorox would flood out and oxidize it. So that's what I did. I took one look at the situation there, and threw the materials I had into the river, the Stanley Pool." (Eventually Lumumba ended up being assassinated under circumstances that remain unclear to this day).

I continued, "What about the anti-Castro plots? Were you aware of the CIA's dealings with Sam Giancana and Johnny Roselli to try to knock him off?"

"No, I knew zero about that. I *was* involved in some of the anti-Castro stuff, but not at the level of these theories that have since come out. There was some assassination planning, but again I was put out of that loop."

Very much in that loop, Gottlieb added, was a little-known figure who worked under him. His name was Raymond Treichler. One of the reasons that Gottlieb said he'd accepted being the poison-courier on the Congo mission was: "I was particularly interested in *not* having Treichler go. I think he would have moved heaven and earth to use it. With the plots to kill Castro, the clandestine services told me to just assign Treichler to them—and stay out of the loop."

Desmond FitzGerald was running the CIA's anti-Castro operations at the time of the Kennedy assassination and eventually placed in charge of the entire clandestine branch. "He'd say, 'Don't bother me with the details, just tell me whether this will or won't work.' I think guys like that can get you in a lot of trouble. One of the Roosevelts, who had been a roommate of FitzGerald's at some point, once told me that he was the most dangerous man he knew."

Gottlieb had known William Harvey, FitzGerald's predecessor in Cuban affairs, "pretty well. When he became head of Executive Action, he certainly talked to me about what we had to offer. Not in any particular operational sense but, you know, just for information."

"What do you mean?"

"Well, like these biologicals, chemicals."

"He was interested in that?"

"Oh, sure. Part of his mission."

"Was Harvey a pretty wild fellow?"

"Well, he was strange. Yeah, I guess he was wild. I mean, when you look at a guy like this who basically has a severe alcohol problem, and think of the responsibilities he was given, you have to wonder about the management of CIA. I mean, here he was brought back from being Chief of Station in Rome because he couldn't stay sober—and given this job planning how to kill foreign leaders! That's unbelievable to me.

"But the CIA, you see, has almost a mythology in it. And Harvey is part of it. He somehow gets a positive image. I didn't think he was either very smart or very stable, yet that's not the aura that he had. That's what frightens you about CIA, creating a government mechanism where guys like that can prosper."

Gottlieb continued, "My view, as somebody who was as close—or not so close—to it all as I was, it's a thing out of the whole cloth. I don't think anything like that ever happened. I don't think the CIA ever had a role . . ."

His voice trailed off momentarily. "In what?" I asked.

"In Kennedy's assassination," Gottlieb said.

I had not yet broached that subject. Nor had I told Gottlieb about my first book. But there was no sense beating around the bush any longer. I sought to home in by paraphrasing the May 12, 1964 testimony by FBI Director Hoover before the Warren Commission. Hoover had been discussing Oswald's two-and-a-half year sojourn in the Soviet Union, working primarily at an electronics factory in Minsk. "But just the day before yesterday," Hoover had said, "information came to me indicating that there is an espionage training school outside of Minsk—I don't know whether it is true—and that he was trained at that school to come back to this country to become what they call a 'sleeper,' that is a man who will remain dormant for three or four years and in case of international hostilities rise up and be used."[79]

When I described Hoover's use of the word "sleeper," Gottlieb said: "You mean a Manchurian candidate? I think that's a perfect example about how a guy of Oswald's personality make-up could use a Manchurian candidate framework to move ahead—like I was saying in general terms before—and then you realize how close you came to: was he hypnotized or was he not hypnotized?"

"What do you mean?"

"Well, here's a guy who has his own moral, political, and economic framework for really hating Kennedy. And he fantasizes because he's a little nuts: 'How can I do something about this man?' And suddenly a situation arises. And someone tells him, 'Look, we've gotta use you and we're gonna hypnotize you, but you don't have to worry about it, we're gonna take care of you.' And so he's undergoing—I'm just running this speculation now—hypnosis, but at some level he says, 'This is great, I can do what I want to do anyway, and they gave me a lovely framework.' And they don't care whether he thinks he's hypnotized or not, as long as he'll go ahead and do the job."

There was a long pause before Gottlieb resumed. "Well, I really can't do any more than speculate. I really had no even beginnings of firsthand knowledge about it."

He clearly wanted to change the subject. He had always believed there was sanction for what he did, Gottlieb said, having personally briefed every President's office on aspects of his research right up to his retirement. A thin smile crossed Gottlieb's face as he added: "I don't know how much you know about the incident that happened on President Nixon's trip." I had no clue what Gottlieb meant, and said so.

"Well, if you remember, he went first to China and then to the Soviet Union in 1971. Nixon had a personal physician with a strange name, Tkach. Dr. [Walter] Tkach was one of the people it was routine for us to brief on LSD, and how he could tell if the President or his entourage had ever been slipped any. One day Dick Helms, who was then Director of the Agency, called me up

---

[79] Hoover on "sleeper": Warren Commission, Volume V, p. 105.

to his office. He said, 'Sid, we got a strange telegram. Tkach himself and some of the secretarial staff on the trip have been acting very strangely.' When all these people came back, John Gittinger, who was the fount of all our knowledge on the behavioral manifestations of LSD, went and interviewed them. And there was no question that they'd been slipped LSD.

"To this day we can't figure out what the Russians were up to, but they were obviously bumbling worse than we were. We might have been crazy, but no one would have let us use LSD operationally like that, thank God!"

"They didn't give it to Nixon, did they?" I asked, unable to hide a smile.

"Well, they never"—Gottlieb laughed out loud—"I don't know whether they tried."

Not long after that, Gottlieb had decided to leave the CIA. Early in 1973, he went to Helms and suggested that the MKULTRA records maintained by Clandestine Services be destroyed. "I said I felt that anybody looking through these, it's not like destroying history, they wouldn't know what to make of it." Helms had agreed. Only a relative handful of MKULTRA documents that had been maintained by the CIA's Administrative branch would survive for future scrutiny.

"Did you ever regret that decision?" I asked.

"There was nothing in there that really mattered," Gottlieb said with a shrug.

He was only 55 when he retired, shortly after the Agency shifted many of his responsibilities to a new Office of Research & Development. His four children were grown, but Sidney and Margaret "were still living in a rather idyllic way outside Vienna [a Virginia suburb of Washington], I had 15 acres there and raised chickens and milk goats. Having been raised in the cement wastes of New York City, that kind of life had always appealed to me. But we felt if we stayed there, it was just too pleasant and wouldn't lead to anything. So we decided to get rid of the house, sell everything, and just take off on a freighter and see what happens."

They spent 47 days with 12 passengers on a Norwegian ship, bound for Australia to visit friends. Then the Gottliebs moved on to India, where Margaret had been raised by missionary parents, and where Sidney would administer a hospital for awhile. Later they traveled to Africa, where he joined a volunteer medical team in Zambia, "used to go out to the squatter settlements around Lusaka and minister to the people."

They had returned to India when Gottlieb's name surfaced during the Church Committee's congressional probe into MKULTRA activities in 1977. The word was that he had fled the United States and, although bitter about the CIA having broken its contract of secrecy about his activities, realized he would have to return.

"We took a very unconventional route," Gottlieb recalled. "The Pakistanis ran these very low-cost buses that start in Nepal and go all the way to Europe for $90. Our companions were the scrubbiest, most hippie-type kids, living on less than a dollar a day. We had a great time on the road to Istanbul."

It was, I thought, an incongruous but fitting sojourn—the man who pioneered LSD research at the CIA heading home with a busload of hippies who surely believed that "acid dreams" began with Timothy Leary.

After testifying behind closed doors before the Church Committee, Gottlieb set out again with his wife, finally ending up in their daughter's town of Santa Cruz, California. He went back to school, got a degree at San Jose State in speech pathology, and began working with children who like himself had a stuttering problem. In the early 1980s, the Gottliebs settled for the last time in the rolling hills of Virginia.

At the end of our interview, he gave me a tour of Blackwater Homestead— the cedar-lined sauna, the indoor swimming pool that he cleaned with ozone rather than chlorine chemicals. We walked out to the garden, where he proudly displayed the sweet corn and sweet potatoes, the small flock of chickens. "We recycle everything that comes from the table, put it on the compost heap."

"One last thing I'm wondering about," I said as Gottlieb saw me to my car, "do you look back on your CIA days in terms of your personal growth today?"

"Well, I'll put it this way," he answered. "I doubt whether I could get where I am now—not that I'm particularly happy about where I am, but I think I've made a good deal of progress—without having worked at the CIA. You know, you have to know what's wrong with things first, before you're motivated to do something about it."

37

Oswald: The Mysterious Formative Years

On May 13, 1968, a most unusual headline—To SLEEP: PERCHANCE TO KILL?—appeared in the *Providence Evening Bulletin*.[80] It began: "A visiting professor of psychology at Rhode Island College believes that hypnosis could have led Lee Harvey Oswald and Jack Ruby to slay their victims."

Dr. George H. Estabrooks was no ordinary visiting professor. He had been a leading adviser to the military on potential applications of hypnosis since the 1930s. In the post-war years, while chairing the psychology department at Colgate University, "Esty" had also provided his expertise to the FBI and CIA.

In the Providence newspaper article, Estabrooks was quoted that "hypnotism is widely used by intelligence agencies of the United States and other countries." The key to creating an effective spy or assassin, he continued, lay in splitting an individual's personality: "It is child's play now to develop a multiple personality through hypnosis." One out of five persons were good subjects, and one out of twenty would prove excellent "for espionage purposes."

The professor went on to say that Oswald and Ruby "could very well have been performing through hypnosis. They would have been perfect cases but I doubt you will find anyone admitting this possibility, especially in *The Warren Report*." Estabrooks concluded by citing the novel and film, *The Manchurian Candidate*, as offering an "entirely possible" scenario.

After stumbling upon this article, I discovered that Estabrooks' papers had been archived at Colgate, where I paid a visit and made photocopies of some. As far back as June 8, 1936, Estabrooks had written to FBI Director Hoover about the possibility of combining drugs with hypnosis, and they had retained a steady correspondence over many years. The papers also revealed an association with the OSS, the CIA's wartime predecessor.[81] Early in 1942, Robert C. Tryon, chief of the OSS's Psychology Division, wrote Estabrooks: "We are very willing, indeed, to examine your plans on the possibility of applying hypnotism to certain problems of modern warfare."[82]

---

[80] Article on Estabrooks: "To 'Sleep'; Perchance to Kill?" by Andrew F. Blake, *Providence Evening Bulletin*, May 13, 1968 (Colgate University archives).

[81] Estabrooks papers: All in Estabrooks Archive, Colgate University, Hamilton, N.Y.

[82] OSS letter: From Robert C. Tryon, Chief, Psychology Division, to Professor G.H. Estabrooks, January 27, 1942.

Some years after the war, Estabrooks would write of having been involved "in preparing many subjects" as "hypnotic couriers" during the war. He would remove from them, "by posthypnotic suggestion, all recollection of ever having been hypnotized."

When using hypnosis for counterespionage purposes, Estabrooks noted: "In hypnotism we would build up their loyalty to this country; but out of hypnotism, in the 'waking' or normal state we would do the opposite, striving to convince them that they had a genuine grievance against this country. . . . Here we would be coming very close to establishing a case of 'dual personality'. . . . That condition, the Dr. Jekyll and Mr. Hyde combination, is a very real one once it is established."[83]

There was also documentation that, as far back as the 1930s, hypnosis was in the planning stage for experiments on children at youth institutions of upstate New York. The director of the Utica Community Chest, Inc., had written Estabrooks: ". . . we have Saint John's Orphan Asylum and the House of the Good Shepherd and in these institutions you could get fifty children from nine to twelve very easily I should think. However . . . it would need a very diplomatic approach."[84] Another letter to Estabrooks, from the Superintendent of the Rome (NY) State School, offered "a group of fifty children . . . if you are not able to use groups of children in Utica."[85]

On June 10, 1959, Estabrooks had sent Hoover information on a proposed research project titled "Hypnotism In Juvenile Delinquency." The outline stated: "Hypnotism is the best device for probing the unconscious to find those unconscious motivations which are leading in the direction of delinquency, and, having found them, to redirect the same."[86]

The surviving MKULTRA files—and they are but a handful compared to what was destroyed—reveal several studies of teenagers in the 1950s. MKULTRA Subproject 102 was a University of Oklahoma study on "intergroup relations," with a stated aim of "devising measures for channeling socially undesirable modes of behavior, exemplified in delinquency, into more constructive modes."[87] Subproject 112 at the University of Indiana revolved around "children's conceptions of occupational role and status."[88]

---

[83] Estabrooks quote: *Hypnotism* by G.H. Estabrooks (N.Y.: E.P. Dutton, 1945).

[84] Letter from Utica Community Chest: Signed by A. J. Derbyshire, Director, to Dr. G. H. Estabrooks, December 17, 1935 (Colgate University Archive).

[85] Rome State School: Letter from Superintendent Charles Bernstein to Dr. G. H. Estabrooks, December 19, 1935 (Colgate University Archive).

[86] Estabrooks/Hoover: Letter, June 10, 1959, with enclosure "Hypnosis in Juvenile Delinquency" (Colgate University Archive).

[87] MKULTRA Subproject 102: National Security Archive, Gelman Library, George Washington University, CIA Behavioral Experiments Collection (John Marks Donation), Box 4, "Adolescent Gangs."

[88] MKULTRA Subproject 112: Ibid, "Vocational Studies in Children."

At an international summer children's camp in Maine, a series of "special studies" into communications skills was conducted. There eleven-year-old boys and girls who spoke different languages would sit down and "interview" each other. A CIA memorandum of November 4, 1959 made brief mention of Subproject 103's hidden agenda: to "assist in the identification of promising young foreign nationals and U.S. nationals (many of whom are now in their late teens) who may at any time be of direct interest to the Company [CIA]."[89]

And there was a 1967 paper co-authored by a long-time MKULTRA subcontractor, Dr. Harold Abrahamson of Mount Sinai Hospital and Columbia University in New York. Titled "Preliminary Method for Study of LSD with Children," it described "a study in which fourteen schizophrenic children were treated with some success with LSD and UML 491."

In mid-February 1994, I paid a visit to the New York City office of Dr. Milton Kline, director of the non-profit Institute for Research in Hypnosis and Psychotherapy, and formerly a consultant to both the FBI and CIA. White-haired and patrician in a dark business suit, Kline was then in his late sixties, also maintaining a private practice in hypnotherapy from a book-lined office suite overlooking Central Park.[90]

In 1959, Dr. Kline had conducted a pioneering experiment to determine whether criminal acts could be carried out under hypnotic suggestion. His findings were published in *The Journal of Genetic Psychology*. "We found out that it is certainly possible to do it," Kline recalled, "although it is not easy."

Based on Kline's work, researchers at the University of Pennsylvania developed what they called a "Machiavellian Scale," where the highest-scoring subjects were those who could more easily be persuaded into anti-social behavior. These traits, Kline explained, were: "Not a lot of empathy for people. Very self-controlled. Rather hard-nosed. The kind of people who don't cry in movies."

Asked what personality characteristics an unscrupulous "programmer" might look for in forging an assassin, Kline pondered for a moment and then replied: "If you're looking for someone to perform an assassination, you'd first have to ask what their gratification would be in performing this act. A lot of assassins do it for political reasons. If there is no political motivation, maybe you have to create one. Or create some other motivation.

"For example," he continued, "in the course of psychotherapy, it's not uncommon for patients to have wishes to kill their parents or their siblings. They hate them, especially if they've been abused. Someone with that kind of traumatic history—having been abused physically, sexually, or emotionally—has a need to get back. In my opinion, they might make a good candidate for an assassin."

---

[89] MKULTRA Subproject 103: Ibid, "Children's Summer Camps."
[90] Kline interview: February 17, 1994, New York City.

I showed Kline the newspaper article where Estabrooks had put forward his theory that Oswald and Ruby could have been programmed through hypnosis. In all the years he knew Estabrooks, Kline said his now-deceased colleague had never mentioned such a thing. Then Kline added, "But I would not say it's far-fetched. I think Oswald was an abused child. As I said, when you get that as a base, the possibility of programming upon it is very real."

Oswald had never known his father, who died before his birth in 1939. For more than a year, at a young age he had been placed by his mother Marguerite in an orphanage, the Bethlehem Children's Home, in New Orleans along with his older brothers. "It was, reportedly, a traumatic experience," according to journalist Anthony Summers. "According to a fellow inmate, the infant Lee more than once witnessed sex between one of the child-minders and teenage girls."[91]

Shortly after Oswald's thirteenth birthday, with both his siblings already in the armed services, he and his mother had moved to New York. Often choosing to stay away from school, Oswald soon faced truancy charges. For three weeks in the spring of 1953, he was remanded to the city's Youth House for psychiatric observation. Dr. Renatus Hartogs, the chief psychiatrist there, later said he found Oswald's personality so intriguing that he chose him as a seminar subject.

As Hartogs would summarize for the Warren Commission, he had seen in Oswald a "cold, detached outer attitude" that viewed his life in a "nonparticipating fashion." Hartogs had also noted Oswald's "vivid fantasy life, turning around the topics of omnipotence and power." His diagnosis had been "personality pattern disturbance with schizoid features and passive-aggressive tendencies."[92]

Hartogs' testimony was crucial to the Warren Commission's developing a pattern of aberrant behavior in Oswald more than ten years before the Kennedy assassination. I decided to do some research into Dr. Hartogs' background. He turned out to have been involved in a landmark court case, *Roy v. Hartogs*, in 1971. He was accused, found guilty and barred from psychiatric practice for having seduced one of his patients, Julie Roy, into a bizarre sexual relationship. This became the subject of a 1976 book, *Betrayal*, co-authored by the alleged victim with Lucy Freeman;[93] ironically, Freeman had previously assisted Hartogs in writing his 1965 psychological study of Oswald and Ruby called *The Two Assassins*.

At Hartogs' trial, the subject of Oswald came up briefly while he was on the witness stand. "Now, doctor, as part of your expertise, did you have occasion

---

[91] Oswald's childhood: *Esquire Magazine* (England), December 1993, "The Secret Life of Lee Harvey Oswald" by Anthony Summers.

[92] Hartogs' diagnosis: See also *The Two Assassins* by Dr. Renatus Hartogs and Lucy Freeman (N.Y.: Zebra Books/Kensington Publishing Group, 1965).

[93] *Roy v. Hartogs* case: *Betrayal* by Lucy Freeman and Julie Roy (N.Y.: Stein & Day Publishers, Giniger Book, 1976).

in 1953 to examine Lee Harvey Oswald?" the opposing attorney asked. After Hartogs responded "Yes," his attorney objected, saying "I don't see the relevance to this." The judge sustained the objection and a luncheon recess was called.[94]

Hartogs' credentials appeared in the court record. He had earned his doctorate in psychology at the University of Frankfurt-am-Main in Germany and come to America in 1940. Late in the decade, he'd obtained his medical degree, internships and psychiatric residency in Montreal. In New York, he'd been a senior psychiatrist at Sing Sing and for the probation department. His time at Youth House was absent from his *curricula vitae*.[95]

Hartogs testified that he was the author of eight books. Among them was one titled *Principles of Suggestion and Auto-suggestion*.[96] This was clearly a reference to a tract about hypnosis.

I contacted Milton Kline, who said he'd known Hartogs in the 1950s. "He was more than just a child psychiatrist, but was involved in some kind of government consultation," Kline added. After recalling how Hartogs had lost his license following his court conviction, Kline continued: "He couldn't continue to practice psychiatry, but he set up shop as a hypnotist in New York, on East Seventy-eighth Street just off Lexington Avenue. I remember he placed quarter-page ads in the newspaper and sent my institute a letter asking if we could use his services. We declined. That's when I became aware that Hartogs must have known a great deal about hypnosis. There is no question in my mind that he was perfectly skilled at it, because he was seeing patients for years.

"There is more than meets the eye about Dr. Hartogs," Kline said.[97]

I then dialed information and found a telephone number for Hartogs, who at the time was in his late eighties and still living in New York. I told him I was curious about his book on "suggestion and auto-suggestion," but he denied having authored it. "I've written all kinds of books, but not that. Maybe it was written by somebody else who probably used my name," he said, and continued: "I'm a Freudian psychoanalyst, not a hypnotherapist. I cannot offer you anything in terms of hypnosis or suggestion. Cross it off your list. What I know about hypnosis and suggestion is outdated, I don't read anything about it anymore."

I was also curious about Hartogs' background in the late 1940s in Montreal, when he worked as a psychologist at the Allen Memorial Institute. For that was the place where Dr. D. Ewen Cameron was known to have performed experiments on psychiatric patients under contract to the CIA, utilizing hypnosis, drugs including LSD, and sensory deprivation. "I knew Dr. Cameron, sure," said

---

[94] Oswald testimony: Ibid, p. 193.
[95] Hartogs' credentials: Ibid, p. 191.
[96] Hartogs' book: Ibid, p. 193.
[97] Kline on Hartogs: Author's telephone interview, January 5, 1995.

Hartogs. "He was a nice man. I don't know what happened to him after I left Montreal and came to New York."

When I brought up Oswald's name, Hartogs brushed the subject aside— "I think he did it on his own"—and indicated that our conversation was over.[98]

I could find no record of the book, *Principles of Suggestion and Auto-Suggestion*, in the Boston Public Library's national database.

Not long after this, I spoke to Dr. Kline again. "I did get a little more information on Hartogs," he told me. "He worked extensively with hypnosis and may have been involved with Dr. Sidney Malitz, who was a professor of psychiatry at the New York State Psychiatric Institute (NYSPI) in the 1950s. Malitz had a number of government contracts, particularly CIA, working with hallucinogenic drugs and personality changes. He was varying from research protocols to work with private patients using some of his drugs. I'm told that Hartogs worked with him for many years, and that he [Hartogs] was a very slippery character."[99]

The NYSPI was part of the Columbia Presbyterian Hospital at 168th and Broadway, not that far from the Oswalds' Bronx apartment on 179th Street. Between 1953 and 1957, it is now known, the Army Chemical Corps funded the NYSPI to the tune of about $140,000, a considerable portion of that money having originated with the CIA. Hospital doctors injected mescaline and LSD into patients who had entered the institute voluntarily for treatment of mental problems. Late in 1953, the NYSPI investigators formed a private corporation, the Research Foundation for Mental Hygiene, Inc., which received at least four lucrative additional contracts for experiments on psychiatric patients. Dr. James Cattell, a former NYSPI team member, testified before Congress in the 1970s that the purpose of the drug tests was to create an "exaggerated mental state (schizophrenia). . . ."

The fact that U.S. government agencies were intentionally inducing a split personality recalled to mind Hartogs' analysis of Oswald's "schizoid features."

In January 1954, Oswald and his mother left New York and returned to live in New Orleans. Sometime in 1955, when he was fifteen, Oswald joined the Civil Air Patrol (CAP), a group of young men interested in flying. Its Senior Squadron Commander was an older fellow then employed as an Eastern Airlines pilot named David Ferrie.

One of the CAP's members, Lawrence Marsh, later spoke to a House Assassinations Committee investigator about his several years with the group in the mid-1950s. "When we would spend the weekend by Dave's for these parties," Marsh said, "he used to practice hypnosis on us, and find out if it were working

---

[98] Hartogs interview: Author's telephone interview, January 21, 1995.
[99] Kline on Hartogs: op. cit.

on us by using a compass or a pin and stick our arms. He was a fanatic about this hypnosis stuff."[100]

In 1994 I contacted another CAP cadet who had been interviewed by the committee named John Irion. "The New Orleans CAP unit, at Lakefront Airport, attracted by and large a lot of underprivileged kids from broken homes," he told me. He remembered Oswald coming, "a recruit if I remember, but he never got much out of that stage. He would sulk and then get argumentative. I would say Oswald was there maybe six months at the most."

Irion also remembered Ferrie's fascination with hypnosis. "He fancied himself as a self-made doctor or psychologist. I personally never submitted to it, because I knew better. It's possible he hypnotized other people, but back then for kids of our age, it was more of a novelty."

Another former CAP cadet, Anthony Atzenhoffer, told the House Assassinations Committee that Ferrie had "wanted the kids to participate in some kind of experiment for Tulane University. They didn't do it."[101] Irion recalled that Ferrie was "constantly at Tulane" during those years.

In September 1975, Charles D. Ablard, General Counsel for the Army, would deliver this testimony before a Senate committee: "We have learned of a 1955 contract with Tulane University which involved the administration of LSD, mescaline, and other drugs to mental patients who had theretofore had electrodes implanted in their brains as a part of their medical treatment. . . ." The project was the brainchild of Dr. Robert Heath, then chairman of the Tulane Medical School's Department of Neurology and Psychiatry, and whose specialty was electrical stimulation of the brain. Heath once stated that the real solutions to mental problems would be found in "controlled manipulation of the pleasure response and . . . manipulation of memory by biological means." Heath acknowledged having taken part in one CIA research project in 1957, testing a purported brainwashing drug on several monkeys.[102]

At some point during his teenage years in New Orleans, Oswald began exhibiting a fascination with communism. He checked out Marx's *Das Kapital* from the local library and tried to persuade a friend to join the Communist Party with him "to take advantage of the social functions." He said he was looking to find a cell of sympathetic Marxists and wrote for information about the "Youth League" of the Socialist Party. His favorite TV program was *I Led Three Lives*, based on the true story of Herbert Philbrick, who penetrated the Communist Party as an FBI informant.

---

[100] Lawrence Marsh: Two-page House Committee report in author's possession.
[101] Atzenhoffer: "Outside Contact Report," October 16, 1978, House Assassinations Committee files.
[102] Heath and 1957 project: *New York Times*, August 2, 1977, "Private Institutions Used in CIA Effort to Control Behavior."

Yet simultaneously, Oswald tried to enlist in the Marines when he was only sixteen. He succeeded a year later, in late October 1956, after moving with his mother to Fort Worth and attending tenth grade for less than a month, three weeks after writing the Socialist Party of America seeking "more information." He soon chose aircraft maintenance and repair as his duty assignment, something David Ferrie had stressed with the boys of the CAP.

By September 1957, he'd been assigned to the Atsugi Naval Air Base just outside Tokyo. Atsugi was the point of origin for the top-secret U2 spy plane flights, whose mission was to photograph military and industrial targets at altitudes high above the Soviet Union and Communist China. As a radar operator, Oswald was at least privy to the existence of the U2s.

Atsugi also contained some twenty buildings identified as the Joint Technical Advisory Group, the cover designation for one of the CIA's main operational bases in Asia. Among the CIA files on MKULTRA released twenty years later, there was a memorandum dated December 1, 1953, headed "SUBJECT: Use of LSD. . . . Only two (2) field stations, Manila and Atsugi, have LSD material," it said.[103] Another sanitized file noted: "Preparing cables to field to find out who has custody and access. Atsugi and Manila. Issuance done only with two CIA employees concurrence and use only with DD/P [Deputy Director for Plans] approval."[104]

Frank Camper was a twenty-year intelligence veteran with numerous FBI and CIA contacts, who served in Vietnam with the elite Special Operations Group and later worked under deep cover penetrating terrorist organizations worldwide. I met Camper at a conference, where he related something told him by an inside source: "Oswald reported a Japanese Communist approach to him to Naval Intelligence and then the CIA picked him up. He fit the profile for MKULTRA." In 1994, Camper wrote me in a letter: "What gives away his high[ly] probable induction in MKULTRA project experiments is the fact he was frequently in the brig or base hospital, was recalled from a unit movement to Formosa to return to the Atsugi hospital, and ended up being assigned to the hospital on a layover or casual basis."

This, Camper believed, "would have given the MKULTRA doctors an opportunity to review Oswald's conditioning and mental state, and correct or note whatever they found wrong."

It was shortly after Oswald's last release from the Atsugi hospital, and reassignment to a Marine squadron at Iwakuni Air Base some 430 miles southwest

---

[103] LSD at field stations: CIA "Memorandum for: Inspector General. Subject: Use of LSD," December 1, 1953.

[104] Atsugi and Manila: CIA "Memorandum for the Record. Subject: Conversation with Dr. Willis Gibbons of TSS re: Olson Case," Lyman B. Kirkpatrick, Inspector General, December 1, 1953.

of Tokyo, that he began referring to the Marines as "you Americans" and denouncing "American imperialism" and "exploitation."

In his book, *The Search for the "Manchurian Candidate,"* author John Marks described an MKULTRA project approved in 1956 to have one of its fronts— the Human Ecology Society—"study the factors that caused men to defect from their countries and cooperate with foreign governments. MKULTRA officials reasons that if they could understand what made old turncoats tick, it might help them entice new ones. While good case officers instinctively seemed to know how to handle a potential agent—or thought they did—the MKULTRA men hoped to come up with systematic, even scientific improvements . . . the purpose of the research was to assess defectors' social and cultural background, their life experience, and their personality structure, in order to understand their motivations, value systems, and probable future reactions."[105]

In the late 1950s, there would be a sudden rash of American defectors to the Soviet Union, including Oswald. It has long been suspected that at least some of these were intentionally dispatched on behalf of the CIA or the military. Whatever the 1956 MKULTRA study fully entailed would, it seems, have been quite useful for such future operations.

In this regard, it is worth making a full circle to an article by Dr. George Estabrooks, published in *Science Digest Magazine* in April 1971. He wrote of a hypnosis experiment that he'd conducted during World War II, "with a vulnerable Marine lieutenant I'll call Jones. Under the watchful eye of Marine Intelligence I split his personality into Jones A and Jones B. Jones A, once a 'normal' working Marine, became entirely different. He talked communist doctrine and meant it. He was welcomed enthusiastically by communist cells, was deliberately given a dishonorable discharge by the Corps (which was in on the plot) and became a card-carrying party member.

"The joker was Jones B, the second personality formerly apparent in the conscious Marine. Under hypnosis, this Jones had been carefully coached by suggestion. Jones B was the deeper personality, knew all the thoughts of Jones A, was a loyal American, and was 'imprinted' to say nothing. . . .

"All I had to do was hypnotize the whole man, get in touch with Jones B, the loyal American, and I had a pipeline straight into the Communist camp. It worked beautifully for months with this subject, but the technique backfired. While there was no way for an enemy to expose Jones' dual personality, they suspected it and played the same trick on us later."[106]

---

[105] Defector study: Marks, 1991, Norton paperback edition, p. 162.
[106] Estabrooks article: "Hypnosis Comes of Age," by G.H. Estabrooks, Ph.D., *Science Digest*, April 1971.

38

Russia and Beyond

Soon after arriving in the Soviet Union in mid-October 1959, Oswald was told by the authorities that his visa had expired and he had to leave Moscow immediately. When his Intourist guide showed up for a meeting in his hotel room, she found that Oswald had slashed his wrist. He was rushed to an emergency room and admitted that same night to the Botinsky Psychiatric Hospital. There, for the next eleven days, he remained under observation.

Former covert intelligence agent Frank Camper described to me what he had heard happened next.[107] "I had a contact with a KGB agent, a guy who has since gone freelance. He told me that, while some of the KGB documentation on Oswald has been released, it is by no means complete. The KGB is saying they did not recruit him, but did watch him for two years. All this is true, but my source said there was a reason they allowed him to stay.

"When Oswald slit his wrist and was in the psychiatric hospital, he showed signs of resistance to questioning or interrogation while under sedation. There was a sub-branch of MKULTRA where people were trained to resist interrogation.

"The doctors told the MVD [the Soviet Ministry of Internal Affairs, which had secret police functions], whom they were reporting to, that Oswald's psychological responses were unusual. He fit a KGB profile for psychologically conditioned agents. They knew U.S. intelligence was running people like this. So they said, let's keep this guy and see what the Americans have run in on us.

"The agent told me that the KGB has not released the particular document about Oswald's psychological profile, because it would compromise their own methods and techniques. But I saw the file."

In a documentary about Oswald aired by PBS' *Frontline* in 1993, a former hospital employee recounted how the KGB arrived at the Botinsky facility when Oswald was about to be discharged. They confiscated Oswald's medical history, discharge paper, and other documents, and spirited the young ex-marine away. A KGB file noted that the Soviet spy agency wished to "study him further."[108]

It was after this that Oswald walked into the American Embassy in Moscow and announced plans to dissolve his American citizenship and, according to

---

[107] Camper on KGB and Oswald: Author's telephone interviews, October 8, 1993 and November 29, 1993.
[108] KGB file: Material provided author by Anthony Summers.

consular official Richard E. Snyder, "has offered Soviets any information he has acquired as enlisted radar operator." John McVickar, another consular official who was in the room, wrote in a memorandum his opinion that Oswald "was following a pattern of behavior in which he had been tutored by a person or persons unknown." Oswald "seemed to be using words he had learned but did not fully understand."[109]

The first journalist to interview Oswald after his defection was Aline Mosby of United Press International. She observed that he talked almost "nonstop" and that his use of phrases such as "capitalist lackeys" and "imperialist running dogs" sounded "as if it were all being given by rote."

Oswald ended up working in an electronics factory in Minsk, being paid a handsome salary by the Russians. Little is known about his day-to-day activities during his first year there, though KGB files reveal that he was under almost constant surveillance. Eduard Shirkovsky, the former KGB Chief of the Byelorussian Republic, told the newspaper *Izvestia* in August 1992 that the KGB had conducted a detailed study of Oswald's personality while in Minsk. "Perhaps some pills were put into his glass, the kind of pills to make him more relaxed, more talkative," Shirkovsky added.

A little more than a year after his arrival in Minsk, Oswald met the attractive Marina Prusakova, daughter of a colonel in the MVD. After a courtship that took place primarily during an eleven-day hospital stay where Oswald underwent an adenoid operation, they were married on May Day 1961. Years later, Marina would remember Oswald's fear of needles, as well as occasional nightmares and talking in his sleep during the year they remained in Russia.[110]

The couple had a baby girl when they crossed the sea in the summer of 1962 aboard the SS *Maasdam*, bound for the U.S. Oswald spent much of his time writing down his political philosophy, presenting himself as a utopian Marxist now disillusioned with Soviet-style communism. Author Edward Jay Epstein, who while researching his book *Legend* enlisted a handwriting expert to examine Oswald's "Historic Diary" and other handwritten statements, would determine that the diary had actually been written in one or two sessions, a "cover story" that omitted "nearly all events that would be inconsistent with his desire to return to the United States." What Oswald penned on the boat back, Epstein believed, "show evidence of having been dictated to him. The way that words are phonetically scribbled down without regard for spelling suggests that he was using words that were unfamiliar to him and hearing them rather than copying them from a book or prepared text. In both cases, he seems to be writing under the discipline of another person."

---

[109] McVickar: Warren Commission, Volume XVIII, p. 153.
[110] Marina Oswald: Author's telephone interview, April 1994.

Although the CIA has always denied having debriefed Oswald upon his return to America, researchers for the 1993 *Frontline* program verified that one did occur. That same year, I interviewed Donald Deneselya, who had worked on James Angleton's Counterintelligence staff. "A routine contract report crossed my desk in the summer of 1962," he recalled. "Oswald's name was not mentioned in the debriefing. But I knew it was him because of the circumstances—a Marine re-defector returning with his family. My assumption was, the Agency had a file on this."[111]

Epstein added in *Legend*: "It is possible that Oswald took a train to Washington, D.C. [upon arriving in New York]. A psychologist code-named Cato on assignment for the CIA claimed to have interviewed a Russian defector at the Roger Smith Hotel who resembled Oswald."[112]

Oswald's older brother, Robert, met him and Marina when they arrived in Dallas that June. In his appearance before the Warren Commission, Robert was suddenly asked by counsel Albert Jenner whether he had seen the film version of *The Manchurian Candidate* (he hadn't), and had "formed an opinion about whether your brother may have undergone some treatment in Russia that may have affected his mind."

Robert Oswald replied: "That perhaps in sheer speculation on my part, that due to the nature of the change in his hair, in the baldness that appeared, I reached the opinion that perhaps something in the nature of shock treatments or something along that line had been given him in Russia."[113]

Later, Oswald would write in an article for *Look Magazine*: "The Commission seemed to be exploring the possibility that Lee could have been subjected to some kind of brainwashing by the Russians, and that the assassination of President Kennedy might have followed some preselected signal."[114]

In Dallas in 1962, the returning Oswalds were soon taken under the wing of George de Mohrenschildt, a mysterious figure who later admitted being in communication about them with J. Walton Moore of the CIA's Domestic Contact Division. In February 1963, de Mohrenschildt introduced Oswald to another young man, Volkmar Schmidt, who had come to Dallas from Germany late in 1960 to work as a geological researcher. De Mohrenschildt later said he arranged the meeting because "Schmidt was fascinated with political ideology . . . [and was] a shrewd analyst of human psychology."

---

[111] Donald Deneselya: Author's interview, October 31, 1993, Washington, D.C.

[112] "Cato": *Legend: The Secret World of Lee Harvey Oswald* by Edward J. Epstein (N.Y.: Reader's Digest Press/McGraw-Hill, 1978), p. 310.

[113] Robert Oswald testimony: Warren Commission, Volume I, p. 331.

[114] Robert Oswald quote: *Look Magazine*, October 17, 1967, "He Was My Brother" by Robert L. Oswald with Myrick and Barbara Land.

Schmidt had been a student in Heidelberg, Germany, of Dr. Wilhelm Kuetemeyer, a professor of psychosomatic medicine who conducted experiments on schizophrenics during World War II. From Kuetemeyer, Schmidt had learned certain techniques that he said he employed with Oswald, seeking to win Oswald's confidence by trying to one-up him on extreme views. (Schmidt also told author Epstein that he was personally fascinated with hypnosis.) That night, Schmidt brought up the name of General Edwin Walker, a right-wing ideologue who lived in Dallas and whom Schmidt compared to Adolf Hitler. "Oswald instantly seized on the analogy," Schmidt would recall, "to argue that America was moving toward fascism. As he spoke, he seemed to grow more and more excited about the subject."[115]

Marina was not sure whether it was that same night, or the next, that she heard Lee talking in his sleep for the first time since Minsk. He spoke so loudly and clearly that she sat up in bed with a start. Oswald was repeating the same words over and over, though she could not understand what he was saying. When she asked her husband about this, he became hostile. Over the ensuing weeks, he would ask several times whether he'd talked in his sleep the night before.

That was the same period when Oswald sent in a mail order for a Mannlicher-Carcano rifle, to be shipped to his "Hidell" alias at his post office box. This was what he used, Marina would testify, in a failed attempt to kill General Walker on April 10. Two weeks later, Oswald moved alone to New Orleans, with Marina joining him in June.

He began having nocturnal problems again, as Marina later described to biographer Priscilla McMillan: "One night he cried, yet when he woke up he could not remember what his dream had been about. He started having nosebleeds, once or twice he talked in his sleep, and one night toward the very end of June he had four anxiety attacks during which he shook head to toe at intervals of half an hour and never once woke up."[116]

When I described Oswald's behavior to hypnosis expert Milton Kline, he responded immediately: "That sounds like an abreaction. This can occur by spontaneous regressions, in terms of someone's mental functioning. But it is more likely to occur on the basis of hypnotically induced experiences, or attempts to recall or relive certain experiences under hypnosis for which there is partial amnesia. What you are describing appears to involve some very conflicting feelings, and perhaps some real feelings of guilt. Particularly having dreams and not being able to recall them is very typical following hypnotically induced trauma.

---

[115] Schmidt/Kuetemeyer: Epstein, *Legend*, p. 204.
[116] Marina quote: *Marina and Lee* by Priscilla Johnson McMillan (N.Y.: Harper & Row, 1977).

The experience is relived via the dream, but the individual represses the dream and typically would then be in a state of depression."[117]

One night during this period, Marina found Lee sitting in the dark, his arms and legs wrapped around the back of a chair and his head resting on top of it, staring at the floor. As she put her arms around him and stroked his head, he was shaking with sobs. Long minutes passed. Oswald told her he was lost and did not know what he should do. At last he rose and returned to the living room, where she followed him. After a silence, he told her he wanted to accompany her back to Russia, and that she should write the Soviet Embassy to that effect. Marina agreed. Unknown to his wife, Oswald then added a letter of his own in English, asking the Embassy to consider his application separately. That same day, July 1, Oswald checked out of the library a biography of Kennedy, *Portrait of a President*. He also took out a book about the 1936 assassination of Louisiana Governor Huey Long. For some reason, Oswald's summer visits to the Napoleon branch library a considerable distance from his home always took place on a Thursday.

On August 9 came Oswald's confrontation with anti-Castro Cubans, while he stood passing out FAIR PLAY FOR CUBA leaflets on a street corner. The incident, which appeared to have been staged in advance and resulted in Oswald's arrest, marked the start of a brief but highly visible role for Oswald as a Castro supporter.

In his book, *The Search for the "Manchurian Candidate"*, John Marks would later recount an interview with a CIA source he called "Deep Trance." The man described a "programmed 'patsy' whom a hypnotist could walk through a series of seemingly unrelated events—a visit to a store, a conversation with a mailman, picking a fight at a political rally. The subject would remember everything that happened to him and be amnesic only of the fact the hypnotist ordered him to do these things. There would be no gaping inconsistency in his life of the sort that can ruin an attempt by a hypnotist to create a second personality. The purpose of this exercise is to leave a circumstantial trail that will make the authorities think the patsy committed a particular crime."[118]

When Oswald was arrested, he presented two forms of identification to the police. One was his Fair Play for Cuba Committee membership card, listing "A. Hidell" as chapter president. Another was a Social Security card in his real name, "which did not bear his signature." After spending a night in jail, Oswald requested to speak to someone from the FBI. Special Agent John Quigley showed up the next morning. He would later maintain he'd never heard of Oswald

---

[117] Kline quote: Author's telephone interview, January 11, 1995.
[118] Programmed patsy: Marks, *The Search for the 'Manchurian Candidate,'* p. 204.

before. Yet in 1961, it was Quigley who had reviewed a Naval Intelligence file on Oswald while the defector was still in the Soviet Union.[119]

In the course of his ninety-minute discussion with Quigley, Oswald said he had met and married his wife Marina in Fort Worth. He showed the FBI agent an FPCC card signed by A.J. Hidell. Since receiving the card, Oswald said he'd spoken several times to Hidell by phone, when "HIDELL would discuss general matters of mutual interest in connection with committee business, and on other occasions he would inform him of a scheduled meeting. He said he has never personally met HIDELL, and he knows HIDELL did have a telephone, but it has now been discontinued."

The FBI report continued: "Last Wednesday, August 7, 1963, OSWALD said he received a note through the mail from HIDELL. The note asked him if he had time would he mind distributing some Fair Play literature in the downtown area of New Orleans. He said HIDELL knew that he was not working and probably had time. HIDELL also knew that he had considerable literature on the committee which had been furnished to him by the national committee in New York."[120]

Who was Hidell? No investigation has ever come up with a real person by that name, and the assumption has been that Oswald made up the alias, probably as a takeoff on "Fidel." But intelligence veteran Frank Camper's discussions with several experts on behavioral conditioning led him to a different conclusion. Camper sees Hidell as Oswald's induced other personality. In his book, *The MKULTRA Secret*,[121] Camper writes:

"It is very possible for one personality to know the other exists, but still consider it as a completely separate entity. This is selective denial at its finest. Oswald could know Hidell's name, and might dimly realize they shared the same body, but feel no responsibility for Hidell's actions. Under pressure, Oswald could (and probably would) go into complete denial about Hidell and have no conscious memory or knowledge of Hidell's actions. The difference comes when it is Hidell acknowledging Oswald. Hidell would always be aware of Oswald, and know and remember everything Oswald did. In multiple personality cases, there is usually one predominant personality. Oswald's MKULTRA conditioning seems to have left his own personality as the surface, or functionality personality, but Hidell manipulated Oswald, not vice versa. . . .

"Oswald's statement to Quigley that Hidell was a person he spoke to on the telephone is one of the many ways some schizophrenics communicate with their other selves. His claim to agent Quigley that he met and married Marina in Fort

---

[119] Quigley and Navy file: WC IV, pp. 432, 438.

[120] FBI report: FBI File No. 100-16601 (CE 826).

[121] Camper quotes: Original manuscript sent to author by Camper, 1995.

Worth seems to indicate total denial of having been in Russia. That had been Hidell, not Oswald."

As Professor George Estabrooks had written in his 1948 book, *Hypnotism*, "We know that dual, and even multiple, personality can be both caused and cured by hypnosis. Moreover, that condition, the Dr. Jekyll and Mr. Hyde combination, is a very real one once it is established."

Not long after the assassination, a U.S. Congressman from Texas named Wright Patman, who had been in the presidential motorcade that day, raised a point along these lines to Washington columnist John Henshaw. "The phony name he [Oswald] used to order a rifle, A. Hidell, seems to be a combination of Jekyll and Hyde," Patman was quoted. "Could it be that Oswald was himself aware of the nature of his mental conflict? Did he keep saying, 'I didn't do it,' because his other self did it?"

Soon after the confrontation that landed him in custody in New Orleans, Oswald had appeared on a local radio program debating Cuban exile Carlos Bringuier and Edward Butler, who worked with an Information Council of the Americas (INCA) disseminating anti-Communist propaganda into Latin America. Butler also served as an informant for the CIA.

When I interviewed Butler by phone in 1995 and asked him to recall his impressions of Oswald, he said:[122] "He was determined, committed, and talked like a man with a piano roll in his head, or what today you would say was a floppy disc. Whether he absorbed propaganda and was self-taught, or was deliberately programmed by someone, I don't know."

You mean you thought it possible that Oswald could have been under some kind of behavioral conditioning? "Yes, I did suspect that," Butler said. "There's no doubt at all you can develop various tendencies in people. Posthypnotic suggestion and post-drug suggestion is obviously something to be considered. At one point, LSD for example was called psychotomimetic, which means 'mimicking psychosis.' The basic problem you have is that, if Oswald was programmed, it was done very effectively. The end result was, he was a lethal weapon."

Tulane University was where Oswald told Cuban exile Carlos Quiroga he'd learned to speak Russian, and where he told Charles Hall Steele his FAIR PLAY FOR CUBA leaflets had originated. Tulane was also a source of MKULTRA experiments conducted by renowned brain researcher Robert Heath. A surviving MKULTRA file dated November 14, 1956, cited Heath's plans to perform toxicity studies on monkeys and added, "He will also evaluate the drug on convicts incarcerated at the [deleted] State Penitentiary."[123] Heath also did research

---

[122] Butler quotes: Author's interview, January 20, 1995.
[123] Heath/MKULTRA: CIA "Memorandum for: Deputy Director, Intelligence, Subject: Investigation and Report on Bulbocapnine," November 14, 1956.

for the Army involving LSD on certain patients in whom he had implanted electrodes.

According to Dr. Milton Kline, "There was also some work that Heath contracted out—I know it went on—using hypnosis to attempt to produce sensory stimulation of those areas of the brain where Heath was using electronic implants. Tulane was a very active place and all sorts of people had contact with Heath, in terms of the kind of research he was doing."[124]

Florence Strohmeyer, who worked under Heath all through the 1950s, told me of one experiment that involved "taking blood to carry on research of a whole bunch of airmen at a base in Albuquerque," trying to determine characteristics of schizophrenia. She also recalled Heath conducting experiments with young people.[125]

In September 1963, Oswald had been seen by a number of witnesses in the small town of Clinton, Louisiana, where he had joined a line of African-Americans seeking to register to vote. Two men had accompanied Oswald in a black Lincoln Continental, and this incident has long fueled speculation that one was David Ferrie and the other was either Clay Shaw or Guy Banister. Most striking in terms of our particular narrative, however, is that Oswald told the voting registrar, Henry Earl Palmer, that he'd been living in Jackson with a doctor who worked at a nearby mental hospital called East Louisiana State.[126] The doctor's name was Frank Silva.

There is no indication that Oswald ever really lived with Dr. Silva, who had left Cuba to come to the U.S. in 1955. However, when interviewed by author Joan Mellen for her biography of Jim Garrison, *A Farewell to Justice*, Silva said he had indeed encountered Oswald one day at the hospital, talking to an attendant about Cuba. Oswald, who said he was applying for a job, then bragged to Silva about how he had been a Marine and was proficient with guns and had plans to go to Cuba. "I'm involved with getting rid of Fidel Castro," Silva recalled Oswald saying, "using my skills as a Marine."[127]

Not mentioned in Mellen's book is the type of doctor that Silva was. According to Dr. Victor Weiss, former clinical director at the hospital, Silva was "mainly the director of the research unit, which was a fairly large one dedicated purely to pharmacology research. The unit was basically designed to make double-blind studies on new anti-psychotic drugs. Silva was one of Heath's fair-haired boys.

---

[124] Kline quote: Author's telephone interview, 1995.

[125] Florence Strohmeyer: Author's telephone interview, January 6, 1995.

[126] Henry Palmer: HSCA interview with Henry Earl Palmer, January 19, 1978.

[127] Silva quotes: *A Farewell to Justice* by Joan Mellen (Washington, D.C.: Potomac Books, Inc., 2005), p. 220.

He was also on the faculty at Tulane, in Heath's department, and he got his appointment at the hospital through Dr. Heath."[128]

A paper co-authored by Heath, Silva, and a few others, and published in *Comprehensive Psychiatry 1960*, was titled: "Comparative Effects of the Administration of taraxein, d-LSD, Mescaline, and Psilocybin to Human Volunteers." The introduction stated, "The patient donors are housed in a special Tulane University Research Unit at the East Louisiana State Hospital, Jackson."[129] The experiments were supported by a grant from the Commonwealth Fund, later identified as having also been a CIA front.

In 1999, the CIA released a memorandum generated more than twenty years earlier. It pertained to "Recent Discovery of Project ZR/ALERT Documents— A Study of the Use of Psychological Programming for Intelligence Purposes." Project ZR/ALERT, according to the memo, concerned "exploration and experimentation by the CI Staff of the use of hypnotism in certain operational situations." CI referred to Counterintelligence, the Agency branch run by James Angleton.

The memo, generated by Bruce T. Johnson for CIA General Counsel Emile L. Julian, went on to say: "Special handling of the documents from Mexico City is called for, I believe. . . . The events described in these documents took place in the summer of 1963, a period in the life of the Mexico City Station which is of intense interest to the HSCA [House Select Committee on Assassination]."

It was suggested that, since the documents "have no bearing upon the investigations" of the HSCA, its Chief Counsel Bob Blakey should be allowed to review them in order to "dispel concerns."[130]

This is the only known reference to Project ZR/ALERT. Not only does its existence in Mexico City coincide with Oswald's visit (or perhaps visits) there, but with a time period in 1963 when Angleton's CI branch was increasingly becoming the Agency's primary repository for everything regarding Oswald's activities.

---

[128] Dr. Victor Weiss: Author's telephone interview, December 13, 1994.

[129] LSD experiments: *Comprehensive Psychiatry*: Volume 1, pp. 370–76, 1960, "Comparative Effects of the Administration of taraxein, d-LSD, Mescaline, and Psilocybin to Human Volunteers" by F. Silva, M.D., R.G. Heath, M.D., et al.

[130] ZR/ALERT: CIA "Memorandum for: General Counsel, Attention: Emile L. Julian," May 17, 1978 (www.maryferrell.org/mffweb/archive/viewer/showDoc.do?docid=26123&relPage ID=2).

39

Programmed to Kill?

The first man to see Oswald, less than two minutes after the last shot rang out in Dealey Plaza, was a motorcycle patrolman named Marion Baker. He'd heard what he was sure was a crack from a high-powered rifle coming from the Texas School Book Depository. Racing inside, Baker glimpsed someone in the lunchroom on the second floor and drew his revolver. A young man stood about twenty feet away, walking to the far corner. When Baker commanded that he turn around, the man obeyed. Baker observed that he was empty-handed, not out of breath, and staring at him impassively. When building superintendent Roy Truly walked in and said he knew the young man, Baker lowered his gun and continued his search.

A clerical supervisor, Mrs. Robert Reid, also saw the young employee come in from the lunchroom holding a bottle of Coca-Cola. "Oh," she remembered saying, "the President has been shot but maybe they didn't hit him." Oswald mumbled something and, seeming "very calm" to Mrs. Reid, kept on walking down the stairs and out the depository's main entrance. When someone, probably a reporter, ran up and asked where he could find a phone, Oswald calmly pointed inside and told the man there was probably a pay phone there.

Slightly more than an hour after the president had been shot, at least fifteen policemen descended on the Texas Theater. The houselights were brought up and patrolman Nick McDonald slowly approached a young man sitting alone near the back, and instructed him to stand up. Oswald did so, saying as he half-raised his hands, "Well, it is all over now." Then he reportedly punched McDonald in the face and reached for a pistol in his waistband. After a brief scuffle, several officers seized the gun and led Oswald out in handcuffs. Twice the twenty-four-year-old ex-Marine stopped, turned around, and hollered at a crowd that had gathered in front of the theater, "I am not resisting arrest."

Shoved into the back seat of a police car between two officers, Oswald remained remarkably serene. One policeman who accompanied Oswald on the ride to headquarters later described his strangely collected behavior as akin to someone who had just been picked up for a speeding ticket. As they neared the station, Sergeant Gerald Hill explained to Oswald that camera crews would probably be awaiting them and, if he wished, he could cover his face. "Why should I hide my face," Hill recalled Oswald saying, "I haven't done anything to be ashamed of."

In a small interrogation room on the third floor of Dallas police headquarters, Oswald identified himself as "Hidell" to one of the first detectives who questioned him. Oswald proceeded to undergo hours of interrogation by homicide captain Will Fritz and District Attorney William Alexander. More than three decades later, Alexander remained extremely troubled by Oswald's curious behavior that afternoon.[131]

"I would say that he was programmed," Alexander told me in a 1994 interview. "I don't know how many murderers, robbers, burglars, pimps, and prostitutes I had talked to in connection with criminal cases—but Oswald's responses were not typical. They were completely atypical. He knew how to avoid a question, and knew how to get right back to you. One way of avoiding interrogation is to answer a question with a question. For the most part, that's what he did, or else make an unwarranted accusation [against his interrogators]."

Alexander continued, "A person's mind can be worked on, where they get an idea and won't give it up. Of course, everybody went 'ha, ha, ha' when I suggested that. It came to me within a few days, but nobody knew what I was talking about. But that guy was under control. It appeared to me that someone had coached him very carefully about how to handle himself in custody. It was as if he had foreseen and anticipated the situation he found himself in. That's my 'Manchurian Candidate' theory."

Also mystified by Oswald's attitude in custody was Frank Ellsworth, an official with the federal Alcohol, Tobacco and Firearms agency, who was called in by Captain Fritz to quiz Oswald about weaponry. As Ellsworth recounted it to me, "I tried to question him shortly after his arrest. But he just sat there with this very self-satisfied smirk on his face. Oswald appeared to be awfully pleased with himself, which struck me as incongruous for a man accused of assassinating the most popular president since Franklin Roosevelt. Particularly with the media out in the hall screaming and hollering like absolute jackals."[132]

When Oswald's brother, Robert, visited him that weekend in his cell, he recorded in a diary: "All the time we were talking, I watched his eyes for any sign of guilt. . . . There was nothing there—no guilt, no shame, no nothing. Lee finally aware of my looking into his eyes, he stated, 'You will not find anything there.'"[133]

According to an FBI report, a New Orleans private investigator named Jack Martin had contacted WWL-TV shortly after the assassination with information about an associate, David Ferrie. "He also told them that FERRIE was an amateur hypnotist and that it was his idea that FERRIE may have

---

[131] Alexander quotes: Author's telephone interview, December 12, 1994.
[132] Ellsworth quotes: Author's telephone interview, 1991.
[133] Robert Oswald: *Look Magazine*, 1967 article, op. cit.

hypnotized LEE OSWALD and planted a posthypnotic suggestion that he kill the president."[134]

As noted earlier, Oswald had been a member of Ferrie's Civil Air Patrol as a teenager and been seen by more than one witness in Oswald's company in the summer of 1963. Not long after Garrison questioned Ferrie early in 1967, he was found dead in his apartment. Police discovered, amid a huge library on hypnotism, several voluminous abstracts on posthypnotic suggestion.

Another report, which appeared in the *Chicago Tribune* on November 27, 1963, had this to say: "One of the more startling TV interviews over the long weekend involved one Bill DeMarr, who was doing a mental act at Jack Ruby's Carousel night club. DeMarr was sure Lee Harvey Oswald was in the club's audience a few nights before and volunteered to help in the act. The FBI hurried over to quiz DeMarr, but no more has been heard of this added bizarre angle."[135] (Thirteen years later, another Carousel employee, Wally Weston, who had first discounted DeMarr's story, claimed that Oswald had indeed been in the club "at least twice" before the assassination.)[136]

Ruby, a known associate of both the police and the mob, was ubiquitous in the post-assassination scene. When D.A. Henry Wade informed reporters that Oswald belonged to the Free Cuba Committee, an anti-Castro organization, it was Ruby who corrected the statement to be Fair Play for Cuba Committee.

Ruby's roommate, George Senator, observed that "the way he talked" seemed very strange on the morning of Sunday, November 24. "He was even mumbling, which I didn't understand," Senator would tell the Warren Commission. "His lips were going. What he was jabbering, I don't know." Watching Ruby get dressed, Senator felt that "he sure had a moody and very faraway look to me. It was a look that I had never seen before on him."[137]

One of Ruby's strippers, Karen Carlin, spoke to her boss that morning on the phone. "I had to keep saying, 'Jack, Jack, are you there?' and he would say, 'Yes.'"[138]

Shortly before eleven o'clock that morning, Ruby left his apartment, casually joined a crowd of policemen and reporters in the basement, and as the accused assassin was let into the piercing glare of TV lights toward a waiting car, cried out "Oswald!" and pumped a single deadly bullet into his abdomen.

---

[134] Martin on Ferrie: FBI File # 89-69, November 25, 1963, report by SA Regis L. Kennedy and Claude L. Schlager.

[135] DeMarr: Referenced in CIA "Memorandum for: Director of Security, Subject: CAIN, Richard Scully," December 19, 1969.

[136] Wally Weston: *Who Was Jack Ruby?* by Seth Kantor (N.Y.: Everest House, 1978).

[137] George Senator: *Case Closed* by Gerald Posner (N.Y.: Random House, 1993), p. 392.

[138] Karen Carlin: *Crossfire* by Jim Marrs (N.Y.: Carroll & Graf Publishers, 1989), p. 419.

Taken to the same jail cell vacated by Oswald early that morning, Ruby asked the police: "What happened?"[139] From that point on, he exhibited an inability to recall his shooting of Oswald with any clarity. Don Roy Archer, the detective charged with placing Ruby in jail, would remember:

"His behavior to begin with was very hyper. He was sweating profusely. I could see his heart beating. We had stripped him down for security purposes. He asked me for one of my cigarettes. I gave him a cigarette. Finally after about two hours had elapsed, the head of the Secret Service came up and I conferred with him and he told me that Oswald had died.

"This should have shocked [Ruby] because it would mean the death penalty. I returned and said, 'Jack, it looks like it's going to be the electric chair for you.' Instead of being shocked, he became calm, he quit sweating, his heart slowed down. I asked him if he wanted a cigarette and he advised me he didn't smoke. I was just astonished at this complete difference of behavior from what I had expected. I would say his life had depended on him getting Oswald."[140]

Ruby's first attorney, Joe Tonahill, told biographer Seth Kantor that "Ruby could have been used by others. It wouldn't have been any problem to reach in and get Ruby to do something like this, through the power of suggestion, through innuendo, without Ruby even realizing it."[141]

An unsigned psychiatric report dated December 27, 1963, stated: "There seems to be no feeling of guilt whatever on the patient's part about the slaying of Oswald. He seems to feel that it was some agent outside of himself that carried out the act."

Before the fifty-two-year-old Ruby was convicted of murder on March 14, 1964, a number of psychiatrists offered their expert diagnoses of his medical condition. In his report, Dr. Walter Bromberg stated that Ruby seemed "pre-set to be a fighter, to attack," and added: "Definitely there is a block to his thinking which is no part of his original mental endowment."[142]

Dr. Roy Schafer of Yale testified at the trial that Ruby "appears to feel not altogether in control of his body actions, as if they occur independently of his conscious will at times."

A leading criminal psychologist, Dr. Manfred Guttmacher, testified that he believed Ruby's brain had been "damaged," but he could not figure out exactly how. At the time of the shooting, Guttmacher believed, Ruby had suffered a "functional psychosis." Asked by Assistant D.A. Alexander whether, by that,

---

[139] "What happened?": Ibid, p. 423.

[140] Don Roy Archer: Ibid, pp. 423–24.

[141] Joe Tonahill: Kantor, op. cit.

[142] Bromberg quote: Memorandum "Was Jack Ruby a 'Manchurian Candidate'?" provided to author by Michael Joseph Levy.

he meant "a psychotic condition for which there is no known organic cause," Guttmacher responded, "Yes."

On April 29, 1964, Dr. Louis J. (Jolly) West came to the Dallas County Jail to examine Ruby. This took place in a private interview room where, according to West, Ruby appeared "pale, tremulous, agitated and depressed." His opinion was that "at this time Mr. Ruby is obviously psychotic." He had sunk into a paranoid state, manifested by delusions, visual and auditory hallucinations, and suicidal impulses. West urged his immediate hospitalization, making him eligible for treatment for a mental disorder, and another doctor soon put Ruby on "happy pills."[143]

The next day, another doctor named Robert Stubblefield, chief of the Psychiatric Department at Southwestern Medical School in Dallas, also came to see Ruby. Although he'd testified that Ruby was sane enough to stand trial, Stubblefield later advised the court that Ruby seemed "currently severely emotionally disturbed, with major paranoid and depressive features."[144]

After that, during Ruby's testimony before the Warren Commission on June 7, 1964, he rambled continually, apparently unable to follow any logical time sequence concerning his movements in the nearly 48 hours between the assassination and his murder of Oswald. At one point, Ruby said, "… and it seems as you get further into something, even though you know what you did, it operates against you somehow, brain washes you that you are weak in what you want to tell the truth about and what to say which is the truth."

His attorney, Melvin Belli, would recall in his book, *Dallas Justice*: "Never once did he voluntarily mention Lee Oswald by name. Never, as far as I could see, was he willing to concede that there had been this living, breathing human being who had died at his hands. It was strange because he had the capacity to summon up sympathy for almost anything."[145]

Dr. West would visit Ruby on two more occasions, writing in a letter dated June 10, 1965: "Today, of course, Ruby has de-compensated into a chronic psychosis.…"

Though unknown to the public at the time, West had been a longtime participant in the CIA's MKULTRA program. A CIA memo on "Interrogation Techniques," dated January 14, 1953, reported; "If the services of Major Louis J. West, USAF (MC), a trained hypnotist, can be obtained … a well-balanced interrogation research center could be established in an especially selected location."

---

[143] West and Ruby: *The Trial of Jack Ruby* by John Kaplan and Jon R. Waltz, 1965, pp. 344–345.
[144] Stubblefield: *The New Republic*, February 11, 1967, "The Last Madness of Jack Ruby" by Ronnie Dugger.
[145] Belli quote: Levy memo, op. cit.

After supervising studies of returning POWs from the Korean War for the Air Force to determine whether they had been "brainwashed," West became chief of psychiatry at the University of Oklahoma (1954–69). There, CIA Subproject 43 was under West's aegis between 1955 and 1957, where he was "cleared through TOP-SECRET," according to Agency files. Included among West's experiments was one with hypnotic suggestion indicating "that more control can be exerted over the autonomic nervous system than has been previously supposed."[146]

During the early 1960s, West conducted animal research using LSD. Indeed, Aldous Huxley reported that West was the doctor who first introduced him to the hallucinogenic drug, at a time when West was simultaneously doing research with hypnosis and mescaline. In 1961, Huxley said West informed him that he was now experimenting with sensory deprivation and had some of the best facilities available.

Reportedly, Dr. Stubblefield, the man who visited Ruby the day after West in the spring of 1964, had also been associated with LSD research and the CIA's MK/ULTRA program.

---

[146] West and CIA: *New York Times*, September 4, 1977, "CIA Tells Oklahoma U. of Mind-Research Role."

40

An MKULTRA Field Operative Talks

"Yeah, okay," Ira Feldman had said over the phone, "come see me but I don't know whether I'll talk to you about all this bullshit." A late August squall was pouring down over Long Island as I walked through the revolving door of a Marriott Hotel at the outskirts of Uniondale, New York. A diminutive man in his seventies looked up from a cushioned chair, an unlit cigar hanging from his mouth.

Ike, as he has always been called, rose slowly to his five-foot-three-inch height, leaning on a long wooden cane. It had a ginseng root for a handle that, he would tell me, had been made for him by a Chinese friend. Dressed in a plaid sport shirt and slacks, he also sported a reddish toupee.[147]

Between 1953 and 1969, Ike Feldman had been an undercover agent for the CIA, though his official capacity was inside the Federal Bureau of Narcotics (FBN, predecessor to today's Drug Enforcement Agency). At both jobs he served as the right-hand man to George White, the leading field officer in the CIA's experiments to control human behavior known as MKULTRA. White had died in 1975, just as MKULTRA and similar programs run by branches of the military were first coming to public attention. In the late 1970s, Feldman had been subpoenaed by a Senate committee investigating drug testing and hypnosis on unwitting American citizens, but was never called to testify. Now he was the last person alive who had worked directly under White's supervision.

I'd located Feldman through another journalist, Richard Stratton, who had written an article about him for *Spin Magazine*. He wanted to set the record straight about certain things. "The LSD," he had told Stratton, "that was just the tip of the iceberg. Write this down. Espionage. Assassinations. Dirty tricks. Drug experiments. Sexual encounters and the study of prostitutes for clandestine use. That's what I was doing when I worked for George White and the CIA."[148]

We entered the Marriott coffee shop and I asked for a quiet corner booth. Feldman ordered a Caesar's salad and an iced tea, keeping his still-unlit cigar tightly clenched between his teeth. No tape-recording, he instructed, but I could take notes.

---

[147] My interviews with Ike Feldman took place on August 17, 1994, and January 19, 1995.
[148] Stratton interview: *Spin Magazine*, March 1994, "Altered States of America" by Richard Stratton.

It was almost a year since I'd interviewed Sidney Gottlieb, and his was the first name I raised.

"I knew Sidney back in 1955, I imagine. He was introduced to me by George White. Then every time he came to San Francisco, I'd pick him up at the airport and take him to White's house. I also had him over to my house. He gave me a book on Zen Buddhism. 'I want you to study it,' Sidney told me. He said he hoped to get into it after he retired. I thought he was an odd duck, but a very capable man."

Then Feldman launched into a few yarns about his career: being recruited into the Office of Strategic Services (OSS, precursor of the CIA) during World War Two by Colonel William "Wild Bill" Donovan, then studying Russian and later Mandarin Chinese after the CIA approached him in the late 1940s. The Chinese classes, at the Army Language School in Monterey, California, were intensive: eight hours a day, seven days a week.

"After I finished that, they sent me to the Far East and I was in charge of an intelligence agency in Korea during that war and after, also Japan and Taiwan. South Korea had its own CIA type thing. I was there at a lot of interrogations when they slapped people around. The [Communist] Chinese had brainwashed these guys. Both outfits were merciless."

He'd wanted to leave the spy world for the private sector, when the CIA called upon him again to work with White in San Francisco. Feldman's conversation was punctuated with epithets, his raspy voice and rough language almost a caricature of James Cagney or Edward G. Robinson in one of the old gangster movies. And his disdain for the majority of his counterparts at CIA came through loud and clear.

"Most of these guys couldn't find their ass with a flashlight," Feldman scoffed. "The fucking soft shoes, the thick glasses, running around making rules for the world. Dulles [CIA Director Allen] was the only good guy, in my view. The rest were follow-me's, do-what-I-tell-yous, but they were *nothin'*! Everybody was just out to feather their own fucking nest. White was something else, though. He knew more people as stool pigeons than we got hair on our head."

"White had varied experience," he went on. "His father was the mayor of Alhambra, California, and Georgie had started out as a newspaper reporter. In the OSS, he made a lot of connections. White's supposedly the guy who got [mobster Lucky] Luciano out of the can. White was 250 pounds and not much taller than I am but powerful. He was completely bald and he always wore moccasins, with a gun tucked in by his belly. He smoked Philip Morris cigarettes like a rat, and drank vodka like it was going out of style."

I knew that Feldman's expertise had been covert testing of drugs, primarily LSD, posing as a racketeer to get prostitutes to lure unsuspecting clients to a CIA safe house, where their drinks would be laced with strange concoctions. It had begun during a conversation with White, which Feldman had described this way to journalist Stratton: "I said, 'Why the hell do you want to test mind-bending drugs?' He said, 'Have you heard of *The Manchurian Candidate?*' I know about *The Manchurian Candidate*. In fact, I read the book. 'Well,' White said, 'that's why we have to test these drugs, to find out if they can be used to brainwash people.' He says, 'If we can find out just how good this stuff works, you'll be doing a great deal for your country.'"

There were a number of universities and colleges, Feldman said, "where experiments were going on. Some were willing participants." He named, specifically, Tulane, Stanford, Berkeley, Yale, and Harvard. "At McGill University in Canada, there were controlled experiments. Students would get paid a certain amount of money. A lot of these guys thought they had a fucking license to go crazy."

For MKULTRA purposes, "In San Francisco, Saint Francis Hospital and another hospital were used. Some people who were given stuff were automatically taken to these hospitals to be detoxified. I also heard of experiments going on with criminals, with their approval—Rikers Island here was one—they were paid a certain amount of money.

"But a lot of these people didn't think they were doing anything bad," Feldman added. "The LSD, or even the brainwashing."

The brainwashing? I asked.

"How the CIA got into brainwashing—I was not mixed up in that," Feldman said. "I knew of an operation to make somebody a different personality. It was done by psychiatrists connected with different hospitals. I mean, these people were indirectly connected with the Agency, but the Agency really had nothing to do with it."

On occasion, according to Feldman, CIA officials from other branches would come around, expressing keen interest in what the MKULTRA program was revealing. One of these was James Angleton, the Agency's chief of counterintelligence. "He came to San Francisco to see me, made me a proposition which I told him to stick up his ass." Related to MKULTRA? I asked. Feldman nodded yes, but would say no more.

Another was William Harvey, who at the time was in charge of the CIA's Cuban desk. "Harvey reminded me of a salesman selling ladies shoes. He was directly involved with us, yes. He was White's compatriot. I met him through White, who must have told him what we were involved in. Harvey was very much interested in it. I went to White and said, 'He wants to know more and more and more.' White told me, 'Don't give him shit.'"

Feldman was aware of the CIA's plotting to eliminate Castro, including a scheme to spike the Cuban Premier's cigars with LSD. "There was one meeting I was at about assassinating Castro, with Dulles, White, and Harry Anslinger from the Bureau of Narcotics. They wanted me to handle it, because I knew some Cubans in San Francisco and in Havana. But Cuba was too tight at that time, Castro had too many friends. So it never went ahead."

One of those involved in the CIA's anti-Castro plotting was Mobster John Roselli. According to Feldman, Roselli also served as one of White's informants. "More than once, White sent me to the airport to pick up Roselli and bring him into the office." Their ties went back to Chicago, where Roselli hailed from originally and where White was the FBN's District Supervisor between 1945 and 1947.

According to the Stratton article on Feldman, "Following a big opium smuggling bust in 1947, Jack Ruby was picked up and hauled in for interrogation, then let off the hook by none other than White. Federal Bureau of Narcotics files indicate Jack Ruby was yet another of White's legion stool pigeons." (Feldman himself had admittedly been tight with L.A. gangster Mickey Cohen, utilizing some of Cohen's "girls" in Operation Midnight Climax, where unsuspecting male clients were lured by prostitutes to a CIA safe house and given cocktails laced with heavy doses of LSD.)

Given what Gottlieb had hinted at, concerning the possibility that Oswald might have been operating under hypnosis, I decided to probe the general line of inquiry with Feldman. "I heard there was hypnosis," he replied, "but I was never present when they were practicing it. But I don't doubt it, because they were trying everything. This particular part of the Agency hired everybody from shoemakers to chemists and biologists."

Then, without any further prompting, Feldman volunteered this: "There was a story that Oswald was hypnotized—and so was Jack Ruby. This story has been kicking around for many years."

You mean kicking around within the Agency? I asked, trying to maintain a cool demeanor. He nodded yes. "The boys would sit down to have a beer, start bullshitting about this thing."

When did you first start hearing these stories? I continued.

Feldman pondered a moment. "Kennedy was killed, what, in '62, no '63, November, right? These stories started kicking around right after January first, the next year."

And was the thought that the Soviets had done it? Or our side?

"The indication was," Feldman went on, more deliberately than usual, "that they thought Marcello and Giancana and possibly another Italian got their heads together, and paid some government people to dose these guys. Because they wanted Kennedy out of the way."

In 1963 Carlos Marcello had been boss of the New Orleans Mob, and Sam Giancana his counterpart in Chicago. Both organized crime figures were known to have been participants in the CIA's attempts to assassinate Castro, and both had also been rumored to have had a hand in Kennedy's demise. Another Italian whose name had been connected to each of those events was the Tampa, Florida gangster Santo Trafficante, Jr.

Later, Feldman elaborated: "I heard rumors that something was given to Oswald days or weeks before he went to the Texas School Book Depository. I also heard he was brainwashed, like the Manchurian Candidate. I heard that when he was in Russia, they started to brainwash him over there. The Russians messed with him, twisted his brains. This affected him for a long time. Then somebody in this country continued to screw around with him. I don't believe it was the CIA. But whoever made the [assassination] plans, he was reintroduced to brainwashing and they gave him something, I don't know what it was. After he got arrested, they claim he would jibber and jabber before he was shot.

"I heard Ruby was tight with the Chicago people, and some in New Orleans. When word came out that Oswald may spill his guts, they sent Ruby in. If Oswald walked, they were afraid he'd involve Giancana, Marcello, and God knows who else. I was told also that Ruby was a doper, a drug user. And after he shot Oswald, he was afraid he would've also talked too much. I don't remember what kind of drugs, but he just loaded up that day. Oswald was one part of the ball field, Ruby was another part. Ruby was a half-assed racketeer, Oswald was a half-assed communist."

I persisted in asking whether he had heard these rumors about mind control from high up in the American government. Feldman nodded. "Very high up. It was State Department people who made these comments. The real rumors came from there. With the Agency, it was just bullshitting like you and I are today."

Then he added: "Look, the Agency was like a great big spider—feet all over and one foot not knowing what the other was doing."

I knew this much after having lunch with Ike Feldman: the possibility that MKULTRA techniques had played a role in the Kennedy assassination was a very real one indeed.

41

Two Caskets, Two Autopsies, Two Brain Exams: The Disappearing Evidence

"Contained within our deposition transcripts and interview reports is unequivocal evidence that there was a U.S. government cover-up of the medical evidence in the Kennedy assassination."

—**Douglas P. Horne**, Former Chief Analyst for Military Records, Assassination Records Review Board

In my many years on the assassination trail, I had never been especially interested in the questions raised by a number of researchers about the physical evidence indicating that someone other than Oswald must have been involved. I'd perused books like David Lifton's *Best Evidence*, but always found the subject a bit too esoteric (and perhaps a little too grisly) for my taste.

My attitude changed, in the course of preparing this book, when it was suggested that I speak with Douglas Horne. He had been an integral part of the third, and last, government body to take witness testimony about the assassination. Established by President Clinton in the wake of Oliver Stone's controversial movie, *JFK*, the Assassination Records Review Board (ARRB) was chartered to locate and declassify records still being kept secret by the CIA, FBI, and other government agencies, and to make them publicly available in a new "JFK Records Collection" in the National Archives. Although Congress did not want the ARRB to reinvestigate or even draw conclusions about the assassination, the staff did take depositions under oath from certain key individuals.

Analysis of the sworn testimony before the ARRB of ten people involved in the autopsy, and others interviewed previously by the HSCA, have led Horne to the inescapable conclusion that a high-level government cover-up was in place from the very afternoon of the president's death. We spoke for more than two hours, in an interview tape-recorded with his permission over the phone. Horne's revelations proved so stunning that I came to believe they should end this book—hopefully opening a new window through which the truth might finally emerge.

How did you end up getting on the Review Board staff?

I'd been with the Navy for twenty years, first as a surface warfare officer on active duty with the Pacific Fleet for ten years—those are the professionals who drive and manage our Navy's surface ships—and after that served the Navy for ten more years in a civil service capacity in Hawaii. I happened to be in Washington, D.C., on Navy business in '94 when COPA [the Coalition on Political Assassinations] was hosting a JFK assassination research symposium. One of the speakers there was Jack Tunheim, who was the head of the five-member Review Board that had been confirmed by the Senate and was about to begin its business. At the end of his talk, he was asked, "Are you hiring staff?" and he said, "Yes, we've just started, it'll take quite awhile and we'll have to get them clearances." (I should point out here that the Board appointed by President Clinton consisted of five VIPs who set matters of broad policy, but worked part-time and only convened about 3 days every month. The staff of 25–28 people hired to support the Board did the lion's share of the work.) The very next day, I submitted a letter to the staff's executive director, David Marwell, saying I'd like to apply for a job. Getting that job turned out to be a very time-consuming process. Most of the people hired were living in the local area and were able to do in-person interviews, so living in Hawaii, I was at a distinct disadvantage. After undergoing a gauntlet of six telephone interviews, I finally received a job offer in March 1995, and started in August. I had to move at my own expense—this was a real test of my motivation—and I took a massive pay cut. I was able to swing it, but just barely. I basically beat the door down through perseverance, and felt the sacrifices were worthwhile because I had always been captivated by the mystery presented by the JFK assassination, and greatly admired Jack Kennedy's presidency.

There were four groups of analysts that comprised the majority of the Review Board staff—teams that examined and worked to declassify military records, CIA records, FBI records, and finally, records of the Secret Service and all the remaining agencies. I was hired as a senior analyst on the military records team. About a year and a half later, after my boss quit, they kicked me upstairs to take his job as chief analyst, or team leader for the military records team.

How did you then get involved in the whole medical records side of things?

The short answer is because the autopsy was performed by the Navy, and the autopsy report was therefore a "military record" that came under the purview of my records team. But that's not the real answer. During the interview process, I learned that Jeremy Gunn—at that time the staff's head of research and analysis (and destined to become its general counsel)—shared a common interest: a fascination with all the medical evidence, and specifically the conflicts within the medical evidence that seemed un-resolvable. Then, not long after I came onboard, the Board granted permission to take the first two medical depositions: sworn interviews of James J. Humes and "J" Thornton Boswell, the two Navy pathologists who conducted the autopsy at Bethesda Naval hospital. I became the research assistant to Jeremy Gunn, and helped him prepare questions for all ten medical evidence depositions related to the autopsy. I also prepared all of the exhibits and assisted Jeremy with them during the questioning of each witness.

When did the light first go on that something was not right with what these doctors were telling you?

It's long been known that Dr. Humes, who was the chief pathologist at the autopsy, prepared a typed statement two days after the assassination saying that he'd burned his preliminary autopsy notes. He had repeated this several times in the years since, each time claiming he'd thrown the notes into his fireplace because they had on them the blood of the president, which he deemed unseemly. Jeremy had reason to suspect that an early draft of the autopsy report had also been destroyed, based upon an analysis of inconsistencies between Dr. Humes' previous testimony about when he wrote the draft, and existing records documenting its transmission to higher authority. Humes had never admitted this before but, under persistent questioning by Jeremy in February 1996, he finally did so.

Jeremy and I were left with the conclusion at the end of the Humes deposition that he was a great liar. The question was, what was he lying about? There were so many times when he would try to deflect our questions with either arrogance or bluff, and other times he would try to play dumb, saying "I'm an old man and I can't remember." We didn't find that convincing.

The second pathologist deposed was Dr. Boswell. After that, there was no doubt about a major medical cover-up. (Boswell was much more forthcoming than Humes, and inadvertently, I think, "gave the store away" on a number of occasions.) It was my idea to use an anatomically correct model of the human skull, which I was allowed to purchase and construct myself, in an attempt to get Boswell to visually identify the true extent of the damage to President Kennedy's skull. (There shouldn't have been any doubt about this 33 years after the autopsy, but unfortunately much eyewitness testimony disagreed with the autopsy photographs and x-rays, and many of the autopsy photos seemed intended to conceal, rather than to reveal the true nature of the head wounds.)

When Boswell had executed a famous two-dimensional sketch of the damage to the skull on the reverse side of the autopsy body chart on November 22, 1963, he'd indicated that a large area of bone was missing from the *top* of the president's skull, but his diagram left unanswered whether any bone was missing from the *back* of the head. While he was still under oath, we asked Boswell to define where there was bone missing, in three dimensions, on the skull model with a marking pen. We wanted to know how much skull bone might have been missing in the back of the head, if any. Of course, we didn't tell him that. And when he soberly, but matter-of-factly marked the area of missing bone on the skull model, it included the entire right rear of the skull behind the ear. Jeremy and I almost fell out of our chairs. Now the autopsy photographs, which show the back of the head to be intact, made no sense whatsoever. Boswell's annotated skull model implied that there must have been a shot that struck Kennedy from the front, a bullet that *exited* from the back of his skull. (Exit wounds are large and avulsive; entrance wounds are small and penetrating.)

So following these first two depositions, Jeremy and I knew that the medical evidence was suddenly of *tremendous* interest. We then pursued the third pathologist involved in the autopsy, Army pathologist Pierre Finck. Dr. Finck used forgetfulness as his defense, which was not convincing, because in a social context, he relayed to us vivid memories of what he was doing in 1938 and the early 1950s—but when it came to the Kennedy assassination, he couldn't remember anything. Even when we showed him a document that he had signed or written and say, "Do you remember this?" he'd respond, "I don't know." We'd say, "Well, is this your signature?" And he'd respond, "Well, it looks like my signature." He was really slippery. But on a couple of answers, Finck provided useful information.

What did you ultimately conclude these three doctors were up to?

I am now convinced—and this insight didn't really come to me until 2006, when I did much of the writing on a manuscript I'm putting together about all this—that Humes and Boswell, who were there at the morgue with the President's body well before the autopsy started and prior to Dr. Finck's arrival, were involved in a covert deception operation from the very beginning. I believe that they were told, for national security reasons, to destroy or suppress any evidence that the president was shot from the front and to record only evidence that he was shot from the rear—even if they had to manufacture some of it. I don't think Finck was initially a part of this deception; the great irony is that even though he was a board-certified forensic pathologist, I believe he was a victim of the Humes-Boswell covert operation. At some point, after the fact, I believe Finck suspected this, but felt he was in so deep by this time, and realized he was so compromised, that he decided not to blow the whistle officially; instead he left a few clues in the record over the years for "CYA" purposes. He was certainly timid and scared when we took his deposition; this was surprising at the time, since the 1992 interview published in the *Journal of the American Medical Association* (JAMA) portrayed him as a "lion," and a person with a good memory and great certitude about the autopsy's events and conclusions. The main point I am trying to make here is that Humes and Boswell had possession of the president's body much earlier in the evening than the official record indicates, and undertook activities to alter the evidentiary record that they did not reveal to Finck.

Can you explain that further?

Let me jump ahead to someone we interviewed later. We were led by a researcher, Kathleen Cunningham, to an ex-Marine who was the sergeant in charge of the security detail at the morgue. Kathleen made clear to us that he was not someone who'd been part of the honor guard, with the white gloves and dress uniforms, whom we read about in William Manchester's book *Death of a*

President. The group this person supervised was *not* the joint service casket team, but was a physical security detail from the Marine Barracks in Washington D.C., dressed in Marine Corps working uniforms, and carrying weapons. We had an "ace" investigator on our staff, Dave Montague, who specialized in locating people, and he and I interviewed this person. The sergeant's name was Roger Boyajian, pronounced "Boy-gen." He had retained an original onion-skin carbon copy of the after-action report that he wrote on November 26, 1963, the day after JFK's funeral, and had shared its contents with Ms. Cunningham. A document like this one that is contemporaneous is priceless, because it's not distorted by fading memories, by time—or by anyone's subsequent theories about the assassination. So I interviewed Boyajian on the phone, and he then mailed me a photocopy of that document, and authenticated it with a letter written above his signature.

He'd gotten to Bethesda really early, before the president's body arrived. One of the entries in his report reads: "1835—President's Casket Arrives." That means 6:35 PM, and indicates that he took notes; every military man in those days had what's called a "wheel book," a little green U.S. government memoranda notebook that fits into your back pocket. The thing is, that's a mind-blowing entry, because it is a well-documented fact that the light-gray Navy ambulance, with the president's bronze casket from Dallas inside, didn't arrive at Bethesda until approximately five minutes before seven, and it sat outside in front of the main building for about 12 minutes or so before being driven around to the back of the morgue. HSCA interviews of FBI agents James Sibert and Francis O'Neill revealed that these two men, assisted *only* by two Secret Service agents, helped carry in this heavy bronze casket (using a dolly), *without* the assistance of the joint service casket team (which was not present when this happened); and a 1964 FBI report provides a time marker for this event of about 7:17 PM. Yet here was Sergeant Boyajian, four days after the assassination, placing the arrival time of the president's body almost forty-five minutes *earlier.*

Now, back in 1979, Dennis David—a Navy petty officer who was standing duty that night at the Bethesda National Naval Medical Center as "Chief of the Day" for the medical school—had told author David Lifton that he'd gathered up a group of sailors at the request of the Secret Service, gone to the back of the hospital to the morgue loading dock, and carried in a cheap, lightweight, unadorned gray (or dull silver-colored) aluminum shipping casket from a *black hearse.* (Not the four-hundred-pound formal bronze viewing casket delivered to Bethesda from Andrews Air Force Base in a light-gray Navy ambulance.) Lifton had asked David to estimate the time, and he'd said around 6:40 or 6:45 PM. This is undeniably a very early casket entry, and of a distinctly different type of casket than the heavy, ornate bronze viewing coffin the president was placed in at Parkland hospital after his death.

After lobbying Jeremy Gunn for months, I was finally allowed to conduct an unsworn interview of Dennis David on the phone. He told the whole story again to me, and nothing had changed from what he originally told Lifton seventeen years previously. He also said that he'd asked Dr. Boswell early the next morning, after the autopsy was over, if the president had been in the casket that he and the sailors had helped carry in that night; he asked the question because although the Secret Service had told him to carry it into the morgue, he and his sailors were not permitted to stay in the morgue and see it opened. Boswell confirmed to Dennis David that he and his sailors had indeed carried the president's body into the morgue early that evening.

All of this corroborates the Lifton hypothesis that the heavy bronze casket that arrived about 45 minutes later that evening at the morgue loading dock, and was quietly carried into the hospital by the FBI and Secret Service at about 7:17 PM, had to be *empty*. It also tells us that we should pay attention to the many people in the morgue who remembered the president's body arriving in a zippered body bag, because those observations are consistent with, and in fact corroborate, the broken chain-of-custody demonstrated by the impossibly early casket entry. Jeremy and I located one additional body bag witness. We interviewed one of the morticians, John Van Hoesen, and he independently recalled—we didn't ask him—that the president's body was in a black zippered pouch. He joins several other, previously known body-bag witnesses: Paul O'Connor, Floyd Riebe, Jerrol Custer, and Captain John Stover. This is extremely significant because when the president's body left Dallas it was wrapped in two sheets, one around the body and one around the head, and was *not* placed inside a body bag.

Here's what this all means: Every time we have a witness who says they saw the president removed from a body-bag, or arrive in a shipping casket, they are in audience one, the early arrival audience that was present during, or immediately after, the "early" 6:35 PM arrival of the President's body documented by Sergeant Boyajian's report. Every time a witness says the president's body arrived wrapped only in sheets, in an expensive bronze casket, they are in audience two, which witnessed JFK reintroduced into the morgue at 8 PM by the joint service casket team. I know this sounds strange, but none of these people were making these stories up; they are all credible witnesses who simply saw different events at different times that evening. The Secret Service, specifically Roy Kellerman, who had been the agent in charge of the Texas trip, was stage-managing these shenanigans as best he could, and attempting to keep the two audiences apart— with the exception of Humes, Boswell, and their Navy superiors, who clearly all knew what was afoot. There was a "shell game" going on with the president's body between its initial arrival at 6:35 PM and the commencement of the official "autopsy-of-record" at 8:15 PM, when the y-incision was made in the chest. A *preliminary* medical examination and other manipulations—what Lifton had speculatively called the *pre-autopsy* autopsy—began about an hour and a half *before* the official one. Afterwards, the president's body was then reintroduced into the bronze casket wrapped in the sheets that it had left Dallas in, was placed in a light gray Navy ambulance (for there was more than one in use that night), and was allowed to be "found" by the joint service casket team. (The casket team, or honor guard, had admittedly lost track of the Dallas casket after its arrival at Bethesda, tearing off in chase of an apparent "decoy" and getting lost in the darkness, on the unfamiliar grounds of the Naval medical complex.) After finding the Dallas casket in front of the hospital in a light gray ambulance, it was formally and very publicly taken into the morgue by them at 8 PM—by these military men from all of the different armed services in their dress uniforms and white gloves—as recorded in the after-action report of the Military District of Washington. It really happened this way. The evidence for three separate casket entries into the morgue (at 6:35 the aluminum shipping casket brought in by Navy sailors, at 7:17 the bronze casket's surreptitious entry by the FBI and Secret Service, and at 8 PM the official "ceremony" or delivery of the bronze casket by the military honor guard) is overwhelming and unimpeachable, and the honest researcher cannot simply be in denial about these events if he takes a scientific, empirical approach to the evidence.

So *why* was this necessary? *Why the shell game?* Because the chain-of-custody of the body had been broken, and it had arrived in the wrong casket and in the wrong wrapping, in order that a clandestine examination (prior to the autopsy proper) and clandestine manipulations (unbeknownst to most autopsy witnesses) could be performed. This covert operation had to be successfully completed, and then covered up, if the country was to buy the simplistic story of the assassination that the government was selling, and so to effectuate the cover-up, the president's body *had to be seen publicly arriving at the morgue in the Dallas casket and the Dallas wrappings.* Hence the 8 PM casket entry, performed by the joint service casket team—whose job it was to stay with the body and carry the casket—and dutifully recorded in the after-action report written by the Army. The size of audience number one, which witnessed the early entry and/or the first casket opening, was small and it was composed of either conspirators (Humes, Boswell, and their superiors), or very low level enlisted people who were muzzled after the fact by threat of court martial.

The varying casket and ambulance descriptions, and the serious timeline discrepancies about when the two caskets entered the morgue, prove there was a serious break in the chain-of-custody of the president's body, which in any medico legal setting (such as a trial or inquest) would invalidate most, if not all, of the autopsy results. I am absolutely convinced that Humes and Boswell were engaged in a deception that centered around getting the body early and performing certain manipulations on it. The two FBI agents on the scene, O'Neill and Sibert, wrote that they were initially barred from entering the morgue, and it is apparent that they were eventually allowed in only as a part of audience number two; hence they recorded in their report dated November 26 that what they sincerely believed to be the first autopsy incision—the Y incision in the chest—happened at 8:15 PM. Dr. Finck didn't arrive until about 8:30 at night (after the brain, lungs, and heart had been removed) and was also unaware of the Navy manipulations performed on the body between the 6:35 PM arrival of the shipping casket, and the 8 PM reintroduction of the body to the morgue in the bronze Dallas casket.

What specific manipulations are you referring to?

Well, here we go—this is the heart of my book, and it is where I differ significantly with the scenario laid out by David Lifton in *Best Evidence*. Lifton believed at the time his book was published that the reason the Dallas wound descriptions by the treatment physicians at Parkland hospital (of a localized *exit* wound in the back of the head and an *entrance* wound in the throat below the Adam's apple) are so different from the Bethesda wound descriptions (of a much larger head wound encompassing additional, and massive damage to the *top and the right side* of the head, and of an *exit* wound in the throat and an entry wound in the high shoulder not seen in Dallas) is because the wounds on the body were tampered with—altered—while the body was in transit between Parkland hospital and the Bethesda complex in Maryland. He wrote in his book that the alteration of the wounds on the body—post-mortem surgery—was performed not only to remove bullets, but to reverse the apparent trajectories first noted in the throat wound and the head wound at Parkland hospital, and thus "fool" the autopsy pathologists into believing that all of the shots came from behind, rather than from in front. Lifton's view in his 1981 book was that the body of the president, the road map of the shooting, was altered to deceive the pathologists. He posited that the back of the head was also *reconstructed* prior to arrival at Bethesda and that its condition not only fooled the Navy pathologists, but also fooled the camera, resulting in the autopsy photos we have today of an intact back of the head.

I have reinterpreted the same body of evidence he examined, and married that body of evidence with certain key HSCA interviews (which are now open-in-full and available to the public), and new findings gleaned from the ARRB interviews and depositions, and have concluded that while the throat wound may possibly have been tampered with in transit, that it was *the Navy pathologists*, Drs. Humes and Boswell, and possibly one of their superiors, who performed the post-mortem surgery that so drastically altered the head wound—enlarging it to four or five times its original size in an attempt to make it appear more or less consistent with a large exit wound caused by a shot fired from behind. In altering the head wound they not only dramatically expanded the size of the rather localized exit wound in the rear of the head seen in Dallas, to encompass the top of the skull and part of the right side, but also surgically removed from the body evidence of an entry wound in the right front of the head. In doing so, they obliterated forensic evidence of a shot fired from the "grassy knoll." Numerous small bullet fragments—many more than the two mentioned in the record today—were removed from the brain, and disposed of, never to be seen again. I also conclude, from a key HSCA staff interview report of an autopsy technician, that they removed a large bullet fragment from the president's back—a significant portion of a bullet found lodged between two of his ribs. The evidence for these claims will be presented in great detail in my forthcoming book.

Furthermore, whereas Lifton believed that the autopsy photos we have today of an intact back of the head were taken immediately after the body's arrival, I am now of the belief that the partial cranial reconstruction seen in these images was performed *after the conclusion of the autopsy* and that the deceptive photographic record of the back of the head that is in the archives today was photographed *after midnight*, after the conclusion of the autopsy, by a different photographer from the one who photographed the autopsy proper. This is how we end up with "autopsy" photographs showing the back of the head intact, which are in stark disagreement with *both* the Dallas and the Bethesda eyewitnesses. A large portion of the rear of the cranium was observed to be missing by *both* Dallas and Bethesda eyewitnesses; the *difference* between their observations is that most of the Bethesda eyewitnesses who saw the body after 8 PM recall *not only* the back of the head missing, but *also* significant portions of the top and right-hand side of the skull, as well.

Most witnesses from the autopsy recall a very large area of missing bone at the back of the head—confirmed for us by the skull diagram Dr. Boswell drew in three dimensions on a model skull. Because this damage does not appear in the autopsy photographs on file at the National Archives, most researchers have believed for many years that the discrepancy is explained by photographic forgery, "special effects" to make the rear of the head look intact when it really wasn't. However, because of the unsworn ARRB medical witness interviews conducted by Jeremy and me, I no longer believe that photographic forgery is the explanation for the perplexing back of the head images. The alternative possibilities—namely, major manipulation of loose and previously reflected scalp from elsewhere on the head, or partial reconstruction of the head by the morticians, at the direction of the pathologists—seem to be a much more likely explanation for these anomalous photos. To be sure, the photos are a lie—for they do create the false impression that the back of the head was intact when the body arrived from Dallas, and they do provide false "evidence" that all eyewitnesses to a blow-out in the right rear of the head were "wrong." But I am as certain as I can be that they are not photographic forgeries.

I was steered toward this opinion by the testimony of the two FBI agents, Sibert and O'Neill. We would never have deposed them if I hadn't insisted on it and persevered. This was about two years into our medical effort, and Jeremy was beginning to doubt the value of the exercise, because the memories were so old and many witnesses' stories kept changing over time. I mean, I was confused, too, but I knew these differing recollections were important. My attitude was, "once these guys are dead, they can't be interviewed by anybody." So Jeremy finally gave the okay to make initial contact with the two FBI agents who had been present at the autopsy. And, to my pleasant surprise, the agents were not only willing to be deposed, they couldn't wait. They were still offended by not having been deposed by either the Warren Commission or the House Select Committee on Assassinations. And what we got from them was a gold mine in some respects.

Both men found the images of the intact back of the head troubling, and inconsistent with the posterior head wound they vividly remembered. O'Neill opined under oath that the images appeared "doctored," by which he meant that the head had been put back together by the doctors. Sibert testified that the head looked "reconstructed"—he actually used that word!

Can you expand upon why you are so certain the back of the head images are not photographic forgeries?

I am virtually certain they are not photographic forgeries because I've looked at them in extremely close detail, and by this I mean I have studied the so-called camera-original color positive transparencies for hours at a time in Rochester, after they were magnified by enhancing software in the Kodak lab where we took them for digital preservation. We didn't see any matte lines, or any discontinuities in the hair. We could see individual pores in the skin in between strands of hair, and all of the grain and resolution seemed consistent across the board in the areas we were looking at. However, I'm convinced that, while *not* "special effects" forgeries, they *are* fraudulent and dishonest. The official Navy photographer, John Stringer, and his assistant Floyd Riebe, left the morgue after the conclusion of the autopsy at about 11:45 PM or midnight. Then a second photographer—Robert Knudsen, who was not a trained medical photographer, but a Navy chief photographer's mate who was a social photographer at the White House—was employed to take the pictures of the head after its reconstruction. And these photographs were later used to misrepresent the condition of the president's head when the body arrived at Bethesda. The real photographs of the exit wound in the rear of the skull would have been deep-sixed. It's that simple. Shortly after the assassination, on two separate occasions, Knudsen showed another government photographer, Joe O'Donnell, two sets of photographs, one with the back of the head blown out (no doubt taken during the autopsy by John Stringer, the photographer of record), and one showing the back of the head intact (which must have been taken by himself, after midnight, following partial reconstruction of the cranium). So I believe Knudsen knew what he was doing and what the intent was, but I do not believe he thought he was doing it for sinister reasons. His family described him to us as a very patriotic American who loved President Kennedy, so I conclude that he, too, like Humes and Boswell, was no doubt given a national security cover story to explain why he was engaged in a subterfuge.

You have been quoted as coming to the conclusion that the autopsy report in the national archives is not the original version. Can you comment on that?

I'm positive the autopsy report in evidence today, Warren Commission Exhibit #387, is the third version prepared—not the sole version, as was claimed for years by those who wrote it and signed it. A careful study of the receipt trail for transmission of the report, the Humes and Boswell deposition transcripts, and the Warren Commission executive session transcripts reveals what happened.

First, Humes and Boswell met about mid-day on Saturday, November 23 (the day after the autopsy) and reviewed a draft of the autopsy report. It is both interesting, and significant, I think, that Dr. Finck was not present. The draft was also reviewed that day by the C.O. of the Naval hospital, Captain Robert Canada. Humes then destroyed both his own autopsy notes, and that first draft, in the fireplace of his home early in the morning of Sunday, November 24. He may have also destroyed the notes of Dr. Finck at that same time. (David Lifton led the ARRB to a very credible witness who signed an affidavit stating that he overheard Finck complaining in 1963 that his notes had disappeared the night of the autopsy, and that he had to reconstruct them from memory afterwards.) So the first autopsy report—a draft that Finck did not see but which was reviewed by Humes, Boswell, and Captain Canada, was burned early Sunday morning before sunrise.

We also know that the three pathologists met, reviewed, and signed an autopsy report during daylight hours on Sunday, November 24. But I do not believe the autopsy report signed on November 24—the second version—is the one in the archives today. I say this because Warren Commission staff director J. Lee Rankin is quoted in an executive session transcript from late in January 1964 as saying that the autopsy [report] shows a bullet fragment (by implication, from the headshot) came out the front of President Kennedy's neck—a conclusion that is most definitely *not* in the autopsy report in the record today. So where is this second version of the autopsy report? Apparently, the Kennedy family got a hold of it in 1965 and it has never been seen since. The evidence for this is a receipt prepared by Vice Admiral Burkley, the president's military physician, on April 26, 1965 which transfers the original autopsy report and seven copies from the Secret Service to Evelyn Lincoln, in compliance with Senator Robert Kennedy's orders to transfer all of the autopsy materials to his custody. So far, so good, but wait! Incredibly, there is a *second* receipt transferring what is described as the "original" autopsy report, only this time it is transferred from the Secret Service to the national archives on October 3, 1967. How could an *original* document be transferred from the Secret Service to Evelyn Lincoln, and then a second time from the Secret Service to someone else? This can only happen if there are two documents, two autopsy reports. The first autopsy report transferred, the one passed to the Kennedy family in April 1965, has disappeared along with various tissue samples and a brain specimen; it is almost certainly the version J. Lee Rankin refers to in the then–Top Secret Warren Commission executive session transcript. The second signed version of the autopsy report transferred by the Secret Service, the one they transmitted to the archives in October 1967, is the item in evidence today; therefore, counting the draft that Humes burned on November 24 in his fireplace, it is (at least) the third version of the autopsy report, overall. Instead of describing a fragment of the head shot exiting the front of the neck, the report in the archives instead describes a bullet—what came to be known later as the so-called "magic bullet"—transiting the body, from the rear to the front, entering high in the shoulder and exiting the front of the neck below the Adam's apple. The autopsy report in the archives today is an *undated* document. Only the transmission letter is dated November 24, and if the report was rewritten as the receipt trail shows it must have been, then the new report could have been substituted in the official record without changing the transmission letter, giving the false impression that it was prepared on November 24. All we know for sure is that the version in evidence today, CE #387, was shown to Parkland hospital doctors in Dallas on December 11, 1963. Its conclusions that a bullet transited the body from back to front were used to get the Dallas doctors to doubt their own conclusions on November 22 that the president had been shot in the throat from the front.

In November 1998 there were two newspaper stories, one put out by the Associated Press, and the other by the Washington Post, *which quoted your ARRB research memo that concluded there were two separate brain examinations after the autopsy on the body, instead of only one, as there normally should be. That sounds incredible. How did you arrive at that conclusion?*

That insight, or rather epiphany, came to me fairly early in our investigation, in May 1996, right before the Finck deposition. Jeremy and I were working on the weekend to get ready for it. He asked me to do a study of all events surrounding the brain exam. (In cases of death due to head trauma, the brain is always examined separately after it has been removed from the body and has been fixed to some extent in formaldehyde.) I sat down and pulled out every piece of testimony and every document I could find. After I finished, I walked into his office and said, "Jeremy, if you just do a time-line analysis, it's clear there were two events. This is really big, and it's also frustrating because we've already deposed Humes and Boswell." He looked at me and said, "I also think there were two brain exams." I was stunned, and asked how he'd come to the same conclusion. "By reading the descriptions of the damage," he said, "and comparing those descriptions to the pattern of damage evident in the brain photographs in the archives. In my opinion, they don't match."

So when we deposed Finck a few days later, we focused in on this one subject, and this is where we got our one big answer from him. The examination of the president's brain clearly took place on November 25, 1963, based upon the consistent testimony of Dr. Boswell and autopsy photographer John Stringer over the years; furthermore, a lab technician at Bethesda, Leland Benson, told the HSCA that he processed brain tissue on Monday, November 25, on the same date identified independently by both Boswell and Stringer as the date of the brain exam. (Humes' answers on this were all over the map, and varied, when he was pressed on the subject.) Finck was known to have been at a brain exam, and wrote in a 1965 report to his boss that he was first contacted about a brain exam by Humes on November 29. When we asked Finck at his ARRB deposition whether the exam he attended had transpired two or three days after the autopsy, or about a week later, he was emphatic in his belief that it occurred at least a week after the autopsy, and as I recall it was just about the only answer he was adamant about. This was consistent with the memorandum he'd written to Brigadier General J.M. Blumberg, his military superior, in February 1965.

We called the Navy photographer, John Stringer, to testify. To our amazement, he disowned the brain photographs in the Archives, for three reasons. First, they were taken on a type of film that he did not use. They also depicted "inferior" views of the underside of the brain that he was certain he did not shoot. And, finally, the photographs of several individual sections of brain tissue that he did photograph—brain tissue that he insisted had been serially sectioned—were not present.

FBI agent O'Neill also swore to us that the brain photos in the Archives could not possibly be of the president's brain, because there was too much tissue present. O'Neill remembered clearly that more than half of President Kennedy's brain was missing when he saw it at the autopsy, following its removal from the cranium. Both O'Neill and Tom Robinson, one the morticians, told us that they recalled that a large portion of the rear of the president's brain was missing, when they saw it outside the body in the morgue during the autopsy. And each man unequivocally demonstrated the location of the absent brain tissue in my presence, by dramatically placing his right hand on the back of the right side of his own head, behind the right ear. By contrast, in the brain depicted in the archives photographs, the right cerebellum is completely intact. Both John Stringer and many of the Dallas treating physicians recalled severe damage to the cerebellum, the structure low in the rear of the human brain.

There is absolutely no doubt that the second brain exam—on a brain not belonging to John F. Kennedy—occurred sometime between November 29 (when Humes contacted Finck) and December 2, because a Navy chief hospital corpsman named Chester Boyers told the HSCA that he prepared brain tissue slides on December 2. It's also my firm belief that Dr. Finck—who had arrived late at the autopsy on November 22 after the brain had been removed, and who was excluded from the review of the first draft of the autopsy report on Saturday, November 23—was used as a "dupe" so that he could "authenticate" the photographs of the second brain specimen, in the event that was ever required. I think Finck knew something was wrong by this time, because he engaged in very clever "CYA" by writing, in his report to Brigadier General Blumberg in February 1965, that the brain he subsequently examined looked different than it had looked at the autopsy—although he benignly attributed the change in its appearance in his written report to an arcane "fixation artifact."

Summarizing, the photographs of President Kennedy's brain, exposed by John Stringer on November 25, were never introduced into the official record because they showed a pattern of damage—missing tissue from the rear of the brain—consistent with a fatal shot from the front, and that evidence had to be suppressed. The photographs of a second brain, taken sometime between November 29–December 2, 1963 by an unknown Navy photographer, *were* introduced into the official record because the brain employed in that exercise exhibited a pattern of damage—to the top-right-side of the brain—generally consistent with a shot from above and behind. So where did that brain come from? I can only remind you that Bethesda was a teaching facility with a medical school alongside the treatment hospital, and specimens would have been on hand at the medical school for teaching purposes; furthermore, there were regular "brain cuttings" about once per week in the D.C. area that were attended by both Navy personnel at Bethesda and Army personnel stationed at the Armed Forces Institute of Pathology, or AFIP. So fixed brains would have been available, one way or another. An accomplished forensic pathologist who viewed the brain photos in the archives at the request of the ARRB told us in 1996 that the brain in these photographs, which appears very gray in the color transparencies, was "very well fixed," and that it had been in a formalin solution for at least two weeks before being photographed, since it showed no traces whatsoever of pink coloration. That ensures it cannot possibly be President Kennedy's brain, which was examined only three days after his death.

Finally, the supplementary autopsy report indicates that the brain depicted in the photographs in the archives weighed 1,500 grams when weighed at the brain exam, which exceeds the weight of an average, normal male brain. This is completely incompatible with a brain that was missing over half of its tissue when observed at the autopsy by FBI agent O'Neill, or a brain that was missing most of the right occipital lobe of the cerebral cortex and much of the right cerebellum, as observed by Dr. McClelland at Parkland hospital.

A short discussion on the autopsy x-rays of the skull is imperative here. I believe that independent researcher David Mantik, who is both an M.D. (a radiation oncologist) and who is also a Ph.D. in physics, has conclusively proven, with his exhaustive optical density measurements of the X-ray materials in the archives, that the three head X-rays in the autopsy collection are *not* originals but are *forged composite copy films* that are simply modifications of the authentic skull X-rays. My own hypothesis and reinterpretation of the medical evidence necessitates that the original head X-rays were exposed *only* after Humes and Boswell had completed their clandestine post-mortem surgery on the skull to remove bullet fragments from the brain and enlarge the head wound. The two lateral skull X-rays, Mantik has demonstrated, had a very dense optical patch superimposed on the copy films *over the occipital-parietal area behind the ear* to mask the blow-out or exit wound seen in Dallas in the back of the head. Mantik also claims that the single anterior-posterior (or "A-P") skull X-ray has had a 6.5-millimeter wide artifact, which is intended to represent a bullet fragment—a "cross section" of the "assassin's bullet"—imposed on the copy film as a special effect, to implicate the Oswald rifle as the supposed murder weapon. To reiterate, the skull depicted in each of the three head X-rays is that of JFK, but artifacts were added to the images during the copying process—through a relatively simple procedure involving applying additional light to specific areas on each film while other areas were masked off—which can now be easily detected using new technology, optical densitometry. I will be offering a quite detailed explanation of Mantik's findings in my forthcoming book.

In short: the autopsy photos are *not* altered photographically (and yet because of manipulations of the scalp after completion of the autopsy, some of them present false and deceptive images of the head wounds). Many authentic autopsy images that are known to have been exposed at the autopsy are *not* in the collection today—they are missing and presumed destroyed. But Mantik's work has persuaded me that the three skull X-rays *are* forgeries—altered copy films created from the original skull X-rays. Both sets of images, together—the autopsy photographs and X-rays—present a distorted and intentionally dishonest depiction of how President Kennedy was killed. Because of the evidentiary importance—the *primacy* (in 1963, anyway if not today)—of photographs and image technology in our culture, and the assumption in those years that they always reflected "reality," these fraudulent collections have been used to fool three official investigations (the Clark Panel, the Rockefeller Commission, and the HSCA forensic pathology panel), and continue to present an enduring lie about what happened to President Kennedy in 1963.

I understand you also did some work in analyzing the Zapruder film. Did that tend to confirm any of this?

We asked Roland Zavada of Kodak, a retired film chemist and a self-taught home movie expert, to do a major authenticity study of the Zapruder film, and he did a very professional job and put a lot of work into it. My own conclusions today about the Zapruder film are in opposition to Zavada's: he thinks it is authentic and I do not. My conclusion is the "minority position" within the research community, and is very controversial, and a lot of people think I'm wrong. But I just don't think his study is conclusive. All of the external indicators on the film are indeed consistent with authenticity—like the date code of when the film came out of the factory, the type of film used, and the processing markings from the lab in Dallas. Well, of course they are. Any conspirator who's going to change a movie and screw up that kind of stuff isn't worth two cents.

But I don't think that's the end of the story, because we uncovered two crucial witnesses from a CIA photo lab who cast serious doubt on the provenance of the film in the archives today.

Here's how it came about. The Review Board held a public hearing on the Zapruder film, which was televised by C-Span. One of the people watching happened to be one of two people who actually magnified individual frames from the Zapruder film the weekend of the assassination and made prints for three briefing boards intended for use in briefing high officials in the government. The individual who watched the Z-film hearing on C-Span was named Morgan Bennett Hunter, and his supervisor in 1963 was Homer McMahon: both were then CIA employees at NPIC, the National Photo Interpretation Center. Homer McMahon was then the head of the still photography color lab at NPIC, and Ben Hunter was his assistant. After Hunter contacted us and told us he had a story to tell us about the Z-film, we asked the CIA to provide clearance for the two men to speak with us and we then interviewed them multiple times.

The story that Homer and his assistant Ben told us was that, on the weekend of the assassination, they had a film brought to them by the Secret Service. The agent said his name was Bill Smith, which I firmly believe is a pseudonym because we ascertained from a roster of employees that the Secret Service had no special agent named 'Bill Smith' onboard in 1963. The Z-film was brought to them at NPIC on either Saturday night or Sunday night after the assassination, because they were positive it was before the president's funeral, which was on Monday. They said that Bill Smith brought what he represented to them as being the original Zapruder film. He did not come from Dallas. He came from Rochester, New York, where he said the film had been developed. And he used a code word for a classified film laboratory that the CIA had paid Kodak to set up and run in Rochester, their headquarters and main industrial facility.

The implications of this are off-scale. This assertion by the Secret Service to two CIA film professionals that the original Z-film was developed in Rochester at a secret CIA-sponsored facility, instead of in Dallas, runs contrary to the paper trail that had traditionally been accepted as ground truth since 1967. We therefore now have an almost-too-good paper trail of typed and signed affidavits prepared by Abraham Zapruder—signed by all of the processing personnel involved with the film on the day of the assassination—which can no longer guarantee the authenticity of the film in the archives. Let me explain what I mean by that. The processing affidavits which attempt to establish the film's chain-of-custody are all dated November 22, the day of the assassination, when Zapruder was running around helter-skelter trying to get his film developed. He went first to a TV station and then some other place, where he was told that since the film's chemistry was proprietary, it had to go to a Kodak lab to be developed. So, yes, these affidavits still do mean that the Kodak lab in

Dallas developed the original film; they establish that Mr. Zapruder exposed three contact prints at the Jamieson film lab in Dallas; and they further establish that he then returned to the Kodak processing plant where the three copies were immediately developed. All of these things happened on November 22, 1963— I don't doubt that for one minute. But I think the affidavits recording these events were probably really executed on Monday, November 25, and back-dated to the 22. (No one I am aware of saw Abraham Zapruder running around Dallas on November 22 with a manual typewriter under his arm.) On Saturday, Zapruder signed a contract with *Life Magazine* for $50,000 for print rights only, permitting them to keep the materials for only one week. Then, on Monday, a new contract was signed for print *and* motion picture rights, and *Life* was to keep the materials forever. Zapruder got a lot more money—$150,000 total now, instead of $50,000—when he renegotiated his deal on Monday. In support of his new contract, I believe he then had to prove the provenance of the film, so he created the appropriate paper trail in the form of the back-dated affidavits.

At the same time this was going on, you have the two men in the NPIC lab being told over that weekend that the original film came from Rochester. I'll tell you why that's important. If Kodak lab technicians in Dallas have developed the original film on the day of the assassination, which they surely did, you can't take them another, altered and reconstructed film two days later and ask them to develop it again. If someone had reconstructed a new, altered Zapruder film on an optical printer in a sophisticated lab, they could not blow their cover by taking the new film back to the same developing lab. So, if someone was involved in creating an altered film, they'd have to develop it at some other Kodak facility. And you didn't have many choices. One choice was the Kodak plant in Chicago, and another was the main plant in Rochester. If the new film was *created* in the classified lab in Rochester, the choice for developing would be obvious.

If the authentic, original film was really shot in slow motion, at 48 frames per second, instead of using the normal speed setting on the camera of 16 fps, and you wanted to remove certain events such as the car stop on Elm Street that over 50 Dealey Plaza eyewitnesses testified to, you would need to remove several frames, and then recreate a film that runs at normal speed, and that is much shorter than the original in terms of total number of frames. Furthermore, if you wanted to eliminate evidence of shots from the front you would need to black out the exit wound in the back of the head in some frames, and even remove some frames showing exit debris in mid-air; and if you wanted the new Z-film to roughly correspond with the pattern of damage in the autopsy photos, you would need to paint on large wounds at the top and the right side of the head in the appropriate frames. The image alteration in these frames would be done using the technique called *aerial imaging* at a facility that possessed a sophisticated optical printer.

I know I'm speculating—I don't know what equipment was in that Rochester photo lab—but this new chain-of-custody for what was represented by the Secret Service to be the original Z-film is very suspicious. All I'm saying is that anyone who believes that the so-called original film in the archives today may be an altered, reconstructed product, and not the true original mentioned in the Zapruder affidavit trail, has valid grounds to be suspicious of it. There are sound reasons, based upon the McMahon/Hunter interviews, to support this possibility. Those who would create a false legend of the shooting by culling the autopsy photo collection and inserting manipulated photos that told a false story of the wounds and the shooting, would of necessity also have to either destroy, or alter, any motion picture evidence of the assassination that was inconsistent with the officially promulgated version of the assassination. And if an original and seven copies of an autopsy report can be successfully switched out and substituted, then so can an original and three copies of a motion picture film. Perhaps a "film switch" is even why Zapruder was allowed to renegotiate his contract with *Life Magazine*; perhaps that additional $100,000 (which was pro-rated over a six-year period) bought his silence and future cooperation. After all, he did see the true original in the Kodak lab the day of the assassination, and did screen it for others (such as Dan Rather) on Saturday, November 23. (Perhaps this is why Dan Rather's contemporaneous account of what he saw in the film that weekend, broadcast on the radio, differs from what we see in the film in the archives today!) It would have been imperative to reliably obtain Zapruder's silence over the switch. This scenario would also explain the accounts we have all heard over the years of others either seeing or possessing different versions of the Zapruder film from the one we know today, if the true original and the three true first-generation copies were not all immediately destroyed.

The reason so many people resist this idea is because the Zapruder film has long been used as a time-clock of the assassination, and considered to be the one thing we can count on in the evidence trail. Based upon the McMahon/Hunter interviews, that approach could now be meaningless. When I study the film on DVD, and concentrate on the still frames associated with the head shot, and see the enormous head wound on the top of the head and the right side that looks "kind of like" the autopsy photos but n ot exactly the same, and which seems to float and jump around a bit on the skull as you view the film, I wonder if the scenario I have laid out above could be true.

What you're implying, of course, is that high-level officials within the American government knew, right from the front, that there was another gunman besides Oswald.

"Shots from multiple directions" is how I would put it. Because of the voice stress analysis work of George O'Toole in the mid-1970s, suggesting that Oswald was *not* lying when he said he was just a patsy and that he did not shoot anyone, I am not yet convinced that Oswald shot *anyone* in Dealey Plaza. He was certainly involved in something—up to his neck—and was probably being "run" by intelligence operatives, and perhaps even engaging in a charade by posing as a leftist Castro sympathizer, but I am not convinced that he shot anyone himself. His shooting skills were below average by the time he was discharged from the Marine Corps, and the murder weapon of record—the war surplus carbine he ordered under an alias—was a terrible weapon in general, and the one he owned was in particularly bad condition, as the FBI later revealed.

What does this indicate to you about the forces behind the assassination?

Well, you can go two ways. If you accept a government cover-up as a given, then it's either a benign one or a sinister one. If it's benign, then the people engineering the cover-up weren't part of the murder plot, but they think that for one reason or another, they can't tell the truth—the truth might endanger the country because it might trigger World War Three if it appears, rightly or wrongly, that there was foreign involvement in the assassination. Or, there might be a real fear that the public would lose faith in our institutions, if we have to admit to our citizenry that "multiple people shot the president and we don't know who they are and we can't catch them." The other alternative, the sinister one, posits that the people performing the cover-up actions—let's say the actors on the ground, Humes and Boswell and the photographers involved—*believe* that they are doing a benign cover-up for national security reasons. *But the people giving them their orders know better, and are part of the assassination plot.*

I believe that the latter scenario detailed above is the most likely one. I'm as sure as I can be that Humes went to his grave thinking that, "Yes, I lied and I obstructed justice, but I did it for the good of national security, and I'm not going to tell anybody because to do so would open the biggest can of worms in history and turn me into a target, so I did my duty and I'm a patriot and that's the way it is." James J. Humes often acted and spoke over the years as if he was harboring some great secrets about the assassination that no one else was smart enough to figure out, and that he was not going to tell any of us what those secrets were because none of us had a need to know—that only he (and "J" Thornton Boswell) did.

Are there records that exist anywhere of who could have contacted Drs. Humes and Boswell at Bethesda and told them to do this?

Yeah, several records, and they've been around a long time. The FBI agents, Sibert and O'Neill, made a list of who was present at the autopsy, at least the people who chose to voluntarily write down their names. One of those is the surgeon general of the Navy, Vice Admiral Edward Kenney, the head of the Navy Medical Corps. During the Clay Shaw trial in 1969, Finck revealed that Kenney had told everybody, "You will not discuss these events with anyone." (Finck also testified at the Shaw trial that an unnamed Army general was in charge of the events in the morgue.) So, in my view, the candidates for directing sinister activity, by name, are Admiral Kenney and Admiral Calvin Galloway, the head of Bethesda NNMC, as well as Captain John Stover, who was the head of the medical school and forced the Navy's autopsy participants to sign those "letters of silence" after the autopsy which were so onerous, and which blatantly and openly threatened the Navy personnel with court martial if they were to discuss the events of the autopsy with anyone. The people we deposed who testified about Stover's attitude and demeanor, like the X-ray technicians and the photographer Stringer, were clearly still scared of this man over thirty years later. And last, but not least, Rear Admiral George Burkley, the president's military physician, tried all night long to limit the scope of the autopsy, and furthermore, appears to have been in charge of coordinating the development of all post-mortem photography. Burkley is almost certainly the person who was responsible for making the many bone fragments from the skull disappear: the three fragments brought into the morgue late in the autopsy by the Secret Service, and the Harper fragment and Burros fragment, from Dallas. I don't see any of these people as the masterminds of an assassination plot, but I believe some of them were knowing participants at the mid-level of the conspiracy, and others had probably been given a national security cover story to justify the cover-up they were involved in.

It's strange, in its final report, the House Committee on Assassinations claimed that none of the twenty-six people present at the autopsy had differing accounts from the general depictions of the wounds seen in the photographs and X-rays.

That statement in Volume 7 is a big lie. That was a major interpretive find by Dr. Gary Aguilar immediately following the release in 1993 of the HSCA's own interview reports and depositions, and he's "spot-on" with his criticism. The House Select Committee's own medical witness interview reports, and its transcript of the deposition of Dr. John Ebersole, the autopsy radiologist, reveal this statement to be untrue, but no one knew this until these reports were released in 1993 by the JFK Act. Robert Blakey suppressed these reports by sealing them for fifty years, and we still would not know about this "big lie" even today, if it had not been for Oliver Stone's movie and the resulting JFK Records Act. This falsehood actually led David Lifton down the wrong path in 1979 and 1980 and caused him to believe that the back of the head was intact when the body was received at Bethesda, simply because he was told by the HSCA in Volume 7 *that the photos were ground truth and that all of the autopsy witnesses agreed with what they showed.* So I say, "shame on you, Robert Blakey," with the utmost invective I can muster, and ask the rhetorical question: "What were you up to in 1978 and 1979?" Your principal medical staff investigator, Andy Purdy, told the ARRB in 1996 that he did not know who was responsible for the statement in Volume 7 that none of the autopsy witnesses disagreed with the autopsy photos and X-rays, and he freely acknowledged that the statement was incorrect. He also told us that he had expected *all* of the HSCA staff's medical witness interview reports and depositions to be published, and was surprised when most of them were instead sequestered for fifty years. By the way, Robert Blakey also suppressed a key August 1978 deposition transcript of photographer Robert Knudsen for fifty years because it presented recollections and assertions incompatible with the HSCA's conclusions about the autopsy photographs; furthermore, no one mentioned anywhere in Volume 7 of the HSCA's report that the deposition was even conducted! In my opinion, Blakey is someone who cannot be trusted to comment accurately or truthfully on the Kennedy assassination. It appears that he was pursuing an agenda in 1978–79 that may have been incompatible with the truth, and if that assessment is correct, then he is undoubtedly still covering his ass today.

At this late date, do you think we will ever know what really happened that day in Dallas?

I think we can prove, based on the medical cover-up, that the official story is not true, and that the government knew that and suppressed what *was* true. Everything else then becomes speculation.

What have you been doing since?

I'm now at the State Department, in a very non-glamorous, nose-to-the-grindstone job as a passport specialist. I review and approve thousands of passport applications every year. It is a way to pay the rent as I work my way toward retirement in about ten years, and to simply keep me afloat while I try to complete my manuscript in my spare time. I have about 730 manuscript pages written already, and that represents only about 60 percent or so of the text. It is my *magnum opus*, a book that will be so massive, and so detailed, that for me to get my message out unfiltered and in an unabridged fashion, it will have to be made available as a "publish on demand" specialty type item sold on the internet, and printed one copy at a time, as each customer pays for it. I will not submit my work to the arbitrary restrictions on length that are imposed by mainstream publishers, nor will I permit an editor to "tone down" the political content of my manuscript. I would rather say exactly what I want to say, in the way I want to say it, and only sell a thousand copies, for example, than water down my life's work into a three-hundred-page puff piece with inadequate detail and inadequate supporting documentation. My goal is to tell the truth as I know it, without anyone watering it down—not to make money. My manuscript is a labor of love, and will be the sharing of an intellectual journey with those who are captivated by the medical evidence, and who have a love of detail. With any luck I will finish the manuscript by the end of 2008, and I hope it will be available to purchase, on-line, as a "print on demand" item, by November 2009. I won't be pulling any punches, and the final section of my book will be a treatise on the political context, and meaning, of the assassination.

INDEX

A

Abels, Cyrilly, 13
Ablard, Charles D., 255
Abrahamson, Harold, 251
Agee, Philip, 84
Aguilar, Gary, 297
AIB (Assassination Information
    Bureau), 3
Alcorn, Dan, 207–209
Aleman, José, 142
Alexander, Bill, 203
Alexander, D.A., 270
Alexander, William, 268, 268n131
Allende, Salvador, 148, 229
Alpha 66, 122, 145–149
    Sprague on, 56
Alsop, Joseph, 37–38
AM/LASH, 47, 89
Ammunition type, 1
AMWORLD project, 229, 233
Anderson, Jack, 142, 146, 63
Angleton, James Jesus, 38, 57, 181,
    192, 204, 214, 260, 266, 275
    Sprague on, 57
Anslinger, Harry, 275
Anson, Robert Sam, 7, 15
Arbenz, 230
Arbor, Ann, 196
Arcacha-Smith, Sergio, 73
Arcega, Victor, 17–25, 18n7, 20n8,
    27–28
Archer, Don Roy, 269, 270n140
Argosy interview with Hemming,
    59–68
    anti-Castro operations, 65
    assassination offers, 60–61, 64
    Castro's involvement, 63
    Cuban exile community in
        assassination, 60
    on Ferris Bryant, 65–66
    Howard Hughes' organization, 64
    Hughes-CIA-Mob link, 65
    International Penetration Force,
        dissolution, 60
    on Jack Ruby, 62
    on John Roselli, 65
    Loran [Lorenzo] Hall's
        involvement, 61–62
    missile crisis, 66
    on Oswald, 62
    on Robert Maheu, 65
Armstrong, John, 125
ARRB (Assassination Records
    Review Board), 211–217
Arsenal, Edgewood, 30, 239
ARTICHOKE Team, 241–242
Artime, Manuel, 228–229, 304
Assassination probe, 29–33, *See also*
    CBS Reports Inquiry; Schweiker,
    Richard
Assignation, assassination, 113–117
Atkin, Herb, 135
Attwood, William, 46–47, 90–91, 222
    on Castro's-revenge idea, 90
Atzenhoffer, Anthony, 255
Augustinovich, Ronald Lee, 118
    on CIA's knowledge before murder,
        116–117

on Oswald's double, 113–117
on President's death, 113–117
Automatic writing, 22
Castillo, 20
Sirhan, 22

B
Baker, Howard, 8
Baker, Marion, 267
Bannister, Guy, 106–107, 265
Barnes, Tracy, 38
Baron, George, 133–136
Barron, Dennis, 87–88
Baumgartner, Alan, 132
Bay of Pigs invasion, 19, 46, 61, 65,
    73, 86, 89–90, 92, 106–107, 122,
    134–135, 141, 143, 160, 223,
    229, 235
Bayle, Pierre, 5
Bayo, Eddie, 141–142
Belin, David, 41–42, 76
Belli, Melvin, 271, 271n145
Bennett, Robert, 9
Benson, Leland, 290
Beret, Green, 59
Bernstein, Carl, 35, 35n19, 37–39,
    52, 99
Bethell, Tom, 101
Betrayal, 89, 91, 98, 107, 252
Billings, Dick, 100
Billings, Richard, 33, 37, 37n25, 141
Binder, David, 38n27
Birch, John, 109–111
Bishop, Maurice, 147–150, 220,
    227, 301
    as the missing link, 147–150
    Veciana and, 147–150
Bissell, Richard, 244
Blake, Andrew F., 249nn80, 81
Blakey, G. Robert, 51, 51n36, 55–56,
    297–298

Bloomfield, L.M., 105
Blumberg, J.M., 290–291
Bohning, Don, 234
Bolden, Abraham, 2
Boothe, Clare, 35, 35n20
Borja, Isidro, 223
Bortner, Harold, 240
Bosch, Juan, 93
Boswell, Thornton, 279–281,
    283–291, 296, 306
Bouhe, George, 134
Boyajian, Roger, 282–283
Boyce, Christopher, 178
Boyers, Chester, 290
Boyle, Tony, 49–50, 54, 57
Brinegar, Johnny, 122
Bringuier, Carlos, 85, 264
Brokaw, Tom, 206
Bromberg, Walter, 270
Broshears, Raymond, 107–108
Brothers, 2
Broutsas, Constantine, 232, 235
Brown, Herman, 134
Bryant, Ferris, Hemming on, 65–66
Buchen, Philip, 12
Bugliosi, Vincent, 2, 34
Buick, Robert Clayton, 227, 227n54
Bundren, Jim, 156
Bundy, McGeorge, 46
Burglar, Watergate, 1
Burkley, George, 50–51, 288, 297
Burnham, David, 49n32, 50, 50nn33,
    34, 52–54
    Sprague on, 52–53
Burroughs, William, 16

C
Cabell, Charles, 91–93
Caesar, Julius, 102
Cagney, James, 274
Calamia, Joe, 156–157

Camera Never Blinks, The, 34
Cameron, D. Ewen, 253
Camper, Frank, 256, 258, 258n107, 263, 263n121
Canaris, Wilhelm, 230
Canon, Jack, 63
Captain Sam, See Augustinovich, Ronald Lee
Carlin, Karen, 269, 269n138
Carmichael, Dan, 132n48
Carré, John le, 8
Carter, Jimmy, 51, 178
Case Closed, 34, 202–204
Castillo, Jean B., 22
Castillo, Luis Angel, 17–28, 18n7, 24n12, 236
    hypnosis session, 19
        David Ferrie, 19
        Lee Harvey Oswald, 19
    trance recollections, 22, 25
Castle, Blarney, 164
Castro, Fidel, 3, 6, 8, 40, 41, 46, 41–48, 59–61, 63–65, 81–84, 89–90, 98, 123, 137–138, 145, 148–150, 160–161, 212, 218–219, 265
    retaliation against Kennedy, question of, 41–48
Cattell, James, 254
Caucus, Black, 51
CBS Reports Inquiry, 29–33
    failures/critics, 29–30
        forensic report, 29
        single bullet implausibivility, 30–31
        Zapruder film analysis, 29
    fatal shot, 31–33
    Oswald's marksmanship, 30
    single-bullet theory, 30
Chandler, Raymond, 133
Charro, Del, 7

Christenberry, Herbert W., 104
Church, Frank, 8
CIA (Central Intelligence Agency), 38
    CIA and the Cult of Intelligence, The, 101
    CIA headquarters visit, 87–88
    CIA's declassified JFK file, speculations about, 76–86
        contradictions, 77
        Garrison Investigation, 84–86
        Mexico mysteries, 82–83
        mysterious Mr. Ruby, 83
        Oswald and the CIA, 78–79
        Oswald and the Cubans, 81
        Oswald and the Russians, 79
        Oswald Rifle, 77–78
Claire, Miss, 43
Clark, Ramsey, 75, 100
Cleaver, Eldridge, 13
Clements, Manning, 130–131
Clinton, Bill, 40, 205, 208–209, 107, 216, 226, 265, 278–279
CMC (Centro Mondiale Commerciale), 105
Cohen, Jeff, 18, 22
Cohen, Jeff, 18, 23, 25
Cohen, Mickey, 276
Colby, William, 87, 177
Colson, Charles, 73, 101
'The Company', 59–68
    ex-CIA man's revelations on, 59–68, *See also* Argosy interview with Hemming
Condon, Richard, 8, 241–242
Connally, John, 30–31, 36, 202
Containment and Change, 197
Coogan, Matthew A., 195, 199–201
Corso, Philip J., 126–127, 126n41
Cory, Richard, 179
County, Dade, 149

Craig, Roger, 120
Cram, Cleveland, 178
Crile, George, 89–90, 142
Cuban connection, 218–224
    Cuban exile and a CIA break-in,
        95–96
    Havana Washington Shadow Play,
        222–224
    Miami Puzzle, 219–224
Cubans connection in JFK murder,
    89–94
Cubela, Rolando, 89
Cuesta, Tony, 221–222, 224
Cunningham, Kathleen, 281–282
Custer, Jerrol, 283
Cypher, James L., 126nn41, 42

D
Daniel, Jean, 46
Daniels, Judy, 3, 4
DaVanon, Joseph, 214
David, Dennis, 282–283
David, Moses, 6
De Lopez, Maria Rodriguez, 86
De Mohrenschildt, Baron George
    Sergei, 55, 85–86, 133–136, 138,
    191, 212, 260, 301
    CIA's interest in, 135
    as Oswald and H.L. Hunt
        middleman, 134
Dean, Harry, 109–112
    background, 110
    first assignment, 110
    and Oswald, 111–112
Dean, John, 102
Deighton, Len, 8
Del Valle, Eladio, 221
DeMarr, Bill, 269, 269n135
Deneselya, Donald, 260, 260n111
Derbyshire, A.J., 250n84
Devereux, Johnny, 63
Devine, Andy, 113, 117

Di Spadafora, Gutierez, 106
Diego, San, 153, 217
Dorfman, Elsa, 209
Double Oswald incidents/mystery,
    See 'Second Oswald'
Downing, Tom, 43, 51, 53–54
Dudman, Richard, 8
Duff, James Arthur, 3
Dugger, Ronnie, 271n144
Dulles, Allen, 3, 38, 44, 46, 101, 193,
    231, 239, 274
Duran, Sylvia, 154
Duvalier, Francois, 135

E
Ebersole, John, 297
Echo from Dealey Plaza, The, 2
Eddowes, Michael H.B., 129,
    129nn43, 44, 130n45,
    131n46, 132
Edwards, Don, 50, 50n33, 53
Ellsworth, Frank, 118–123, 268,
    268n131
Eloriaga, Antonio Reyes, 18,
    21–23, 18n7
Emery, Wilbur, 23
Emily, Jennifer, 2n5
Epstein, Edward J., 259–260,
    260n112, 261
Epstein, Jason, 15, 24
Ervin, Sam, 43
Estabrooks, George H., 22,
    249–250, 252, 249nn80, 82,
    250nn83, 84, 85, 86, 257,
    257n106, 264
Evidence, disappearing, 278–306
    Horne's revelations, 278–306
        autopsy report, 288–289
        brain examinations after
            autopsy, 289–292
        forces behind assassination, 296
        head images, 287

on house committee on
assassinations report, 297–
298
medical records, 279–280
medical records, manipulations
in, 281–287
as review board
staff, 278–279
second gunman involvement,
295–296
Zapruder film analyses,
292–295

F

Fadeykin, Ivan, 225
Fallon, Dean, 109
Farewell to Justice, A, 226
Fatal shot
CBS Reports, 31–33
FBI informant, memories of, 109–
112, *See also* Dean, Harry
Feisst, Ernest, 106
Feldman, Ira, 273–277, 273n147
Felker, Clay, 4
Fensterwald, Bernard, Jr., 23, 76,
86, 94, 95, 152, 164, 168, 172,
195, 228
Fenton, Clifford, 144
Ferrell, Mary, 72–73
Ferrie, David, 19, 32, 73–74, 85,
92–93, 98–99, 101–102, 106–108,
195, 221, 236, 255, 265, 268–269,
269n134, 305
Finck, Pierre A., 281, 285, 288–290,
296, 306
Fitzgerald, Christopher, 96, 97, 133
Fitzgerald, Deborah, 95
FitzGerald, Desmond, 38, 47, 65, 95,
214, 228–229, 232–233, 245, 303
Flammonde, Paris, 106
Fleites, Armando, 301
Fonzi, Gaeton, 145–146, 207–209

Ford, Gerald, 5–16, 17, 36, 41–42, 48,
94, 100
Freed, Donald, 15
Freeman, Lucy, 252, 252nn92, 93
Fritz, Will, 268

G

Gagarin, Yuri, 148
Gallen, Richard, 70n37
Galloway, Calvin, 296
García, Herminio Díaz, 221–222
Garrison, Jim, 6, 10, 19, 32, 48, 59,
73–75. 76, 84–85, 92–93, 97–108,
118, 221, 265, 269, 299
Garrison investigation, 73–74
CIA, 84–86
vindication of, 97–108
Gatlin, Maurice, 107
Gervais, Pershing, 103–104
Giancana, Sam, 12–13, 67, 140–142,
245, 276
Gibbons, Willis, 256n104
Gibbs, Lois, 190
Gillin, Edward G, 236
Gillin, Edward G., 236, 236n71
Gittinger, John, 247
Goldwater, Barry, 15
Golitsin, Anatoli, 174–175
Golovachev, Pavel, 79
Golz, Earl, 129n43, 131n47,
132n49
Gonzalez, Henry, 43, 50, 50n34,
53–54, 74
Sprague on, 53–54
González, Reinaldo, 145
Gottlieb, Sidney, 238–249, 274, 276,
305
Green, Wilson, 239
Gregory, Dick, 6, 8, 10, 12–14, 15
Griffin, Burt. 194
Groody, Paul, 130, 132
Guevara, Che, 39, 59, 64, 150

Gunn, Jeremy, 279–282, 286–287, 289
Guttmacher, Manfred, 270

H
Hall, Loran, 69, 71, 139–144
    Bayo's team and, 142
    Hemming on, 61–62, 142
    Lee Harvey Oswald and, 139–140
    Santo and, 140
    Trafficante association with,
        139–142
Halperin, Morton, 39
Hancock, Larry, 233n61
Hand, Frank, 127
Harbin, Philip, 135
Harker, Daniel, 222
Harris, Louis, 100
Hart, Gary, 42–43
Hartmann, Thom, 234n63
Hartogs, Renatus, 252–254, 252n92,
    253nn95, 96, 254n98
Harvey, Bill, 232
Harvey, William, 232, 245, 275
    Harvey and Lee, 125
Havana's missing pieces, 221–222
Havana–Washington Shadow Play,
    222–224
Heath, Robert, 255, 264–266,
    264n123, 266n129
Hecksher, Henry, 229–235, 230nn58,
    59, 232n60, 233n61, 235nn67,
    68, 304
Hedegaard, Erik, 1n3
Helms, Dick, 246–247
Helms, Richard, 26, 32, 38, 44, 47, 57,
    78, 95, 101, 130, 179, 235, 237
Hemming, Gerry Patrick, 59–68,
    69, 142, 214, 300, *See also* Argosy
    interview with Hemming
    Loran Hall and, 142–143
Hendrix, Hal, 38, 38n26
Hensen, Eldon, 213

Henshaw, John, 264
Heritage of Stone, A, 99
Hersh, Seymour, 7
Hidell, A.J., 129, 155, 241, 262–264
Hill, Capitol, 43
Hill, Gerald, 267
Hitler, Adolf, 230, 261
Hoesen, John Van, 283
Hoffa, Jimmy, 221
Hoover, J. Edgar, 7, 36, 44–45, 78,
    125–126, 125n39, 155, 161–162,
    212, 227, 227n53, 237, 237n73,
    246, 246n79, 249–250
Horne, Douglas P., 278–306, *See also*
    under Evidence, disappearing
Horrock, Nicholas M., 26n14,
    242n77
Houdini, Harry, 9
Hougan, Jim, 18n7
House investigation, 49–58
    House Assassinations
        Committee, 39
    Sprague interview, 51–52
        on Alpha 66, 56
        on assassination, 55–56
        on David Burnham, 52–53
        on David Phillips, 55
        on George de Mohrenschildt, 55
        as HSCA's chief council,
            51–52
        Henry Gonzalez, 53–54
        on James Angleton, 57
        on matters beyond
            assassination, 54–55
        on Santo Trafficante, Jr., 57
        on Tip O'Neill, 57
Howard, Lawrence, 69–72, 143,
    162, 300
HSCA (House Select Committee
    on Assassinations), 49–50, *See also*
    House investigation
Hughes, Howard, 63–65, 234

Humes, James J., 279–281, 283–285, 287–291, 296, 306

Hunt, E, Howard, Jr., 1, 1n3, 9, 14, 46, 80, 91, 105, 227, 234

Hunt, H.L., 121, 124, 134
  Masen on, 124

Hunter, Edward, 26

Hunter, Morgan Bennett, 293, 295

Hussein, Saddam, 199

Huxley, Aldous, 272

Hypnosis involvement, 17–28, 250–257, *See also* Castillo, Luis Angel
  Hypnotism, 22, 264

I

Ike Feldman, *See* Feldman, Ira

Illig, William, 50–51

Irion, John, 255

Italian rifle study, 1, 1n1

Itek, photo-analysis corporation, 29

J

Jackson, C.D., 34–35, 35n18, 35, 35n19

Jackson, Fort, 161

James, Daniel, 39, 39n28

James, Rosemary, 103

Janis, Brooke, 7

Jean, B., 20, 24

Jelisavcic, Michael, 227, 227n53

Jenner, Albert, 260

JFK movie, 40, 194

Joannides, George, 1, 1n4

Johnson, Lyndon, 44

Johnson, Robert, 1, 37, 44, 47–48, 61, 63, 90, 100, 127–128, 213

Johnson, T. Bruce, 266

Joling, Robert, 29

Jolla, La, 7, 10–11, 15

Jones, Penn, 118

Julian, L. Emile, 266, 266n130

JURE *(Junta Revolucionaria)*, 234–235

K

Kampiles, William, 178

Kantor, Seth, 269n136, 270

Kaplan, John, 271n143

Karbainov, Alexander, 183

Katz, Bob, 196

Keating, Kenneth, 38

Keeney, John C., 12

Kellerman, Roy, 283

Kelley, Clarence, 8

Kennedy, Edward, 48

Kennedy, Jacqueline, (Jackie), 31, 73

Kennedy, John F.
  addressing United Nations, 162
  assassination, *See all other index entries*
  Bay of Pigs invasion, 19, 46, 61, 65, 73, 86, 89–90, 92, 106–107, 122, 134–135, 141, 143, 160, 223, 229, 235
  and the Cuban Connection, 218–224
  Cuban Missile Crisis, 92–93, 148, 160. 212, 218, 219–221
  Fidel Castro's retaliation, 40–42
  JFK Records Act, 211, 297
  JFK movie, 40, 194–195, 278
  nuclear test ban treaty, 1963, 81, 161–162
  Portrait of a President, 262

Kennedy, Regis L., 269n134

Kennedy, Robert, (Bobby) 2, 21, 47, 57, 67, 73n38, 90, 99, 159, 195, 198–199, 221, 228, 288

Kenney, Edward, 296

Kevin, Art, 144

KGB *(Komitet Gosudarstvennoi Bezopasnosti)*

visit to, 182–190
Kharlamov, Sergei, 188–189
Kirk, Claude, 65
Kirkpatrick, Lyman B., 237, 237n72, 256n104
Kissinger, Henry, 8
Klein, Ken, 144
Kline, Milton, 243, 243n78, 251–254, 251n90, 253n97, 254n99, 261, 262n117, 265, 265n124
Knudsen, Robert, 287, 298
Kohly, Mario Garcia, 91–94
Kohn, Howard, 7, 14
Koresh, David, 75
Kostikov, Valery V., 80, 185
Kuetemeyer, Wilhelm, 261, 261n115

L
Lane, Mark, 15, 36, 45
Lansky, Meyer, 84, 62–63, 67, 97
Lanz, Pedro Diaz, 64
Lardner, George, Jr., 50n34
Lawford, Peter, 57
Leary, Timothy, 6, 248
Lee, Andrew, 178
Legend, 259–260
Lesar, Jim, 207–209
Levi, Edward, 8
Levy, Michael Joseph, 270n142
Lewis, Anthony, 36
Liddy, Gordon, 63
Liebacher, Ernest, 214
Life Magazine, 37
    DID OSWALD ACT ALONE? A
    MATTER OF REASONABLE
    DOUBT, 37
    END OF NAGGING
    RUMORS: THE CRITICAL
    SIX SECONDS, 35
The Warren Report, 36–37

Lifton, David, 192, 278, 282–284, 288, 297
Lincoln, Evelyn, 288
Lindsay, Franklin A., 29
Lodge, Henry Cabot, 219
Logue, Lester, 143
Lone-gunman theory, 36
Long, Huey, 262
Long, Russell, 99
Loomis, Bob, 202
Luce, Clare Booth, 35, 39, 41
Luce, Henry, 37

M
Maas, Peter, 199
MacArthur, Douglas, 193
Machiavellian Scale, 251
Madden, Ray, 43
Magruder, Jeb, 63
Maheu, Robert, 65
Mailer, Norman, 215–216
    on Newman's work, 216
Malitz, Sidney, 254
Malone, John, 125
Malonem, William Scott, 51n36
Man Who Knew Too Much, The, 2, 17, 151, 191–195
Manchester, William, 281
Manchurian Candidate
    Manchurian Candidate, The, 241
    Oswald as, question of, 236–237
Mansfield, Mike, 8
Mantik, David, 291–292
Marcello, Carlos, 73, 98–99, 106, 221, 276
Marchetti, Victor, 32, 85, 101, 105, 176
Marcos, Ferdinand, 20, 20n8
Marcuse, Herbert, 10–11
Marks, John, 26, 240n75, 243, 250n87, 257, 257n105, 262
Marrs, Jim, 130, 269n138

Marsh, Lawrence, 254, 255n100
Marston, Dave, 43, 47–48
Martello, Francis, 227
Martin Luther King Assassination, The, 199
Martin, Jack, 98, 107, 268, 2 69n134
Martino, John, 141–142, 220
Marwell, David, 279
Marx, Herman, 63
Masen, John Thomas, 122–124
Mason, Paul, 103
McClelland, John, 8, 291
McCloy, John, 37
McCone, John, 66, 81
McCord, James, 14, 86, 164, 168, 216
McDonald, Nick, 267
McGovern, George, 8
McKeown, Robert Ray (The Gunrunner), 33, 136–138
on Carlos Prío, 136–137
illegal weapons supply by, 137
on Jack Ruby, 137
Lee Oswald visiting, 137
McLeavy, Maryann, 173
McMahon, Homer, 293, 295
McMillan, Priscilla Johnson, 261, 261n116
McVickar, John, 259, 259n109
Meador, Vaughn, 3
Mecom, John, 134
Media, the CIA, and the Cover-Up, 34–40
Medina, Juan, 163
Melanson, Philip, 195, 198–199
Mellen, Joan, 226
Mellen, Joan, 73n38, 226, 265, 265n127
Mengele, Josef, 203–204
Meredith, James, 66
Messianic, Napoleon, 8–9

Mexico mysteries, 82–83
Miami Puzzle, 219–224
Milteer, J.A., 47
Mitchell, John, 103–104
MKULTRA program/files, 26, 237, 250, 257, 273, 275
field operative talks, 273–277
Molder, John, 15
Montague, Dave, 282
Montgomery, Slew, 74–75
Moody, Osmant, C., 64
Moore, Edwin, G., 178
Moore, Jim, 135
Moore, Walter, G., 134
Moore, Walton, J., 134–135, 260
Morales, David, 220
Morgan, Robert, 90
Morley, Jefferson, 1n4, 2
Morrow, Robert, 89, 91, 98, 106–107
revelations, 92–94
on Shaw, 106
Morton, Fred, 155, 156
Mosby, Aline, 259
Motyka, Joe, 211

N
Nagell, Richard Case, 17, 151, 152–165, 166, 182, 188–189, 192, 202, 205–206, 211–217, 222, 225–229, 231, 233, 235, 225n50, 236, 303
alerting CIA officials, 212
contract to kill Lee Harvey Oswald, 152–165
on KGB, 192
Nagell Saga, new clues in, 225–235
on Soviets hand, 215
Nagy, Ferenc, 106
New questions, 76–86, *See also under* CIA
Newman, John, 213–216

on Nagell, 213–214
Nhu, Madame, 3
Nitze, Paul, 177
Nixon, Richard, 9, 32, 43, 46, 73,
　101–102, 168, 175–176, 246–247
Norton, Linda, 132
Nosenko, Yuri, 168, 174–177, 180
Novel, Gordon, 72–75, 101, 107
Novel, John le Carré, 187
Nuñez, Orlando, 95–96

O
O'Connor, Paul, 283
O'Donnell, Joe, 287
O'Leary, Jeremiah, 52
O'Neill, Francis, 282, 284, 286–287,
　290–291, 296
O'Neill, Tip, 51, 53, 57
　Sprague on, 57
O'Toole, George, 86, 295
Odio, Sylvia/Odio sisters, 69–70, 70n37,
　96, 143, 145, 162, 223, 235, 235n66
　"Odio incident", 70
　Odio's testimony, to Warren
　　Commission, 143
Oglesby, Carl, 194–198
Oliva, Erneido, 304
Ólivier, Alfred, G., 30
Olson, Frank, 240, 244, 240n75
Oltmans, Willem, 134, 136, 139
Orne, Martin, 243
Osborn, Howard, J., 85
Oswald, Lee Harvey, *See also* 'Second
　Oswald'
　behavior to hypnosis, 250–257, 261
　craniotomy, 132
　and the Cubans, 81
　dead body investigations, 130–132
　different names of, 128
　height discrepancies, 129
　Hemming on, 62
　Manchurian candidate?, 236–237

marksmanship, 30
　CBS Reports, 30
　mysterious formative years, 249–257
　Nagell's contract to kill, 152–165
　Oswald File, The, 129
　Oswald Rifle
　　CIA analysis, 77–78
　Oswald's Tale, 215
　Oswald–CIA link, 78–79,
　　211–217
　Oswald-Ruby Connection, 32
　and the Russians, 79
Oswald, Leon, 120, 235
Oswald, Marguerite, 110, 112
Oswald, Marina, 79, 86, 131–132,
　132n48, 134, 154, 259n110, 302
　reflections of, 205–210
Oswald, Robert, 260, 260nn113, 114,
　268n133
Oswald, William Stout, 128
*Our Man in Mexico: Winston Scott and
　the Hidden History of the CIA*, 2

P
Pacepa, Ion Mihai, 225, 225n51
Padron, Amador Odio, 145
Paisley, Eddie, 171
Paisley, Jack, 172
Paisley, John, Russian spy, 166–181,
　214
　death mystery, 172–175
　Paisley Puzzle, 166
Paisley, Maryann, 168, 170–175,
　177–181
Paley, William, 37
Palmer, Henry Earl, 265, 265n126
PANEL TO REJECT THEORIES
　OF PLOT IN KENNEDY
　DEATH, 36
Parish, Orleans, 98
Patman, Wright, 264
Pawley, William, D., 141–142

Permindex, S.A., 106
Pfeiffer, Carl, 27n15
Philbrick, Herbert, 255
Philby, Kim, 29
Phillips, David Atlee, 40, 49,
    55, 216, 220, 223, 227–230, 233,
    235, 301
    Sprague on, 55
Pic, John, 128
Pitts, J.E., 129
Polgar, Tom, 229–233, 235, 229n56
Policoff, Jerry, 34n16, 35, 35nn18, 21,
    37n24, 49n32, 51n36
Popkin, Richard H. (Professor
    Popkin), 3, 5–16, 17–18, 21–22,
    120, 153–154, 157
    journalists visiting, 7
        Brooke Janis, 7
        Howard Kohn, 7
        Lee Townsend, 7
        Marty Schramm, 7
    telegrams, 7–8, 14
    The Popkin Papers, 6
Porter, Katharine Anne, 13
Porter, Marina Oswald, 205–210
Porter, Robert, 92
Posner, Gerald, 34, 202–204, 206,
    269n137
    Hitler's Children, 203
    Mengele: The Complete Story, 203
    Warlords of Crime, 203
    Zhe Bio-Assassins, 203
Post, 89
Pratkins, Solomon, 84
Preyer, Richardson, 147
Price, C.J., 130
Principles of Suggestion and
    Autosuggestion, 253–254
Programmed to Kill?, 267–272
Prusakova, Marina, 259
Puerto Rico, 17, 153, 235
Purdy, Andy, 297

Q
Quigley, John, 262–263, 263n119
Quiroga, Carlos, 264

R
Raganc, Frank, 221
Rankin, J.L., 78, 155, 159, 237,
    288–289
Rather, Dan, 31, 34, 34n17, 37,
    137, 295
Ray, James Earl, 14, 86, 168, 199
Ray, Manuel, 223, 234–235, 234n64
Rebozo, Bebe, 7
Reclaiming History, 2, 34
Regnery, Henry, 91
Reid, Robert, 267
Reily, William, B., 128
Rhodes, James, 73, 101
Ricey, S., 163
Richard, Condon, 241
Richard, Sprague, 33
Richter, Bob, 32–33
Riebe, Floyd, 283, 287
Robert Kennedy Assassination, The, 199
Robertson, Randolph, 209
Robinson, Edward, G., 274
Robinson, Tom, 290
Rockefeller Commission's report, 26
Rockefeller, Nelson, 6, 8, 17n6, 29
Rodriguez, Arnesto, 86
Rodriguez, Arturo, 218–219, 223
Rodriguez, Manuel, O., 122
Rolling Stone article, 37
Roosevelt, Franklin, 268
Rose, Earl, 130–131, 131n47
Roselli, John, 65, 67, 140–142
Roselli, Johnny, 245
Roselli, Mobster John, 276
Rosenthal, David, 8
Rous, Alberto, 18n7
Rowley, James, 163
Roy, Julie, 252, 252n93

Ruby, Jack, 1, 3, 32, 44–46, 56, 62,
    76, 83–84, 92, 93, 98, 105–106,
    129–130, 136–137, 140–141, 158,
    164, 198, 203, 249, 252, 269–272,
    270n142, 271nn143, 144, 276–277
    Hemming on, 62–63
    McKeown on, 137
Ruffin, Roger, 14
Rusconi, Jane, 194
Rush to Judgment, 36
Russell, Bertrand, 9
Russell, Dick, 39n28, 133, 151, 159,
    166, 218
Russell, Richard, 126–127, 158, 225
Russian connection, 258–266
Russo, Perry, 102

S
Salandria, Vincent, 36
Salant, Richard, 39, 39n29
Salisbury, Harrison, 37
Santiago, Felipe Vidal, 219, 223
Sargent, Frank, 200
Schafer, Roy, 270
Schellenberg, Walter, 230
Schlager, Claude, L., 269n134
Schmidt, Volkmar, 260–261
Schonfeld, Maurice, 29
Schorr, Daniel, 14
Schramm, Marty, 7
Schweiker, Richard, 41–49, 145, 148,
    150, 207
    reopening assassination probe, 41–48
Schweitzer, Albert, 129
Scott, Peter Dale, 12, 128
Scott, Winston, 2, 39, 233, 233n62
*Search for the Manchurian Candidate,
    The*, 26, 257, 262
'Second Oswald', 119–124
    mystery, 125–132
    Ronald Lee Augustinovich on,
        113–117

The Second Oswald, 5, 9, 120
Sergei Kharlamov, 188–189
Sevareid, Eric, 37
Seymour, Bill, 71
Seymour, William, 69, 143, 300
Shackley, Ted, 232
Shadrin, Nicholas, 176–177
Shaw, Clay, L., 32, 76, 84–85, 92–93,
    97–107, 164, 265
Sheridan, Walter, 73n38, 102
Shipman, Tim, 1n1
Shirkovsky, Eduard, 259
Shur, Gerald, 104
Sibert, James, 282, 284, 286–287, 296
Sichel, Peter, 230–232, 230n57
Silva, Frank, 265–266, 265n127,
    266n129
Silver, Bob, 24
Silverberg, David, 187–189
Silverglate, Harvey, 207
Single-bullet theory, 30, 203
    CBS Reports, 30
Sirhan, Sirhan, 15, 21–22, 24, 57, 198
Sirica, John, 86
Six Seconds in Dallas, 36
Slawson, W. David, 125, 126n40, 131
Smith, Arnholt, C., 14
Smith, Bill, 293
Smith, K. Wayne, 170–171, 218
Smith, Sergio Arcacha, 73
Smith, Snuffy, 7
Smith, Wayne, K., 170, 179
Snyder, Richard, E., 259
Socarrás, Carlos Prío, 136–138
Spiegel, Herbert, 24
Sprague, Howard, 29
Sprague, Richard A., 49–51, 49n32,
    50n34, 51n35, 55, 299, *See also
    under* House investigation
Sprague, Richard E., 25, 102
Stanley, Joan, 208–209
Stanton, Frank, 32

Stokes, Carl, 147
Stolley, Richard, 35
Stover, John, 283, 297
Stratton, Richard, 273, 275–276,
    273n148
Streicher, Julius, 230
Stringer, John, 287, 289–291, 297
Strohmeyer, Florence, 265, 265n125
Stubblefield, Robert, 271–272
Sturgis, Frank, 59, 61, 63, 137
Styron, William, 202
Sullivan, William, 126
Sulzberger, Arthur Hays, 37
Summers, Anthony, 258n108, 35n20,
    38n26, 126, 252, 252n91
Summit, Camp David, 180
Sword, Gerald, 170, 181
Szulc, Tad, 89

T
Talbot, David, 2, 228
Tallaro, Patrick F., 226
Tanenbaum, Bob, 56–57
Texas A&M bullet study, 1, 1n2
Thomas, Herman, 23
Thompson, Josiah, 30–31, 36
Thornberry, Homer, 155, 157, 213
Thurmond, Strom, 126
Thyssen, Fritz, 230
Tkach, Walter, 246–247
Tom, Kane, 114–115
Tonahill, Joe, 270, 270n141
Toro, Sara del, 145
Townley, Richard, 102
Townsend, Lee, 7
Trafficante, Santo, Jr, 57, 62, 89,
    139–142, 220–221, 276
    Sprague on, 57–58
Treichler, Raymond, 245
Truly, Roy, 267
Tryon, Robert, C., 249, 249n82
Tunheim, Jack, 279

Turner, Admiral Stansfield, 179
Turner, Bill, 14
Twyman, Noel, 217

V
Veciana, Antonio, 145–150, 220, 233,
    301, *See also* Alpha 66
Vogel, Wolfgang, 163

W
Wade, Henry, D.A., 269
Wagener, Phil, 171, 176, 179
Waldron, Lamar, 37n24, 234n63
Waldron, Martin, 37
Walker, Edwin, 121–123, 219, 261
Wall, John, 103
Waltz, Jon, R., 271n143
Ward, Hugh, 107
Ware, John, 203
Warren Commission, 125–127
    conclusions, 29–30
        single-bullet theory, 30–31
    on Oswald's physical appearance,
        128–131
Warren Report, The, 36–37, 129
Warren, Earl, 11, 15
Watson, Marvin, 46
Wayne, John, 111–112
Wecht, Cyril, 30–32
Weems, George, 173
Weisheit, Oscar, G., 154
Weiss, Victor, 265, 266n128
Wescott, Ray, 169
West, Louis, J., 271, 271n143
Weston, James, 29
Weston, Wally, 269, 269n136
White, George, 273–274
White, Thomas B., 163
Willens, Howard P., 78
Williams, Dave, 3
Willoughby, Charles, 193
Wilson, Edwin, 199–200

Wilson, John, 83–84, 140
Wilson, Norman, 171, 179
Wise, David, 202
Wisner, Frank, 239
Witnesses, 133–138
    Baron George Sergei de
        Mohrenschildt, 133–136
    Gunrunner (Robert Ray
        McKeown), 136–138
    Witnesses, The, 36
Worth, Fort, 256
Wright, Jim, 56–57

Y
Yankee and Cowboy War, The, 195
Yawkey, Tom, 173
Yeltsin, Boris, 188–189

Z
Zapruder film, 36–37
    analysis, 29, 292–295
    conspiracy in, 31
Zapruder, Abraham, 34–37,
    292–295
Zavada, Roland, 292